The Communicator's Commentary

Ezekiel

THE COMMUNICATOR'S COMMENTARY SERIES
OLD TESTAMENT

Lloyd J. Ogilvie

General Editor

The Communicator's Commentary

Ezekiel

Douglas Stuart

WORD BOOKS, PUBLISHER • DALLAS, TEXAS

Library of Congress Cataloging in Publication Data
Main entry under title:

The Communicator's commentary.
    Bibliography: p.
    Contents: OT18. Ezekiel / by Douglas Stuart
    1. Bible. O.T.—Commentaries.   I. Ogilvie, Lloyd
John.   II. Stuart, Douglas, 1943–.
BS1151.2.C66   1986   221.7'7   86–11138
ISBN 0–8499–0424–2 (v. OT18)

Printed in the United States of America

5 6 7 8 9 9   AGF   9 8 7 6 5 4

To my brother, Streeter,
expert communicator
of the Word

Contents

HOPE AND DANGER IN THE FUTURE: EZEKIEL 33:1–39:29

VISION OF THE NEW TEMPLE AND LAND: EZEKIEL 40:1–48:35

Editor's Preface

God has called all of His people to be communicators. Everyone who is in Christ is called into ministry. As ministers of "the manifold grace of God," all of us—clergy and laity—are commissioned with the challenge to communicate our faith to individuals and groups, classes and congregations.

The Bible, God's Word, is the objective basis of the truth of His love and power that we seek to communicate. In response to the urgent, expressed needs of pastors, teachers, Bible study leaders, church school teachers, small group enablers, and individual Christians, the Communicator's Commentary is offered as a penetrating search of the Scriptures of the Old and New Testament to enable vital personal and practical communication of the abundant life.

Many current commentaries and Bible study guides provide only some aspects of a communicator's needs. Some offer in-depth scholarship but no application to daily life. Others are so popular in approach that biblical roots are left unexplained. Few offer impelling illustrations that open windows for the reader to see the exciting application for today's struggles. And most of all, seldom have the expositors given the valuable outlines of passages so needed to help the preacher or teacher in his or her busy life to prepare for communicating the Word to congregations or classes.

This Communicator's Commentary series brings all of these elements together. The authors are scholar-preachers and teachers outstanding in their ability to make the Scriptures come alive for individuals and groups. They are noted for bringing together excellence in biblical scholarship, knowledge of the original Hebrew and Greek, sensitivity to people's needs, vivid illustrative material from biblical, classical, and contemporary sources, and lucid communication by the use of clear outlines of thought. Each has been selected to contribute to this series because of his Spirit-empowered ability to help people live in the skins of biblical characters and provide a "you-are-there" intensity to the drama of events of the Bible which have so much to say about our relationships and responsibilities today.

The design for the Communicator's Commentary gives the reader an overall outline of each book of the Bible. Following the introduction, which reveals the author's approach and salient background on the book, each chapter of the commentary provides the Scripture to be exposited. The New King James Bible has been chosen for the Communicator's Commentary because it combines with integrity the beauty of language, underlying Hebrew and Greek textual basis, and thought-flow of the 1611 King James Version, while replacing obsolete verb forms and other archaisms with their everyday contemporary counterparts for greater readability. Reverence for God is preserved in the capitalization of all pronouns referring to the Father, Son, or Holy Spirit. Readers who are more comfortable with another translation can readily find the parallel passage by means of the chapter and verse reference at the end of each passage being exposited. The paragraphs of exposition combine fresh insights to the Scripture, application, rich illustrative material, and innovative ways of utilizing the vibrant truth for his or her own life and for the challenge of communicating it with vigor and vitality.

It has been gratifying to me as editor of this series to receive enthusiastic progress reports from each contributor. As they worked, all were gripped with new truths from the Scripture—God-given insights into passages, previously not written in the literature of biblical explanation. A prime objective of this series is for each user to find the same awareness: that God speaks with newness through the Scriptures when we approach them with a ready mind and a willingness to communicate what He has given; that God delights to give communicators of His Word "I-never-saw-that-in-that-verse-before" intellectual insights so that our listeners and readers can have "I-never-realized-all-that-was-in-that-verse" spiritual experiences.

The thrust of the commentary series unequivocally affirms that God speaks through the Scriptures today to engender faith, enable adventuresome living of the abundant life, and establish the basis of obedient discipleship. The Bible, the unique Word of God, is unlimited as a resource for Christians in communicating our hope to others. It is our weapon in the battle for truth, the guide for ministry, and the irresistible force for introducing others to God.

A biblically rooted communication of the Gospel holds in unity and oneness what divergent movements have wrought asunder. This commentary series courageously presents personal faith, caring for individuals, and social responsibility as essential, inseparable dimensions of biblical Christianity. It seeks to present the quadrilateral Gospel in its fullness which calls us to unreserved commitment to Christ, unrestricted self-esteem in His grace, unqualified love for others in personal evangelism, and undying efforts to work for justice and righteousness in a sick and suffering world.

A growing renaissance in the church today is being led by clergy and laity who are biblically rooted, Christ-centered, and Holy Spirit-empowered. They have dared to listen to people's most urgent questions and deepest needs and then to God as He speaks through the Bible. Biblical preaching is the secret of growing churches. Bible study classes and small groups are equipping the laity for ministry in the world. Dynamic Christians are finding that daily study of God's Word allows the Spirit to do in them what He wishes to communicate through them to others. These days are the most exciting time since Pentecost. The Communicator's Commentary is offered to be a primary resource of new life for this renaissance.

It has been very encouraging to receive the enthusiastic responses of pastors and teachers to the twelve New Testament volumes of the Communicator's Commentary series. The letters from communicators on the firing line in pulpits, classes, study groups, and Bible fellowship clusters across the nation, as well as the reviews of scholars and publication analysts, have indicated that we have been on target in meeting a need for a distinctly different kind of commentary on the Scriptures, a commentary that is primarily aimed at helping interpreters of the Bible to equip the laity for ministry.

This positive response has led the publisher to press on with an additional twenty-one volumes covering the books of the Old Testament. These new volumes rest upon the same goals and guidelines that undergird the New Testament volumes. Scholar-preachers with facility in Hebrew as well as vivid contemporary exposition have been selected as authors. The purpose throughout is to aid the preacher and teacher in the challenge and adventure of Old Testament exposition in communication. In each volume you will meet Yahweh, the "I AM" Lord who is Creator, Sustainer, and Redeemer in the unfolding drama of His call and care of Israel. He is the Lord

11

who acts, intervenes, judges, and presses His people into the immense challenges and privileges of being a chosen people, a holy nation. And in the descriptive exposition of each passage, the implications of the ultimate revelation of Yahweh in Jesus Christ, His Son, our Lord, are carefully spelled out to maintain unity and oneness in the preaching and teaching of the Gospel.

I am pleased to introduce the author of this commentary on Ezekiel, Douglas Stuart. Professor Stuart received his Ph.D. from Harvard University and has taught for many years at Gordon-Conwell Theological Seminary in Massachusetts. Currently he is Professor of Old Testament and Chair of the Division of Biblical Studies at the seminary. Many readers will already know Doug Stuart from his scholarly writings, including his outstanding study of Hosea, Joel, Amos, Obadiah, and Jonah in the Word Biblical Commentary series.

In his introduction to this commentary on Ezekiel, Professor Stuart notes that "Ezekiel is one of the less-often preached or taught books of the Bible." He attributes this to Ezekiel's historical particularity, daunting length, confusing apocalypticism, and frequent repetition. A member of my congregation recently confirmed this observation to me when he returned from a business trip. On Sunday morning Jon faithfully attended a church. Joining one of the adult Sunday school classes, Jon was surprised to hear its teacher begin: "Well, today we start our study of Ezekiel. This is a very hard book. I really can't figure out what's happening in the first few chapters. So I'll just read the text and then read from a commentary. I hope this makes some sense to you."

If only this disarmingly honest communicator had access to Doug Stuart's work! Professor Stuart has written in the hope that "this commentary will help you, the communicator, to be able to understand and utilize the entire book, not merely the few chapters usually paid attention to, and to convey their abundant value to your audience." I believe that this hope will be realized! As you use this commentary, it will become a trusted friend—guiding you through the intricacies of ancient history and language, wisely interpreting obscure prophetic visions, and always suggesting contemporary applications. Doug Stuart's academic expertise undergirds each comment, yet he writes in a straightforward manner for all communicators of Scripture.

This commentary will help you to hear afresh the timeless message of Ezekiel. As the community of God's people, we need to be reminded again of our call to obey God and of His judgment upon our sin. Yet we also need to remember, both corporately and individually, God's promise of renewal: "I will give you a new heart and put a new spirit within you; I will take the heart of stone out of your flesh and give you a heart of flesh" (Ezek. 36:26).

This promise will be fulfilled in fresh, new ways as you use this commentary. I commend it to you as a guide for personal and church renewal as you teach and preach from Ezekiel.

LLOYD OGILVIE

Introduction

Ezekiel is one of the less-often preached or taught books of the Bible. There are several reasons for this. As an Old Testament prophetical book, it is bound to suffer somewhat from the same neglect that applies to most prophetical books. To be understood, these books require some appreciation of the history of Israel as it intersects with the history of the ancient Near East, some appreciation of the prose and poetic speech forms employed routinely by the prophets, and some knowledge of the Mosaic covenant on which the blessings and curses of the prophets are based. In short, these books require effort, and the more effort a book requires, the less likely it is to be read—or preached.

Ezekiel also is a large book, not the kind that is usually picked as the subject for Bible studies or sermon series. Then there is the matter of its apocalyptic content. Ancient apocalyptic literature, such as is found in parts of Ezekiel, Daniel, Isaiah, Zechariah, and Revelation, is so different from anything usually encountered in modern literature that the casual reader finds it genuinely difficult to fathom.

But perhaps more daunting than any of these other factors is the way that Ezekiel is a repetitive book. For example, the vast majority of the first twenty-four chapters is given over to the message that Jerusalem will fall to the Babylonians—a message told and retold dozens of times, from every conceivable angle, again and again and again. There is much to be learned from these chapters about the certainty of God's judgment, about His faithfulness to His promises, about the wages of sin, about national and individual unrighteousness, about forgiveness, about the role of God in history, about the communicator's responsibility to proclaim God's message steadily and consistently as the years go by, and so on. But there's no escaping the fact that there is a lot of space in those first twenty-four chapters devoted to a single topic in a manner that can tend to put off the casual reader or the busy expositor.

Likewise, the large number of oracles against the foreign nations of Ezekiel's day (Chapters 25–32) are not likely to be chosen as subject matter for sermons or lessons. And any seasoned communicator can tell at a glance that Chapters 40–48, nine full chapters consisting mostly of measurements and building descriptions, is not the sort of material on which a great preaching or teaching career is likely to be built. What's left, Chapters 33–39, is the section from which most sermons on Ezekiel are preached. It is my hope that this commentary will help you, the communicator, to be able to understand and utilize the entire book, not merely the few chapters usually paid attention to, and to convey its abundant value to your audience.

The Date of Ezekiel

Ezekiel dates many of his prophecies, and all the dates fall between 593 and 571 B.C., as the table below demonstrates:

Chapter	Date
1:2	593
8:1	592
20:1	591
24:1	588
26:1	586
29:1	587
29:17	571
30:20	587
31:1	587
32:1	585
32:17	585
33:21	585
40:1	573

Within the four large blocks around which all of the book is organized (Chapters 1–24, before the fall of Jerusalem; Chapters 25–32, oracles against foreign nations; Chapters 33–39, hope and danger in the future; Chapters 40–48, vision of the new temple and land), the prophecies that are dated are arranged in strict chronological order. Ezekiel may have done this, or it may have been the work of a disciple or a later inspired editor. At any rate, Ezekiel is, as a result, one of the most readily datable books in the Bible. We can see how this prophet of the Exile had a ministry that spanned dozens of years, during which he preached God's message to people who were by no means always ready to receive it.

The Historical Situation

Ezekiel was taken into exile during the second of three deportations of Israelites to Mesopotamia by the Babylonians (605 B.C., 598 B.C., and 586 B.C., respectively). These deportations, each successively greater in numbers of people involved, were part of the death throes of the nation of Israel. It was, by any measure, a crisis time, a turning point in the history of the people of God.

Assyria had conquered the part of Israel referred to as Samaria (the ten northern tribes) in 722 B.C. That part of the promised land was then integrated into the Assyrian Empire, and the Babylonians inherited it when they completed their conquest of the Assyrians in 605 B.C. Under their powerful king, Nebuchadnezzar the Great, the Babylonians then set out to subdue the rest of the Fertile Crescent— including little Judah.

By 598 B.C., Ezekiel and large numbers of the leadership of Judah were in exile after the siege and resulting capitulation of Jerusalem under the young Israelite king, Jehoiachin (2 Kings 24:10–16). A puppet king, Zedekiah, was then installed on the throne in Jerusalem. Foolishly thinking he could lead his weakened remnant successfully against the Babylonians, Zedekiah initiated a rebellion, which resulted in a furious Babylonian retaliation, culminating in the fall of Judah after a two-year siege of Jerusalem (2 Kings 24:17–25:26).

Judah was never again an independent nation; thereafter the land was always under the domination of one foreign empire or another (first Babylon, then Persia, then Greece, then the Seleucids, then Rome, etc.). All those passages about the end of Judah in Chapters 1–24 were well warranted. This was the time when the world's most special nation was coming to an end, and it was a time when people needed to hear what was in store for other nations (Chapters 25–32) and for the true Israel in the future (Chapters 33–48).

Ezekiel the Man

We know nothing about Ezekiel apart from the book of his prophecies, and there is little in it of a biographical or autobiographical nature. Reading prophetical books for biographical information is wrongheaded anyway, since the bits and snatches of personal information are virtually always merely incidental to one prophecy or another, and are not provided as having merit in themselves.

We do know, however, that Ezekiel was a priest, the son of a priest named Buzi (1:3), that he was an exile in Babylon living in the region of the Habur Canal (1:3), that he was married until the death of his wife in exile (24:18), that he had sufficient credibility to be consulted by Israelite elders in the exile community (8:1), and that he gave some of his prophecies from his house (8:1; 20:1). If the "thirtieth year" mentioned in 1:1 refers to Ezekiel's thirtieth year, as many believe, this would give a precise sense of the prophet's age corresponding to the dated prophecies. (He would have been about fifty-two years old when he delivered his last dated prophecy, around 571 B.C., predicting the plunder of Egypt by the Babylonians [29:17–21].) This is virtually all we really know about Ezekiel. What God wanted us to have from this book was His divine message, not a portrait of the messenger.

The Unity of the Book

Ezekiel is a highly structured book, obviously arranged thematically, and, within its four major sections, also largely or entirely chronologically. Attempts to suggest that one or more of these sections (usually the great vision of Chapters 40–48) is inauthentic—that is, the product of a later, anonymous writer—have not been successful. Stylistically the book is remarkably consistent, even though its subject matter is varied. It is especially evident that the book is unified theologically, making it hard for those who tend to look for conflicting theologies in biblical materials to make much of a case for such disunity in Ezekiel.

Of Special Note

Ezekiel is a big book with a great many valuable themes and issues. Nevertheless, it may be of use to mention a few by way of introduction, as long as the reader realizes that these do not at all exhaust the riches to be found in this collection of prophecy.

The reliability of God's word. To an audience that found it hard to imagine that God would ever allow Jerusalem to fall to foreign conquest, Ezekiel preached repeatedly, almost incessantly, that Jerusalem would indeed be destroyed (Chapters 1–24). It was, and God's word, once widely doubted, was vindicated. To a discouraged exile community that saw the other nations of the world doing fine while their nation lay in ruins, Ezekiel preached lengthy oracles predicting the doom of those very nations whose prosperity seemed at the time unlikely ever to end (Chapters 25–32). All that he said came true, much of it in the lifetime of his audience, as the rapidly unfolding events of the early sixth century B.C. proved the words the Lord had given him to have been accurate beyond any possibility of human invention. To a people who seemed to themselves small and whose discouragement after the final conquest of Judah was surely very great, he preached about a new age, including the vast increase of God's people, their coming new relationship to the Lord, and the holiness God would bring about in their midst, in spite of the fact that they could not hope to manage it on their own. In this, his inspired words remarkably anticipated the Christian experience and look forward to the rewards and characteristics of eternal life in heaven.

The glory of God. Ezekiel was moved to portray dramatically the relationship of the glorious presence of God to His blessing. His visionary witnessing of the divine glory leaving the temple (Chapter 10) and later returning (Chapter 43) is a symbol of the transition from the old age to the new in Christ.

Individual responsibility. In Chapters 18 and 33 are contained some of the most thorough, carefully expressed, and absolutely clear discourses on the topic of the responsibility of the individual for his or her own sins found anywhere in the Bible. These passages provide a valuable correction to the potential errors of fatalism, rigid determinism, and blame-avoidant judgmentalism.

Israel's long history of sin. Throughout the book reference is made to the fact that the punishment of the loss of the promised land and its attendant miseries of population decimation, exile, and deprivation were not arbitrarily or suddenly decided upon. Rather, they had been earned many times over as the centuries had gone by and Israel stubbornly continued in its steady pattern of sin and disobedience to the law of God.

The power of national leadership for good or bad. Israel's past kings and the kings of other nations (particularly Tyre and Egypt) play a considerable role in certain of Ezekiel's prophecies (especially Chapters 19, 29–32, and 34). Without the support and/or guidance of these national leaders, their nations would not have entered into the practices for which the nations fell under the condemnation of God. Ezekiel uses the special word "prince" (Hebrew, *naśî'*) to designate Israel's past and future leaders, and his prophecies reassure his audience—then and now—that the messianic king will rule justly and will administer his assignments in the coming kingdom for good and not for ill (especially Chapters 44–46).

God's holiness and our responsibility for obedience. A holy God cannot tolerate disobedience, which defies people and institutions, and therefore separates them from God's saving blessing. Again and again Ezekiel's prophecies describe the disobedience of God's covenant shown by Israel or other nations, and in the magnificent vision of Chapters 40–48 the prophet is allowed to see the new promised land and its holy city and temple, all symbolizing the orderliness and peace with God that obedience to a holy God brings.

God's transcendence. The book begins and ends with visions. These visions are of a great God and what He can and will do. He is not limited to Israel's tiny boundaries or narrow interests. He is a universal God who will judge all the nations, untie the bonds that keep His people oppressed and downtrodden, free them from their slavery to sins of all sorts, and rule the nations. He will give His people a home forever, where they will enjoy His presence and worship Him rightly, the Gentile and the Jew both sharing in the eschatological kingdom, citizens of the eternal promised land.

An Outline of Ezekiel

SECTION ONE

Before the Fall of Jerusalem

Ezekiel 1:1–24:27

CHAPTER ONE

Visions of God

Ezekiel 1:1–28

Ezekiel's prophecy is filled with visions. No other Old Testament book contains so many vivid pictures of what God caused a person to see. In that sense, Ezekiel is an exceptional book, since a majority of the sixteen prophetical books in the Old Testament do not contain vision reports. Daniel has several in its latter chapters. Isaiah has some, as do Jeremiah, Amos, and Zechariah. It was obviously not necessary for a prophet to see visions to receive God's revelation. Visions were, however, one way for God to convey His truth through a prophet to His people.

A well-established tenet of learning theory is that people remember pictures better than they remember words. Popular books on how to improve one's memory and memory specialists who can dazzle an audience by memorizing hundreds of names in just a few minutes depend on this fact: the best way to remember words (or names) is to associate them with pictures in your mind. Then by remembering the pictures you can usually come up with the words.

Sociologists often describe the present era as a visual age. People are more oriented to what is visual than to what is merely spoken or written. The average American sees almost thirty hours of television a week (not to mention what he or she sees in movies, filmstrips, slides, snapshots, etc.) but would probably find it an intolerable burden to have to read any combination of written materials for that many hours. Besides this, people simply see more than they talk or listen. Except for those whose vision is impaired, seeing is a bigger part of life than words could ever be. The skillful communicator must realize this and use it to good advantage. Whether one is preaching, teaching, writing, or counseling, getting a message across effectively involves communicating in a way that will allow people

27

to form mental images. Unless what we say is clear and vivid enough that people can somehow "see" what we're saying, they are not as likely to remember it long enough for it to do any good.

God knows this and always has. Thus the Bible, while containing no photographs or drawings, is nevertheless liberally provided with word-generated images, things that can be visualized. Truths do not need to be changed or simplified to be vivid. The Bible is packed with stories that the mind's eye can follow, poetry that conjures up images in our heads, parables, similitudes, analogies, and other literary forms that turn on the visual imagination or memory. Among the prophetical books, then, Ezekiel is an example of an almost constant use of "visual" literature. Ezekiel tells us what he saw, and no other Bible author, with the possible exception of John the Apostle, the writer of Revelation, "saw" so much.

THE HEAVENS OPENED

1:1 Now it came to pass in the thirtieth year, in the fourth *month,* on the fifth *day* of the month, as I *was* among the captives by the River Chebar, *that* the heavens were opened and I saw visions of God.

2 On the fifth *day* of the month, which *was* in the fifth year of King Jehoiachin's captivity,

3 the word of the LORD came expressly to Ezekiel the priest, the son of Buzi, in the land of the Chaldeans by the River Chebar; and the hand of the LORD was upon him there.

Ezek. 1:1–3

These verses are like the title page of a book, or the information on its dust jacket or front cover. They are not intended to be exciting or dramatic, but to orient us in as simple and direct a fashion as is possible to the subject matter of what follows. While it is quite true that you can't judge a book by its cover, a good descriptive title and mention of the author's name still provide a great deal of important information. If we saw a title like *China: 1900–1950* by Yi Po Ling on the cover of a volume in a used book store, we would know at once that here was a book about a specific Asian country in a specific time period, almost surely a history, and probably written by someone who was a native of that country and a speaker of its language.

From the longer title in Ezekiel we glean an even greater amount of information. Verse 1 gives us a precise closing date for Ezekiel's visionary ministry. Verses 2 and 3, on the other hand, identify the day on which Ezekiel saw his first vision. Jehoiachin was exiled in 598 B.C. (2 Kings 24:8–17) and replaced with a puppet king, Zedekiah, by the Babylonians who conquered Jerusalem in that year (2 Kings 24:17–18). The Jews in the first exile (the one of 598 B.C.) in Mesopotamia, of whom Ezekiel was a member, refused to recognize the puppet Zedekiah as their king. They considered Jehoiachin to be the last legitimate Judean king, even though he had reigned only three months before being deposed and exiled (2 Kings 24:8). Thus Ezekiel dates his prophecies according to the amount of time that had elapsed since Jehoiachin had left Jerusalem in 598 B.C. The final prophecies (presumably those of chapters 40–48) were therefore delivered not later than the "thirtieth year" (568 B.C.) while the first prophecy (1:4 and following) was the result of Ezekiel's experience in 593 B.C., "the fifth year of King Jehoiachin's captivity."

Verse 1, in the first person and thus spoken by Ezekiel himself, functions as an introduction to the entire book and makes two paramount points: (1) Ezekiel was among the exiles; (2) he saw revelatory visions. Virtually everything we read in this extensive book was first reported to that defeated community of expatriate Jews forcibly deported to Mesopotamia by the Babylonians, an unknown number of whom (probably a few hundred) lived where Ezekiel did at the city of Tel-Abib along the Chebar River. This river was in fact a great irrigation canal that took water from the Euphrates River at the city of Nippur and carried it in a large semicircle through the countryside until it rejoined the Euphrates downstream near the city of Uruk.

Because the word "Tel" in the name Tel-Abib can mean "ruined mound," it is quite possible that the Judean exiles were allowed to live there in order to rebuild and repopulate a destroyed or abandoned city. Such a policy would have been advantageous to the Babylonians, who could use these Jewish settlers to reclaim land. For the Jews, however, it was a discouraging life. They were displaced, hopelessly distant from the type of economy and society they understood, and far out of range of ever worshiping at the Jerusalem temple as the Law required. In other words, they could no longer even carry on their religion normally, since properly worshiping God involved temple sacrifice at Mount Zion (Deuteronomy 12).

Yet to these despairing deportees God encouragingly revealed His will through the visions He gave to His prophet Ezekiel. As verse 3 tells us, Ezekiel was a priest. He was trained in the elaborate procedures for appearing ritually pure before God at the temple and properly butchering and/or cooking food for the sacrificial meals. That God should later reveal through him many specifics about the rituals and standards of worship in the new temple (chaps. 40–48) is especially understandable in the light of this training.

"The hand of the Lord was upon him" (v. 3). This idiomatic expression indicates in part God's acceptance and approval of Ezekiel, but its central emphasis is that God *was in charge of* Ezekiel, supervising his experiences and directing his life (cf. 1 Chron. 4:10; Ezra 7:6), just as any of us would hope that God would direct our lives for good.

CREATURES IN THE WIND

1:4 Then I looked, and behold, a whirlwind was coming out of the north, a great cloud with raging fire engulfing itself; and brightness *was* all around it and radiating out of its midst like the color of amber, out of the midst of the fire.

5 Also from within it *came* the likeness of four living creatures. And this *was* their appearance: they had the likeness of a man.

6 Each one had four faces, and each one had four wings.

7 Their legs *were* straight, and the soles of their feet *were* like the soles of calves' feet. They sparkled like the color of burnished bronze.

8 The hands of a man *were* under their wings on their four sides; and each of the four had faces and wings.

9 Their wings touched one another. *The creatures* did not turn when they went, but each one went straight forward.

10 As for the likeness of their faces, *each* had the face of a man; each of the four had the face of a lion

on the right side, each of the four had the face of an ox on the left side, and each of the four had the face of an eagle.

11 Thus *were* their faces. Their wings stretched upward; two *wings* of each one touched one another, and two covered their bodies.

12 And each one went straight forward; they went wherever the spirit wanted to go, and they did not turn when they went.

13 As for the likeness of the living creatures, their appearance *was* like burning coals of fire, like the appearance of torches going back and forth among the living creatures. The fire was bright, and out of the fire went lightning.

14 And the living creatures ran back and forth, in appearance like a flash of lightning.

Ezek. 1:4–14

Ezekiel's first vision began with a storm out of the north (v. 4). He saw a dark cloud, illumined round the edges as if by the backlighting of the sun, what seems to have been lightninglike fire, and a glowing center of brightness. The fact that the storm came from the north is significant. It hints that this storm has something to do with God, since one symbolic way of describing God's abode in Bible times was to depict it as in the north (Ps. 48:2; Isa. 14:13). Moreover, storms and clouds were often associated with theophanies (appearances of God: Isa. 29:6; Job 38:1; Pss. 29:3–9; 104:3). Indeed we look forward to the fact that the Lord Jesus will return with the clouds (Matt. 24:30; 26:24; 1 Thess. 4:17) that will accompany His second coming in fulfillment of this same association between storms/clouds and theophany (cf. Exod. 13:21; Lev. 16:2; etc.).

As the vision progressed, Ezekiel's attention was drawn to four *"living creatures"* (v. 5). From their description in verses 5–11 it is clear that they fit the general category of cherubim, known to us both from other accounts in the Old Testament (1 Kings 6:24–27; Exod. 25:18–22; etc.) and also from ancient Near Eastern throne sculpture (cf., e.g., *Zondervan Pictorial Bible Encyclopedia*, 1:789). Cherubim are sometimes likened to the "animals" of the angelic creation. (The creation of angels and angelic life was separate from and is therefore not described in Genesis 1–3). In the Bible, they are often depicted as

God's beasts of burden, as it were, the creatures that draw His divine chariot (see vv. 22–28).

In the present passage the emphasis is not really on their appearance, even though "appearance" (vv. 5, 13, 14) and "likeness" (vv. 5, 10, 13) are words used often in the context. Rather, the point made is that as Ezekiel gradually began to make sense of these unusual creatures that he was seeing, he could tell that they were oriented omnidirectionally. Later (vv. 15ff.) Ezekiel describes how the creatures were stationed at the four sides of the divine chariot, each facing in a different direction, yet all—by reason of having four faces—were able to see at once in any direction. Here he also notes (v. 10) that their faces represented man, lion, ox, and eagle. These were traditionally the four most impressive of the land and air animals: man, chief over all; the lion, chief of the wild animals; the ox, chief of the domesticated animals; and the eagle, chief of the birds of the air. Intelligence, strength, ferocity, freedom, etc. were all wrapped up in one in these special angelic creatures.

Ezekiel saw that when they flew bearing God's chariot they did not need to turn to face the intended direction of their flight, because they were already oriented to all directions (v. 12). He also notes how fiery and brilliant was their appearance (vv. 13–14).

So here we have special creatures, supernatural and unusual, coming out of a cloud lined with fire. So far, Ezekiel hasn't told us everything about his vision, but from what we already know, two things are evident. (1) Something that is supernatural and that involves God on the move is about to happen. (2) It is happening in Mesopotamia, to exiles who thought themselves hopelessly removed from God's presence and out of the picture religiously, as well as economically and politically.

In terms of images familiar in our day, it might well be that some people looking for God would expect Him to choose symbolically to manifest Himself via a space shuttle, or perhaps the biggest, longest, most impressive limousine anyone had ever seen. Maybe they would look for Him to choose to appear as if out of the mushroom cloud of an atomic blast, or a grand volcanic eruption, or a terrible hurricane. In fact, God's most direct, self-manifestation to date has been very different. He came as a human being, in remarkably humble circumstances, living and dying in a rather obscure part of the world. Yet we beheld His glory even more brightly than Ezekiel did (John 1:14).

In Ezekiel's day God chose means that readily conveyed something of His greatness and His special nature, so that His prophet and the people to whom His prophet relayed the message would not miss the importance of what was about to take place.

This visual display, and those that follow in the book, were by no means ends in themselves. The purpose was not simply to dazzle Ezekiel, but to point to a message. God is on the move, He is allowing Himself to be seen, He is appearing even in what people thought was a godforsaken place. What an enduring message of hope! How important it is for us to remember that God is never confined, never limited, never distracted, never disinterested in His people.

WHEELS IN WHEELS

1:15 Now as I looked at the living creatures, behold, a wheel *was* on the earth beside each living creature with its four faces.

16 The appearance of the wheels and their workings *was* like the color of beryl, and all four had the same likeness. The appearance of their workings *was*, as it were, a wheel in the middle of a wheel.

17 When they moved, they went toward any one of four directions; they did not turn aside when they went.

18 As for their rims, they were so high they were awesome; and their rims *were* full of eyes, all around the four of them.

19 When the living creatures went, the wheels went beside them; and when the living creatures were lifted up from the earth, the wheels were lifted up.

20 Wherever the spirit wanted to go, they went, *because* there the spirit went; and the wheels were lifted together with them, for the spirit of the living creatures *was* in the wheels.

21 When those went, *these* went; when those stood, *these* stood; and when those were lifted up from the earth, the wheels were lifted up together with them, for the spirit of the living creatures *was* in the wheels.

Ezek. 1:15-21

Because of the language of verse 16, *"a wheel in the middle of a wheel,"* much misunderstanding about the nature of Ezekiel's vision has occurred. There have been suggestions that a little wheel was somehow encased in a big one; that the smaller wheel was perhaps a rim; that the wheels counter-rotated in opposite directions as part of a propulsion system of some sort; that the wheels were symbolic of key truth hidden within a larger corpus of fact; or even that Ezekiel was seeing the workings of a flying saucer.

In fact, the explanation is not complicated, and it relates to the omnidirectional emphasis already made in the preceding passage in connection with the cherubim. The two sets of wheels were within each other in the sense of being interconnected on different axes. One wheel intersected the other at right angles so that no turning was necessary to go in any of the four main directions, as verse 17 says. (Each wheel could, of course, go in two directions since a wheel can go forward or backward equally easily.) Moreover, the wheels were so closely linked to the cherubim (v. 22), which they were right beside (v. 15), that there was no lack of response to the cherubim's leading (v. 19). Together, the cherubim all flying in concert and the wheels always ready to go without needing to turn provided a means of conveyance that could go anywhere, in any direction, immediately (v. 21).

That was the point: the spirit of the living creatures was in the wheels so that this chariot could move fast. God was moving—and fast! Ezekiel and his compatriots needed to be encouraged and challenged. Ezekiel's vision provided him with a vivid symbol of the fact that nothing was keeping God from going wherever He wanted to. Just as He had protected these people and controlled their fortunes in Palestine, He was now prepared to protect and direct their lives in exile in Babylon. God had wheels! He was not limited. He could go anywhere anytime.

The concept of God shared by Ezekiel's countrymen, the Judean exiles, had been too small. They had assumed, like many peoples of ancient times, that gods had jurisdiction only over their own nations. But here was evidence of a different sort of jurisdiction. One God, the God, was traveling the earth, in control of it all. His supremacy might just mean that their situation was not so hopeless after all.

Thus ultimately the chariot vision is a vision of hope for a people who needed encouragement to hope once again. A vision of God's mobility was for them a message not to despair but to anticipate: in what way was God on the move and how did it concern them? The following passages provided the answer.

FIRMAMENT AND THRONE

1:22 The likeness of the firmament above the heads of the living creatures *was* like the color of an awesome crystal, stretched out over their heads.

23 And under the firmament their wings *spread out* straight, one toward another. Each one had two which covered one side, and each one had two which covered the other side of the body.

24 When they went, I heard the noise of their wings, like the noise of many waters, like the voice of the Almighty, a tumult like the noise of an army; and when they stood still, they let down their wings.

25 A voice came from above the firmament that *was* over their heads; whenever they stood, they let down their wings.

26 And above the firmament over their heads *was* the likeness of a throne, in appearance like a sapphire stone; on the likeness of the throne *was* a likeness with the appearance of a man high above it.

27 Also from the appearance of His waist and upward I saw, as it were, the color of amber with the appearance of fire all around within it; and from the appearance of His waist and downward I saw, as it were, the appearance of fire with brightness all around.

28 Like the appearance of a rainbow in a cloud on a rainy day, so *was* the appearance of the brightness all around it. This *was* the appearance of the likeness of the glory of the LORD.

So when I saw *it*, I fell on my face, and I heard a voice of One speaking.

Ezek. 1:22-28

The English word "firmament" translates the Hebrew *rāqî'a*, a word conveying the sense of something spread out, extensive. Verses

22–24 describe the firmament as gemlike, supported by the cherubim, whose wings made a great roar as they flew around bearing the firmament. Verses 25–26 reveal that the firmament functioned as a kind of platform for God's throne. The "likeness" on the throne was that of God, who, as verses 27–28 tell us, could not really be seen except in general shape, and whose most "visible" feature was His glorious shining brightness. Firmament, throne, wheels, and cherubim together, commanded by the voice of God (v. 25), constituted an impressive picture of God's giant, fiery, air chariot driven by the King of kings Himself, which had touched down right there at the obscure town of Tel-Abib.

A previously unknown prophet might now have a firsthand experience of the power and majesty of God Himself. No wonder Ezekiel tells us that he fell on his face (v. 28). In ancient times it was standard practice for people to lie face down on the ground when they appeared before a monarch. In Egypt, at certain times at least, appearing before the Pharaoh required formal groveling: rolling from stomach to back seven times before being allowed to rise at the command of the Pharaoh. Here Ezekiel is privileged to hear the voice of God speaking to him. He did not seek this audience with God, but rather God sought him out and showed him a token of His splendor and power. What follows then, we may expect, ought to be an indication of what God has in store for Ezekiel and his countrymen, a revelation to them of what God is about to do.

Let us hope that the majesty of God would always cause us, similarly, to respect and honor Him. His glory is not something reserved for Old Testament-era visions, but part of what we are to manifest as a result of His indwelling us (2 Cor. 3:7–18). We must show forth His glory, not merely be impressed by it. As Christ revealed the Father, so we are to imitate the Son (1 Cor. 4:16; 1 Thess. 1:6; cf. Eph. 5:1).

God is truly a glorious being. It will be our pleasure to behold and adore that glory in heaven, but we ought not to ignore our opportunity to get in practice now. By prayer, meditation, worship, and study of His words and deeds in Scripture, we can renew our own contact with God's glory in a strengthening, even impelling way. Then, just as Ezekiel's vision of God's glory led to action on behalf of God, we can act with confidence to do God's will, reminded by His glory of the certainty of our success.

CHAPTER TWO

Five Commissions

Ezekiel 2:1-3:27

Ezekiel now learns of his call. God has for him an almost intolerable assignment. He must preach a message likely to be rejected as ridiculous to a group of people, the Israelites, whose long history has been characterized by their rebelliousness against God and many of whom are in exile in a foreign country as a result. To a bitter, hostile, unreceptive audience he must faithfully convey God's word even if no one listens.

Again and again God reminds Ezekiel of the necessity of his task and of the need to be faithful to it. No fewer than five times God commissions His prophet in symbolic ways to undertake the assignment, hard though it may be. Ezekiel even has to experience the inability to speak (the fifth commission) as a forceful experiential reminder of the fact that he has no authority to make up on his own what he says to his fellow Israelites. Rather, only God can, as it were, loose his tongue. He must let God speak through him, and not invent anything himself or take his message from anyone else. Originality is usually prized among writers and speakers. Yet there was to be no originality in Ezekiel's doctrine. In all five commissions he is reminded that his job is to convey and not to create. The great king has arrived among the exiles to give him his assignment. He must be faithful.

FIRST COMMISSION (REBELS)

2:1 And He said to me, "Son of man, stand on your feet, and I will speak to you."

2 Then the Spirit entered me when He spoke to

37

me, and set me on my feet; and I heard Him who spoke to me.

3 And He said to me: "Son of man, I am sending you to the children of Israel, to a rebellious nation that has rebelled against Me; they and their fathers have transgressed against Me to this very day.

4 "For *they are* impudent and stubborn children. I am sending you to them, and you shall say to them, 'Thus says the Lord GOD.'

5 "As for them, whether they hear or whether they refuse—for they *are* a rebellious house—yet they will know that a prophet has been among them.

6 "And you, son of man, do not be afraid of them nor be afraid of their words, though briers and thorns *are* with you and you dwell among scorpions; do not be afraid of their words or dismayed by their looks, though they *are* a rebellious house.

7 "You shall speak My words to them, whether they hear or whether they refuse, for they *are* rebellious."

Ezek. 2:1–7

Good parents make sure that their children hear what they need to hear: warnings about safety, advice about associations and habits, counsel about the proper directions in life, etc. Sometimes a parent must repeat a type of warning or advice over and over to be sure that a child gets the message. Everyone is capable of listening without paying attention, and the Children of Israel were no exception.

But Israel's refusal to *"hear"* (vv. 5, 7) went even beyond this. The verb šāmaˤ, rendered "hear," can also carry the connotation "heed/obey," as it does in this case. Ezekiel had every reason to believe that his fellow Israelites in exile could actually hear what he said to them. What he had reason to be unsure of, however, is whether they would accept his words as those of God or ignore them. Israel's history is full of examples of the people's listening to false prophets instead of true prophets of the Lord (e.g., 1 Kings 20; Jer. 14:14–16; Isa. 59:13). When false prophets told the people what they wanted to "hear," for example, that they would prosper even though they had lived selfishly and did not acknowledge God or worship Him exclusively, the people tended to "hear." But Ezekiel was being required to announce judgment and to call for repentance, an unpopular message of the sort the people had plenty of practice not "hearing."

God addresses him (vv. 1, 3, 6, and about ninety times hereafter) as "son of man" (Hebrew, *ben ʾādām*) in a manner that emphasizes his humanity as over against God's supernatural greatness and power. The expression "son of" can have a special idiomatic sense in Hebrew. "Son of" indicates a close relationship even when it does not literally connote sonship. For example, in Jon. 4:10 the leafy gourd that sheltered Jonah is called "a son of a night," meaning that it lasted only one night. Jesus calls a person of peaceful intentions and hospitality literally "a son of peace" in Luke 10:6. A person deserving to die is literally a "son of death" in 1 Sam. 10:31. Thus Ezekiel, as "son of man" is the human. Later, the term took on the symbolism of *The Human* and became a Messianic term connoting in effect a new Adam, but here it stresses Ezekiel's inferiority to and dependence on God, who alone is sovereign.

In light of the characterization of the Israelites as rebels (vv. 3, 5, 6, 7), transgressors (v. 3), and impudent and stubborn (v. 4), it is no wonder that Ezekiel might be afraid to go to them as a prophet. Who wants a career full of hostility? Who could enjoy the kind of angry criticism and contempt that would be as painful to endure as thorns or scorpions? What modern-day pastor would choose to take a parish where he or she was guaranteed a hostile rejection from the congregation? Is it easy for a missionary to set off for a tribe or territory where he or she is sure to meet not merely hostile disapproval of God's message, but rejection *personally*? There are many modern-day saints who understand from experience exactly what Ezekiel was called to endure, but there are few who enjoyed the process. Rare is the person who can set out on a task knowing that people will hate him or her for doing it. But this is exactly what Ezekiel was called to do. His faithfulness stands as a challenge to ours.

THE SWEET SCROLL

2:8 "But you, son of man, hear what I say to you.
Do not be rebellious like that rebellious house; open
your mouth and eat what I give you."

39

9 Now when I looked, there was a hand stretched out to me; and behold, a scroll of a book *was* in it.

10 Then He spread it before me; and *there was* writing on the inside and on the outside, and written on it *were* lamentations and mourning and woe.

3:1 Moreover He said to me, "Son of man, eat what you find; eat this scroll, and go, speak to the house of Israel."

2 So I opened my mouth, and He caused me to eat that scroll.

3 And He said to me, "Son of man, feed your belly, and fill your stomach with this scroll that I give you." So I ate, and it was in my mouth like honey in sweetness.

Ezek. 2:8–3:3

The command to eat the scroll given him from God represents both the first act of obedience on the part of Ezekiel and also a divine means of encouragement to the newly called prophet. Scrolls were no more appetizing in Bible times than they would seem to be today. Yet by his obedience to this unusual command, Ezekiel shows himself to have accepted God's call to be a prophet to his fellow exiles and also demonstrates that he is willing to do whatever God commands him to do as part of the process. The Israelites were indeed rebellious. Ezekiel could not be if he were to serve God responsibly (2:8). The *"scroll of a book"* (Hebrew, *megillat-sēper*) would not be a dainty thing but a big, thick papyrus or leather roll. Indeed, Ezekiel reports that *"He caused me to eat that scroll"* as if it were something he would otherwise expect to choke on and not be able to consume. To his apparent surprise, however, it was as sweet as honey when he actually ate it (3:3).

This incident reminds us of Jesus' teaching that people cannot live only on food but need also the Word of God to sustain their lives (Matt. 4:4), a teaching which Jesus repeated from its original statement in Deut. 8:3. It is not food as usual that will give Ezekiel the strength he needs to carry on his difficult ministry, but rather God's Word. It must fill him (3:3) so that he preaches only what God has given him to preach and nothing else.

This is also the meaning of the fact that the scroll is written on both sides, *"on the inside and on the outside"* (2:10). It was completely

40

covered with writing, so that neither Ezekiel nor anyone else could add anything to it. Scrolls in ancient times were not normally written upon this way, but were blank on one side. Perhaps the writing on both sides also served to alert Ezekiel to the sheer amount of communication that God was calling him to do.

Characteristic of Ezekiel's obligatory preaching would be lamentation, mourning, and woe (2:10). In the Hebrew these words function as synonyms for one another, so there is no suggestion here that his message had three slightly differing facets or the like. Rather, what Ezekiel had to bring to his fellow exiles was a message of bad news, and plenty of it. In fact, when Jerusalem fell in 586 B.C. (chap. 33), God immediately gave to Ezekiel a message of hope for the future of Israel. So his preaching was not entirely negative throughout his career. But the bulk of it was indeed bad news for those to whom it was addressed, the Jews in exile as well as the Jews in Judah and Jerusalem, and the many nations of the Fertile Crescent whose actions in opposing and oppressing one another would not remain unpunished by the Righteous Judge of all nations.

Correspondingly, the faithful communicator of the Word of God has no right to soften the blow that hearing the truth may bring to those caught up in sin. While no preacher, teacher, evangelist, or counselor should want to emphasize the negative out of proportion to the positive, and while the gospel represents by its very essence good news announced to the whole world, there is also the inescapable fact that God has appointed a time at which He will judge the world. There is a hell, and it will receive for destruction those who have rebelled against God. To hide this from people is to do them no favor. Lovingly, sensitively, but honestly and seriously, the warning must be heard along with the invitation.

SECOND COMMISSION (POOR LISTENERS)

3:4 Then He said to me: "Son of man, go to the house of Israel and speak with My words to them.

5 "For you *are* not sent to a people of unfamiliar speech and of hard language, *but* to the house of Israel,

6 "not to many people of unfamiliar speech and of hard language, whose words you cannot

understand. Surely, had I sent you to them, they
would have listened to you.

7 "But the house of Israel will not listen to you,
because they will not listen to Me; for all the house
of Israel *are* impudent and hard-hearted.

8 "Behold, I have made your face strong against
their faces, and your forehead strong against their
foreheads.

9 "Like adamant stone, harder than flint, I have
made your forehead; do not be afraid of them, nor be
dismayed at their looks, though they *are* a rebellious
house."

Ezek. 3:4–9

Again God's commission to Ezekiel concerns the importance of
perseverance. The term "house of Israel" (Hebrew, *bêt yiśrāʾēl*) is
used three times in this short passage (vv. 4, 5, 7) and "house" alone
is used once as well (v. 9). A more meaningful translation might be
"family of Israel" and "family" (v. 9). The Israelites are a people descended from a common ancestry, who are God's people as well as
merely being a nation among others. And they are Ezekiel's own
people, the folks he grew up with, the people whose language is also
his mother tongue (vv. 5–6).

Yet familiarity can breed contempt. Jesus' comment that a prophet
receives honor everywhere but the place he is from (Matt. 13:57)
reflects a fact that Ezekiel must confront. Foreigners would have listened to him (v. 6b), perhaps even with the level of acceptance that
Jonah found among the citizens of the Assyrian chief city, Nineveh
(Jon. 3:5), because he would have been someone new, an outsider,
not someone to whom they were accustomed. But Ezekiel was, as it
were, just another former Judean temple priest, of whom there were
probably plenty among the exiles, and the fact that he would approach his own people with a prophetic message would be nothing
impressive to them.

Even the most eloquent evangelist knows how much more difficult
it is to call a family member or a close friend to faith and repentance
than to call a total stranger. The pastor knows how much less likely
his or her advice is to be taken well by his or her spouse or children
or siblings than by those in the congregation to whom he or she is

more formally, professionally connected. Yet those close to us need us, too. We do not usually have the luxury of calling in outside specialists. Nobody will care for our families, friends, the people we grew up with, neighbors, close associates, etc., in the same way that we will. So even though it can be harder and more awkward, we must still go to them. They are our own, as the house of Israel was Ezekiel's own.

In addition to the description of the Israelites as *"impudent"* (v. 7), repeated from 2:4, Ezekiel hears his people also described as *"hard-hearted"* (v. 7). This is not really a new designation, since it is a synonym of "stubborn" used in 2:4, which it reflects in company with impudent (v. 7). It is, however, the same essential term used at points in Exodus to describe Pharaoh's attitude (*qāšāh lēb*; cf. Exod. 7:3) and thus may have sent to Ezekiel the rather unsettling message that he might be running into the same kind of opposition that Moses encountered almost a millennium before, in trying to bring God's Word to a hostile audience.

Again God encouraged Ezekiel by symbolically strengthening his face and forehead (vv. 8–9). We talk about "facing" difficult situations. The Hebrew idiom is comparable. Ezekiel learns that it will be hard to go back again and again to face an unreceptive, resentful audience and tell them what God wants them to hear, but he also learns that God will give him the strength and resolve to do it.

Perhaps the key statement in the present passage is found in verse 7, *"Israel will not listen to you, because they will not listen to Me."* Ezekiel must understand that the rejection he encounters is not ultimately personally directed, though it may appear so. If he speaks only what God has given him, adding nothing of his own making to the inspired word (2:10; 3:4), then he can at least have the confidence that any lack of acceptance of his message is not his fault.

This we too must guard against. The gospel we preach cannot be our own reformulation, our own selection, our own creative construction. It must be God's word. We want to clarify, not invent. Originality should have no premium with the faithful communication of God's message. If others reject God's message, we cannot stop that. But let us be sure it is not our way of telling God's message that is the problem.

THIRD COMMISSION (LIFTED BY THE SPIRIT)

3:10 Moreover He said to me: "Son of man, receive
into your heart all My words that I speak to you, and
hear with your ears.

11 "And go, get to the captives, to the children of
your people, and speak to them and tell them, 'Thus
says the Lord GOD,' whether they hear, or whether
they refuse."

12 Then the Spirit lifted me up, and I heard behind
me a great thunderous voice: "Blessed *is* the glory of
the LORD from His place!"

13 *I* also *heard* the noise of the wings of the living
creatures that touched one another, and the noise of
the wheels beside them, and a great thunderous noise.

14 So the Spirit lifted me up and took me away,
and I went in bitterness, in the heat of my spirit; but
the hand of the LORD was strong upon me.

15 Then I came to the captives at Tel Abib, who
dwelt by the River Chebar; and I sat where they sat,
and remained there astonished among them seven
days.

Ezek. 3:10–15

God continues to address Ezekiel not by his name but by the title
"Son of Man" (v. 10) so as to remind him of his inferior, dependent
relationship to God. He continues also to emphasize Ezekiel's special
ministry to his own people (*"children of your people"*), those whose
circumstances were the same as his own, that is, exile. And now,
Ezekiel reports that he was actually taken from wherever he had
been until this point (somewhere by himself, outside the city?) and
was brought by God's Spirit back to where the other captives who
lived at Tel-Abib were located.

Ezekiel was not yet able to begin preaching the divine message to
them. He had been overwhelmed by his visions, conversations, and
lately his experience of being carried from one location to another
by the Spirit (v. 14). So he remained *"astonished"* (Hebrew, *mašmîm,*
"overwhelmed," "desolated") for an entire week. Probably this means
that he was having little contact with others, staying inside and
keeping quiet. It does not necessarily mean that he was unable to
speak or the like (see below, 3:22–27).

44

By the end of this passage, a week has passed since Ezekiel's first sighting of the storm cloud out of the north (1:4). The date is still the same unspecified month in the fifth year of Jehoiachin's captivity, 593 B.C., but we move from the fifth day to the twelfth in these verses. From 1:4 to 3:15a, a lot happened in the course of a single day.

But it was not just the rapidity of major revelatory events that left Ezekiel so devastated. Verse 14 tells us about his resultant *"bitterness"* and *"heat of spirit"* as well as his realization that *"the hand of the Lord was strong upon me."* The bitterness and heat (anger and agitation) that he felt were understandable. His life had been changed by the call of God from what may well have been a quiet, perhaps even comfortably secure existence to one characterized, according to God's promise, by difficulty, rejection, and hostility. The word *"but"* should read *"and"* in verse 14, since the idea of the Lord's hand being "strong" (Hebrew, *hāzāqāh*) upon someone is a way of conveying that one has been forced into a difficult set of circumstances. We already learned from 1:3 that the Lord's hand (control) was on Ezekiel. Now we know that it was not always a pleasant experience.

But that is something all of God's servants can acknowledge, if they are honest enough to admit it. We sometimes attempt to avoid any impression that our lives are not constantly happy and that we are not always confident and positive, for fear that if we are more frank, people will conclude that the Christian's life is not sufficiently different from the non-Christian's life. We forget that faithfulness and love are to characterize the demeanor of the Christian, not coziness and freedom from hardship. Thus "testimonies" often tell only of *past* misery and *present* bliss, not just in terms of one's relationship to God, but as if all of life had become trouble free. Nowhere in the Bible is reality avoided in this way, however. The trials of life, major and minor, are to be expected and are not embarrassments to God's people. It is how we respond to discouragement and to the "heavy hand of God" upon us that represents an effective testimony. What Ezekiel had found out about his life ahead was genuinely painful to him, and his reaction of dismay was entirely reasonable. However, he neither gave up nor hid his distress. That should be an example to us.

In verse 10, *"receive into your heart"* simply means "commit to memory" (cf. Luke 2:51). It does not imply some special level of acceptance or emotional agreement, but the need for Ezekiel to be accurate.

In verse 12, the statement, *"Blessed is the glory of the Lord from His place"* is apparently the result of a scribe's copy mistake, at a time when the Hebrew letter *mem* could easily be mistaken for the Hebrew letter *kaph*. Thus an original *berûm* ("as . . . arose") was miscopied into *barûk* ("blessed . . ."). It would be best, then, to translate "I heard behind me a great thunderous sound [Hebrew, *gôl*] as the glory of the Lord arose from its place," which fits the context completely and lets us know that God's great omnidirectional chariot was taking off and Ezekiel's inaugural vision had come to an end.

FOURTH COMMISSION (WATCHMAN FOR ISRAEL)

3:16 Now it came to pass at the end of seven days that the word of the LORD came to me, saying,

17 "Son of man, I have made you a watchman for the house of Israel; therefore hear a word from My mouth, and give them warning from Me:

18 "When I say to the wicked, 'You shall surely die,' and you give him no warning, nor speak to warn the wicked from his wicked way, to save his life, that same wicked *man* shall die in his iniquity; but his blood I will require at your hand.

19 "Yet, if you warn the wicked, and he does not turn from his wickedness, nor from his wicked way, he shall die in his iniquity; but you have delivered your soul.

20 "Again, when a righteous *man* turns from his righteousness and commits iniquity, and I lay a stumbling block before him, he shall die; because you did not give him warning, he shall die in his sin, and his righteousness which he has done shall not be remembered; but his blood I will require at your hand.

21 "Nevertheless if you warn the righteous *man* that the righteous should not sin, and he does not sin, he shall surely live because he took warning; also you will have delivered your soul."

Ezek. 3:16–21

Once Ezekiel again heard the Word of the Lord, his week-long period of recuperation was over. Verse 16 says that the Word of the

Lord "came" to Ezekiel, similarly to 1:3. This is one of fifty times that this expression is used, and there are many other places in the book where it could have been said, but where some other, usually similar, expression for hearing God's Word was employed instead. The expression does not imply that Ezekiel physically had to be reached by God's Word, but means simply "Ezekiel had/got God's Word." The emphasis is on Ezekiel's own lack of creative involvement: he passes on what he hears and learns unchanged, so that his own hearers can know that his message comes directly from God.

We are also told that God made Ezekiel as a watchman. This was an assignment, not an invitation. As a prophet, he would have to do the job required of him, and this one carried with it extensive responsibility. Prophets are often likened to watchmen in the Old Testament (Isa. 56:10; Jer. 6:17; Hos. 9:8; Hab. 2:1) because they must be aware of what is happening and especially what is coming in the future, because they have to try to arouse their fellow citizens to take account of the threats that they face, and because they are responsible for the fate of a community—others expect them not to fail to warn the populace of important events or of danger. For God to talk of *"My mouth"* (v. 17) is merely an idiomatic way of saying "directly from Me" and implies nothing about God's having physical characteristics.

The first kind of warning Ezekiel must be prepared to give is a warning to evil people. *"You shall surely die"* (v. 18) represents the standard language of capital punishment laws in the Pentateuch (e.g., Exod. 21:12; Lev. 20:10) and is the very thing that God warned Adam and Eve would be the consequence of their disobedience in eating the forbidden fruit (Gen. 2:17). In other words, eternal death or the second death (Rev. 20:14) is not in focus here. The judgment yet to come will determine that. Here the issue is death in this world from accident, warfare, disease, or any other proximate cause that God might choose to inflict on a wicked person or group.

Is there any hope for such people? Yes, indeed. As verse 19 suggests, the purpose of the prophet's warning is to produce a turning from iniquity to righteousness, thereby sparing their lives. However, if people thus warned did not repent and change because they hadn't been warned, then *Ezekiel* would be guilty of their "blood," which would be "required" of him (v. 18). This is the language of vengeance, which the Bible reminds us is God's right alone (Deut. 32:35; Heb.

10:30). Vengeance involves punishing someone in return for something harmful they have done. Ezekiel would be held responsible for the earthly death of a wicked person put to death by God (symbolically told, "You shall surely die") because he had failed to place before that person the challenge that might have allowed him to exercise his free will to stop breaking God's covenant. If, however, Ezekiel faithfully gives the warning, his obligation would be discharged. All responsibility would then rest on the warned person.

The second kind of warning applies to the righteous person (vv. 20–21). If he has stopped being righteous and has committed transgressions against God's law, he is in danger of earthly death just as the wicked person is. Note that *"stumbling block"* (Hebrew, *miškōl*) in verse 20, like its Greek translation *skandalon* in the New Testament, means figuratively some factor or event that serves as a problem or barrier or source of harm. In other words, the righteous and the wicked are not differentiated here as to how they might die. The wicked person's hearing God tell him he will die (v. 18) and the righteous person's tripping over a stumbling block are merely two comparable ways of describing earthly death at the hands of an angry God.

The righteous, therefore, need a warning too, if for no other reason than to help keep them from turning away from righteousness (v. 21). Paul's stern advice to Christians, "let him who thinks he stands take heed lest he fall" (1 Cor. 10:12) is of the same sort. People who choose to rebel against God are in danger of incurring divine wrath.

Later in Ezekiel's ministry he again was called to refer to his commission to be a watchman (33:1–11). There as well as here, the important doctrine of individual responsibility is stated prominently. People are responsible to do what they know they ought to. If a person does not realize, for whatever reason, that a responsibility is incumbent on him or her, then an excuse for not carrying out that responsibility may be appropriate. But if a person consciously disregards God's direct warning, that is another matter. As a watchman, Ezekiel faithfully discharged his individual responsibility, so that the guilt for those who disobeyed God was not his but their own.

But how does this responsibility involve the modern-day Christian? Much the same, indeed, as it involved Ezekiel. If a person is called by God to convey his word (witness) to any person or audience, he or she is not free to fail to fulfill the terms of the call. In this regard, the modern preacher, counselor, evangelist, missionary, teacher, writer, or the like, whether layperson or professional, is not so different from any person who takes on a responsible task. Failure to live up to the responsibility implied in the task is bound to do harm, and such failure ought to be called to account. Here we do not talk about ability but about willingness. Important jobs carry important responsibilities, duties that cannot be avoided.

As for those gifted and called to speak God's Word, they must take refuge in the faithful fulfillment of their responsibility and not mistakenly depend for satisfaction on the results. Those who seek to persuade people should not forget that people, once informed, are responsible for their own choices. We cannot let the effectiveness of our lives be hampered by regret or self-condemnation for what others refuse to do with the Word of God we have faithfully conveyed to them.

FIFTH COMMISSION (DUMBNESS)

3:22 Then the hand of the LORD was upon me there, and He said to me, "Arise, go out into the plain, and there I shall talk with you."

23 So I arose and went out into the plain, and behold, the glory of the LORD stood there, like the glory which I saw by the River Chebar; and I fell on my face.

24 Then the Spirit entered me and set me on my feet, and spoke with me and said to me: "Go, shut yourself inside your house.

25 "And you, O son of man, surely they will put ropes on you and bind you with them, so that you cannot go out among them.

26 "I will make your tongue cling to the roof of your mouth, so that you shall be mute and not be one to rebuke them, for they *are* a rebellious house.

27 "But when I speak with you, I will open your mouth, and you shall say to them, 'Thus says the Lord GOD.' He who hears, let him hear; and he who refuses, let him refuse; for they *are* a rebellious house."

Ezek. 3:22–27

In this final stage of Ezekiel's orientation to the difficult role of prophet, he learns the importance of submission to the divine word. God must have a prophet who will not act on his own, but who will appear and speak in public only when God's spirit moves him to do so.

Again the *"hand of the Lord"* is upon Ezekiel, meaning that he is under God's control (v. 22). He is commanded to go out to *"the plain"* (Hebrew, *biqʿāh*), the same word, perhaps referring to the same place, translated "valley" here as well, since a *biqʿāh* is a space between mountains as opposed to the broad plains one can find all over Mesopotamia.

In the valley, he once again saw the glory of the Lord that had so impressed him in his initial vision (1:28) and which had gone with the divine chariot when that first vision had ended (3:12). Ezekiel once again fell on his face (v. 23; cf. 1:28) because he knew that he was once more in the presence of the great King of kings. Once more (v. 24; cf. 2:2) the Spirit of God entered into him and set him on his feet. Thus God was still accepting him and would deal with him as an approved servant. (For a sovereign to invite a suppliant to stand meant that he at least was willing to do business with him.)

Ezekiel must now undertake his first enactment prophecy. An enactment prophecy, also called "dramatic prophecy" or "symbolic action prophecy," is something like the ancient equivalent of a speech based on visual aids. We who are used to seeing speakers with charts, slides, films, overhead projector transparencies, or other visual aids know how useful such devices may be to the communication process. Similarly, prophets frequently were called to act out their messages, or some key component of them, so as to dramatize by visual impact the point being made. God had already given His own visually dramatic message (chap. 1). Now Ezekiel began along similar, though much less spectacular, lines.

This first enactment prophecy was for Ezekiel's benefit mainly. Later he would do or create things that symbolized a message for the Israelites in exile or for other nations. But the fifth commission's enactments are directed at Ezekiel himself, so that he might learn obedience by them.

Three kinds of confinement are required of him in this enactment. First, he must stay at home (v. 24). This symbolizes his need from now on to appear formally in public only on official business as God's representative. Such a prohibition would not prevent him from ever setting foot outside his house in the future, but his *public service* from now on must be limited to his role as a prophet. Second, and closely related, he must be tied up (v. 25). This symbolizes that he is God's prisoner, subject to God's will. The Apostle Paul, literally a Roman prisoner, likewise saw himself as a prisoner of Christ (e.g., Philemon 1). The Hebrew literally says "they will put ropes on you and bind you" but "they" can be just as indefinite in Hebrew as in English. In other words, this is not an enactment that Ezekiel was forced into, but something he arranged. Friends or family would publicly tie him up now and again to symbolize his restriction to God's ministry. He would not, however, actually be tied up constantly. Third, Ezekiel would be denied speech. This *was* an involuntary action and probably the most miserable of the three. For the tongue to cling to the roof of the mouth (v. 26) is an idiomatic way of saying that one cannot talk (cf. Job 29:10; Ps. 137:6). God says that Ezekiel cannot be a "reprover" (Hebrew, *môkîaḥ*) to the Israelites in exile, meaning that he cannot *on his own* criticize them even though they are, as has been said often already and is said again here, rebellious (vv. 26–27). He must learn to wait for God to give him the message. This God promises to do (v. 27).

Note the doctrine of individual responsibility once again in verse 27: *"He who hears, let him hear; and he who refuses, let him refuse."* Jesus uses this same essential language frequently (e.g., Mark 4:9, 23; 7:16). People are free to react by acceptance or rejection of God's message. God invites response but does not force it.

Any Christian would do well to take to heart God's instruction to Ezekiel in this passage. We do not have the right *on our own* to criticize or condemn people. We have no authority to be reprovers to anybody. We cannot set the standards people should meet, nor pick the time to confront them according to those standards. Rebuke and reproof must come from the Lord. Only when what people are doing clearly violates what He has commanded, and only as we are called and commissioned by God to have a ministry of authoritative communication to a given group, of whatever size, can we expect God's blessing. Otherwise, we may well become nothing more than complainers, whose criticisms of others are seen only as self-interested and whose negative spirit brings no glory to God.

When prominent persons have unintentionally created needless controversy or aroused needless opposition in the press, it has usually been the result of ill-prepared, inadequately thought out reactive attacks, or critical pronouncements. When Christians most open themselves up to distrust is not simply when they say hard things, but when their words are perceived as self-serving rather than God-serving. If God calls us to rebuke someone or some group, or even our whole culture, we must surely do so—but on His terms, according to His standards, under His authority.

CHAPTER THREE

Four Symbolic Portrayals of Jerusalem's Coming Siege

Ezekiel 4:1–5:17

Here begin Ezekiel's prophecies directed toward others than himself. In this section of the book the city of Jerusalem and punishment for the sin of its inhabitants constitute the focus of the prophecies. There is no way to tell how much time elapsed after Ezekiel's initial confinement (3:24) and his receiving the summons to build a model of Jerusalem under siege (4:1), the first of the four enactment prophecies that dominate these two chapters. Probably it is still 593 B.C., about five years before the Babylonian armies of Nebuchadnezzar actually instituted the two-year siege that brought Jerusalem finally to defeat in 586 B.C. (2 Kings 25:1–10).

All four enactment prophecies, unusual as they were, had the purpose of calling attention to the coming disaster in Judah's capital. That siege is then described in some detail in 5:12–17. Ezekiel's fellow exiles surely did not expect a second Babylonian invasion of Judah and a second siege of the city ending in its destruction. From their point of view what had happened to them, deportation and resettlement, was probably about as severe a consequence of Babylonian displeasure as they would likely see.

They could not be aware, as God was, of the increasing scheming on the part of the puppet king, Zedekiah, to declare independence from Babylon and break the existing treaty with its monarch (2 Kings 25:20; 2 Chron. 36:13). They could not assume that this pro-Babylonian administration could turn against its benefactors and thus incur Nebuchadnezzar's wrath. But even more important, they did not seem to understand the extent of God's anger against His people. In reality, however, the first siege, capture, and exile of which they had been part (2 Kings 25:10–16) was only a token of what was to come.

EZEKIEL BUILDS A MODEL OF JERUSALEM

4:1 "You also, son of man, take a clay tablet and lay it before you, and portray on it a city, Jerusalem.

2 "Lay siege against it, build a siege wall against it, and heap up a mound against it; set camps against it also, and place battering rams against it all around.

3 "Moreover take for yourself an iron plate, and set it *as* an iron wall between you and the city. Set your face against it, and it shall be besieged, and you shall lay siege against it. This *will be* a sign to the house of Israel."

Ezek. 4:1–3

Most of us have built models: houses from clay, planes or cars from kits, perhaps a village scene from papier-mâché. Ezekiel had undoubtedly built things from clay and wood as a child. Now he was actually called by God to build a model, but one that had nothing to do with play.

God told him to take a clay tablet, that is, a flat block of moist clay not yet baked, and *"portray"* (draw) on it a map of Jerusalem. Clay tablets used for writing were almost never larger than a foot square, and this may have been the size of Ezekiel's tablet.

Presumably using clay and sticks, the prophet built replica siege works: ramps climbing to the tops of walls, close-by encampments for the soldiers besieging the city (who would always be on the lookout for any fleeing inhabitants or any relaxation of defenses), and battering rams to pound against the gates. Jerusalem, like most ancient major cities, was surrounded by a large double wall. The two solid segments, stone on the outside and brick or stone on the inside, were filled in the middle with tamped earth or rubble. The wall was as high as fifty feet at places and as wide as thirty, depending on the terrain and accessibility. Getting into a well-defended city was no easy matter for an enemy force. As a result, a common tactic of ancient warfare was to besiege a city so as to weaken its resistance gradually.

Ezekiel was told to add an iron plate (cooking pan; probably of the sort bread dough and other food was fried on) to the usual features of the model. The plate constituted a barrier between Ezekiel's face and the city. He thus symbolized God, who by "hiding His face" from His people, fulfilled covenant curse predictions against them (Lev. 26:17; Deut. 31:17, 18; 32:20). Ezekiel himself was also separated from the city and its sinfulness and rebellion by the plate, as a symbol of God's independence from its rebellious character. The whole enactment prophecy is then a "sign" to the Israelites that God has rejected them and separated Himself from them. A bleak prediction indeed!

Ezekiel probably did all this in front of his house in the little exile village of Tel-Abib. As people would pass by they would see the model and could hardly help inquiring about it. Ezekiel would then explain what God had told him to do and what it meant. The message would be clear enough: Jerusalem's days were numbered. Since all the exiles had once lived, if only temporarily, in Jerusalem, this prediction would have a particularly powerful impact.

The purpose of God in this prophetic act was hardly limited to letting Ezekiel and his countrymen in on the future. More important was their need to see that God was not about to let the sins of the city He had chosen go unpunished. The wickedness of the people in the days of Zedekiah was just as bad as it had ever been (2 Kings 25:19–20) and had not ended with the first exile. Therefore, God was about to "cast His people from His sight."

War and its ravages, including the awful effects of siege, are one kind of curse God promised the Israelites if they broke His covenant (e.g., Deut. 28:52–57). Sin cannot go unpunished. When the covenant is broken, the offender must pay.

This brief passage ought to serve as a reminder to us who are partners to the New Covenant. God is not mocked. We reap what we sow (Gal. 6:7). For us the ultimate enemy is not, of course, Babylon, but death, the wages of sin. Our siege is by temptation, not by battering rams and earthworks. We desperately need God's armor against it (Eph. 6:10–17) and His strong refuge from it (Pss. 46:1, 7, 11; 59:16). We can, moreover, rejoice in the fact that unless we deliberately will it, nothing can separate us from the love of God (Rom. 8:31–39) like the iron plate separated Ezekiel from his model of Jerusalem. The disobedient national kinsmen of the prophet needed to fear God's coming wrath. For those in Christ, all such fear is removed.

DAYS OF PUNISHMENT

4:4 "Lie also on your left side, and lay the iniquity of the house of Israel upon it. *According* to the number of the days that you lie on it, you shall bear their iniquity.

5 "For I have laid on you the years of their iniquity, according to the number of the days, three hundred and ninety days; so you shall bear the iniquity of the house of Israel.

6 "And when you have completed them, lie again on your right side; then you shall bear the iniquity of the house of Judah forty days. I have laid on you a day for each year.

7 "Therefore you shall set your face toward the siege of Jerusalem; your arm *shall be* uncovered, and you shall prophesy against it.

8 "And surely I will restrain you so that you cannot turn from one side to another till you have ended the days of your siege."

Ezek. 4:4–8

The prophet must undertake a long, painfully slow enactment prophecy lasting a total of 430 days, 390 of those days representing 390 years of Israel's (the North's) punishment for iniquity (v. 5) and 40 days representing 40 years of Judah's punishment for iniquity (v. 6). The total of 430 years is especially significant, since that is the length of time that the Israelites were in Egypt (Exod. 12:40). What else do these figures signify?

The numbers are somewhat rounded off in order to add up to 430, a number any of the exiles would know represented bondage and captivity, servitude to others in a foreign land. Note that Ezekiel's actions symbolize bearing iniquity, that is, undergoing punishment. The most basic punishment is rejection from God's presence (cf. Lev. 26:17, 24, 28, 41; Deut. 31:17–18; 32:19–20) which can include but is not limited to exile. The North, Israel, was rejected by God already in 931 B.C. when it was cast away as a result of the apostasy encouraged by Solomon (1 Kings 11:31–36). The ongoing civil war that immediately followed sealed the split of north and south, and virtually guaranteed that Northerners would stay away from true orthodox worship in Jerusalem (1 Kings 13:19–24, 26–33; 14:30).

The North went into exile in 722 B.C. (2 Kings 17:5–23), and its exile would not end until the Judean exile also ended in 539 B.C., with the famous decree of Cyrus stating that deported Israelites all over the former Assyrian and Babylonian empires could return home (Ezra 1:1–4). Accordingly, the punishment of (Northern) Israel may be dated from 931 B.C. to 539 B.C., 392 years, rounded off to 390 by Ezekiel. (In the complex dating system of ancient times, where parts of years were counted as whole years for purposes of dating, it could even have been added up as 390 years exactly.) The Judean punishment was to last (by the minimum reckoning) literally 47 years (586 to 539 B.C.), but this number was rounded off in the present prophecy to 40 because of the interest in having the symbolic addition total 430.

Moreover, "forty" is a number that could be used in Hebrew speech figuratively to indicate the general notion of "several dozen," and thus the rounding down of forty-seven to forty would not have raised any questions among the exiles of Ezekiel's day. Also, the tradition of the Israelites' wandering forty years in the wilderness was so prominent in their history that Ezekiel's audience could hardly have missed the comparison between their own present "wilderness" sojourn and the original one described in Numbers.

Another round number, seventy, was also used elsewhere in exile predictions (Jer. 25:12; 29:10), figured on another basis, from initial Babylonian control over the Fertile Crescent (605 B.C.) to Babylonian defeat in 539 B.C. (actually sixty-six years) or possibly from the destruction of the Jerusalem temple (586 B.C.) to its reconstruction in the days of Haggai and Zechariah (516 B.C.).

It should be noted that the Septuagint text of Ezek. 4:5 reads 190 rather than 390, but this probably reflects a copyist's error rather than another way of figuring Israel's punishment (i.e., 722 B.C. to 539 B.C., 183 years rounded up to 190).

Ezekiel's body in this enactment prophecy represents the weight of Israel and Judah's sins. His sides represent the respective divisions of the total nation that must bear that weight, or punishment. Before the prophet started his enactment, he had once more to face the siege model he had built (v. 7). Then he had to bare his arm as an indication of readiness for action (cf. Isa. 52:10), thus symbolizing

God's readiness for action against the city. Next he had to prophesy (preach) against the city, warning it that its iniquities would result in its siege and capture. Finally, he allowed himself to be tied up again as God required (v. 8; cf. 3:25; *"restrain"* should be "tie up with cords") and began the long ordeal of lying on his side.

The passage does not imply that Ezekiel lay on his side around the clock for over a year, any more than the words "Our pastor preached for two months from Colossians" would imply continuous nonstop oratory for sixty days. Comparisons with other enactment prophecies (e.g., Isaiah 20) make clear that these actions were done for public benefit now and again, but certainly not continuously. The following passage (4:9–17) states that Ezekiel had to be up and around cooking, eating, and preaching during the same 430 days, and he obviously had to do many other things as well. In fact, judging from the date formula in 8:1, *all* the events between 1:2 and 8:1 took place in just over a year, not merely Ezekiel's lying on his side.

At any rate, we can imagine the prophet bound, lying on his side in front of his house next to the siege model he had built (4:1–3) at a time (or times) of the day when people would pass by, thus fulfilling God's command. People might scoff or joke about him, they might do their best to ignore him, they might become rather weary of seeing him out there tied up on his side, but they could not ignore his message. Every time they saw him that way they would be reminded that God was punishing His people, all twelve tribes, North and South. They were in exile because they were sinners!

Ezekiel for his part was learning, as he had been learning from the day of his call, that serving God as His spokesman involved personal sacrifice and no little hardship. He had to endure discomfort, both from the ropes that bound him and the steady lying on one side. What he had to do restricted his freedom and may have cost him considerable respect. After all, a rebellious people are not likely to take warmly to a prophet whose message is steadily critical of them.

But there was, nevertheless, an element of hope in what Ezekiel was doing. Eventually his days of lying on his side would come to an end. That conveyed something to the thoughtful listener of the fact that the years of captivity for Israel and Judah would come to an end, too, just as the years of captivity in Egypt had eventually ended with the exodus. So there was an end in sight, a termination point for the punishment. For the Judeans, that end was "forty" years away, a generation or so (cf. Num. 14:27–35). There was thus a bright side to this tedious enactment process, a hopeful objective as an antidote to total despair. On the other hand, consider the situation from a personal point of view. God's faithful servant Ezekiel was working to communicate a result he *himself* would not see. He did not return to Zion from exile. Others would not return either. He was to die in captivity.

God's servants may have to undertake tasks involving a lot of tedium, patiently carrying out responsibilities less than entirely pleasant, regularly doing things they would much rather not have to be involved in. Preparing for a Sunday school class week after week, leading a Bible study year by year, visiting shut-ins steadily as time goes by, patiently shaping the behavior of and caring for children as the years come and go, laboring to bring about social change; these sorts of things are hardly always enjoyable. Faithfulness involves sticking to tasks where the reward cannot necessarily be experienced right away. Loyal Christian servants may not see in this life the rewards of their steady labors, but we carry on because God's work is never done in vain, no matter how hard it may be (1 Cor. 15:58).

FAMINE IN THE CITY

4:9 "Also take for yourself wheat, barley, beans, lentils, millet, and spelt; put them into one vessel, and make bread of them for yourself. *During* the number of days that you lie on your side, three hundred and ninety days, you shall eat it.

10 "And your food which you eat *shall be* by weight, twenty shekels a day; from time to time you shall eat it.

11 "You shall also drink water by measure, one-sixth of a hin; from time to time you shall drink.

12 "And you shall eat it *as* barley cakes; and bake it using fuel of human waste in their sight."

13 Then the LORD said, "So shall the children of Israel eat their defiled bread among the Gentiles, where I will drive them."

14 So I said, "Ah, Lord GOD! Indeed I have never defiled myself from my youth till now; I have never

eaten what died of itself or was torn by beasts, nor has abominable flesh ever come into my mouth."

15 Then He said to me, "See, I am giving you cow dung instead of human waste, and you shall prepare your bread over it."

16 Moreover He said to me, "Son of man, surely I will cut off the supply of bread in Jerusalem; they shall eat bread by weight and with anxiety, and shall drink water by measure and with dread,

17 "that they may lack bread and water, and be dismayed with one another, and waste away because of their iniquity".

Ezek. 4:9–17

Ezekiel must add to his regimen of lying on his side the daily discipline of eating skimpy meals and drinking a meager amount of water. Again, these would be a public display. Privately the prophet was free to supplement these poor siege-type rations and to cook normally. But as an enactment prophecy, the special public diet would remind all who saw Ezekiel preparing and eating it of the horrible starvation that accompanied a long siege.

This kind of famine is predicted in Deut. 28:52–57. The desperation of the hungry under siege is described as leading even to family cannibalism. Ezekiel's compatriots had already experienced one siege, a short one of less than three months' duration (2 Kings 24:10–12). That siege ended in surrender because the king at that time (598), Jehoiachin, knew that it could lead only to the starvation of the entire city. The siege Ezekiel was predicting, however, was to be of greater duration (two years, in fact; 2 Kings 25:1–8) and was to produce the sort of terrible famine within the surrounded city that Ezekiel's enactment prophecy was designed to predict (2 Kings 25:3).

The odd mixture of grains and legumes that the prophet was commanded to turn into a dough and then a bread (v. 9) symbolized the make-do food preparation that would be necessary during the long siege. Spelt, the last grain mentioned, produces a particularly poor-quality flour. He could eat only twenty shekels of the resulting bread a day as his public diet (v. 10). Since a shekel is less than half an ounce, that comes to about eight ounces! The water he was permitted to drink, a sixth of a hin (v. 11), was only about a pint, and he was allowed to drink that only once a day (this is what the expression implies; cf. 1 Chron. 9:25) to symbolize the need to ration the city's water supply while it was under siege. What a diet!

Ezekiel was required to make his bread in the same general shape as barley cakes were made (v. 12). These cakes were the simple flat round coarse loaves that constituted a main food of the poor (Judg. 7:13; John 6:9, 13). He was also told—at first and as a kind of test—to bake it by burning dried human waste as the heat source, something God knew would immediately offend Ezekiel's priestly sensibilities in light of the Pentateuchal cleanliness laws. Thus we may be sure that God was not so much trying to get Ezekiel to violate his own priestly responsibilities as to be reminded of how many compromises of what is usual and normal would have to be made by those cooped up in Jerusalem under overwhelming enemy pressure. When Ezekiel protested the use of human waste as a fuel source (requiring, presumably, handling; v. 14), God graciously substituted what He had obviously planned all along, cow dung as cooking fuel. Cow dung was—and is—a common fuel in the Near East, and its use in cooking fires was, as far as we know, not unusual in any way, and not a violation of the orthodox Israelite cleanliness regulations.

The passage ends with a divine pronouncement, which Ezekiel probably repeated countless times to those who inquired about his meals, or even just stopped to watch. The famine would require paltry food and drink portions, and these would contribute to the anxiety and dread (v. 16) that those under the siege would experience. They would not know if the enemy might give up and withdraw or be driven off by friendly forces (the hope of all who ever tried to wait out a siege), or whether their meager rations would eventually dwindle to nothing, and they would all die from starvation or be captured and killed, no longer having the strength to defend their strongly walled fortress city. The result of the ongoing process of siege would thus be, as verse 17 describes it, dismay (a sense of disgust) at each other's gaunt, sick appearance, and the slow attrition of death from the famine.

The last four words of verse 17, *"because of their iniquity,"* are in one sense the most important of the passage. Everything that Ezekiel's symbolic actions are pointing to is a punishment for sin. What will happen to the holy city is not a matter, ultimately, of human warfare, but of divine judgment. Just as the covenant curses predict, defeat in war is a result of God's wrath against His people for their disobedience (e.g., Lev. 26:17, 37; Deut. 28:25, 49, 52; 32:23–24, 30, 42).

There are two especially interesting lessons in all of this. One is the way that actions have power to draw attention to one's message. What Ezekiel *does* provides the effective framework for what he *says*. While enactment prophecy may not be an accepted mode of prophetic speech (preaching) today, there is still undeniably a connection between one's behavior and the convincingness of one's words. Those who advocate prayer had better do some. Those who preach evangelism should be about the business of evangelizing. Those who call for good works ought to glorify God with their own. And so on. The divine word still gains acceptance in part by its being heard from the lips of those who obey it as well as speak it.

Second, where nations are concerned, God's anger against iniquity may take the form of warfare. Of course, it could be argued that all wars have involved nations less than entirely righteous on both sides. But beyond this, we must recognize that sometimes the judgment of God is meted out in this life against an unrighteous nation by means of war. The substantial destruction of Germany and Japan during the Second World War, for example, can hardly be isolated from the sovereign controlling action of God. Aggressors and oppressors were vanquished because of their monstrous iniquity. This being the case in principle, it behooves the citizens of all nations to consider when confronted by an enemy whether or not their sins as a people have had anything to do with the distress they face.

A SWORD AGAINST THE CITY

> 5:1 "And you, son of man, take a sharp sword, take it as a barber's razor, and pass *it* over your head and your beard; then take scales to weigh and divide the hair.
> 2 "You shall burn with fire one-third in the midst of the city, when the days of the siege are finished; then you shall take one-third and strike around *it* with the sword, and one-third you shall scatter in the wind: I will draw out a sword after them.

3 "You shall also take a small number of them and bind them in the edge of your *garment.*

4 "Then take some of them again and throw them into the midst of the fire, and burn them in the fire. From there a fire will go out into all the house of Israel.

5 "Thus says the Lord GOD: 'This *is* Jerusalem; I have set her in the midst of the nations and the countries all around her.

6 'She has rebelled against My judgments by doing wickedness more than the nations, and against My statutes more than the countries that *are* all around her; for they have refused My judgments, and they have not walked in My statutes.'

7 "Therefore thus says the Lord GOD: 'Because you have multiplied *disobedience* more than the nations that *are* all around you, have not walked in My statutes nor kept My judgments, nor even done according to the judgments of the nations that *are* all around you'—

8 "therefore thus says the Lord GOD: 'Indeed I, even I, *am* against you and will execute judgments in your midst in the sight of the nations.

9 'And I will do among you what I have never done, and the like of which I will never do again, because of all your abominations.

10 'Therefore fathers shall eat *their* sons in your midst, and sons shall eat their fathers; and I will execute judgments among you, and all of you who remain I will scatter to all the winds.

11 'Therefore *as* I live,' says the Lord GOD, 'surely, because you have defiled My sanctuary with all your detestable things and with all your abominations, therefore I will also diminish *you;* My eye will not spare, nor will I have any pity.

12 'One-third of you shall die of the pestilence, and be consumed with famine in your midst; and one-third shall fall by the sword all around you; and I will scatter another third to all the winds, and I will draw out a sword after them.

13 'Thus shall My anger be spent, and I will cause My fury to rest upon them, and I will be avenged; and

they shall know that I, the LORD, have spoken *it* in My zeal, when I have spent My fury upon them.

14 'Moreover I will make you a waste and a reproach among the nations that *are* all around you, in the sight of all who pass by.

15 'So it shall be a reproach, a taunt, a lesson, and an astonishment to the nations that *are* all around you, when I execute judgments among you in anger and in fury and in furious rebukes. I, the LORD, have spoken.

16 'When I send against them the terrible arrows of famine which shall be for destruction, which I will send to destroy you, I will increase the famine upon you and cut off your supply of bread.

17 'So I will send against you famine and wild beasts, and they will bereave you. Pestilence and blood shall pass through you, and I will bring the sword against you. I, the LORD, have spoken.'"

Ezek. 5:1–17

A poetic expression of covenant warnings for violation of God's law in Deuteronomy promises "I will sharpen my flashing sword" (Deut. 32:41; cf. Lev. 26:25, 33; Deut. 32:24). This is typical of the many instances where the "sword" (Hebrew, *hereb*) symbolizes coming warfare and death in the Bible (e.g., 1 Sam. 12:10). Ezekiel's audience knew the association of "sword" with "warfare/death" very well. It was part of the common language of their culture. When they saw that Ezekiel was handling a sword in a symbolic enactment prophecy, therefore, there would have been no doubt in their minds that he was predicting someone's death. That "someone" was the people of Jerusalem.

In this final prophetic instruction among the four portraits of Jerusalem's coming siege, God commanded Ezekiel first to shave off his hair and beard using the sword as a razor (v. 1). The prophet then had to divide the hair carefully into thirds, not because God was planning to apportion the judgment that was to follow for Jerusalem exactly in thirds, but because careful, measurable preparation and enumeration in prophetic revelation is intended to convey God's *planning and preparation,* which are always thorough and precise.

From verse 2 it is clear that Ezekiel was to perform this enactment prophecy concurrently with the others, presumably toward the end of the 430 days of publicly lying on his side and eating starvation rations. The hairs he had cut were to be disposed of when *the days of the siege are finished,"* that is, as a symbol of what would happen to Jerusalem's population when the city fell to the attackers (586 B.C.) and the people were exposed to the will of the invader, Babylon. Some of the hairs were burned, some cut up with the sword, and some thrown to the wind (v. 2). A few were at first saved in Ezekiel's clothing (v. 3), but even some of those were taken out again and burned (v. 4).

There are clear meanings to all these enactments. Beginning at verse 5 God explains through Ezekiel what significance these symbolic actions have in terms of prediction. At verse 12 we actually read the meanings. Burning the hairs symbolized that there would be a group that would die from disease during and after the siege. Fever so often accompanies disease that the burning symbolism is highly appropriate. Cutting some hair with the sword symbolized that a group that would be killed by the soldiers of the Babylonian army, venting their pent-up frustration at the population that had held out so long against them. Such people would in many instances literally die by the sword. The others would be exiled (scattered *"to all the winds"*) just as the third group of hair was thrown to the wind. Exile was seen in ancient times as a fate from which one never returned, in the same way that hair scattered to the winds is virtually impossible to reclaim. But that wasn't all! The small group spared so far in all this destruction would be further decimated (i.e., like the hair taken from the garment and burned) by famine, wild animals, disease, bloodshed, and more death (vv. 16–17). These latter miseries are also standard types of covenant curses associated in the Pentateuch with disobedience to God's law (famine: Lev. 26:26, 29, etc.; wild animals: Lev. 26:22, Deut. 32:24; disease: Deut. 28:21, etc.; bloodshed: Deut. 32:42).

Disobedience was exactly Jerusalem's problem, as God's words to Ezekiel make clear. Jerusalem was, in fact, more guilty than the pagan nations around it because Jerusalem knew God's covenant (*"statutes . . . judgments"*) and broke it anyway (v. 6). Moreover, their disobedience literally exceeded the pagans', inasmuch as in certain ways by *any* measure they were worse than their nonbelieving neighbors. Even the pagans thought so (v. 7). Accordingly, it was appropriate that Jerusalem be punished openly and internationally, by the Babylonian siege and by exile to various nations, that is, *"in the sight of the nations"* (v. 8).

Among the extreme horrors attendant to the whole process would be the practice of cannibalism (v. 10), itself a predicted judgment for violating the covenant (Lev. 26:29; Deut. 28:53–56). So great were the abominations of the people of Jerusalem that this awful fate also awaited them as they slowly were starved by the surrounding armies. The Book of Lamentations describes in considerable detail the fact that all these judgments did indeed come to pass upon Jerusalem at the time of its long siege and subsequent fall to Babylon in 588–586 B.C. (Lam. 1:7–14; 2:20–22; 4:4–10; etc.).

Why such a heavy emphasis upon the sins and resulting punishment of Jerusalem? Because Jerusalem was *the* holy city, God's sanctuary (v. 11). Already in Deuteronomy 12, as the law was preached to the Israelites by Moses before they had even entered the promised land, the plan of God to establish a single city at which He would be worshiped was revealed. Other nations had a multiple-shrine worship system. The Canaanites, in fact, could be accused of worshiping on practically "every hill" (Deut. 12:2). But with Israel's divinely revealed expectation of worship at one site only came an emphasis upon the necessary holiness of that site (Jerusalem). God's name dwelt there (1 Kings 8:29), and it had to be a place of righteousness, a light to the Gentiles. Instead, it had become a place full of idolatry (2 Kings 23:4–14) and a capital from which evil kings reigned over an evil populace (e.g., 2 Kings 24:19–20).

Thus Jerusalem had failed to fulfill its calling. Later when Jesus wept over the city (John 11:35), his disappointment was similar. Here was a great ancient city specially entrusted by God with divine care and blessing, specially entrusted to witness to the eternal message, yet a city that simply had failed to accomplish the uprightness and faithfulness reasonably expected of it. Jerusalem, the chosen city of a chosen people, was unwilling to respond to its special place in God's plan.

It is always somewhat saddening to witness wasted potential. It is even more grievous to see potential shirked by reason of outright arrogance and/or willful disobedience. God, who is the Sovereign

Judge of all the earth, was not about to allow His chosen city to refuse its obligation and turn its back on Him yet again. So the city must be decimated by disease and death, and its surviving population deported to face yet more difficult circumstances.

In this wasted potential is a lesson for every Christian and every church. The seven churches in Revelation 2 and 3 were excoriated for their failure to be obedient, not realizing their potential to serve the Lord. Individuals who likewise have heard God's claims cannot risk failing to respond. Jerusalem was to be holy and was not, thus, it met with tragedy. The Christian's call is also to be holy (1 Pet. 1:14–15). That call cannot be ignored, lest tragedies of another sort result.

CHAPTER FOUR

Coming Judgment

Ezekiel 6:1–7:27

Although Ezekiel employed a few symbolic actions to introduce some of the prophecies that he now was called upon to preach to his people (facing the mountains, 6:2; clapping and stamping, 6:11; perhaps making a chain, 7:23), the bulk of chapters 6 and 7 is devoted to relatively straightforward predictions of doom and disaster for the nation of Israel. Ezekiel's audience of exiles would understand, of course, that his words applied to what was left of the old Israel, that is, Judah and Jerusalem, since the North had already fallen to the Assyrians in 722 B.C. and had been captured into the control of the Babylonians in 609 B.C. when the Assyrian Empire fell.

It was difficult for the Israelites in exile to believe that their beloved homeland would really be given away and destroyed at the will of its own God. Even the captives' personal experience of exile had not convinced them that in the immediate future Jerusalem would fall and Israel would never again be an independent nation. Therefore Ezekiel was required to preach prophecy after prophecy of doom so that by repetition, if nothing else, the message might have a chance to get through to a stubborn people (see chaps. 1–3). The passages in chapters 6 and 7 are a part of those many prophecies on the same subject, Israel's coming doom.

A particular emphasis of the present set of prophecies is the totality of the destruction that will bring to an end the current complacent life of the Judeans not yet exiled. Through Ezekiel God taught Judah to expect not merely an invasion and capture, but a grand-scale annihilation of Judean society.

FACING THE MOUNTAINS

6:1 Now the word of the LORD came to me, saying:

2 "Son of man, set your face toward the mountains of Israel, and prophesy against them,

3 "and say, 'O mountains of Israel, hear the word of the Lord GOD! Thus says the Lord GOD to the mountains, to the hills, to the ravines, and to the valleys: "Indeed I, *even* I, will bring a sword against you, and I will destroy your high places.

4 "Then your altars shall be desolate, your incense altars shall be broken, and I will cast down your slain *men* before your idols.

5 "And I will lay the corpses of the children of Israel before their idols, and I will scatter your bones all around your altars.

6 "In all your dwelling places the cities shall be laid waste, and the high places shall be desolate, so that your altars may be laid waste and made desolate, your idols may be broken and made to cease, your incense altars may be cut down, and your works may be abolished.

7 "The slain shall fall in your midst, and you shall know that I *am* the LORD.

8 "Yet I will leave a remnant, so that you may have *some* who escape the sword among the nations, when you are scattered through the countries.

9 "Then those of you who escape will remember Me among the nations where they are carried captive, because I was crushed by their adulterous heart which has departed from Me, and by their eyes which play the harlot after their idols; they will loathe themselves for the evils which they committed in all their abominations.

10 "And they shall know that I *am* the LORD; I have not said in vain that I would bring this calamity upon them."'"

Ezek. 6:1–10

Idolatry was the standard means of worship in the ancient world. It was believed by all the nations with which Israel had contact that by manufacturing the likeness of a god or goddess, part of the essence of that divinity could be brought close to a group of humans. Idols were understood actually to represent a god, much as in voodoo a doll is thought to represent an individual by those who practice "black magic." What is done to the doll will be done to the person it represents according to this way of thinking. In a way, the doll *is* the person. Likewise, in a way, the idol *is* the god.

We call this "prelogical" religion, but it was the norm in biblical times. All religions everywhere were idolatrous—with one exception. Those Israelites who obeyed the Mosaic covenant did not employ idols in their worship. But since everyone else did, that made nonidolatry such a minority religion and so completely out of step with prevailing beliefs, that sticking to it was terribly difficult. It is safe to say that nonidolatrous Israelites were considered somewhat crazy by their idolatrous neighbors and friends. How could they worship a god without his idol? If their god was not represented among them by means of an idol, how could they expect that they were "reaching" him when they prayed or sacrificed?

So few Israelites had sufficient faith against this sort of societal pressure and religious mind-set that orthodoxy became a minority view in Israel, and idolatry prevailed during most of the nation's history. From the miraculous days of the conquest (Josh. 24:23) to the last whimper of Judean independence (2 Kings 23:26–27; 24:9, 19) the siren call of idolatry was all but irresistible to most of the descendants of Abraham.

The fact that it was the majority view, however, in no way made idolatry right. It represented the most basic sort of covenant disobedience (Exod. 20:3–5) and required judgment. Because idolatry was practiced mostly on the hilltop shrines (the infamous "high places") in Canaan (1 Kings 14:23; 2 Kings 7:10), it was appropriate for the Lord to instruct Ezekiel to face west toward the mountains of Israel in order to denounce Israel's idolatry and to predict desolation as a result of it (v. 2). His prophecy against the mountains (v. 3ff.) is thus a literary device (cf. 2 Sam. 1:19, 21, 25) and not intended to suggest that the mountains themselves were guilty. The real guilty party was the idolaters themselves, not an aspect of the geography. Indeed, by including also the ravines and the valleys, the prophecy shows that Israel in general—meaning the nation as a whole—is to suffer destruction.

Verses 4, 5, and 7 speak of those who will be slain. The prospect for Judah is mass death. When the Babylonian armies have completed the siege of Jerusalem they will move throughout the countryside eliminating all opposition. Finally the sacrifice altars and incense altars (v. 4) would then be silent, no longer the bustling business centers of a ritually oriented, idolatrous religious system, but broken-down testimonies to God's wrath against the disobedient. Death is the required judgment for idolatry (Deut. 28:21). The nation as a whole must suffer, and thus necessarily the people (cf. Deut. 32:25). The invading Babylonians certainly had no special compassion for their Israelite foes. Thus Ezekiel relays God's promise of corpses and scattered bones (v. 5) as an imagistic way of portraying the awful military carnage to come.

Again in verse 6 the two types of altars used to worship at the high places are mentioned. The *"altars"* (Hebrew, *mizbeḥōt*) were used for the cooking of animal meat devoted to the idol at whose shrine the altar stood. Incense altars (Hebrew, *ḥammānîm*) were small stands on which hot coals vaporized the sweet-smelling gobs of pitch that were dropped on them by the idol priests. All this was done in the presence of the idols themselves. These we know about from the few that have been uncovered archaeologically as well as from the descriptions of them in the Old Testament. They were merely relatively crude sculptures of stone or wood. None were of solid metal, though some, like the golden calves (young bulls) made by Israel's Jeroboam (1 Kings 12), in imitation of the original model fashioned by Aaron (Exodus 32), had a metal overlay on the wood.

People who worshiped via idols would typically go up to the high place where a given idol's shrine was located, bringing meat for cooking (still alive so that it could be prepared and eaten fresh) and perhaps money to purchase the burning of some incense. They would bow to the idol (prostrating themselves, not merely bowing at the waist) and also kiss it (1 Kings 19:18). Then they would eat and relax (Amos 2:8), often partaking of ritual sex with a cult prostitute as a symbolic stimulation of the divine powers of fertility (Amos 2:7; Num. 25:6–8; Hos. 4:14). The whole system was materialistic, selfish, and degenerate! Idolatry was a self-interested way of practicing religion, in which adequate sacrificing supposedly produced gratitude on the part of the god represented by the idol, who then was obligated to bless the worshiper materially. The worshiper could indulge his or her own self-interest without interference. No ethical standards existed, no structured covenant with laws about loving one's neighbor. Obedience to a cult demanded only payment in food and money. The idolater was free to live a fully selfish life.

Against this complete distortion of true religion that now dominated the practices of His own people, the Lord could only bring judgment. The *adulterous heart* (v. 9) that had led Israel to reject its covenant with God would have to learn its lesson. But even in the awful destruction that was coming, there would be some who would be spared, since God had long ago promised not to annihilate His people utterly (Deut. 4:27–31). And so here again He promises through Ezekiel that a remnant (vv. 8–9) would escape to witness the whole process of desolation and subsequent deliverance, and to realize that God did not take lightly His own commitment to enforce His covenant.

What idolatry most reveals about the people who practice it is not merely another faith, but also an actual lack of faith. Modern idolatry, like the ancient Israelite-Near Eastern kind, is essentially materialistic (1 John 2:15–17; 5:21). Instead of full reliance on God, while we may not deny His existence, we don't trust Him to take care of us materially. Thus we do everything we can to gain worldly possessions, to secure our future, to have a "comfortable" retirement, to succeed in a competitive world. With this comes the danger of "losing our own souls" because we cannot serve God and money (Matt. 6:24). When we fail to trust God for our needs, we go far beyond the bounds of providing for our basic requirements and can thus trap ourselves in modern idolatry, which is nothing other than materialism (1 Tim. 6:6–10).

CLAP AND STAMP

> 6:11 'Thus says the Lord GOD: "Pound your fists and stamp your feet, and say, 'Alas, for all the evil abominations of the house of Israel! For they shall fall by the sword, by famine, and by pestilence.
> 12 'He who is far off shall die by the pestilence, he who is near shall fall by the sword, and he who

remains and is besieged shall die by the famine. Thus will I spend My fury upon them.

13 'Then you shall know that I *am* the LORD, when their slain are among their idols all around their altars, on every high hill, on all the mountaintops, under every green tree, and under every thick oak, wherever they offered sweet incense to all their idols.

14 'So I will stretch out My hand against them and make the land desolate, yes, more desolate than the wilderness toward Diblah, in all their dwelling places. Then they shall know that I *am* the LORD.'"'

Ezek. 6:11–14

These verses continue the theme of God's denunciation of idolatry and repeat some of the imagery already mentioned in verses 1–10 (v. 13 especially). They also conclude somewhat similarly to verses 1–10 in that the result of the coming destruction will be a recognition—even if a grudging one—on the part of the rebellious house, Israel (cf. 2:3–3:9) that *"I am the Lord."* In other words, the Israelites would know that the Lord was the same Lord who had delivered His people from slavery in Egypt, had brought them miraculously into the promised land, had defended them supernaturally from their foes, and, indeed, controlled the destinies of all nations. Israel had to a substantial degree forgotten just who their Lord was and desperately needed reminding.

Some of their forgetting was a predictable though still inexcusable result of their present circumstances. They were dominated by foreigners, partly scattered already in exile, facing even further decline as a power in Palestine. It was hard for those who had yielded to the dominant polytheistic thinking of the day to avoid the conclusion that their national god, Yahweh (the Lord), was not very effective any more. Gods like Marduk, the national god of Babylon, seemed to be in the ascendancy. The other gods were, of course, no gods at all, but idols, the work of human hands. As concepts they were merely the creation of selfish human minds. There was no way the Lord could restore His people as long as their faith was placed in such nonsense. Destruction of idolatry was essential.

So God told Ezekiel to clap (*"Pound your fists"* is a less likely translation) and stamp, signs of pleasure and delight (cf. Ezek. 25:6) at the impending fall of what was left of Israel. This is not intended to convey God's delight at the misery His people would endure, but symbolically represents the sort of taunting rejoicing that Israel's enemies would have at their downfall because of the nation's idolatrous unfaithfulness. Ezekiel was later commanded to sing a number of taunt songs or mocking dirges against Israel's foes (e.g., chaps. 27, 28, 31, and 32), but here, since Israel itself had become a foe of the Lord by its constant, repeated disobedience, it deserved a taunt of its own.

The words of mourning in this taunting lament are introduced by *"Alas"* (Hebrew, ʾaḥ, an interjection of grief or pain) associated with death or loss (v. 11). Ezekiel is then told that the nation will fall by *"the sword, by famine, and by pestilence."* These three miseries, that is, war, starvation, and disease, were three major kinds of covenant punishments. The three together were sometimes used by the prophets to convey the full range of punishments mentioned in Leviticus 26 and Deuteronomy 28–32 (cf. 2 Sam. 24:13; Jer. 27:13; 29:17). God's word to Ezekiel then elaborates on these three traditional punishments in a manner designed to give them even more of an impact: no matter where the Israelites are, one way or another they will die (v. 12). Even if they are not present at the siege inside Jerusalem, they will still meet their end. God's anger at disobedience must be satisfied, and He promises that it will be. Some individuals might escape by His grace, but the nation in general must be annihilated.

The passage ends with a predictive description of desolation. In a typically hyperbolic way, the description portrays a distant barrenness beyond that which was well known as an example of barrenness: the extreme northern wilderness approaching Riblah (the erroneous textual reading *"Diblah"* must be corrected), a city in the northern Syrian district of Hamath on the Orontes River. Israel would be a scorched, empty wasteland according to this scenario. On desolation as a covenant punishment, see Lev. 26:32–35, 43; Deut. 29:23.

Perhaps the most intriguing theme of the passage is found in verse 12, where the inescapability of God's judgment is made evident. Naturally, people a long distance from Jerusalem, or Judah, would tend to think of themselves as secure from any disaster that might befall that area as a result of the Babylonian invasion and siege. Some actually inside Jerusalem might also have thought themselves to be protected, as they relied on the city's massive walls and extensive defense preparations to save them. But hope in human means of escape was useless in the face of divine wrath. The only means of escape from divine wrath is divine mercy. God Himself must make the rescue possible. Nothing human can be counted on. In Christ's death and resurrection this has indeed been accomplished. Whether people are "far off" or "near," they are still in danger of destruction unless they find forgiveness, and the only source of it is the grace of God as a result of trusting in Christ. That way alone, an otherwise inevitably desolate life, followed by an inevitable death, can be avoided. Hope in God is the human being's only true, fruitful hope.

BEHOLD THE END

7:1 Moreover the word of the LORD came to me, saying,

2 "And you, son of man, thus says the Lord GOD to the land of Israel:
'An end! The end has come upon the four
corners of the land.
3 Now the end *has come* upon you,
And I will send My anger against you;
I will judge you according to your ways,
And I will repay you for all your
abominations.
4 My eye will not spare you,
Nor will I have pity;
But I will repay your ways,
And your abominations will be in your midst;
Then you shall know that I *am* the LORD!'
5 "Thus says the Lord GOD:
'A disaster, a singular disaster;
Behold, it has come!
6 An end has come,
The end has come;
It has dawned for you;
Behold, it has come!
7 Doom has come to you, you who dwell in the
land;

> The time has come,
> A day of trouble *is* near,
> And not of rejoicing in the mountains.
> 8 Now upon you I will soon pour out My fury,
> And spend My anger upon you;
> I will judge you according to your ways,
> And I will repay you for all your
>   abominations.
>
> 9 'My eye will not spare,
> Nor will I have pity;
> I will repay you according to your ways,
> And your abominations will be in your midst.
> Then you shall know that I *am* the LORD who
>   strikes.'"
>
> *Ezek. 7:1–9*

Chapter 7 continues from chapter 6 the theme of prophecies directed generally to the entire *"land of Israel"* as 7:2 states explicitly. Most of chapter 7 appears to be written in a semipoetic style. Some of the modern versions have treated the chapter as poetry as the NKJV does, while others have not (e.g., RSV, NIV). There is much repetition in these verses and a considerable degree of paronomasia, or play on words. For example, in verse 6 the sound of the Hebrew word *haqqēṣ,* "the end," is mimicked by *hēqîṣ,* "awakened" (NKJV, *"dawned"*). Or at the end of verse 9, the Lord calls Himself in Hebrew *Yahweh makkeh,* "The Lord Attacker," a play on the many divine place names such as *Yahweh yirʾeh* (Jehovah-jireh, "The Lord sees") in Gen. 22:14 and *Yahweh nissî* (Jehovah-nissi, "The Lord is my banner") in Exod. 17:15. Such literary devices are intended to catch the attention of the audience and make more memorable the message, which in this case is a message Ezekiel must state repeatedly, even tediously, so that a "stiff-necked" audience is able to comprehend it instead of merely hear it.

Verse 2b begins the message itself, after the rather standard introduction in verses 1–2a. The first subsection of this passage runs from verse 2b to verse 4. It mentions that the end "has come," just as the following subsection (vv. 5–9) mentions that disaster "has come" and the section after that, beginning in verse 10, mentions that the day "has come." The Hebrew word *bāʾ,* translated here "has come" can also mean "is coming" and thus there is created a certain degree of uncertainty as to the exact timing of the events about which Ezekiel warns. Some of the usages of *bā'* by themselves would be grammatically almost certain to mean "has come" while others would by themselves mean "is coming." That they are mixed purposely here suggests to the listener that there is an urgency to the timing. A process has started which will conclude quickly: it is not completed yet, but will not be delayed for long, either. God's words through Ezekiel are thus designed to shake his listeners out of their complacency. In verse 2 the expression *"four corners of the land"* is an idiomatic way of saying "the whole land" and is not intended to say anything literal about the geography.

God emphasizes that His anger is not arbitrarily or capriciously sent upon Israel, but comes as a result of what the Israelites have done (v. 3). Their "ways" are in fact "abominations" (Hebrew, *tô'abōt*), practices that God despises and that are so unacceptable that of themselves they constitute serious crimes against God's law. Any number of evil practices could be included under the category of "abominations," though idolatry and polytheism would head the list, because these constitute rejection of the very basics of the Lord's relationship to His people.

The time for pity, for giving one more chance was long gone (v. 4). The people had had generations of prophets to listen to and obey if only they had been willing. What was now to be expected? Punishment! "Repay" (Hebrew, *nātan 'al*) conveys the sense of punishment in a fitting manner. The nation must get exactly what it deserves, and so its disobedience is "thrown back" at them. The result, again (cf. 6:14) is a recognition of the person and power of the true God (*"you shall know that I am the Lord"*).

"Disaster" (Hebrew, *rā'āh*) in verse 5 may also be translated "trouble," "misery," or the like. The word translated "singular" in the NKJV, Hebrew *'āḥat*, is textually uncertain; other ancient manuscripts have the equivalent of "Disaster after disaster" rather than "A disaster, a singular disaster," and we cannot be sure of the original reading. At any rate the nation's fate would be negative, not positive. Verse 6 reiterates the finality of what was said in verses 2 and 3, and verse 7 reinforces the severity of the prediction, introducing the concept of "the day," which will figure prominently in verses 10ff. The Hebrew does not say "A day of trouble" but "The day, panic/trouble." Ezekiel's audience already knew what "the day" referred to:

the day that Amos (5:18), Isaiah (13:16), and others had often predicted as the occasion of the Lord's intervention to punish Israel for its long history of sin.

It is evident from the mention of those "in the land" and "in the mountains" that the prophetic oracles against "land" (7:2) and "mountains" (6:2) are really intended for their inhabitants, not the topographical features themselves. Ezekiel must remind his audience that the day of the Lord will be a day of difficulty, not rejoicing (v. 7). As ever, the people were assuming that the Lord would never punish His own people (cf. Amos 5:18ff). Verses 8 and 9 largely reiterate what has already been said, with the exception of the ending of verse 9, *"The Lord who strikes."* God was the attacker, the one whose proxy—the Babylonian army—had come to hurt Israel, rather than to help it (cf. Joel 2:11, 25).

From what we can reconstruct about the time at which Ezekiel delivered this prophecy (about 592 B.C.) we can guess that one thing the Israelites surely thought they had on their side was time. The exile of 598 was several years now in the past. Zedekiah had presumably not openly shown any signs of rebellion against Babylon, if he had even thought in that direction (2 Chron. 36:13). It would have seemed unlikely to the casual viewer that anything could happen in the near future to break the calm that prevailed. Babylon was stably in control of the Fertile Crescent, including Palestine, or so it seemed. Few people would be looking for a change, an "end."

So it is in our own day. Not many are looking for the end, let alone preparing for it or anxiously awaiting it. But the end draws near, and with it exactly the same necessary divine wrath on ungodliness that has always accompanied God's decisive acts of intervention in human history. Lack of preparation for God's judgment is a sad reality. Most people simply will not heed such warnings and will be caught unaware and unprepared to face their creator and judge. People of Noah's day were not ready for anything as cataclysmic as the flood. They thought they had plenty of time (Matt. 24:38–39). And so it was in Ezekiel's day regarding the fall of Judah. "It can't happen now," they thought. And so it is in ours. Yet because we simply do not know when that day will come, we ought to be all the more, not less, watchful (Matt. 24:42–44).

Behold the Day

7:10 'Behold, the day!
Behold, it has come!
Doom has gone out;
The rod has blossomed,
Pride has budded.

11 Violence has risen up into a rod of wickedness;
None of them *shall remain,*
None of their multitude,
None of them;
Nor *shall there be* wailing for them.

12 The time has come,
The day draws near.

'Let not the buyer rejoice,
Nor the seller mourn,
For wrath *is* on their whole multitude.

13 For the seller shall not return to what has been sold,
Though he may still be alive;
For the vision concerns the whole multitude,
And it shall not turn back;
No one will strengthen himself
Who lives in iniquity.

14 'They have blown the trumpet and made
everyone ready,
But no one goes to battle;
For My wrath *is* on all their multitude.

15 The sword *is* outside,
And the pestilence and famine within.
Whoever *is* in the field
Will die by the sword;
And whoever *is* in the city,
Famine and pestilence will devour him.

16 'Those who survive will escape and be on the
mountains
Like doves of the valleys,
All of them mourning,
Each for his iniquity.

17 Every hand will be feeble,
And every knee will be *as* weak *as* water.

79

18 They will also be girded with sackcloth;
   Horror will cover them;
   Shame *will be* on every face,
   Baldness on all their heads.

19 'They will throw their silver into the streets,
   And their gold will be like refuse;
   Their silver and their gold will not be able to
      deliver them
   In the day of the wrath of the LORD;
   They will not satisfy their souls,
   Nor fill their stomachs,
   Because it became their stumbling block of
      iniquity.

20 'As for the beauty of his ornaments,
   He set it in majesty;
   But they made from it
   The images of their abominations—
   Their detestable things;
   Therefore I have made it
   Like refuse to them.

21 I will give it as plunder
   Into the hands of strangers,
   And to the wicked of the earth as spoil;
   And they shall defile it.

22 I will turn My face from them,
   And they will defile My secret place;
   For robbers shall enter it and defile it.'

                                              Ezek. 7:10–22

This passage is about the Day of the Lord as a time when Israel's
pride will be destroyed. The day "has come" (grammatically more
likely: "is coming") when the doom God has stored up for His disobedient people must now be released (v. 10). We are invited here to
imagine a rod (stick) blossoming, perhaps in a manner similar to the
miraculous budding of Aaron's rod in the wilderness. In that instance, the rod was a sign to the rebellious (Num. 17:10), as Ezekiel's
compatriots have already been labeled repeatedly (2:5, etc.). In this
instance the rod starts out as pride, then shows itself as one of the
aspects of pride, "violence" (v. 11; the term implies oppression and
exploitation of people more than it does physical harm [cf. Prov.
16:29; Amos 3:10] and should probably be translated something like

"mistreatment"). Then the rod grows into a full staff: wickedness. In other words, this little metaphorical story tells us how Israel's pride has caused it to become a wicked nation in which wrongdoing prevails. As elsewhere in the chapter (see 7:1-9) there are a number of plays on words present. "Rod" (Hebrew, *maṭṭeh*) can also mean "tribe" (e.g., 1 Kings 7:14), so that the pride and wickedness of the tribe of Judah are also alluded to here. Thus the statement that *"none of them shall remain"* (said various ways three times) is referring to the Judeans. So complete will be their destruction that it will be as if no one will be left to mourn the dead. (This was not literally intended, however; cf. v. 16).

After we are again reminded of the urgency of the hour (v. 12a; cf. vv. 6-7), the logical flow of the passage begins to center on Judah's trust in material wealth and its accompanying business practices. In Deut. 8:17-18 God had warned the Israelites against the very pride that they are now exhibiting: "You say in your heart, 'My power and the might of my hand have gained me this wealth.' [But] remember the Lord your God, for *it is* He who gives you power to get wealth." This warning went unheeded, so now commerce as the people have known it must cease.

The buyer can no longer rejoice at getting a good deal. The seller can no longer "mourn," that is, wear a long face as a claim that he has been gotten the best of in a transaction, thus making the buyer a satisfied customer. Buyer and seller alike, *"their whole multitude"* (v. 12), are doomed to experience the wrath of God. Another pun shapes the wording of verse 13. Just as the seller cannot return ("go back," Hebrew, *šûb*) to what he has already sold, since the buyer now owns it, Ezekiel's vision cannot return ("go back," Hebrew, *šûb*) either. In other words, there's no turning back the judgment that's coming. The sinner cannot protect against his or her fate.

In light of the fact that what is coming for the Judeans is God's punishment, not merely an invasion by a human army, an attempt at defense is ultimately futile. The people of Jerusalem and Judah can prepare all they want. It won't help. God is going to punish them all (v. 14). "Sword, famine, and pestilence" (cf. chaps. 4 and 5) here portray the siege (v. 15). Outside the besieged city are the enemy troops ("sword"). Inside, without enough food and sanitation, in close quarters, famine and disease are characteristic.

There will be, of course, people who escape (v. 16), the purpose-fully extreme language of verse 11 notwithstanding. But their existence, also, will be pitiable. Like mourning doves they will bemoan their past sinfulness, too late to make amends with a righteous God. Defeated, with all the fight knocked out of them (v. 17), they will assume the posture of mourning, wearing the rough camel's hair clothing ("sackcloth") that people wore to make themselves miserable and thus keep all thoughts of selfish enjoyment aside. They might also have put dirt on themselves as mourners sometimes did to call attention to their misery (2 Sam. 13:19; Jer. 6:26; Jon. 3:6), but the emphasis here is on how these people would instead be "covered" with horror and shame. Shaving the head was a common means of showing mourning also (Isa. 3:24; 15:2; Ezek. 27:31) because loss of one's hair and beard were considered unpleasant and self-abnegating (2 Sam. 10:4–5).

What's to be done with all the wealth accumulated by mistreatment of others (cf. Isa. 5:8; Amos 5:11–12)? It certainly won't bribe God when He comes in judgment against Judah! The people who formerly relied on their wealth as protection and power will throw their money into the streets. It is useless against the wrath of God. Note especially the charge (v. 19) that wealth *became their stumbling block of iniquity.* This is exactly the sort of warning one reads often in the New Testament (Matt. 6:19–24; Luke 6:24–25; 1 Tim. 6:6–10, 17–19; James 5:1–6) yet is widely ignored by Christians in America today, where wealth is virtually never viewed as dangerous, but always as desirable.

Precious metals and gems, given to the idol smiths so that idols could be adorned for display, will do the rebellious Israelites no good in the day of their destruction. The enemy will carry off their wealth (2 Kings 25:13–17) as the spoils of war. But note how the passage ends: God will even reject ("turn My face from"; cf. Lev. 26:17; Deut. 31:17–18; 32:20) His own temple ("My secret place"). The holy house itself would be plundered (2 Chron. 36:18; Jer. 52:18–19) and destroyed (2 Kings 25:9)! This rejection of Israel's worship place had long ago been predicted if disobedience had prevailed (Lev. 26:31), and now it was coming to pass.

As the saying goes, "You can't take it with you." Carefully built-up worldly wealth has no value whatever in eternity. Death makes all people equal financially. Yet wrongdoing is so often economically based. There is no kind of evil that people will avoid if the money is right (1 Tim. 6:10). In spite of this, in the final analysis, wealth means little. It does the individual no real good. What counts is how one has lived before God. We are tempted to amass wealth as if we could live on earth forever, even though it is the last thing that could help us to live forever in heaven. As Paul says, "Some people, eager for money, have wandered from the faith and pierced themselves with many griefs" (1 Tim. 6:10, NIV).

For those inclined to save up treasure, another avenue of action is open: storing up treasures in heaven (Matt. 6:20). The Judeans of Ezekiel's day prided themselves on their prosperity and trusted in it. And they suffered bitterly as a result when God called them to account for their lives. How much better to live in a manner faithful to God, always expending energy for His purposes rather than our own, paying attention to people because they are in God's image rather than because they can help us advance in life, using our time to love God and neighbor rather than to make ourselves lovely to others? The Israelites made a terrible mistake by reason of their pride. It is sad that the same sort of mistake should be repeated so constantly still.

CRIMES OF BLOOD

7:23 'Make a chain,
    For the land is filled with crimes of blood,
    And the city is full of violence.
24 Therefore I will bring the worst of the
      Gentiles,
    And they will possess their houses;
    I will cause the pomp of the strong to cease,
    And their holy places shall be defiled.
25 Destruction comes;
    They will seek peace, but *there shall be* none.
26 Disaster will come upon disaster,
    And rumor will be upon rumor.
    Then they will seek a vision from a prophet;
    But the law will perish from the priest,
    And counsel from the elders.

27 'The king will mourn,
    The prince will be clothed with desolation,

And the hands of the common people will
   tremble.
I will do to them according to their way,
And according to what they deserve I will
   judge them;
Then they shall know that I *am* the LORD!'
                             Ezek. 7:23–27

The Hebrew words translated "make a chain" are unfortunately not entirely comprehensible, and the other ancient texts do no agree with the Hebrew wording. Accordingly we cannot even be sure that verse 23 represents another brief prophetic enactment. More likely, verses 23–27 carry on the theme of coming destruction by providing instances of the awful effects of the invasion and occupation of Judah by its enemies.

It is noteworthy that the land is described as "filled with crimes of blood," and then in poetic parallel fashion, the city, Jerusalem, is "full of wrongdoing" (NKJV, "violence," v. 23). For the unscrupulous rich people of Judah, life in these days when Babylon was dominant was not unpleasant. They exploited the poor by controlling large tracts of land and giving short shrift to their tenant farmers, as well as by lending at usurious interest rates to people who ended up unable to pay except by forfeiting their houses and land. So, as a fitting punishment, the exploiters will have their property, so diligently collected, just given away to others in one sudden event. Others will get for free what these had labored for (cf. Deut. 28:30). Moreover, their illegal, heterodox sanctuaries will be ruined, losing their (fake) holiness as foreigners smash them (v. 24; cf. Lev. 26:31).

From such destruction there can be no respite (v. 25). It will affect everyone because it will be nation-wide and city-wide in its scope. Therefore the person who seeks to get away from the coming trouble and find peace will not succeed. Of course, when cataclysmic changes such as a grand-scale military invasion occur, people naturally want to know what to do next. They need guidance, and in ancient times people sought guidance by religious means far more routinely than is now the practice (v. 26). But God says that He will have withdrawn Himself from His people (cf. Deut. 31:17–18) so that they will have no revelation from their prophets, or instruction (Hebrew, *tôrāh*, NKJV, "law") or advice from their community leaders. Everyone will be in a panic; no one will know what to do.

Even the king ("prince" is a parallel term, not indicating royal family but referring to the king; cf. 44:3; 46:6–8; 46:16–18) will suffer, just as will the commoners. From the highest to the lowest, all will experience the agony of invasion, eventual capture, and the full ravages of war. Why? Because this is exactly what they deserve (v. 27)! Their rebellion and neglect of proper responsibility to God necessitates punishment. Only then will they realize who God is and how they should have been obeying Him all along (cf. 6:14; 7:4; 7:9).

The real enemy, then, was within. Israel's foe was not so much the Babylonians as its own sinfulness. Nothing that lay in their future by way of judgment need have happened. They had brought it all on themselves because their sinfulness was so regular and so widespread. There was simply no doubt that this nation had broken its covenant with the Lord. The evidence was overwhelming, and no one with anything but a distorted perspective could fail to realize that. God's covenant cannot be violated without consequences, and the Israelites had to learn this the hard way. Everyone had to learn the lesson; no one was exempt from—could escape—the terrible truth.

Isn't the real enemy often within? When you fail to live the way God desires, whom do you have to blame but yourself? If a church doesn't evangelize, or care for the needs of people, or support missions, or influence its community, is God to blame? Is it the fault of Satan, whose temptations are so attractive as to be irresistible? Hardly. The problem is internal, not external; it is a matter of will, obedience, and discipline on the part of people themselves. The challenge of a passage like this is in its implicit warning that we, too, are not above disobedience, not beyond failure to accomplish God's will. If we fail, we have no one to blame but ourselves. The Righteous Judge knows that, and we should admit it, as well.

CHAPTER FIVE

Visions of the Temple

Ezekiel 8:1–11:25

As a visionary prophet, Ezekiel was not limited to his own geographical environs for firsthand observation on matters of concern to the Israelites. God had shown Himself to be sovereign over all the earth, not just Canaan, by His dramatic appearance to Ezekiel in Mesopotamia (chaps. 1 and 2). This same sovereignty could also put Ezekiel's spiritual eyes anywhere on earth. In chapters 8–11 the temple at Jerusalem constitutes the locale for a great set of observations and revelations about Israel's guilt and coming punishment.

From 11:24–25 it appears that Ezekiel did not physically leave his home in Mesopotamia where the elders of the exile were seated with him (8:1), even though his visions were extensive and he describes himself as being "lifted up" by the hair (8:3). God did not lack the ability to transport Ezekiel miraculously in full person to Jerusalem. That would have been easy enough. But there was no need to do so. God was everywhere and fully capable of showing to Ezekiel's spirit anything He wanted him to see.

What Ezekiel sees in Jerusalem is both infuriating and sad. Evidence of the provocation of God to wrath was everywhere (cf. 8:17–18) in the open sin of the people. And, as well, Ezekiel had to witness the departure of God's glory from the temple with all its terrifying implications (chap. 10). Yet the element of hope looms in these prophecies as well. God's promise to restore His people eventually (11:16–20) provides a beam of encouragement through the gloom of the nation's current sinfulness and coming judgment.

A TOUR OF THE TEMPLE

8:1 And it came to pass in the sixth year, in the sixth *month*, on the fifth *day* of the month, as I sat in my house with the elders of Judah sitting before me, that the hand of the Lord GOD fell upon me there.

2 Then I looked, and there was a likeness, like the appearance of fire—from the appearance of His waist and downward, fire; and from His waist and upward, like the appearance of brightness, like the color of amber.

3 He stretched out the form of a hand, and took me by a lock of my hair; and the Spirit lifted me up between earth and heaven, and brought me in visions of God to Jerusalem, to the door of the north gate of the inner *court*, where the seat of the image of jealousy *was*, which provokes to jealousy.

4 And behold, the glory of the God of Israel *was* there, like the vision that I saw in the plain.

5 Then He said to me, "Son of man, lift your eyes now toward the north." So I lifted my eyes toward the north, and there, north of the altar gate, was this image of jealousy in the entrance.

6 Furthermore He said to me, "Son of man, do you see what they are doing, the great abominations that the house of Israel commits here, to make Me go far away from My sanctuary? Now turn again, you will see greater abominations."

7 So He brought me to the door of the court; and when I looked, there was a hole in the wall.

8 Then He said to me, "Son of man, dig into the wall"; and when I dug into the wall, there was a door.

9 And He said to me, "Go in, and see the wicked abominations which they are doing there."

10 So I went in and saw, and there—every sort of creeping thing, abominable beasts, and all the idols of the house of Israel, portrayed all around on the walls.

11 And there stood before them seventy men of the elders of the house of Israel, and in their midst stood Jaazaniah the son of Shaphan. Each man had a censer in his hand, and a thick cloud of incense went up.

12 Then He said to me, "Son of man, have you seen
what the elders of the house of Israel do in the dark,
every man in the room of his idols? For they say,
'The LORD does not see us, the LORD has forsaken the
land.'"

13 And He said to me, "Turn again, *and* you will
see greater abominations that they are doing."

14 So He brought me to the door of the north gate
of the LORD's house; and to my dismay, women were
sitting there weeping for Tammuz.

15 Then He said to me, "Have you seen *this*, O son
of man? Turn again, you will see greater abominations
than these."

16 So He brought me into the inner court of the
LORD's house; and there, at the door of the temple of
the LORD, between the porch and the altar, *were* about
twenty-five men with their backs toward the temple
of the LORD and their faces toward the east, and they
were worshiping the sun toward the east.

17 And He said to me, "Have you seen *this*, O son
of man? Is it a trivial thing to the house of Judah to
commit the abominations which they commit here?
For they have filled the land with violence; then they
have returned to provoke Me to anger. Indeed they
put the branch to their nose.

18 "Therefore I also will act in fury. My eye will
not spare nor will I have pity; and though they cry in
My ears with a loud voice, I will not hear them."

Ezek. 8:1–18

Precisely fourteen months after the first vision (1:2), that is, 592
B.C., Ezekiel received a vision while at home in Tel-Abib, with leaders ("elders") from the exiled community present (v. 1). This is one of
four occasions specifically mentioned (cf. 14:1; 20:1; 33:31) on which
the prophet received a revelation with a group of people sitting before him waiting for a word from the Lord. Presumably it was often
the case that groups from the exiles would come to Ezekiel to inquire
of the Lord through him (cf. also 2 Kings 4:38; 6:1, 32). It was the
sixth month (September–October) at the end of summer.

What Ezekiel begins to see is a vision of God (v. 2), fiery and
bright, visible only in a sort of general shape by which He allows

Himself to be "seen," similarly to 1:26–27. In this vision, Ezekiel also apparently felt the sensation of being pulled up into the sky by "the form of" a hand (v. 3). It was the Spirit who transported him (cf. 3:14; 11:24; 37:1; 43:5) since God has no actual "hand." Note that he was brought "in visions" to Jerusalem; he was still physically in his home among the exiles.

There were three gates from the outer to the inner court of the Jerusalem temple. They faced north, east, and south. The northern gate was the one used by the king and was thus perhaps the most prominent. At that gate was some kind of idol, which Ezekiel here calls the "image of jealousy," that is, a rival to Yahweh (v. 3). It may have been something like the image of the goddess Asherah that had stood in the temple during the days of Manasseh (2 Kings 23:6) or perhaps a sculpture of an angel guarding the doorway. We do not know, but it is obvious that it had become during the first temple's latter days an object of worship contrary to the Mosaic covenant (Exod. 20:4–5).

In addition to seeing idol worship of this sort (vv. 5–6) Ezekiel also noted the presence of God's glory (v. 4) just as he had seen it previously (1:28). In spite of the abominations practiced there, God had still not removed His merciful presence from His "house," so great was His patience toward His people. Then the prophet, in order to see even "greater abominations" (v. 6), had a vision of himself digging through a wall to reach a secret door to a closed room, where he saw full-blown pantheistic idolatry underway (vv. 10–11). This idolatry involved Israel's very leadership ("elders") and was presided over by a secret traitor to orthodoxy, Jaazaniah.

This individual was from a prominent family in Jerusalem. His father had been secretary of state in the cabinet of the last righteous king, Josiah (2 Kings 22:3), and one of his brothers was well known as a defender of Jeremiah (Jer. 26:24). How tragic, then, that this member of a great and faithful Judean family should be a leader of animal worship! Pantheism, the belief that the gods are part of everything and that everything is a god or part of one, was widespread in the ancient world. It could take forms that seem silly to us today. The Egyptians, for example, worshiped the dung beetle (scarab) because it was alive! All life to them was divine. So here we have a report of a visionary scene of people appealing to the spirits of various animals, represented by their images on the walls of a room, using incense smoke to symbolize the animals' glory. The room they were in was probably a *liŝkāh*, one of the many chambers built into the temple complex and used, as true religion degenerated, for pagan worship and banqueting (cf. Neh. 13:4–9).

Verse 12 makes it clear that Ezekiel's vision was just a sampling of the sort of idolatry widespread in Judah at that time. It is not likely that people actually thought that the Lord could not see them when they did this sort of thing in private, but rather that they assumed that the Babylonian victory in 598 B.C. meant that the promised land was no longer the Lord's land (*"The Lord does not see us, the Lord has forsaken the land"* [v. 12]). Many ancient peoples believed that gods were limited in their influence to specific territories and could abandon or be driven from them. Ezekiel knew better (cf. chap. 1), but many of the Judeans did not.

But Ezekiel still had more—even worse things—to see. Back where he had first arrived, at the north gate, he now saw Tammuz worship (v. 14). Tammuz is the Hebrew form of Dumizi(d), the dying and rising Sumerian-Babylonian god of plant life, whose death was mourned (*"women . . . weeping* [v. 14]) every fall when the crops died and trees shed their leaves, and whose coming back to life was celebrated every spring with the sprouting of nature. But even that was not all the paganism going on (v. 15)! In the inner court of the temple yard, right before the temple building, where only priests were allowed, Ezekiel saw men (priests) turning away from the temple and toward the sun, doing obeisance to it. The sun had been worshiped as a god at the temple for decades (2 Kings 23:5, 11) but presumably not at the very entrance to the holy place itself by priests, with their backs to the Lord! Worshiping the sun and worshiping Tammuz were further evidences of national degeneration into nature worship, a truly primitive religion.

This "violence" (read "wrongdoing," v. 17) could not go on without judgment. The Hebrew words here translated *"put the branch to their nose"* are obscure, but probably should be rendered something like "are a stench to my nose" referring to how offensive these actions are to the Lord. He promises swift, unbridled punishment (v. 18) for such a total desecration of His holy place and covenant.

There are two things about Ezekiel's vision of the temple that ought especially to be a lesson to us. First, it was Israelites who were doing all the "abominations" he viewed. It was foolish enough that any people should worship idols and nature. But for Israelites, who had known the true God and had access to His truth via His gracious covenant with them, such practices were simply atrocious. Yet it is a fact that knowing the truth does not prevent people from ignoring or abandoning it (cf. Rom. 1:21–22) to their own detriment. People are capable of throwing away the only truth that could save them in favor of a lie that appeals to their tastes or habits. Second, they thought they could get away with what they were doing because God was limited in His power (v. 12). They underestimated God, somewhat in the same way that people today take the approach that they may do as they please, since God does not exist, or care, or have the power to call them into judgment. Were they naive? Yes. Were they degenerate? Of course. Were they unusual? Unfortunately, no. Nothing they did is all that different from the foolish practices people are capable of in our own day and in our own society—thinking themselves smart all the while they are foolishly practicing what to God are abominations.

SEVEN EXECUTIONERS

9:1 Then He called out in my hearing with a loud voice, saying, "Let those who have charge over the city draw near, each *with* a deadly weapon in his hand."

2 And suddenly six men came from the direction of the upper gate, which faces north, each with his battle-ax in his hand. One man among them *was* clothed with linen and had a writer's inkhorn at his side. They went in and stood beside the bronze altar.

3 Now the glory of the God of Israel had gone up from the cherub, where it had been, to the threshold of the temple. And He called to the man clothed with linen, who *had* the writer's inkhorn at his side;

4 and the LORD said to him, "Go through the midst of the city, through the midst of Jerusalem, and put a mark on the foreheads of the men who sigh and cry over all the abominations that are done within it."

5 To the others He said in my hearing, "Go after him through the city and kill; do not let your eye spare, nor have any pity.

6 "Utterly slay old *and* young men, maidens and little children and women; but do not come near anyone on whom *is* the mark; and begin at My sanctuary." So they began with the elders who *were* before the temple.

7 Then He said to them, "Defile the temple, and fill the courts with the slain. Go out!" And they went out and killed in the city.

8 So it was, that while they were killing them, I was left *alone*; and I fell on my face and cried out, and said, "Ah, Lord GOD! Will You destroy all the remnant of Israel in pouring out Your fury on Jerusalem?"

9 Then He said to me, "The iniquity of the house of Israel and Judah *is* exceedingly great, and the land is full of bloodshed, and the city full of perversity; for they say, 'The LORD has forsaken the land, and the LORD does not see!'

10 "And as for Me also, My eye will neither spare, nor will I have pity, *but* I will recompense their deeds on their own head."

11 Just then, the man clothed with linen, who *had* the inkhorn at his side, reported back and said, "I have done as You commanded me."

Ezek. 9:1–11

In this part of the vision, Ezekiel is still spiritually present at the Jerusalem temple, and the action appears to follow virtually immediately after the Lord's promise of punishment for Israel in chapter 8.

"Those who have charge over the city" (v. 1) are Jerusalem's guardian angels. The fact that they are called *"men"* in v. 2 is merely typical of the language of angelic visions. Not only people (Heb. 1:14) but nations (Daniel 10) and cities have angels that are, as it were, assigned to them by God. Angels do not, of course, have any authority of their own; they simply do what God wants done. So these angels in charge of Jerusalem are a means by which God may choose to impose His will on the city's populace. Here their presence foreshadows the coming brutal invasion of the city after the siege will end in 586 B.C. (2 Chron. 36:17, 19; Lam. 1:15; 2:3–8), so they appear as destroying warriors with battle weapons (v. 2; cf. Rev. 9:14–15). The seventh angel, however, has a different task. His dress is linen, typical of angels not on bloody assignments (e.g., Ezek. 10:6–7; Dan. 12:6–7),

indicating his heavenly origin (cf. Ezek. 44:17–18; Rev. 19:8, 14). His task will depart significantly from that of the six others, as we learn in vv. 4 and 11.

Verse 3 describes the initial movement of the glory of the Lord as it prepares to leave the temple altogether (chap. 10). Normally this glory would be evidenced at the ark, in the holy of holies, the innermost room of the temple building. The top of the ark was decorated with cherubs (Exod. 37:7–9) where the "mercy seat" represented the presence (glory) of God. But now the glory shifts to the threshold, at the front of the building. The Lord, still Ezekiel's guide in the vision, then instructs the linen-clad angel to mark the foreheads of all believers who do not share in the city's corruption, but lament it. The word for "mark" in v. 4 in Hebrew is *taw*, the final letter of the Hebrew alphabet, which in Ezekiel's day was shaped like an "X." Some commentators have suggested that this signified Christ or the cross, but in Ezekiel's day, it merely signified an "X," nothing more.

What is important to remember about the marking process is its relationship to the doctrine of individual responsibility so strongly asserted in the book (cf. chap. 3). While God may judge nations, cities, cultures, etc. as a group, He is not an arbitrary, unfair judge. Those who have turned against the evils of their own people will be spared by God's judgment, even if from an earthly point of view they may be caught up in the fate of the corporate entity to which they belong. Thus we all recognize that the president of the United States and the Communist party leader in the Soviet Union could decide to destroy both nations in a nuclear war, and Christians as well as non-Christians would lose their lives in the process. But *God's* judgment that would follow would be based not on national or corporate associations or involvements, but on whether or not an individual's relationship with God was right or not. Likewise, in Ezekiel's Jerusalem, corrupt as the city was, the righteous were still to remain faithful and not give up or give in to the practices and ideals of the surrounding culture.

The rest of the populace would be destroyed (v. 5), including women and children. Total elimination of the population is associated with Old Testament holy war (Deuteronomy 20), which is a divine war of extermination of a wicked society in which the human soldiers are merely agents of God's wrath. Thus the implication for Ezekiel and his eventual audience was clear: The coming destruction represented *God's* condemnation, not just a political-military success for the Babylonians in Palestine.

The first to be slain in the vision were Jerusalem's leaders ("elders") who, as we know from 8:16, were the most offensive of the abominators. It is they who defiled the temple by having the gall to worship the sun at the very porch of the temple building. As the slaughter proceeded after that throughout the city, Ezekiel assumed the role of intercessor for his people, much as Amos had done when the Lord threatened total annihilation of Israel in his day (Amos 7:2–6) or as Moses had done when the Lord had considered doing away with Israel because of its rebelliousness at Sinai (Exod. 32:10–14). In fact, verse 11, which reports that the "man in linen" had done his task well, reassures us that as a matter of principle we may be confident that God will indeed spare the innocent and provide a remnant who may by reason of their faithfulness escape the divine wrath.

Again, the complacency of the people is an issue (v. 9). They think that God is limited, off the scene somehow (cf. 8:12). The people were so self-centered that they could not imagine the Babylonians dominating the Fertile Crescent unless the Lord had no role to play in Israel. It simply did not occur to them that the Babylonian success was precisely the outworking of God's plan *against* His people.

The principle of individual responsibility is, of course, two-sided. If the individually righteous are to be spared, the individually wicked are not. So God reminds Ezekiel that He will carry out the covenant punishments He committed Himself to enforce (Leviticus 26, Deuteronomy 28, etc.). The final enforcement of justice, after frequent opportunities for the guilty to repent, is not a time for leniency ("pity," v. 10) but for firm execution of the appropriate punishments. There *is* a "sin unto death" (1 John 5:16) that requires firm requital and cannot be overlooked. Judah and Jerusalem had come to exactly that point, and Ezekiel's visionary experience showed him so.

THE THRONE CHARIOT AT THE TEMPLE

10:1 And I looked, and there in the firmament that was above the head of the cherubim, there appeared something like a sapphire stone, having the appearance of the likeness of a throne.

94

2 Then He spoke to the man clothed with linen, and said, "Go in among the wheels, under the cherub, fill your hands with coals of fire from among the cherubim, and scatter *them* over the city." And he went in as I watched.

3 Now the cherubim were standing on the south side of the temple when the man went in, and the cloud filled the inner court.

4 Then the glory of the LORD went up from the cherub, *and paused* over the threshold of the temple; and the house was filled with the cloud, and the court was full of the brightness of the LORD's glory.

5 And the sound of the wings of the cherubim was heard *even* in the outer court, like the voice of Almighty God when He speaks.

6 Then it happened, when He commanded the man clothed in linen, saying, "Take fire from among the wheels, from among the cherubim," that he went in and stood beside the wheels.

7 And the cherub stretched out his hand from among the cherubim to the fire that *was* among the cherubim, and took *some of it* and put *it* into the hands of the *man* clothed with linen, who took *it* and went out.

8 The cherubim appeared to have the form of a man's hand under their wings.

9 And when I looked, there were four wheels by the cherubim, one wheel by one cherub and another wheel by each other cherub; the wheels appeared *to have* the color of a beryl stone.

10 *As for* their appearance, all four looked alike— as it were, a wheel in the middle of a wheel.

11 When they went, they went toward *any of* their four directions; they did not turn aside when they went, but followed in the direction the head was facing. They did not turn aside when they went.

12 And their whole body, with their back, their hands, their wings, and the wheels that the four had, *were* full of eyes all around.

13 As for the wheels, they were called in my hearing, "Wheel."

14 Each one had four faces: the first face *was* the

face of a cherub, the second face the face of a man,
the third the face of a lion, and the fourth the face of
an eagle.

15 And the cherubim were lifted up. This *was* the
living creature I saw by the River Chebar.

16 When the cherubim went, the wheels went beside them; and when the cherubim lifted their wings
to mount up from the earth, the same wheels also did
not turn from beside them.

17 When *the cherubim* stood still, *the wheels* stood
still, and when *one* was lifted up, *the other* lifted itself
up, for the spirit of the living creature *was* in them.

18 Then the glory of the LORD departed from the
threshold of the temple and stood over the cherubim.

19 And the cherubim lifted their wings and
mounted up from the earth in my sight. When they
went out, the wheels *were* beside them; and they
stood at the door of the east gate of the LORD's house,
and the glory of the God of Israel *was* above them.

20 This *is* the living creature I saw under the God
of Israel by the River Chebar, and I knew they *were*
cherubim.

21 Each one had four faces and each one four
wings, and the likeness of the hands of a man *was*
under their wings.

22 And the likeness of their faces *was* the same
as the faces which I had seen by the River Chebar,
their appearance and their persons. They each went
straight forward.

Ezek. 10:1–22

Much of this chapter is devoted to a description of God's impressive chariot throne, and the description parallels that of chapter 1
extensively. Ezekiel's original audience was probably changing to
some extent as time went by, and such repetitions were not a problem to them, but probably quite welcome. Even to us, who can read
chapters 1 and 10 side by side if we wish, this second lengthy description of the chariot has considerable value. It links indisputably
the departure of the glory from the temple (vv. 4, 18) with the appearance of God (chap. 1) so that no reader can miss the point that
as part of His judgment God Himself is actually now abandoning the

place where He was once worshiped. The description is again so lengthy and carefully done that it is obvious how impressed Ezekiel must have been with what he saw. Elisha had seen a vision of the "chariot of Israel" (2 Kings 2:11), but who else had ever seen the chariot of God?

In verse 1 Ezekiel's description focuses temporarily on the sapphire-like throne above the cherubim (cf. 1:26), which is the point from which God could be heard speaking to the angel in linen. This figure had completed the task of sparing the righteous (9:4) and now is assigned an opposite sort of job—bringing God's judgment fire on the city. A raging fire was visible in the midst of the cherubim, as if the chariot were itself made of fire, which is at least how it appeared (1:4; cf. 2 Kings 2:11). This fire would constitute not just any fire but the very fire of God, since the chariot was God's own. Fire in the Bible is often a symbol of God's judgment against wickedness (Gen. 19:24; Deut. 28:24; 32:22; Amos 1–2), and thus the scattering of coals of fire over Jerusalem would symbolize divine destructive wrath.

In chapter 1 Ezekiel never identifies the cherubim by name, though it is obvious who the unusual angelic animals are. Here he calls them cherubim from the start and concludes the chapter (vv. 20–22) by emphasizing their identity. The reason for this is the extremely close association of cherubim and the *presence* of God. In the modern day, people lining a street waiting for a presidential motorcade to come by know that if they are to catch a glimpse of the president, they must look for the black limousine. The president will not be found on a motorcycle or in a station wagon, but inside a black limousine. So far as a presidential motorcade is concerned, where the limousine is, there is the president. Ancient Israelites had a similar sort of expectation: where the cherubim are, there is God. Of course, they did not think that God was to be found only on His "throne" or chariot anymore than we would think that the president could be found only in a motorcade. But from the beginning of the construction of the tabernacle and its furnishings at Sinai, the cherubim were the supernatural "animals" on which the throne of God was depicted as resting (Exod. 37:7–9), and the ark on which this depiction appeared was the same ark that stood in the temple. Moreover, the temple itself was filed with carvings of cherubim (1 Kings 6:29, 35; 7:29, 36) and God was routinely portrayed as borne by cherubim in Old Testament literature (e.g., Pss. 18:10; 80:1; 99:1). Thus Ezekiel's audience, by hearing so much about cherubim in this chapter, could not help but realize that if the cherubim were moving, God was moving too. That is the point of the passage.

The "outer court" (v. 5) was the court at the furthest edge of the temple complex. For the noise of the cherubim's wings to be audible there was an indication of what a great roar their wings made in motion! The chariot was still just over the temple porch (v. 4). Since cherubim are guardians of the throne, protectors of the Lord, it was they who gave the fiery coals to the angel (v. 7). An angel would presumably not be authorized to tamper with or touch God's chariot throne.

Most of verses 8–22 repeats or connects with what was stated in chapter 1 about the cherubim and God's chariot, with the exception of verses 13, 18, and 19. Verse 13 mentions that the wheels were addressed by name, thus emphasizing that the wheels had an intelligence of their own, something implicit but not explicit in chapter 1 (vv. 18–21). Then in verses 18 and 19 the glory of God mounts the chariot again. In other words, that glory had briefly lifted from off the chariot in 10:4, but now again rejoined the chariot so that God was once again enthroned on it. And finally the chariot progressed to the east gate of the temple, at the very edge of the temple complex, poised to leave the city (which it does in 11:23).

It is noteworthy that the throne-chariot, bearing the glory of God, came *to* Ezekiel in exile but departed *from* Jerusalem. The presence of God is a sign of His favor (Deut. 4:29, 31) whereas the absence of God is a sign of His rejection (Deut. 31:17, 18). The passage symbolizes the fact that it is exiles to whom God has entrusted continuation of true religion and a right relationship with Himself. Those remaining in Jerusalem could not be trusted. They had proved themselves unworthy and unreliable, having failed to learn any lesson from the invasion and exile of 598 B.C. After the period of the exile was complete, it would be returning exiles like Zerubbabel and Jeshua (Hag. 1:15; Zechariah 3–4) or later, Ezra and Nehemiah, who would help restore orthodox faith and practice to Judah—not the "people of the land" who had never been taken into exile and had thus stayed in Judah all along. Just as the same burning coals that symbolized the purity of God's presence at the throne chariot could also be used as a means of destruction for the city in the early part of the vision of chapter 10, the same people sent into exile could later be the ones who preserved true worship, having been purified in their faith by the ordeals they underwent.

Earthly status means nothing to God. If a mere deportee like Ezekiel is willing to do God's will, he may be chosen over the official leadership of the nation in Jerusalem. If national leaders are corrupt, they will be rejected and destroyed along with all the rest. There is no pulling rank with God, no appeal to personal prestige in order to secure His favor. Faithful obedience is the hallmark of the Lord's servants; there are no worldly credentials that make any difference to Him (cf. Phil. 3:3–8).

JUDGMENT ON JERUSALEM'S EVIL LEADERS

11:1 Then the Spirit lifted me up and brought me to the East Gate of the LORD's house, which faces eastward; and there at the door of the gate were twenty-five men, among whom I saw Jaazaniah the son of Azzur, and Pelatiah the son of Benaiah, princes of the people.

2 And He said to me: "Son of man, these *are* the men who devise iniquity and give wicked counsel in this city,

3 "who say, '*The time is* not near to build houses; this *city is* the caldron, and we *are* the meat.'

4 "Therefore prophesy against them, prophesy, O son of man!"

5 Then the Spirit of the LORD fell upon me, and said to me, "Speak! 'Thus says the LORD: "Thus you have said, O house of Israel; for I know the things that come into your mind.

6 "You have multiplied your slain in this city, and you have filled its streets with the slain."

7 'Therefore thus says the Lord GOD: "Your slain whom you have laid in its midst, they *are* the meat, and this *city is* the caldron; but I shall bring you out of the midst of it.

8 "You have feared the sword; and I will bring a sword upon you," says the Lord GOD.

9 "And I will bring you out of its midst, and deliver you into the hands of strangers, and execute judgments on you.

10 "You shall fall by the sword. I will judge you at the border of Israel. Then you shall know that I *am* the LORD.

11 "This *city* shall not be your caldron, nor shall you be the meat in its midst. I will judge you at the border of Israel.

12 "And you shall know that I *am* the LORD; for you have not walked in My statutes nor executed My judgments, but have done according to the customs of the Gentiles which *are* all around you."'"

13 Now it happened, while I was prophesying, that Pelatiah the son of Benaiah died. Then I fell on my face and cried with a loud voice, and said, "Ah, Lord GOD! Will You make a complete end of the remnant of Israel?"

Ezek. 11:1–13

In chapter 11, Ezekiel is commanded to preach two messages: one of doom, the other of deliverance. To the leaders of Jerusalem, some of whom are mentioned by name in verses 1–13, he is required to prophesy that some will be killed and others exiled as a result of their willful disobedience of God's commandments. To the Diaspora, on the other hand, those who are already in exile and longing for the Lord's favor, he can announce a message of hope for return to the land of Canaan and enjoyment once again of God's mercy and protection (vv. 14–25).

This message was exactly the opposite of what Jerusalem's leaders considered appropriate. They saw the exiles as unfortunate victims of their own bad luck and poor judgment for having somehow gotten exiled instead of having been spared as the present leaders had been. Of course, the present leaders could hardly be expected to exercise the best judgment; they were mostly inferior leaders who had been left behind by the Babylonians in 598 when the best of the leadership was taken capture and deported. But in their self-importance they seem to have considered themselves somehow the favored few, who, feeling secure in their wisdom and in the upgrading of the city's fortifications that had undoubtedly taken place in the latter years of Zedekiah's reign, believed that Jerusalem could hold out against any foe.

Their byword was the enigmatic saying of verse 3, which seems to be a boast of some sort, an arrogant expression of confidence that they, as the new overlords of the city and territory, had now been given "the land as a possession" (v. 15) and that it would never be taken away from them. The Hebrew wording of their boast is difficult to understand. It says literally, "Not build houses near? It is the pot, we are the meat!" The English translations all attempt to smooth out this terse aphorism, but its exact sense must remain a matter of conjecture. Perhaps it implies that the people could go ahead to build, that is, making long-term plans (cf. Jer. 32:6–15) because they belonged in Jerusalem like meat in a cooking pot whereas the exiles were like the entrails, hooves, etc. of an animal—discarded as unfit to go into the pot for cooking.

In Ezekiel's vision the city's leaders appeared as twenty-five men at the east gate of the temple (v. 1), which is where the throne chariot was at this time (10:19). In effect, God paused there to give Ezekiel the important messages of chapter 11 before departing. The two leaders mentioned by name, Jaazaniah and Pelatiah, are otherwise unknown to us (it's a different Jaazaniah from 8:11), but they had, under the king, obviously risen to considerable power. And their counsel was defiant of the Lord: "we can keep on with our current practices; we're in no danger of exile," they thought.

Verses 6 and 7 are predictive. The policies of the city's leaders have made it inevitable that large-scale slaughter of the remaining populace will take place. And the leaders, so secure that Jerusalem is for them a safe haven, will not be able to stay in the city but will be taken out by the enemy and killed (v. 9). This prediction was fulfilled in 586 B.C. at Riblah in Hamath (west Syria) when the city's leaders were killed in the presence of Nebuchadnezzar, the king of Babylon (2 Kings 25:18–21). The very sword (warfare) that they feared in verse 8 would come upon them in verse 10. The city would not be a refuge (v. 11), but they would be, as it were, thrown out of the pot as meat unfit to eat.

Why? Because of disobedience. In virtually every generation of ancient Israel, orthodox Yahwism, the true revealed religion of the Mosaic covenant, was ignored by a majority of people. Much as in America today, true devotion to God was practiced by only a minority. The *"customs of the Gentiles"* (v. 12) prevailed. Those included materialistic idolatry, exploitation of the poor, ritual sex as a part of worship, and so on (cf. 2 Kings 23).

Finally, in this vision, Ezekiel sees one of the corrupt leaders, Pelatiah, collapse and die (v. 13) as a dramatic foreshadowing of the mass executions that would later take place at Riblah. Ezekiel's response mirrors that of Amos when the latter saw similar visions of judgment (Amos 7:2–3, 5–6). Evil as a person like Pelatiah was, and evil as the people of Judah and Jerusalem were, it was hard for Ezekiel to imagine that his own people were to be utterly extinguished. Fortunately, this was not the plan of God, as the reassuring message of verses 14–25 makes plain.

Arrogance, self-confidence, and willful disobedience are the triple sins of the nonexiled Judeans described in this passage. Each of these sins by itself is dangerous, but together they cry out for the wrath of God to be imposed upon the nation. That the leaders are mentioned by name is no accident. Large groups always have leaders, people who function as the catalysts for the actions and perspectives of a class or category. For a society to be so led astray, as the society of ancient Judah was, that it would neither expect nor fear the coming judgment of God, it had to give a lot of credence to its leaders. Yet all societies tend to do exactly that: they allow to rise to leadership the sorts of people who reflect, appeal to, and will carry out the values and expectations of the majority. The passage thus is not just about corrupt leaders but is about them as reflections of and manifestations of a corrupt society. That is why Ezekiel can discern in the death of one the coming death of all.

As for arrogance and self-confidence, it is remarkable how often such attitudes are found in people least qualified in actual fact to hold them. The truly skillful, able, gifted person is free to be humble and to acknowledge the grace of God in his or her accomplishments. As for disobedience, it is the foolish, not the wise, who fail to learn from the punishments of the past. Ezekiel's contemporaries in Jerusalem saw no danger in disobedience to the divine covenant. They obviously could not imagine themselves getting into trouble for what they were doing. Underestimating the power of God to enforce His Law, they became the objects of the enforcement! But disobedience to divine commands never goes unnoticed.

HOME WITH A NEW HEART

11:14 Again the word of the LORD came to me, saying,

15 "Son of man, your brethren, your relatives, your countrymen, and all the house of Israel in its entirety, *are* those about whom the inhabitants of Jerusalem have said, 'Get far away from the LORD; this land has been given to us as a possession.'

16 "Therefore say, 'Thus says the Lord GOD: "Although I have cast them far off among the Gentiles, and although I have scattered them among the countries, yet I shall be a little sanctuary for them in the countries where they have gone."'

17 "Therefore say, 'Thus says the Lord GOD: "I will gather you from the peoples, assemble you from the countries where you have been scattered, and I will give you the land of Israel."'

18 "And they will go there, and they will take away all its detestable things and all its abominations from there.

19 "Then I will give them one heart, and I will put a new spirit within them, and take the stony heart out of their flesh, and give them a heart of flesh,

20 "that they may walk in My statutes and keep My judgments and do them; and they shall be My people, and I will be their God.

21 "But *as for those* whose hearts follow the desire for their detestable things and their abominations, I will recompense their deeds on their own heads," says the Lord GOD.

22 So the cherubim lifted up their wings, with the wheels beside them, and the glory of the God of Israel *was* high above them.

23 And the glory of the LORD went up from the midst of the city and stood on the mountain, which *is* on the east side of the city.

24 Then the Spirit took me up and brought me in a vision by the Spirit of God into Chaldea, to those in captivity. And the vision that I had seen went up from me.

25 So I spoke to those in captivity of all the things
the LORD had shown me.

Ezek. 11:14–25

Ezekiel's question of 11:13 needed an answer. He reflected the same concerns his countrymen in exile had in the early 580s as to the future of the nation of Israel. Was he actually seeing a vision indicating the annihilation of his people? Or could some of them somehow be rescued even from the fate he and others had already experienced?

As far as we can tell, it would have been the farthest thing from Ezekiel's mind, and certainly as well from the minds of his fellow Israelites in exile, that *they* might be the ones to re-inhabit Jerusalem and Judah and prosper again there as a people. If any group could survive all the coming miseries at the hands of the Lord and His human agents of punishment, the Babylonians, surely it would have to be some of the people who were left in Judah and Jerusalem, not yet scattered among the nations by the awful punishment of exile. There seemed to be no likelihood that people deported and resettled throughout the seemingly all-powerful Babylonian Empire, hundreds of miles from home, second-class citizens in the places where they now lived, stripped of all political influence, could ever hope to return from exile and repopulate the holy nation.

This passage thus represents an ironic reversal: the promise of death and exile to those who have escaped it, and the promise of life and a return home to those facing death in exile. Such ironic reversals are common in Old Testament literature (e.g., the story of Joseph's rising from slavery to international power, the protection of Moses within Pharaoh's household, the choosing of David over his brothers) and the New Testament as well ("The first shall be last, and the last shall be first").

In verse 15 the ironic reversal is anticipated by what is said about the identity of *"the house of Israel in its entirety."* The true Israel is comprised of "brothers, relatives, and kinsmen" of Ezekiel. These terms are all synonyms of one another and not intended literally to apply to blood relatives, but to apply figuratively to all those who believe in and obey the Living God. Contrasted to them are the "inhabitants of Jerusalem," whose attitudes and practices are further detailed in verse 21. They are idolaters and practice the personal and

104

social immorality (abominations) forbidden by the Mosaic covenant. For such people deliverance is not appropriate—proper punishment is. Thus their behavior will come down *on their own heads,* a common expression in the Old Testament indicating that they will get directly and exactly what they deserve (cf. Judg. 9:57; 2 Chron. 6:23).

Arrogantly critical of those in exile, the present citizenry of Jerusalem wanted nothing to do with the exiles, mistakenly assuming that fortune had smiled upon them so that they had escaped the first exile. But God had other plans. No matter how distant or how widely dispersed His people were, He would bring them home (vv. 16–17; cf. Joel 3:6–8), and it would be they who would rid Jerusalem and Judah of the idolatry and religious heterodoxy practiced there (v. 18). This is exactly what happened historically. When the Jews began to return from captivity after the decree of Cyrus in 539 B.C. (Ezra 1, 3) they found Jerusalem to be continuing in the corrupt practices and false religion that had caused the Lord to abandon it in the first place. As late as the time of Ezra (Ezra 6–10) and Nehemiah, that is, 458–420 B.C., Jews returning to Zion from exile were correcting abuses and reestablishing righteous religion and obedience to the Mosaic Law. It turned out to be the exiles who, after living in pagan lands so long, came back pure enough to clean up Jerusalem (v. 18). God had shown them in exile how offensive full-blown pagan idolatry really was (Deut. 4:27–28), and in their distress they had repented and converted to true worship of the Lord (vv. 19–20, fulfilling Deut. 4:29–30), something those who had lived all along in the holy city had never humbled themselves to do.

Ezekiel had learned what may be considered a key message of the book: he and people of like mind were at the center of God's will even though their circumstances made them seem like castaways and a bunch of nobodies. The leaders of Jerusalem, on the other hand, looked to the casual observer as if they had it made and could expect to enjoy a long and prosperous life in the capital of Judah. In reality, *they* were the castaways! Their days were numbered, and in a few short years the horrible miseries of siege and bloody defeat predicted in chapters 4–7 would come upon them.

Now it was time for God symbolically to abandon His headquarters. The throne-chariot, conveyed by the cherubim, took off (v. 22) and could be seen by Ezekiel clearly outside the city limits (v. 23). This was a sign that the rejection of wicked Jerusalem had finally come to pass. Ezekiel felt himself brought back home to Mesopotamia (Chaldea) and the vision was over (v. 24). The faithful prophet then relayed to all who would listen what he had seen (v. 25).

How easy it is for any of us to forget that God has made foolish the wisdom of this world (1 Cor. 1:20). He has put down the proud and mighty and exalted the lowly (Luke 1:51–52). We are inclined to choose our leaders and those to whom we give respect because of their obvious position and prestige. To almost any of us, those Jerusalemites that Ezekiel saw in his temple vision would have seemed, as they seemed to themselves, the favored ones of God, the people blessed and called to be in charge. But God's design was otherwise. Those who looked foolish, who were at the low end of things—the Judean exiles in Babylon—were the ones God had in mind to exalt. Of course their exaltation was dependent on their repentance and turning to God, but this was beginning to happen as the exiles saw the enormity of their plight and realized that their only hope was in the Lord.

God doesn't work much with proud people, but with the humble He does great things. From the proud of Jerusalem He departed with His glory. To the humble of the exile He promised a great future. Which kind of group would we have tended to want to be a part of in Ezekiel's day? Which sort of group are we among right now?

CHAPTER SIX

Bags Packed for Deportation

Ezekiel 12:1–28

Although Ezekiel's visionary visit to Jerusalem was over, his responsibility to preach about the approaching fall of the city to the Babylonians remained constant. Through chapter 24 of the book he continues to describe the sinfulness of Judea and Jerusalem, the inevitability of their downfall, and some of the details of the process of Babylonian conquest and deportation of the population. He also provides certain overviews of Israel's history, emphasizing the tragedy of how an elect nation could fall so far into disgrace by reason of their disobedience to the Holy One.

In chapter 12 the topic is deportation, both its inevitability and its proximity in time. Not only will the survivors of siege in the city be taken into exile, but this whole disastrous sequence of events is near at hand! Every generation realizes that sometime in the future, wars or disasters are going to take place. Ezekiel's generation, like others, had the sense that peace would not prevail forever. They knew something about history and realized that good times tend eventually to give way to bad times. But every generation hopes that it will be later, not sooner, that things get worse. Everyone wishes that the inevitable hard times will not come until he or she is off the scene. In America, huge national budget deficits are tolerated because they bring prosperity in the short run; the fact that all that borrowed money must be paid back in the future is some other generation's problem. Energy wastefulness is easy to indulge in, as long as the supply is good for a few more decades. Let someone else worry about heat and power after we're gone!

But the deportation of Jerusalem wasn't going to wait. It could not be delayed by anyone other than God, and through Ezekiel He makes clear in this chapter that the nation must prepare for the inevitable.

HEADING OFF TO EXILE

12:1 Now the word of the LORD came to me, saying:

2 "Son of man, you dwell in the midst of a rebellious house, which has eyes to see but does not see, and ears to hear but does not hear; for they *are* a rebellious house.

3 "Therefore, son of man, prepare your belongings for captivity, and go into captivity by day in their sight. You shall go from your place into captivity to another place in their sight. It may be that they will consider, though they *are* a rebellious house.

4 "By day you shall bring out your belongings in their sight, as though going into captivity; and at evening you shall go in their sight, like those who go into captivity.

5 "Dig through the wall in their sight, and carry your belongings out through it.

6 "In their sight you shall bear *them* on *your* shoulders *and* carry *them* out at twilight; you shall cover your face, so that you cannot see the ground, for I have made you a sign to the house of Israel."

7 So I did as I was commanded. I brought out my belongings by day, as though going into captivity, and at evening I dug through the wall with my hand. I brought *them* out at twilight, *and* I bore *them* on *my* shoulder in their sight.

8 And in the morning the word of the LORD came to me, saying,

9 "Son of man, has not the house of Israel, the rebellious house, said to you, 'What are you doing?'

10 "Say to them, 'Thus says the Lord GOD: "This burden *concerns* the prince in Jerusalem and all the house of Israel who are among them."'

11 "Say, 'I *am* a sign to you. As I have done, so shall it be done to them; they shall be carried away into captivity.'

12 "And the prince who *is* among them shall bear *his belongings* on *his* shoulder at twilight and go out. They shall dig through the wall to carry *them* out through it. He shall cover his face, so that he cannot see the ground with *his* eyes.

13 "I will also spread My net over him, and he shall be caught in My snare. I will bring him to Babylon, *to* the land of the Chaldeans; yet he shall not see it, though he shall die there.

14 "I will scatter to every wind all who *are* around him to help him, and all his troops; and I will draw out the sword after them.

15 "Then they shall know that I *am* the LORD, when I scatter them among the nations and disperse them throughout the countries.

16 "But I will spare a few of their men from the sword, from famine, and from pestilence, that they may declare all their abominations among the Gentiles wherever they go. Then they shall know that I *am* the LORD."

Ezek. 12:1–16

"Back" from Jerusalem (though he had been there only in vision, not in body) Ezekiel now hears a reminder of what God had stressed to him in his original call (2:3–3:11), that the Israelites were not disposed to hearing or obeying God's Word (v. 2). Thus chapter 12 seems to provide a kind of new departure point, though not a new subject. God requires of His prophet yet another enactment prophecy by which he will dramatize the coming exile of Jerusalem. Ezekiel's audience was made up of people who had been exiled after the first Babylonian capture of Jerusalem in 598 B.C. None of them who paid attention could fail to understand the general nature of the prophet's actions, since they alluded to exile. But how specifically they were to be applied to events now around 588 B.C., ten years after their own exile, must certainly have been a question raised by those who witnessed Ezekiel's actions. Ezekiel therefore explained his actions as he undertook them, in inspired response to questions from his "audience" (v. 9).

He first was commanded to gather his belongings as if for a long trip (v. 3). Apparently the Babylonians allowed their prisoners to bring whatever personal belongings they could carry when they were taken into exile. A bag or two would constitute the bearable limit on a forced walk of several hundred miles' duration. Animals, carts, etc., would be of no help to the Israelites, having been seized by their captors for their exclusive use.

Openly (vv. 3–4), probably in front of his house, Ezekiel made preparations for a trip. He did this apparently all day (v. 4) so that by nightfall virtually everyone in the small Tel-Abib community would have had a chance to see him packing, or at least hear that he had been doing so. Finally when evening had come, Ezekiel was to depart (v. 4) by digging through his wall (v. 5). We do not know if this meant the wall of his house per se or of his courtyard because we do not know the structure of his dwelling unit in Tel-Abib. If he had a courtyard-style house, a crowd could be expected to gather to watch him loosen the bricks at one spot to make a hole in the courtyard wall and then crawl through. The crowd would understand that breaking through a wall was symbolic of exile, since the conquering armies would systematically break the walls through at various points in order to enter the city. Amos makes a similar prediction: "You will go out through the breaks in the walls, each one straight ahead" (Amos 4:3).

Ezekiel also had to cover his face (v. 6) so that he could not see where he was going ("see the ground"). The eventual blinding of Zedekiah (2 Kings 25:7) was thus predicted. All this he did (v. 7), engendering considerable interest and discussion on the part of his fellow captives. The next day (v. 8) God revealed to him the words he should say in response to the questions asked the night before (v. 9) by those who watched him walk away from his home as if an exile.

His reply first concerns the "prince" of Jerusalem, a term used routinely in the Book of Ezekiel to refer to the king. Zedekiah was the king of Jerusalem at this point. He was a puppet king installed on the throne by the Babylonians after the surrender of Jehoiachin in 598 B.C. Zedekiah's eventual rebellion against the Babylonians (2 Kings 25:20) sealed his fate. Once the Babylonians conquered Jerusalem, Zedekiah would be punished severely (2 Kings 25:6–9). Thus Ezekiel's "burden" (v. 10), that is, prophecy, pointed to the fact that both king and people would be taken prisoner, the government and the resident citizenry being, for all practical purposes, eliminated. The end of the nation of Judea as an independent state was at hand.

Verses 12–14 allude to Zedekiah's frantic escape attempt, his lack of success, his capture by the Babylonians, and his being taken blind to Babylon, where he died (2 Kings 25:4–7). Beginning with

110

verse 14 the prophecy stresses that the Babylonians are merely the proximate agents in all this. God is the real mover, the ultimate enemy of the wicked people of Jerusalem. It was important for the defeated Judeans to know this, as verse 15 makes clear. They had considered the Lord to be ineffective, defeated among the gods. They would learn otherwise.

The covenant God had made with His people at Mount Sinai centuries before contained an important provision. No matter how severely God might punish His people for violations of the covenant, He would not completely destroy them. There would always be a people of God, however few, however different from the original group (Lev. 26:42–45; cf. Exod. 32:10; Deut. 4:30–31). So in spite of the sword, famine, and pestilence (v. 16, a standardized way of referring to the full range of divine punishments), some of the people would survive. They would then be in a position to confess their sins, testifying to the fact that their nation had been exiled not because of a fault or weakness of its God, but because of its own rebellions against Him. Something as awful as the Exile would thus have a useful side: the truth of God's greatness would be heard by many people outside of Israel. This in fact, was exactly what happened as people like Daniel and his three colleagues, as well as Ezra, Nehemiah, and others witnessed to the Lord's goodness and power before the peoples among whom they lived in exile.

Several aspects of the prophecy deserve emphasis. First, there is the fact that now even the government was known to be coming to an end. God's hand is over all governments. Whether they know it or not, all national leaders will one day answer to Him for how just and generous their rule has been (cf. Rom. 13:1–5; 14:10–12). No human leader ever exalts himself without eventually being abased (Dan. 2:21).

Second, it is interesting to note that God gave Ezekiel's audience time to reflect on the symbolic actions they had seen the prophet doing. Even Ezekiel did not seem to know all the implications of his dramatic motions until the following day, when the specifics were revealed to him (vv. 8–16). Can it be that our own failure to reflect carefully and patiently on what we have learned from God is sometimes at the root of our problems?

Third, the prophecy shows that God is interested in more than simply punishing the disobedient people of Jerusalem and Judah.

His concern is also for the ultimate purpose of glorifying His name among the Gentiles as a witness to them (v. 16) so that the truth of God may be ever more widely known. This should be our concern as well. Even adversity should serve to remind us of our responsibility to proclaim God's faithfulness, since nothing that happens to us is the result of His fault or failure. He alone is always good, and His purposes always just.

No Delay in Departure Time

12:17 Moreover the word of the LORD came to me, saying,

18 "Son of man, eat your bread with quaking, and drink your water with trembling and anxiety.

19 "And say to the people of the land, 'Thus says the Lord GOD to the inhabitants of Jerusalem *and* to the land of Israel: "They shall eat their bread with anxiety, and drink their water with dread, so that her land may be emptied of all who are in it, because of the violence of all those who dwell in it.

20 "Then the cities that are inhabited shall be laid waste, and the land shall become desolate; and you shall know that I *am* the LORD."'"

21 And the word of the LORD came to me, saying,

22 "Son of man, what *is* this proverb *that* you *people* have about the land of Israel, which says, 'The days are prolonged, and every vision fails'?

23 "Tell them therefore, 'Thus says the Lord GOD: "I will lay this proverb to rest, and they shall no more use it as a proverb in Israel." But say to them, "The days are at hand, and the fulfillment of every vision.

24 "For no more shall there be any false vision or flattering divination within the house of Israel.

25 "For I *am* the LORD. I speak, and the word which I speak will come to pass; it will no more be postponed; for in your days, O rebellious house, I will say the word and perform it," says the Lord GOD.'"

26 Again the word of the LORD came to me, saying,

27 "Son of man, look, the house of Israel is saying, 'The vision that he sees *is* for many days *from now,* and he prophesies of times far off.'

28 "Therefore say to them, 'Thus says the Lord
GOD: "None of My words will be postponed any more,
but the word which I speak will be done," says the
Lord GOD.'"

Ezek. 12:17-28

The present passage is made up of two distinct revelatory messages to Ezekiel, verses 17–20 and verses 21–28. The first message calls for fear on the part of the people of Jerusalem and Judah (called Israel here again) since in fact the doom of the land is about to take place. The second message confirms that the punishment will come soon, rather than in some future time and to some distant generation of Israelites.

Ezekiel was still presumably involved in the process of eating a starvation diet in public (4:9–17) during the 430 days of lying publicly on his side (4:4–8). To the message conveyed by the diet itself, that is, that the Babylonian siege would bring starvation to Jerusalem's inhabitants, he now is commanded to add another message, conveyed by the way in which he would eat. The bread and water had to come to his lips in quaking hands, eaten and drunk with a fearful expression! This would suggest that the siege of Jerusalem would not go in favor of the Israelites, but against them. People can hold out for a long time under adverse conditions if they have reason to believe that victory will eventually be theirs. But if it begins to look as if all will be lost and the sacrifices and self-denial of the past months and years will lead only to the enemy's brutal conquest and to exile, then they eat their meager rations not with confidence but with anxiety and dread.

The word translated "dread" in verse 19, Hebrew, *šimmāmôn*, sounds in Hebrew like it would be related to the verb translated "will be emptied" (NKJV, "may be emptied"), *tēšām*. By this play on words, the prophet's message links the attitude he portrays in his actions of eating with a prediction of deportation. And the reason for such a judgment from God is, once again, the wrongdoing ("violence"; cf. 7:11, 23; 8:17) that characterized the nation's social and religious behavior (v. 19). The result will be desolation (Hebrew, *šemāmāh*, another related sound), which is a fulfillment of warnings in the Mosaic covenant such as Lev. 26:31–35 and Deut. 28:51, 29:23.

Again, the Lord will show Himself alive, well, and all-powerful by such acts (*"You shall know that I am the Lord"*). He will be honored and His truth vindicated when the land is emptied of its inhabitants, since He alone will have done exactly what He had promised to do, that is, keep His covenant, including its provisions for punishing those who might break it.

The wording of verse 21 (*"And the word of the Lord came to me, saying, . . ."*) indicates the beginning of a new revelation, received perhaps the same day, but more likely some days later, although still during the symbolic siege period of 430 days begun in chapter 4. In this revelation, two "proverbs" or popular sayings are refuted. The first, stated in verse 22 (*"The days are prolonged, and every vision fails"*) represents a kind of skeptical view about the messages of the prophets that was apparently quite popular among the people of the exile, perhaps even among those still in Jerusalem at this time. It refers to more than just Ezekiel's words, encompassing the sorts of things, positive and negative, that prophets were heard to say during the decade or so after the first surrender of Jerusalem in 598 B.C. We can imagine people thinking back on the predictions of doom for Jerusalem and Judah that had been going on since Amos (e.g., 2:4–50), Hosea (e.g., 5:10–14), Micah (e.g., 1:8–9), and Isaiah (e.g., 22:1–14) in the eighth century, and that had continued right up to Ezekiel's current dramatic performances in exile at Tel-Abib in the early 580s. All had predicted the destruction of the city and the desolation of the land, but these had in fact simply not yet taken place! Generations had lived and died since Amos's first prophecies around 760 B.C., yet Jerusalem still stood, secure, fortified, populated, surrounded by huge walls, and ruled by a son of David. (Zedekiah, the king, was in the lineage of David as all Southern kings had been.) So what was there to worry about? Time kept moving along, each successive vision (Hebrew, *ḥāzôn*, meaning also "revelation") came and went, and none of it had yet come true.

It might seem that we could hardly blame people for wondering why it had taken so long for the prophets' words to come true if they were really speaking for God. This skepticism had a point. But we cannot ultimately sympathize with them because in fact they were severely underestimating and misunderstanding the power of God to do what He was doing. They mistook His mercy and patience for His inability or disinterest. He was waiting, giving them another chance, calling them to change. They were taking it all as evidence that He was not a force to be reckoned with.

The same sort of situation prevails in our own day with regard to the promised return of Christ. For well over nineteen hundred years people have been asking the question recorded in 2 Pet. 3:4, "Where is the promise of His coming? For since the fathers fell asleep all things continue as they were from the beginning of creation." Once the Lord does return, of course, no one will ask this skeptical question again. But in the meantime, we can hardly be surprised that it is asked routinely, often mockingly. The forbearance of God will always be mistaken by many people for the nonexistence or at least impotence of God.

At any rate God commands Ezekiel to reply to the people that the proverb in question is about to become a thing of the past and suggests a slightly revised wording with an entirely different meaning: *"The days are at hand, and the fulfillment of every vision"* (v. 23). In the Hebrew this involves just a few sound changes compared to the original proverb.

Verse 24 makes it clear that some people were also influenced in their thinking by false prophets, who gave reassuring prophecies that all would be well, that any doom was still far away chronologically. In fact it would be the very generation that Ezekiel was addressing that would see the destruction of Jerusalem come to pass (v. 25) because the time of delay had run out. Once again God will "say the word," that is, reveal it through Ezekiel, but this time He will also "perform it" right away. And in just a year or two, when the city of Jerusalem would have fallen, its temple destroyed, and its populace taken away in chains, the performance of God's Word was to be all too evident!

Ezekiel then—or thereafter—received a third message, concerning yet another proverb, one that applied rather directly to Ezekiel himself. Some people were apparently quite willing to believe that his words about the coming Babylonian invasion of Judah and Jerusalem were true. Perhaps they saw that Ezekiel's message was entirely consistent with what the Law and the earlier prophets had already foretold and, therefore, had to be true. Indeed, such people may have been more or less orthodox in their credence of what the Scriptures then in existence taught. But it was the timing they hoped would spare them. So they believed the report but put its fulfillment off in time so that they themselves could still experience peace. Even good King Hezekiah had held this attitude a century earlier (2 Kings 20:19), not worrying about the future as long as the present was pleasant.

For this sort of expectation God had a silencing reply (v. 28): *"None of My words will be postponed any more."* This was it! Ezekiel and his fellow Israelites were living in the last days of Judah. Theirs was to be the generation to witness the end. *"The word which I speak will be done,"* says the Lord.

People always manage to come up with excuses for not taking God's Word seriously. They remain unconvinced of what it says, either because it can't be proved to their satisfaction (e.g., prophecies don't come true fast enough), or because they think it can't apply to them, or because they don't trust the one who speaks the word, or whatever. Rebelliousness (v. 25) can take many forms, some of them even quite pious ("How do I know which preacher to believe, which church is right?"). In Ezekiel's day it was "How do I know which prophet is correct (v. 24), which prophecy applies to me (v. 27)?" A true commitment to God does not allow such convenient shrugging off of duty and faith. If God is God, His word is true. If He has said it, it will come to pass (v. 28). We can never hide behind "timing" or "interpretational problems" or any other device to avoid taking seriously God's commands and promises. God does what He says He will do.

CHAPTER SEVEN

False Prophets and Idolatry

Ezekiel 13:1–14:23

The four sections of prophecy that are found in chapters 13 and 14 all give further, specific evidence of the ways in which God's coming judgment against His people is justified by their ongoing rebellion against Him. Undoubtedly some among Ezekiel's fellow exiles and many left still in Jerusalem doubted that the first exile—the one in which Ezekiel had been taken—and a coming exile, if there was to be one, could be fair to the nation. Most Israelites of the time may have seen themselves as innocent, accidental, unfortunate victims of the tyrannical Babylonian Empire's gobbling up territory to feed its voracious appetite for supremacy in the Fertile Crescent. It was apparently not widely believed in Judah that the nation deserved what had happened or was about to happen to it. Accordingly, through Ezekiel, God reviewed the corruption of true religion in the life of His people and effectively provided an argument that would silence honest criticism: the people were so wayward that their destruction was inevitable if God was to be true to His covenantal promise to punish those who broke His law.

False prophecy and idolatry are the main concerns of this section of the book. Both men (13:1–16) and women (13:17–23) were involved in false prophecy, earning a living by telling people what they wanted to hear, though it was not a genuine word from the Lord. And the people themselves, as 14:1–11 points out, practiced a kind of idolatry of the heart, even in exile. The nation was so full of unrighteousness that even famous ancient worthies like Noah could not manage to help it survive (14:12–23).

With this section of the book the typical prophetic indictments against the Israelites come to a temporary halt. Next will follow more reflective sections, including allegories illustrating the nation's character and behavior patterns.

PROPHECY AGAINST PROPHETS

13:1 And the word of the LORD came to me, saying,

2 "Son of man, prophesy against the prophets of Israel who prophesy, and say to those who prophesy out of their own heart, 'Hear the word of the LORD!'"

3 Thus says the Lord GOD: "Woe to the foolish prophets, who follow their own spirit and have seen nothing!

4 "O Israel, your prophets are like foxes in the deserts.

5 "You have not gone up into the gaps to build a wall for the house of Israel to stand in battle on the day of the LORD.

6 "They have envisioned futility and false divination, saying, 'Thus says the LORD!' But the LORD has not sent them; yet they hope that the word may be confirmed.

7 "Have you not seen a futile vision, and have you not spoken false divination? You say, 'The LORD says,' but I have not spoken."

8 Therefore thus says the Lord GOD: "Because you have spoken nonsense and envisioned lies, therefore I *am* indeed against you," says the Lord GOD.

9 "My hand will be against the prophets who envision futility and who divine lies; they shall not be in the assembly of My people, nor be written in the record of the house of Israel, nor shall they enter into the land of Israel. Then you shall know that I *am* the Lord GOD.

10 "Because, indeed, because they have seduced My people, saying, 'Peace!' when *there is* no peace— and one builds a wall, and they plaster it with untempered *mortar*—

11 "say to those who plaster *it* with untempered *mortar*, that it will fall. There will be flooding rain, and you, O great hailstones, shall fall; and a stormy wind shall tear *it* down.

12 "Surely, when the wall has fallen, will it not be said to you, 'Where *is* the mortar with which you plastered *it?*'"

13 Therefore thus says the Lord GOD: "I will cause a stormy wind to break forth in My fury; and there shall be a flooding rain in My anger, and great hailstones in fury to consume *it.*

14 "So I will break down the wall you have plastered with untempered *mortar,* and bring it down to the ground, so that its foundation will be uncovered; it will fall, and you shall be consumed in the midst of it. Then you shall know that I *am* the LORD.

15 "Thus will I accomplish My wrath on the wall and on those who have plastered it with untempered *mortar,* and I will say to you, 'The wall *is* no *more,* nor those who plastered it,

16 '*that is,* the prophets of Israel who prophesy concerning Jerusalem, and who see visions of peace for her when *there is* no peace,'" says the Lord GOD.

Ezek. 13:1–16

After the standard introductory clause, *"And the word of the Lord came to me,"* Ezekiel hears a new sort of command. He must prophesy not to the people in general but to other prophets! Preaching to other preachers is one of the most difficult assignments a pastor can undertake. If one's audience is made up of people who are equally as (or more) expert than the speaker, the speaker tends to be intimidated. But this sort of thing was sometimes part of the difficult job description of an ancient orthodox prophet. Others had done it (e.g., Hos. 4:5, 12; Mic. 3:5–7; Isa. 9:15–16; Jer. 23:9–40), and Ezekiel had to follow suit. God had a word for the fakers who purported to be telling His truth, giving forth His revelations, and Ezekiel, a true prophet, had to deliver that word.

There were many other prophets among the Israelites, both in Palestine and with the exiles in Mesopotamia. Ezekiel was hardly the only one. True prophets of the Lord at this time included Daniel, Habakkuk, Obadiah, Jeremiah, and possibly Joel. The false prophets, however, were legion. They were *"the prophets of Israel who prophesy"* (i.e., are actively prophesying at the present) and who *"prophesy out of their own heart"* (i.e., make up the words they say in their own

mind, v. 2). To them Ezekiel was to say, *"Hear the word of the Lord!"* —
a rather ironic change since this is exactly the sort of thing they said
routinely in connection with their own false prophecies (v. 6).

What this says about the process of prophetic inspiration is instructive. Ezekiel and other true prophets never made up anything.
They knew that God gave them their messages, they were not fabri-
cating what they said but merely repeating it. False prophets, on the
other hand, were not gifted by God as prophets, so they had to fake
what they said. They may have thought that that was what true
prophets did too, since if you have never had a revelation from God,
how would you know what it was like to get one? People who pretend to be Christians in our own day are sometimes acting from the
same perspective. Their experience of God is not genuine, but as
outsiders to a genuine experience they have no way of knowing what
a genuine knowledge of God would actually be like.

Because the false prophets fabricated their messages themselves
(v. 3), they deserved punishment ("woe") for being deceivers. In the
same way that impersonating a police officer is a crime in modern
society, because it harmfully defrauds people who trust and obey
the police, impersonating a true prophet of the Lord was, by God's
law, a fraudulent misleading of Israelites in Ezekiel's day. What the
Lord needed was repentance and a change of behavior so that on the
"day of the Lord" (cf. 7:5–19), when the Babylonians attacked, many
might be spared because they had heeded the words of warning
instead of having been deceived by false words of reassurance.

The true prophets were providing warnings of destruction over
and over again. By assuring people that all was well and that no military danger lay ahead, however, the false prophets were like "jackals
in the ruins" (NKJV, "foxes in the deserts" is a misleading translation;
v. 4). Jackals would move into ruined or abandoned cities regularly in
the ancient Near East (cf. Lam. 5:18; Isa. 13:21) and would certainly
not improve such places. True prophets would have done otherwise:
repairing the holes ("gaps") in the defense walls and preparing the
city for the coming battle (v. 5), not doing no good, like jackals. Since
the false prophets were not the Lord's emissaries, what they envisioned was simply falsehood (NKJV's "futility" is misleading). All they
did was guess at the future and hope that their guesses were confirmed by events (v. 6). But since God had not spoken through them,
what they said was a lie (v. 7).

This of necessity provoked God's wrath and rejection (a covenant curse, cf. Lev. 26:28, 41; Deut. 31:17–18). Such prophets could have no part in the new Israel (v. 9). The new nation would be purified and would reenter the land according to the promises God had been making through other true prophets as well as through Ezekiel (11:14–20).

The deceptive proclamations of peace (cf. Mic. 3:5, Jer. 6:14; 8:11) that such false prophets have always been noted for are like shaky, poorly built walls covered with whitewash (NKJV, "untempered mortar"). The whitewash makes the walls look good, but in fact they cannot withstand even heavy weather (vv. 10–11, 13–14). When Paul called the high priest in Jerusalem a "whitewashed wall" (Acts 23:3), he was similarly indicating that Ananias was a phony, since his command to punish Paul was inconsistent with the Law he was pledged to uphold. The false prophets were inconsistent with God's truth. They made their living from contributions, and when they gave assurances of peace and prosperity people paid better than when they predicted gloom and distress. Thus their "whitewashed wall" would fall, and their own fall (v. 14) would be symbolized thereby as well. False reassurance (the wall) and false prophets (those who whitewashed it, v. 15) would alike be destroyed by God when the reality of Jerusalem's destruction came to pass.

False prophecy was not simply a phenomenon of ancient times. It is very much a modern-day problem also, and Christians must know how to deal with it. Certain religious "leaders," some with major media access, give conflicting advice about current events and the future. Books appear regularly purporting to marshal evidence for coming changes and telling the reader how to cope or prepare. Mystics and psychics, non-Christian yet often claiming spiritual authority, issue projections and capture the imagination of "weaker brothers." Who should you believe? Is it safe to ignore them all?

The answer is still basically the same as the answer God gave through Ezekiel: the phonies are the ones who make their money by telling you what you want to hear whether or not it is consistent with what God has already proclaimed. The true prophets are the ones who emphasize what God has already spoken and whose preaching is devoted to telling you what God has said regardless of how appealing it may be to you personally. The true prophets' words, like a good wall, stand. The false prophets' words, like a whitewashed, faulty wall, will eventually be proven false (cf. Deut. 18:18–22).

PROPHECY AGAINST PROPHETESSES

13:17 "Likewise, son of man, set your face against the daughters of your people, who prophesy out of their own heart; prophesy against them,

18 "and say, 'Thus says the Lord GOD: "Woe to the *women* who sew *magic* charms on their sleeves and make veils for the heads of people of every height to hunt souls! Will you hunt the souls of My people, and keep yourselves alive?

19 "And will you profane Me among My people for handfuls of barley and for pieces of bread, killing people who should not die, and keeping people alive who should not live, by your lying to My people who listen to lies?"

20 'Therefore thus says the Lord GOD: "Behold, I *am* against your *magic* charms by which you hunt souls there like birds. I will tear them from your arms, and let the souls go, the souls you hunt like birds.

21 "I will also tear off your veils and deliver My people out of your hand, and they shall no longer be as prey in your hand. Then you shall know that I *am* the LORD.

22 "Because with lies you have made the heart of the righteous sad, whom I have not made sad; and you have strengthened the hands of the wicked, so that he does not turn from his wicked way to save his life.

23 "Therefore you shall no longer envision futility nor practice divination; for I will deliver My people out of your hand, and you shall know that I *am* the LORD."'"

Ezek. 13:17–23

Since God makes a point of addressing Ezekiel once again by the title Son of Man (v. 17), as He does usually at the beginning of distinct, self-contained passages, and since He commands him to prophesy separately from the command given in verse 2, it is

122

reasonable to conclude that at verse 17 we are at the start of a new section and that verses 17–23, in spite of their proximity in place and theme to verses 1–16, contain a message of their own.

That message is directed toward women exclusively and as such is one of the few prophetic passages in the Old Testament where females are subject to criticism (others are Amos 4:1–3, Isa. 3:16–4:1; 32:9–13). Women are usually simply assumed to be part of whatever group is addressed in the general prophetic oracles. Here, however, "daughters who prophesy" (falsely) are the issue. Women prophets were common in both the Old Testament (e.g., Exod. 15:20; Judg. 4:4; 2 Kings 22:14; Neh. 6:14) and the New Testament (Luke 2:36–38; Acts 21:9; 1 Cor. 11:5), spiritual gifts not being limited by gender (Joel 2:28–29). And so in Ezekiel's day women could be accepted by the people as having prophetic authority, which they could turn selfishly to their own advantage every bit as well as the men had done (vv. 1–16).

While women prophets probably undertook a wide range of activities, the practices Ezekiel concentrates on are what we would associate with magic and divination. Two things the women prophets commonly did were (1) the sewing of something like muffs around their wrists (NKJV, "magic charms") and (2) covering people with large veils that would shroud their whole bodies (v. 18). Because the Hebrew word for veil (*mispāḥāh*) contains the sound of the Hebrew word for bird trap (*paḥ*; cf. Amos 3:15; Isa. 24:17) and perhaps because the veils were something like large nets, God's word through Ezekiel likens these women to hunters of birds. The women false prophets, in other words, trapped the people who came to them for advice like a hunter traps a bird. In this case their prey was the lives (NKJV, "souls") of the people who consulted them and were led astray by their untrue prophecies, disobeying the Laws of God (Lev. 19:31, etc.) in the process.

The ultimate judgment for such phonies and deceivers was death and destruction, just as it was for all the other evildoers in Jerusalem (cf. also Lev. 20:27), and the death penalty was also reserved for those who visited such false prophets seeking information (Lev. 20:6). These capital punishments are not mentioned in the present passage because they were so obvious that they required no statement. What instead was predicted was the end of witchcraft, so that God's people could be free from its "snare" (vv. 20–21). These women practitioners of the occult had corrupted the nation. Their advice discouraged good people and encouraged wicked people (v. 22), and the nation needed rescue from them (v. 23).

Modern-day fortune tellers are rather similar to the women described in this passage. Fortune tellers, interestingly, are usually women, and they tend to dress in a rather elaborate manner, often wearing clothing or jewelry associated with the occult arts, comparable to the "muffs" on the prophetesses in ancient Israel (v. 18). They tend to give their advice in darkened rooms, where the attitude of the inquirer is influenced in an eerie way, and this corresponds to the veil put over the inquirer in Ezekiel's description (v. 18). They are paid for what they do, just as the ancient women were (v. 19), and their advice is always dangerous (v. 19) because it leads people astray from the truth of God, that truth being the only way to live and not die eternally. They are frauds, who envision "lies" (NKJV, "futility," v. 23) because their predictions are fabrications made up from their own minds (v. 17), just as was done in Ezekiel's time.

Why then do people go to such phonies and pay them for their services? Indeed, why are fortune tellers big business in some societies and even in some subcultures in the supposedly advanced, modern, and sophisticated United States? The answer is a combination of fear and hope. Everyone tends to fear that the future may not be pleasant and wants to be able to prepare against that unpleasantness. Moreover, everybody tends to hope that there may be some way to do better in the future, to gain something, to accomplish something, perhaps even to have surprisingly good fortune come one's way. Fortune tellers and false prophets of all sorts trade upon the strength of the fear and hope found in gullible people.

Only God, however, knows the future. In broad terms He has told it to us, so that we may be comforted by it (4:18) and thus impelled to good works confidently done with the assurance that God's good will eventually triumph (1 Cor. 15:58). But the vast majority of specifics are not to be known! God expects us to trust Him, not ourselves or some vision of things to come. It is by faith that we will please Him, not by clever reaction to inside information about what is to befall us. No one else, no matter how appealing his or her personality may be, can ever know more than what God has revealed, and He has revealed nothing to the practitioners of the occult.

IDOLS IN THE HEART

14:1 Now some of the elders of Israel came to me and sat before me.

2 And the word of the LORD came to me, saying,

3 "Son of man, these men have set up their idols in their hearts, and put before them that which causes them to stumble into iniquity. Should I let Myself be inquired of at all by them?

4 "Therefore speak to them, and say to them, 'Thus says the Lord GOD: "Everyone of the house of Israel who sets up his idols in his heart, and puts before him what causes him to stumble into iniquity, and then comes to the prophet, I the LORD will answer him who comes, according to the multitude of his idols,

5 "that I may seize the house of Israel by their heart, because they are all estranged from Me by their idols."'

6 "Therefore say to the house of Israel, 'Thus says the Lord GOD: "Repent, turn away from your idols, and turn your faces away from all your abominations.

7 "For anyone of the house of Israel, or of the strangers who dwell in Israel, who separates himself from Me and sets up his idols in his heart and puts before him what causes him to stumble into iniquity, then comes to a prophet to inquire of him concerning Me, I the LORD will answer him by Myself.

8 "I will set My face against that man and make him a sign and a proverb, and I will cut him off from the midst of My people. Then you shall know that I *am* the LORD.

9 "And if the prophet is induced to speak anything, I the LORD have induced that prophet, and I will stretch out My hand against him and destroy him from among My people Israel.

10 "And they shall bear their iniquity; the punishment of the prophet shall be the same as the punishment of the one who inquired,

11 "that the house of Israel may no longer stray from Me, nor be profaned anymore with all their

transgressions, but that they may be My people and
I may be their God," says the Lord GOD.'"

Ezek. 14:1–11

Idolatry was the standard method of religion in ancient times. Ancient peoples believed that any depiction of a thing somehow par-
took of the essence of that thing, no matter how crude or artificial
the depiction might be. A picture of a tree contained part of the
essence of the tree; a statue of a god contained part of the essence of
that god. Where that statue was, the god was of necessity at least
partly present. Anything offered to a god's statue was offered directly to the god.

This sort of thinking, now called prelogical, was nevertheless per-
vasive among ancient peoples. Moreover, along with idolatry went a
whole system of beliefs and practices. Materialism, for example, was
commonly a part of idolatry since idols were understood to want and
accept any food or money offered to them and to be bound to repay
the generous worshiper with prosperity. In reality, of course, the
food or money went to the idol's priests, but the worshipers believed
that the idol benefited and repaid in kind. Thus, in a general sense,
idolatry was a system of serving one's own selfish interests by partaking in an appealing, ritualistic, but not genuine or true, religious
practice.

This was what even the leaders of the exiled community in the
early 580s were doing, and thus God through Ezekiel denounces
their folly. The elders had probably come on the occasion described
in these verses to consult Ezekiel or to ask him questions about one
of the prophecies (vv. 1, 3). While they were at his home, God, who
"looks on the heart" (1 Sam. 16:7), gave Ezekiel a message for them
exposing their real motives and attitudes. The diagnosis: idolatry!
The prophet had already reported to many of these same people
about the abominable idolatry he had seen practiced by the community leaders in Jerusalem (11:25, cf. chap. 8). Now his own associates were found guilty of a form of the same violation. Such a sin
risked God's cutting off His word from them (v. 3). The Lord could
not ignore this sort of abomination that their attitudes represented.
He could not simply continue revealing Himself to those who were
flirting with disobedience to a basic provision of His covenant
(Exod. 20:4–5).

Because we are told that this idolatry was "in their hearts," it is likely that the people had not yet openly practiced it. Rather they found that living among the Babylonians—a successful, powerful, more numerous, and more advanced people culturally—increasingly influenced them to imitate Babylonian ways. In other words, the idolatry the exiled Israelites saw in their new Mesopotamian surroundings had begun to look better and better to them. They began to try to think of how they might do it themselves. They were in the process of talking themselves into it, as it were. This represented a divided loyalty of the sort that violated the first commandment, "You shall have no other gods before Me."

So what was Ezekiel to do in response to such people coming to him to ask what word he had from the Lord? Verse 4 provides the answer: he was to let them know that God would "answer" them according to their idolatry. The Hebrew verb, 'nh (Niphal), here carries the sense of "respond," and the overall meaning is something like what the greedy outlaw used to say in the western movie to those who wanted to split the loot with him: "I'll give you what's coming to you, all right!" God would "answer" them, then, not by a prophetic message but by His wrath. The purpose was to purify the people, to "seize" them "by their heart" (v. 5) so that they would be wholly loyal to the Lord. In other words, God's judgment against idolaters was for the sake of proper belief, a generous act of cleansing so that His people might not continue estranged from Him who alone could save them, but might turn to Him away from idolatry (v. 6).

The true prophet, one like Ezekiel, was not allowed to give any answer to an inquirer who was bent on idolatry. God would give the "answer" directly (v. 7) by bringing about death (cutting off the idolater from the midst of the people, v. 8). Of course, a false prophet would still be inclined to give a prophecy to any inquirer who paid the going rate, and even a true prophet might conceivably be tempted likewise. Verse 9 addresses this possibility. It specifies that any prophet who yielded to the temptation to sell his skill to an idolater for money—whether he or she was a true or a false prophet— would be punished by God via that false prophecy that he or she gives. God will use the very act of sin (in this instance, false prophecy) as the initial means of punishment. Does this suggest that God is the author of evil? Hardly. Rather, it's a case of abandonment as punishment. In the manner of Rom. 1:18-32, God abandons such

127

people to the sort of thing their corrupt passions lead them to do. This abandonment is referred to by the term "induce" (NKJV) or "incite" (Hebrew, *pth*) but it has virtually the same sense of rubbing people's noses in their sin, as it were. Deut. 4:28 relates the equivalent sort of thing: idolaters will be exiled and forced to practice idolatry in exile until they see how empty and foolish it is.

Here, God will force false prophets to prophesy falsely all the more and then destroy them (v. 9), so that the prophet and the idolater who consulted him or her both end up being cut off (v. 10). Purification of God's people is the purpose and result of this punishment (v. 11), so that the proper faithful relationship between God and His people may be restored.

The principle of punishment by abandonment to sin is illustrated throughout our world every day. Is the drug user happy? In fact, the more he or she uses drugs, the more enslaved by them he or she becomes. Is the greedy person satisfied? The more that person seeks to gain, the more elusive the gain becomes. Are the oppressors made secure by their brutal denial of rights to their people? They become, in fact, more and more suspicious, protective, and fatalistic about their chances to remain in power in light of the enormous hatred their policies inspire. Does free sex satisfy? Statistics show that is the surest road to lack of fulfillment, conflict, and incompatibility. And so on. We reap what we sow. When we seek God's will and do it, we escape transgression and enjoy God's favor. When we seek our own way, God may give it to us, but it turns out to be a punishment.

FOUR SEVERE JUDGMENTS

14:12 The word of the LORD came again to me, saying:
13 "Son of man, when a land sins against Me by persistent unfaithfulness, I will stretch out My hand against it; I will cut off its supply of bread, send famine on it, and cut off man and beast from it.
14 "Even *if* these three men, Noah, Daniel, and Job, were in it, they would deliver *only* themselves by their righteousness," says the Lord GOD.
15 "If I cause wild beasts to pass through the land, and they empty it, and make it so desolate that no man may pass through because of the beasts,

16 *"even though* these three men *were* in it, *as* I live,"
says the Lord GOD, "they would deliver neither sons
nor daughters; only they would be delivered, and the
land would be desolate.

17 "Of *if* I bring a sword on that land, and say,
'Sword, go through the land,' and I cut off man and
beast from it,

18 "even *though* these three men *were* in it, *as* I live,"
says the Lord GOD, "they would deliver neither sons
nor daughters, but only they themselves would be delivered.

19 "Or *if* I send a pestilence into that land and
pour out My fury on it in blood, and cut off from it
man and beast,

20 "even *though* Noah, Daniel, and Job *were* in it, *as*
I live," says the Lord GOD, "they would deliver neither
son nor daughter; they would deliver *only* themselves
by their righteousness."

21 For thus says the Lord GOD: "How much more it
shall be when I send My four severe judgments on
Jerusalem—the sword and famine and wild beasts
and pestilence—to cut off man and beast from it?

22 "Yet behold, there shall be left in it a remnant
who will be brought out, *both* sons and daughters;
surely they will come out to you, and you will see their
ways and their doings. Then you will be comforted
concerning the disaster that I have brought upon Jerusalem, all that I have brought upon it.

23 "And they will comfort you, when you see their
ways and their doings; and you shall know that I
have done nothing without cause that I have done in
it," says the Lord GOD.

Ezek. 14:12–23

This prophecy predicts four kinds of miseries for the unfaithful
population of Jerusalem, in keeping with the overall theme of Chapters 1–24, that is, the sin and resulting punishment of the holy city.
The four judgments are introduced somewhat gradually but summarized in verse 21 as the sword (warfare resulting in defeat), famine
(caused largely by the enemy invasion, which confines the defenders
to the walled-in city; cf. chap. 4), wild animals (a Pentateuchal type

of curse introduced here for the first time in the book), and pestilence (contagious disease, again largely the result of confined, unsanitary living conditions under siege).

These four judgments were prominent among those predicted by God to the Israelites at Mount Sinai when the escapees from Egypt first joined in covenant with the Lord (Leviticus 26) and again at the time that the Israelites were about to launch their conquest of the promised land just before Moses' death (Deuteronomy 28–32).

"Sword" curses (predictions of punishment by war) are found in such verses as Lev. 26:25, 33 and Deut. 32:24, 41–42. For famine curses, see Lev. 26:26, 29, 45 and Deut. 28:53–56, 32:24. Wild animal curses occur in Lev. 26:22 and Deut. 32:24; and pestilence curses in Lev. 26:14 and Deut. 28:21–22; 32:24. We list these references from the Pentateuch in order to emphasize that Ezekiel is here commanded to announce the imposition of types of judgment punishments known for more than eight hundred years! God is doing nothing to His people suddenly or without plenty of warning. For dozens of generations these warnings about the consequences of disobedience were well known. They had been heard since the days of Moses, whenever the Law was read. Failure to repent and obey the Lord was Israel's problem; lack of warning was not.

A particularly striking feature of this prophecy is its mention of three ancient pre-Israelite worthies: Noah, Danel, and Job. The NKJV and most modern English versions spell Danel as if it were Daniel, Ezekiel's fellow exile and the main human figure in the Old Testament Book of Daniel. But the person mentioned here is not that Daniel but a figure from the second millennium B.C. or earlier, known to us from Ugaritic stories about him from 1500–1200 B.C. This Danel, like Noah and Job, lived on earth in the days before the nation of Israel had come into existence. These three men were famous for living righteous lives in contrast to the prevailing wickedness of the societies of their day (e.g., Gen. 6:5–12; 7:1; Job 1:1, 22).

In ancient Israel, as elsewhere in the ancient Near East, it was apparently rather common for people to think in terms both of guilt by association and righteousness by association. Ezekiel already had been called on to denounce guilt by association and to proclaim the principle of individual responsibility (3:16–21, etc.). Now he must expose the parallel folly of righteousness by association. Of course, in His mercy God did sometimes spare a city or nation because of righteous people in it who prayed to Him for His compassion. He was willing, for example, to spare Sodom on the basis of Abraham's prayer if enough righteous people were found there (Gen. 18:20–33), and He did delay His judgment upon Judah because of the righteousness of good King Josiah (2 Kings 22:16–20). However, it seems to be the case that the Judeans of Ezekiel's day misinterpreted such generous, merciful acts of God as guarantees of their own safety. They presumed that because Jerusalem and Judah still had in them good people (and they surely did in the person of such prophets as Jeremiah, Habakkuk, and Obadiah, for example, or such godly people as Baruch, Jeremiah's disciple and supporter) that God would never bring Himself to give the nation totally over to its enemies. Many probably had already concluded that the exile of 598 B.C. was the worst thing that would happen to Judah and that the little state had nowhere to go but up from now on.

Had they considered the stories of people like Noah and Job more sensibly, they might not have been so sanguine about Judah's chances. After all, Noah's righteousness did not prevent the extinction of his generation. And Job's goodness covered not even his close associates (Job 42:7–8), let alone his original family. Abraham's intercession for Sodom proved ultimately futile, as well. And the righteousness of Josiah could not sustain Judah beyond the time of his own death.

At any rate, the passage effectively drums in the point that Judah was beyond saving in the early 580s. It does this by its fourfold repetitive pattern. First, the punishment of famine is predicted (v. 13), and then it is stressed that Noah, Danel, and Job could effect no righteousness by association that would relieve the nation from its misery (v. 14). By reason of their faithfulness to God they themselves could escape, but others could not. Then wild animals are predicted (v. 15) with a similar word about the powerlessness of the three worthies to stop it. This time the point of Judah's corruption is rubbed in further by the claim that the three could not even realize the sparing of their own families (v. 16)! By this language, the curse of Lev. 26:22 is alluded to: "I will also send wild beasts among you, which shall rob you of your children . . . and make you few in number; and your highways shall be desolate." The language of the sword punishment statement is similar (vv. 17–18) as is the language of the disease punishment statement (vv. 19–20). No one could fail to get the point of such clear, repetitious condemnation of Judah. But the condemnation is intensified even further, with God's assertion that (since Noah, Danel, and Job were not in Judah) the coming fate of the Southern Kingdom and its capital would be even worse (v. 21).

Yet there would be some who would escape—not by reason of their righteousness, but as part of those experiencing the punishment of exile rather than immediate destruction. When those already in Mesopotamia in exile saw the second wave of exiles coming among them in 586 B.C. and realized how corrupt and godless they were, they would "be comforted." The verb *niḥḥam/niḥam*, here "be comforted," can also mean "change your mind." In other words, the exiles would no longer regard the destruction of Judah's capital as an excessive, unwarranted judgment, but a punishment well deserved and appropriate to God's justice (vv. 22–23).

The vain hope of Ezekiel's contemporaries that God would never destroy Judah and Jerusalem is not unlike the rather soft-hearted thinking of many in our time who cannot imagine that a loving God would ever destroy anyone in hell (Matt. 10:28), no matter how evil and rebellious that person might have been. "Everyone has some good in him," they say, and they are right. But just as some good people cannot rescue a corrupt society, some good in a person cannot rescue that person from judgment. The opportunity to do good is given to all people. The patience of God is great. The desire of God that all should turn to Him is well known. But it is equally true that those who turn against God, rejecting His law and His truth, must eventually endure His wrath. Soft-pedaling such a reality does no favor to anyone.

CHAPTER EIGHT

Three Revealing Allegories

Ezekiel 15:1–17:24

In the next several chapters of Ezekiel (17–23) a variety of allegories are used to illustrate the rise and fall of the nation of Israel or some part of it, such as the city of Jerusalem. An allegory is a specially composed fictional story that, while not literally true, is figuratively true in that it points directly to things that really did or will happen. It is a kind of comparison story in which the specific details have been changed from the true events it points to but which still captures the sense of the actual situation and events. Each major detail of an allegory corresponds to a fact of some sort in real life. The minor details have little significance other than helping the story move along.

THE VINE

15:1 Then the word of the LORD came to me, saying:

2 "Son of man, how is the wood of the vine *better* than any other wood, the vine branch which is among the trees of the forest?

3 "Is wood taken from it to make any object? Or can *men* make a peg from it to hang any vessel on?

4 "Instead, it is thrown into the fire for fuel; the fire devours both ends of it, and its middle is burned. Is it useful for *any* work?

5 "Indeed, when it was whole, no object could be made from it. How much less will it be useful for *any* work when the fire has devoured it, and it is burned?

6 "Therefore thus says the Lord GOD: 'Like the wood of the vine among the trees of the forest, which

I have given to the fire for fuel, so I will give up the inhabitants of Jerusalem;

7 'and I will set My face against them. They will go out from *one* fire, but *another* fire shall devour them. Then you shall know that I *am* the LORD, when I set My face against them.

8 'Thus I will make the land desolate, because they have persisted in unfaithfulness,' says the Lord GOD.'

Ezek. 15:1–8

Israel is often compared to a grapevine in the Old Testament (Gen. 49:22; Deut. 32:32; Ps. 80:8–11; Isa. 5:1–7; Jer. 2:21; Hos. 10:1; etc.). It is likely that the Israelites of Ezekiel's day were accustomed to this comparison and that other prophets had used it in their hearing. Grapevines grow rather well in the climate and terrain of the land of Canaan, and wine became a major domestic and export product in ancient Israel. But, as Jesus later reminded his hearers (John 15:6), the only good thing about a grapevine is its grapes. The vine itself is a virtually useless wood that has no value at all, other than its ability to burn. It cannot be cut into furniture because it is far too pliable and weak. A section of it cannot even be carved to make something as simple as a peg on which to hang something (v. 3) because it bends and cracks too easily for that purpose.

In this allegory, then, God compares Israel not to the fruit of the vine, as the Israelites flatteringly thought of themselves, but to the vine itself, to that which they were really closer to in terms of current worth. They were a people who had borne no fruit, and their uselessness—except as something to be destroyed by fire—was now evident (cf. Matt. 7:19). It should be noted that Jesus' use of a similar image (John 15:9–17) is a demonstration of His humility and servanthood—as the vine He exists not for His own advantage but for the sake of the fruit.

The allegory begins with questions to Ezekiel (cf. 37:1–14) which he would then be expected to repeat to his listeners virtually in the form that we have it here in Chapter 15. To the first question, about how grapevines have better wood than other trees, the answer is obviously "no way" (v. 2). To the second question, about useful implements made from the grapevine, the answer is "No, nothing" (v. 3). Thrown into the fire, grape wood often burns only partially, with the charred thick trunk not entirely consumed (v. 4). Here, the allegory points to Israel's current situation in Ezekiel's era.

Northern Israel was already "burned up" by the Assyrian invasion and exile of 722 B.C. Most of Judah and many of the inhabitants of Jerusalem were "burned up" by the Babylonian invasion and exile of 598 B.C., the one in which Ezekiel had been taken. What was left in Jerusalem could be compared with a mostly burned grapevine. If an unburned vine has no use, a mostly burned one certainly has none (v. 5). Jerusalem is not only like a grapevine destined for fire (v. 6) but like a charred portion of a vine that did not get completely consumed in the first fire (598 B.C.) but will be consumed totally when thrown into a second fire (586 B.C.), that is, the second Babylonian invasion and exile. In this manner God will have rejected His people ("set My face against them") because of their unfaithfulness (v. 7) as manifested in the many evils identified in earlier chapters of the book.

The allegory thus functions as a prediction of desolation, fulfilling the desolation curses of the Mosaic covenant (Lev. 26:32–35, 43; Deut. 29:23). It had a particularly literal fulfillment of a sort as well in that the invading Babylonians practiced a scorched earth policy, burning whatever they could to destroy their enemy's possessions, especially within their cities (2 Chron. 36:10). Since such burning of cities had been common since the time of the Israelite invasion of Canaan in Joshua's day (e.g., Josh. 6:24; 8:19; 11:11), few in Ezekiel's audience could have missed an allusion to Jerusalem in the allegory of the vine. Jerusalem's full desolation was indeed near.

The Christian application of this part of the Book of Ezekiel has already been made by Christ Himself. Christians show their genuine relation to Christ by bearing the fruit of love (John 15:9–17). Otherwise they are unproductive vine branches, detached from the good vine, suitable only for burning. We can produce nothing aside from Christ. Attachment of our branches to any other vine would be as useless as no attachment at all. Faithful Israelites loved God and kept His commandments. Unfaithful ones did neither. Faithful Christians bear the proper fruit (Gal. 5:22); unfaithful ones bear nothing useful.

JERUSALEM THE WAYWARD WOMAN

16:1 Again the word of the LORD came to me, saying,

2 "Son of man, cause Jerusalem to know her abominations,

3 "and say, 'Thus says the Lord GOD to Jerusalem: "Your birth and your nativity *are* from the land of Canaan; your father *was* an Amorite and your mother a Hittite.

4 "*As for* your nativity, on the day you were born your navel cord was not cut, nor were you washed in water to cleanse *you*; you were not rubbed with salt nor wrapped in swaddling cloths.

5 "No eye pitied you, to do any of these things for you, to have compassion on you; but you were thrown out into the open field, when you yourself were loathed on the day you were born.

6 "And when I passed by you and saw you struggling in your own blood, I said to you in your blood, 'Live!' Yes, I said to you in your blood, 'Live!'

7 "I made you thrive like a plant in the field; and you grew, matured, and became very beautiful. *Your* breasts were formed, your hair grew, but you *were* naked and bare.

8 "When I passed by you again and looked upon you, indeed your time *was* the time of love; so I spread My wing over you and covered your nakedness. Yes, I swore an oath to you and entered into a covenant with you, and you became Mine," says the Lord GOD.

9 "Then I washed you in water; yes, I thoroughly washed off your blood, and I anointed you with oil.

10 "I clothed you in embroidered cloth and gave you sandals of badger skin; I clothed you with fine linen and covered you with silk.

11 "I adorned you with ornaments, put bracelets on your wrists, and a chain on your neck.

12 "And I put a jewel in your nose, earrings in your ears, and a beautiful crown on your head.

13 "Thus you were adorned with gold and silver, and your clothing *was of* fine linen, silk, and embroidered cloth. You ate *pastry of* fine flour, honey, and

oil. You were exceedingly beautiful, and succeeded to royalty.

14 "Your fame went out among the nations because of your beauty, for it *was* perfect through My splendor which I had bestowed on you," says the Lord GOD.

15 "But you trusted in your own beauty, played the harlot because of your fame, and poured out your harlotry on everyone passing by who *would have* it.

16 "You took some of your garments and adorned multicolored high places for yourself, and played the harlot on them. *Such* things should not happen, nor be.

17 "You have also taken your beautiful jewelry from My gold and My silver, which I had given you, and made for yourself male images and played the harlot with them.

18 "You took your embroidered garments and covered them, and you set My oil and My incense before them.

19 "Also My food which I gave you—the pastry of fine flour, oil, and honey *which* I fed you—you set it before them as sweet incense; and *so* it was," says the Lord GOD.

20 "Moreover you took your sons and your daughters, whom you bore to Me, and these you sacrificed to them to be devoured. *Were* your *acts* of harlotry a small matter,

21 "that you have slain My children and offered them up to them by causing them to pass through *the fire?*

22 "And in all your abominations and acts of harlotry you did not remember the days of your youth, when you were naked and bare, struggling in your blood.

23 "Then it was so, after all your wickedness—'Woe, woe to you!' says the Lord GOD—

24 "*that* you also built for yourself a shrine, and made a high place for yourself in every street.

25 "You built your high places at the head of every road, and made your beauty to be abhorred. You offered yourself to everyone who passed by, and multiplied your acts of harlotry.

26 "You also committed harlotry with the Egyptians, your very fleshly neighbors, and increased your acts of harlotry to provoke Me to anger.

27 "Behold, therefore, I stretched out My hand against you, diminished your allotment, and gave you up to the will of those who hate you, the daughters of the Philistines, who were ashamed of your lewd behavior.

28 "You also played the harlot with the Assyrians, because you were insatiable; indeed you played the harlot with them and still were not satisfied.

29 "Moreover you multiplied your acts of harlotry as far as the land of the trader, Chaldea; and even then you were not satisfied.

30 "How degenerate is your heart!" says the Lord GOD, "seeing you do all these *things*, the deeds of a brazen harlot.

31 "You erected your shrine at the head of every road, and built your high place in every street. Yet you were not like a harlot, because you scorned payment.

32 "*You are* an adulterous wife, *who* takes strangers instead of her husband.

33 "Men make payment to all harlots, but you made your payments to all your lovers, and hired them to come to you from all around for your harlotry.

34 "You are the opposite of *other* women in your harlotry, because no one solicited you to be a harlot. In that you gave payment but no payment was given you, therefore you are the opposite.'

35 'Now then, O harlot, hear the word of the LORD!

36 'Thus says the Lord GOD: "Because your filthiness was poured out and your nakedness uncovered in your harlotry with your lovers, and with all your abominable idols, and because of the blood of your children which you gave to them,

37 "surely, therefore, I will gather all your lovers with whom you took pleasure, all those you loved, *and* all those you hated; I will gather them from all around against you and will uncover your nakedness to them, that they may see all your nakedness.

38 "And I will judge you as women who break wedlock or shed blood are judged; I will bring blood upon you in fury and jealousy.

39 "I will also give you into their hand, and they shall throw down your shrines and break down your high places. They shall also strip you of your clothes, take your beautiful jewelry, and leave you naked and bare.

40 "They shall also bring up an assembly against you, and they shall stone you with stones and thrust you through with their swords.

41 "They shall burn your houses with fire, and execute judgments on you in the sight of many women; and I will make you cease playing the harlot, and you shall no longer hire lovers.

42 "So I will lay to rest My fury toward you, and My jealousy shall depart from you. I will be quiet, and be angry no more.

43 "Because you did not remember the days of your youth, but agitated Me with all these *things*, surely I will also recompense your deeds on *your own* head," says the Lord GOD. "And you shall not commit lewdness in addition to all your abominations.

44 "Indeed everyone who quotes proverbs will use *this* proverb against you: 'Like mother, like daughter!'

45 "You *are* your mother's daughter, loathing husband and children; and you *are* the sister of your sisters, who loathed their husbands and children; your mother *was* a Hittite and your father an Amorite.

46 "Your elder sister *is* Samaria, who dwells with her daughters to the north of you; and your younger sister, who dwells to the south of you, *is* Sodom and her daughters.

47 "You did not walk in their ways nor act according to their abominations; but, as *if that were* too little, you became more corrupt than they in all your ways.

48 "*As* I live," says the Lord GOD, "neither your sister Sodom nor her daughters have done as you and your daughters have done.

49 "Look, this was the iniquity of your sister Sodom: She and her daughter had pride, fullness of food, and

abundance of idleness; neither did she strengthen the hand of the poor and needy.

50 "And they were haughty and committed abomination before Me; therefore I took them away as I saw *fit*.

51 "Samaria did not commit half of your sins; but you have multiplied your abominations more than they, and have justified your sisters by all the abominations which you have done.

52 "You who judged your sisters, bear your own shame also, because the sins which you committed were more abominable than theirs; they are more righteous than you. Yes, be disgraced also, and bear your own shame, because you justified your sisters.

53 "When I bring back their captives, the captives of Sodom and her daughters, and the captives of Samaria and her daughters, then *I will also bring back* the captives of your captivity among them,

54 "that you may bear your own shame and be disgraced by all that you did when you comforted them.

55 "When your sisters, Sodom and her daughters, return to their former state, and Samaria and her daughters return to their former state, then you and your daughters will return to your former state.

56 "For your sister Sodom was not a by-word in my mouth in the days of your pride,

57 "before your wickedness was uncovered. It was like the time of the reproach of the daughters of Syria and all *those* around her, and of the daughters of the Philistines, who despise you everywhere.

58 "You have paid for your lewdness and your abominations," says the LORD.

59 'For thus says the Lord GOD: "I will deal with you as you have done, who despised the oath by breaking the covenant.

60 "Nevertheless I will remember My covenant with you in the days of your youth, and I will establish an everlasting covenant with you.

61 "Then you will remember your ways and be ashamed, when you receive your older and your younger sisters; for I will give them to you for daughters, but not because of My covenant with you.

62 "And I will establish My covenant with you.
Then you shall know that I *am* the LORD,
63 "that you may remember and be ashamed, and
never open your mouth anymore because of your
shame, when I provide you an atonement for all you
have done," says the Lord GOD.'"

Ezek. 16:1–63

In this chapter is contained the longest single allegory of the entire
Bible. Prostitution (harlotry) is the most frequent metaphor in the allegory, and by it Jerusalem's unfaithfulness to the Lord is compared
to a prostitute's unfaithfulness, which of course occurs repeatedly
and over a long term. Another common metaphor in the allegory is
that of nakedness, and not just here, but often in the prophetical
books. "Naked" and "exile" are basically the same word in Hebrew.
Exile means exposing, taking away from protection or covering, and
that also is what nakedness is, so the idea of nakedness became for
the prophets a common way of talking about the coming exile.

Because the chapter speaks of sexual promiscuity and even
nymphomania (vv. 28–29) it can be somewhat embarrassing to read
through it. However, those who would wish to teach or preach on
this chapter (or its even more explicit counterpart in chap. 23) can do
so quite successfully and with decorum as long as they take care to
concentrate attention on the facts to which the allegory points,
namely, the long history of infidelity to the Lord manifested by the
holy city—and not on the erotic aspects of the allegory itself. In
Jewish Rabbinic tradition, Ezekiel was a book reserved for study by
mature students rather than beginners partly because of the delicate
nature of Chapters 16 and 23.

The allegory is introduced (v. 1) by the usual reference to
Ezekiel's receipt of the Word of the Lord and by a clear explanation
(v. 2) that the purpose of the allegory was to point out Jerusalem's
"abominations," that is, actions and practices objectionable to God.
Jerusalem is addressed directly beginning in v. 3 and continuing
through the end of the chapter, and the effect is a sort of tragic
"This Is Your Life."

The Amorites, described symbolically in verse 3 as the ethnic
stock of Jerusalem's "father," were merely the general population
source of which the Canaanites were part. The Hittites were one of

the local ethnic groups in Canaan, possibly Hurrian in origin, and somehow traditionally linked with old Jerusalem before the Israelite conquest. The Hittites may have predated the Jebusites who dominated the city in Joshua's day (Josh. 15:63). In the allegory they are the ancient city's "parents." Jerusalem had a long history, going back to at least 4000 B.C. according to carbon-14 dating evidence, and thus the allegory has a vast sweep historically.

Verses 4–6 portray Jerusalem as an abandoned baby girl, denied the cutting of the umbilicus as well as the washing, salting, and diapering that were all part of loving baby care in ancient Palestine. (The salting was a carry-over from the practice of preserving meat. Since salt kills bacteria, it was a fairly effective, though primitive, kind of hygiene.) But the Lord loved this "baby," Jerusalem, and by His all-powerful Word decreed that she should live. This part of the allegory points to Jerusalem's early years, as in Abraham's day (Gen. 14:18–20) when the city was an independent city-state, as is confirmed by the fourteenth-century B.C. Amarna Letters, a major Egyptian archaeological find.

Later God chose Jerusalem as His special city (Deut. 12:5, 11, 14), and when David captured the central, fortified part of the city from the Jebusites, he made it crown property, separate from any of the tribal holdings, and also the nation's capital (2 Sam. 5:7–9). Jerusalem thereafter had special status as God's chosen place, and the language of verses 7–8 points to this. Verses 9–14, in turn, point to the city's splendor, its beautiful temple as constructed by Solomon, its wealth, etc., all portrayed via the dress, adornments, and diet of a lovely young woman in the flower of her attractiveness.

The infidelity of the city (vv. 15ff.) began with Solomon's introduction of idolatry and his creation of multiple shrine sites for the idolaters to worship at (1 Kings 11:1–10). The wealth and beauty of the city became increasingly devoted to idols (vv. 17–19; cf. Hos. 2:8), and the religious practices of Israel's Canaanite neighbors were progressively adopted by the people, even to the extent of practicing child sacrifice (vv. 20–21; cf. 2 Kings 23:10; Jer. 32:35). The people of Jerusalem and Judea had forgotten that it was the Lord who had given them their land and city (v. 22). As Israel's paganism increased (vv. 23–25), their tendency to ignore the Lord and depend for their security on international alliances grew. Judah and Jerusalem were taken advantage of by Egypt, Philistia, Assyria, and Babylon in succession (see 1 Kings 18–20 for examples) as the people sought to imitate or find refuge in other nations' ways (vv. 26–29). Jerusalem, Judah's capital, became more and more unwilling to turn to the Lord (v. 30). In the process, the city lost much more than it gained as other nations exploited and controlled the Judeans (vv. 31–34).

At verse 35 the future comes into focus. Jerusalem's past infidelity to God has been described, and now we learn what God is going to do about it. He will cause her enemies to attack and exile her population (vv. 36–37, "nakedness," of course, being a Hebrew synonym of "exile") and to destroy her wealth and leave her desolate (vv. 38–41) because of His fury against His former "bride" (vv. 42–43).

At verse 44 the allegory returns to retrospective, adding the element of comparison of Jerusalem to history's most notorious city, Sodom (see Genesis 18–19) as well as to another long-destroyed city, Samaria. Jerusalem, since the time of its Hittite origin (cf. v. 3), here called its "mother," had been independent (vv. 44–45). Samaria and its "daughters" (Hebrew, bānôt, the standard word for "suburbs" or "adjacent villages") and Sodom and its "daughters" were once like Jerusalem (vv. 46–52) though Jerusalem itself had even worse behavior in some ways than they (vv. 47–48). Arrogance, conspicuous materialism, a leisure class living well by exploiting the poor (v. 49), along with idolatry and its related degeneracies, resulted in the destruction of Sodom. Similar sins led to Samaria's destruction. Jerusalem "comforted" those cities (v. 54) and "justified them" (v. 52) by copying their ways. So having broken the Lord's covenant, thus rejecting Him, Jerusalem must now face His rejection of her.

Amazingly, in spite of Jerusalem's long history of evil, the allegory makes it clear that God will not reject her forever. Her captivity will end (v. 53) and God will honor His promise of old (e.g., Deut. 4:31) to reestablish His covenant with her (vv. 60–62), make her pure and secure, elevated above neighboring cities like Samaria and Sodom (v. 61), forgiven and righteous again (v. 63). The allegory is not literal and therefore does not intend to indicate that the people of Sodom would actually return from exile (v. 53) or that Sodom or Samaria would become great cities again (v. 61). Instead it points to the fact that in addition to the restoration of Jerusalem, God will one day bless other cities as well, forgiving many people their sins, and that He will eventually establish an existence where righteousness prevails and rebellion against Him is no more.

It is encouraging to realize that we are already in that "everlasting covenant" if we are in Christ (Gal. 3:29). Our future home is the new Jerusalem, which we will inhabit joyfully in fulfillment of this promise of faithfulness on God's part (Rev. 21:22–27). It will have in it none of the abominations of old—none of the arrogance, materialism, idolatry, etc.—that caused its demise and desolation in Ezekiel's day. But it will represent once again the dwelling place of God with His people, a true eternal home for the saints. It would not be going too far to say that for those who prefer country life, Jerusalem will seem rural, and for those who like the city, it will be urban! For Jerusalem in the Scriptures becomes ultimately itself a metaphor for eternal, peaceful, and blissful life with God rather than a literal dwelling place, as if it were actually a giant heavenly city holding all the redeemed of the ages inside its physical walls.

This happy ending to the allegory, however, is not the only part of it that has meaning for us. The history of Jerusalem's sin is very much a mirror for our own past state. When we sinned against the God who loves and cares for us, we made ourselves undeserving of His rescue. When we who without Him were lost and helpless, grew to ignore Him and even openly rebel against Him, imitating those we admired in the world rather than imitating His Son, we acted no better than the harlot Jerusalem in the allegory. Yet there was always hope for us, because God still loved us. No matter how far we may have degenerated, we were not too distant to be redeemed, if only by faith we would respond to God's call. In His mercy He has even loved the "citizens of Sodom," as it were. And they are we!

This is good news. As the allegory has a happy ending after a miserable beginning, so can the life of anyone who finds Christ. Therefore let us never forget that no one is beyond redemption and that no disobedience cannot be overcome by true conversion to Christ.

THE TWO EAGLES, THE CEDAR, AND THE VINE

17:1 And the word of the LORD came to me, saying,
2 "Son of man, pose a riddle, and speak a
parable to the house of Israel,
3 "and say, 'Thus says the Lord GOD:

"A great eagle with large wings and long
pinions,

144

Full of feathers of various colors,
Came to Lebanon
And took from the cedar the highest branch.
4 He cropped off its topmost young twig
And carried it to a land of trade;
He set it in a city of merchants.
5 Then he took some of the seed of the land
And planted it in a fertile field;
He placed *it* by abundant waters
And set it like a willow tree.
6 And it grew and became a spreading vine of
    low stature;
Its branches turned toward him,
But its roots were under it.
So it became a vine,
Brought forth branches,
And put forth shoots.

7 "But there was another great eagle with large
    wings and many feathers;
And behold, this vine bent its roots toward him,
And stretched its branches toward him,
From the garden terrace where it had been
    planted,
That he might water it.
8 It was planted in good soil by many waters,
To bring forth branches, bear fruit,
And become a majestic vine."

9 "Say, 'Thus says the Lord GOD:

"Will it thrive?
Will he not pull up its roots,
Cut off its fruit,
And leave it to wither?
All of its spring leaves will wither,
And no great power or many people
Will be needed to pluck it up by its roots.
10 Behold, *it is* planted,
Will it thrive?
Will it not utterly wither when the east wind
    touches it?
It will wither in the garden terrace where it
    grew."'"

145

11 Moreover the word of the LORD came to me, saying,

12 "Say now to the rebellious house: 'Do you not know what these *things mean?'* Tell *them,* 'Indeed the king of Babylon went to Jerusalem and took its king and princes, and led them with him to Babylon.

13 'And he took the king's offspring, made a covenant with him, and put him under oath. He also took away the mighty of the land,

14 'that the kingdom might be brought low and not lift itself up, *but* that by keeping his covenant it might stand.

15 'But he rebelled against him by sending his ambassadors to Egypt, that they might give him horses and many people. Will he prosper? Will he who does such *things* escape? Can he break a covenant and still be delivered?

16 '*As* I live,' says the Lord GOD, 'surely in the place *where* the king *dwells* who made him king, whose oath he despised and whose covenant he broke—with him in the midst of Babylon he shall die.

17 'Nor will Pharaoh with *his* mighty army and great company do anything in the war, when they heap up a siege mound and build a wall to cut off many persons.

18 'Since he despised the oath by breaking the covenant, and in fact gave his hand and still did all these *things,* he shall not escape.'"

19 Therefore thus says the Lord GOD: "*As* I live, surely My oath which he despised, and My covenant which he broke, I will recompense on his own head.

20 "I will spread My net over him, and he shall be taken in My snare. I will bring him to Babylon and try him there for the treason which he committed against Me.

21 "All his fugitives with all his troops shall fall by the sword, and those who remain shall be scattered to every wind; and you shall know that I, the LORD, have spoken."

22 Thus says the Lord GOD: "I will take also *one* of the highest branches of the high cedar and set *it* out. I will crop off from the topmost of its young twigs a

tender one, and will plant *it* on a high and prominent mountain.

23 "On the mountain height of Israel I will plant it; and it will bring forth boughs, and bear fruit, and be a majestic cedar. Under it will dwell birds of every sort; in the shadow of its branches they will dwell.

24 "And all the trees of the field shall know that I, the LORD, have brought down the high tree and exalted the low tree, dried up the green tree and made the dry tree flourish; I, the LORD, have spoken and have done *it*."

Ezek. 17:1-24

This allegory displays some features of a fable. A fable is a story in which animals, plants, or inanimate objects talk or act with human characteristics, as in Jotham's fable in Judges 9. Here neither the eagles nor the plants talk, but their actions come close to being "intelligent" and thus effectively portray in a symbolic way the actions of the kings of Babylon, Egypt, and Judah, as well as the people of Judah as a nation.

The allegory tells the story of Judah's diplomacy from the time of the first exile in 598 B.C. to the second exile (still future here) in 586. It is just unclear enough without explanation in the way that it is first posed (vv. 1-10) that Ezekiel's compatriots who heard it must have been at least somewhat baffled as to the referents for the various major points of the story. But the explanation in verses 12-21 makes the whole intent clear and also establishes the fact that Zedekiah, the "vine," would be punished not only for breaking his covenant with the Babylonians, but for the ultimately more serious crime of breaking the Mosaic covenant with the Lord (v. 19) that he should have kept at all costs.

This allegory, like the one in Chapter 16, ends on a positive note of hope and forgiveness for the nation. The "cedar" (Israel, or more specifically its remainder state of Judah) will be revisited, rescued from exile, and resettled in the land of Judah to dwell there in safety. In spite of its terrible leadership (the vine) and failed history of diplomacy, the nation has going for it the most important asset it could ever possess: God's loyalty. He has established for Himself a people and will never let them disappear from the earth, neither be assimilated into the land of their captors nor be annihilated by conquest or oppression. Though the generation in power in Ezekiel's day has done great wrongs, the nation as an entity may look forward to future deliverance and return from exile.

This allegory differs from others Ezekiel was commanded to tell his audience because of its opaqueness, so he was to tell it as a riddle (v. 2). The fact that the tree is a cedar and that its location is in Lebanon means nothing special; these are just details that help to create a story line. Babylonian kings had long come to Lebanon for forest products, there being virtually no timber in Mesopotamia, so Ezekiel's allegory likens Israel to a tree of Lebanon whose top (the leadership of the nation deported in 598 B.C.; cf. 2 Kings 24:14) was taken back to Babylon, the "land of trade" (center of commerce and wealth at that time, v. 4). "Young twig" in verse 4 could be better translated "top section" or the like. The "seed" of verse 5 is young Zedekiah, the member of the royal family descended from David, whom Nebuchadnezzar placed on the throne in Jerusalem as his puppet king (2 Kings 24:17).

For a while, Zedekiah was loyal to Nebuchadnezzar as represented by the vine's orientation in verse 6. But eventually Judah's king began to get ideas about rebellion. The Babylonians taxed the Judeans heavily and were their conquerors, after all. Egypt, by comparison, seemed a more suitable ally, and the Judean king knew that the Egyptians had for decades been fierce enemies of the Babylonians. Indeed, good King Josiah had lost his life in a battle designed to stop the Egyptians from coming to the aid of the Assyrians against the Babylonians in 609 B.C. (2 Kings 23:29). Following the futile example of the Israelite King Hoshea, who in the 720s had hoped Egypt might come to Israel's aid against Assyria (2 Kings 17:4), Zedekiah thought that the Pharaoh, the other "eagle" (v. 7), might help him against the Babylonians (v. 15). As far as we know, Egypt never provided much help other than selling war horses to Judah (v. 15), which proved useless in the siege the Babylonians mounted against Jerusalem (v. 17). Thus the "vine," Judah's leadership after 598 B.C., was bound to die. It had tried to change its roots and move its location (vv. 6–7) and thus became exposed, easy to pull up (v. 9) and remove (exile). Without the protection of the Babylonian treaty relationship that kept Zedekiah on his throne, how could he possibly hope to survive (v. 10)?

God was Zedekiah's real enemy. The king's most serious rebellion was not against his agreement with Nebuchadnezzar but against his responsibility to God (v. 19). Thus God would cause his punishment, exile, and imprisonment in Babylon (2 Kings 25:7), the capture of his army (vv. 25:5, 11), and the dispersion into exile of the rest of the people of Jerusalem (2 Kings 25:11–21). Defeated and deported, the formerly rebellious people now would join the first wave of exiles in a foreign land. But God's plan was not finished. God would go back to that same cedar top (the wording of v. 22 is intended in the original to indicate the same item as vv. 3–4 describe) and place it high in the land of *Israel* (v. 23), not Babylon, and make it a great dwelling place for His people (on birds in trees representing people thriving under someone's care see Dan. 4:20–22; Hos. 14:5–7).

The allegory concludes with yet another statement from God about the importance of people knowing that He was in control of human events and history. Most of these statements have taken the form "you shall know that I *am* the Lord" (e.g., 16:62). Here, however, the allegory keeps its free imagery right to the end, expressing the certainty that "all the trees" (all nations) would know that God can cause nations to rise and fall at His pleasure. This theme gave condolence to the Israelites in exile who knew the stories of Daniel (e.g., Dan. 2:21; 4:17) and Ezekiel's preaching: even as awesome an empire as the Babylonians controlled could fall if God willed it. And even as puny a people as the defeated Judeans in exile could be reestablished if God chose to make it happen.

Who exactly is the cedar top of verse 22? It cannot be King Jehoiachin and his nobles exiled in 598 B.C. They died in Babylon. It certainly cannot be Zedekiah and his associates. Zedekiah is the "vine" who rebelled and was uprooted to wither in Babylon. The new cedar top must, however, be someone in the royal lineage, a son of David, someone under whose "branches" all who will can dwell in safety, someone pleasing to God in contrast to the evil kings. It is of course, Christ, who is the ultimate deliverer of God's people, the sovereign of history, the only one in whom all people can have hope for salvation. Christ is called the Branch, in consonance with this chapter's allegorical language, in Isa. 11:1 and elsewhere (cf. Isa. 4:2; Jer. 23:5, 33:15; etc.). Israel's real hope as a nation could never rest merely in diplomacy or political change. Only the coming of Christ could fulfill the expectations of the allegory. The new, future king would rule from Zion over a righteous people. Gone would be the futile rebellions and machinations of the past.

CHAPTER NINE

The Principle of
Individual Responsibility

Ezekiel 18:1–32

A significant contribution of the Book of Ezekiel to biblical theology is its clear, extensive teaching about individual responsibility, the fact that people are fully responsible before God for their own actions and not punished for the sins of others.

As obvious as this principle might seem to Christians today, it was not necessarily the majority opinion in biblical times. Moreover, even today among some religions of the world that are fatalistic, or among some Christian groups that are excessively deterministic, there remains a tendency to assume that God causes all actions, including sin (!) so that people are punished for what they have to do anyway. Biblically, however, sin is presented always as a matter of choice, even though it is also often a matter of habit. Fatalistic Israelites, who believed that God sometimes punished one person for another's sins, had even coined the proverb quoted in Ezek. 18:2. Thus part of God's correction of His people's stubbornness and rebellion was the correction of their wrongheaded thinking about responsibility for sin.

THE SOUL THAT SINS WILL DIE

18:1 The word of the LORD came to me again, saying,
2 "What do you mean when you use this proverb concerning the land of Israel, saying:

'The fathers have eaten sour grapes,
And the children's teeth are set on edge'?

3 "*As* I live," says the Lord GOD, "you shall no longer use this proverb is Israel.

4 "Behold, all souls are Mine;
  The soul of the father
  As well as the soul of the son is Mine;
  The soul who sins shall die.
5 But if a man is just
  And does what is lawful and right;
6 If he has not eaten on the mountains,
  Nor lifted up his eyes to the idols of the house
    of Israel,
  Nor defiled his neighbor's wife,
  Nor approached a woman during her impurity;
7 If he has not oppressed anyone,
  But has restored to the debtor his pledge;
  Has robbed no one by violence,
  But has given his bread to the hungry
  And covered the naked with clothing;
8 If he has not exacted usury
  Nor taken any increase,
  But has withdrawn his hand from iniquity
  And executed true judgment between man and
    man;
9 *If* he has walked in My statutes
  And kept My judgments faithfully—
  He *is* just;
  He shall surely live!"
  Says the Lord GOD.

10 "If he begets a son *who is* a robber
   Or a shedder of blood,
   Who does any of these *things*
11 And does none of those *duties*,
   But has eaten on the mountains
   Or defiled his neighbor's wife;
12 If he has oppressed the poor and needy,
   Robbed by violence,
   Not restored the pledge,
   Lifted his eyes to the idols,
   Or committed abomination;
13 If he has exacted usury
   Or taken increase—
   Shall he then live?
   He shall not live!
   If he has done any of these abominations,

He shall surely die;
His blood shall be upon him.
14 *"If,* however, he begets a son
Who sees all the sins which his father has done,
And considers but does not do likewise;
15 *Who* has not eaten on the mountains,
Nor lifted his eyes to the idols of the house of
    Israel,
Nor defiled his neighbor's wife;
16 Has not oppressed anyone,
Nor withheld a pledge,
Nor robbed by violence,
But has given his bread to the hungry
And covered the naked with clothing;
17 *Who* has withdrawn his hand from the poor
And not received usury or increase,
But has executed My judgments
And walked in My statutes—
He shall not die for the iniquity of his father;
He shall surely live!

18 *"As for* his father,
Because he cruelly oppressed,
Robbed his brother by violence,
And did what *is* not good among his people,
Behold, he shall die for his iniquity."

Ezek. 18:1–18

It wasn't easy to be defeated, in exile from one's homeland at the whim of a great military power, impoverished, and looking forward to one's remaining years eking out a hardscrabble existence on foreign soil in what amounted to a resettlement camp. Ezekiel and his contemporaries had endured humiliation and discouragement, and many of them undoubtedly took psychological refuge in the popular little epigram quoted in verse 2, *"The fathers have eaten sour grapes and the children's teeth are set on edge."* This saying had been learned in Palestine before the exile, perhaps in the hard times of increasing Babylonian pressure in the 590s, to judge from its being mentioned and similarly rejected in Jeremiah (Jer. 31:29).

It was an appealing saying, since its subtle message was that the present generation was not responsible for all the disasters that had come upon it but had merely inherited conditions and problems that previous generations had set in motion. The attitude expressed in the saying, then, was one of both fatalism ("you can't do anything about the way things are") and irresponsibility ("you don't have to do anything about your own situation since it isn't your fault").

Of course, we can easily appreciate how that sort of thinking could have come about. If there is a chance to blame another person or situation for your own problems, human nature being what it is, you'll certainly be tempted to do so. Most people are blame-avoidant to some degree, all too willing to consider the idea that their problems are not of their own making. It is doubly hard to face difficulties while also knowing that we are the sole cause of them. It is usually somewhat easier to face hardships with an attitude of innocence, as if *we* at least aren't to blame for what we are now experiencing. The people of Jerusalem of Ezekiel's day were all too willing to say that they had *inherited* a situation of disaster, since this meant that they could claim not to have *caused* it.

This does not mean that there was no truth at all in the saying of verse 2. We would not expect a "proverb" that had no truth at all to have gained any popularity. But its truth was limited. God does "visit the sin" of one generation on another (Exod. 20:5), in the sense that He does not stop the effects of a person's sin when that person's life stops and does not limit the effects of a person's sin only to that person. (For more on this, see below under Ezek. 18:19-32.) But that is hardly the same as saying that God actually punishes one person for another person's sin. Moreover, it is quite true that the exile of the Judeans in 586 B.C. was the result of a long history of sin by many generations of Israelites (Deut. 4:25-28; 2 Kings 17:7-23; 22:16-17; etc.). Yet that is not the same as saying that an innocent group endured the punishment of a guilty group. The exile and accompanying punishments for the Israel of Ezekiel's day were deserved by that generation *along with* all the generations who had sinned against the Lord before them.

God therefore forbids the use of this misleading "sour grapes" proverb any more (v. 3). It was never accurate, and He solemnly charges the nation by an oath taken symbolically upon His own life ("As I live") that it must not be used. He now teaches the people in a carefully reasoned discourse about the nature of individual responsibility. First, everyone belongs to God (v. 4). Accordingly, God is in control of all lives, and everyone can therefore be assured that His judgment will be fair and true. Judgment doesn't just happen; God controls it. Only those who actually deserve to die because of their sin will die.

Next (vv. 5–9) follows a rather lengthy description of what constitutes the sort of behavior that will *not* cause a person to die but to be acceptable to God and thus to live. It is important to realize that this description is not advocating what we call "works righteousness." That is, God does not here make the point that the better you behave, the more likely you are to go to heaven, without any concern for any other factors in the process. Instead, what God says about the behavior of a righteous person must be seen in regard to God's covenant. It is God who saves, not works, and it is through faith that salvation comes—in the Old Testament as well as in the New. However, there is no real faith where there are no real works of righteousness. Good works prove true faith. Faith without works is dead, just as James says (James 2:17).

Paul's strong teaching on the essential linkage of faith and works in Ephesians is comparable. After explaining that it is the grace of God through faith, not works, that saves (Eph. 2:8–9) Paul immediately adds: "For we are His workmanship, created in Christ Jesus for good works, which God prepared beforehand that we should walk in them" (Eph. 2:10). It is the very design of God that His people should be characterized by good works—they are created in Christ for this purpose while on earth.

Thus Ezek. 18:4–9 calls us to do such things as avoiding false religion, lust, and sexual immorality (v. 6); practicing generosity to the needy as opposed to cheating or robbing others (v. 7); living honestly and decently (v. 8); and in general keeping God's laws (v. 9). This kind of living—upright and just—is what ought to, indeed, *must* characterize true believers. In other words, God's people had better act like they are God's people. The person who claims to belong to God but lives as if he or she belongs to the world does in fact belong to the world and not to God.

In verses 10–13 a related teaching appears, this time involving directly the question of a second generation, which, according to the false attitudes of the people of Ezekiel's day, could indeed suffer for the first generation's sins. But the message is clear: the second generation will suffer for its own sins, no one else's. Thus the child who is a criminal (v. 10), practices false religion or sexual immorality

(v. 11), exploits others (vv. 12–13), etc. will die for his own sins, regardless of his parents' righteousness or lack thereof.

Verses 14–18 consider what might be called a corollary, a corresponding situation, but with some key changes. In these verses the focus is on a child (the Hebrew *bēn* may be translated "child" as well as "son") who has a parent who does the sorts of things that constitute disobedience to God's law, as described in the preceding verses, but who does not himself or herself do such things. The parent is guilty; the child is not. That child will not die for the iniquity of his or her parents (v. 17) but will live. The parent, on the other hand, having disobeyed God, will die for his or her own sin (v. 18).

So whether the first generation is evil and the second evil also, or whether the first generation is evil and the second good, or vice versa, each generation and each person in each generation will receive from the Lord what they individually deserve. It is important to note that the terms "live" (Hebrew *ḥāyāh*) and "die" (Hebrew *mût*) refer to ultimate eternal punishments, not to living longer or dying sooner in this life, as the next section of the book (18:19–32) makes clear. The rewards for righteousness and punishments for sin are God's eternal prerogatives, not something that just happens in the course of life on earth. On earth the things that happen to people may or may not have a correspondence to what their eternal judgment will hold in store. As the Book of Job points out in a variety of ways, in *this* life the wicked often prosper and the righteous often suffer (e.g., Job 21, 24), just the opposite of what God will bring about at the final judgment.

Two Kinds of Judgment. How we understand the judgment of God depends partly on which sort of judgment we are talking about. In this world, in this life, there is a kind of divine judgment that does involve innocent people in the results of the sins of others. It is corporate or group punishment. That is, in this world God does indeed punish entire *groups* for the sins that they *as groups* commit, even when some members of the group may be innocent. Such groups are often nations, cities, or other political entities, but they may also be societal groups such as priests or prophets, or economic groups such as businesses or trade guilds, or such voluntary associations as churches.

The general rule is that "nations are judged in this world, and individuals in the next." More specifically, one may substitute for "nation" any corporate entity, that is, group. On the judging in this world of priests and prophets, see Hos. 4:4–13; of cities including innocent inhabitants, see Gen. 18:16–33; of a whole nation including innocent people (by drought), see 1 Kings 17:1–12; of nations in war, including some innocent citizens, see Josh. 6:21; of churches, see Rev. 3:16.

Was everyone in Hitler's Germany deserving of the destruction that the Allies necessarily wrought on that nation? Do all the people of any nation that goes to war against another support the war? Do all the soldiers even support it? Many who had nothing to do with starting or pursuing a war may die in it nonetheless, and many who do not endorse a group's evils may suffer its judgment. Conversely, of course, unrighteous people can be "carried along" by a group's overall righteousness, so that even though they as individuals are not deserving of God's favor, they share in the blessings with which He blesses the whole group. If the group on balance—overall— meets with God's favor, all its members may share in that favor. If the group on balance meets with God's wrath, all its members in this life may well suffer that wrath.

With regard to *eternal* punishment, however, the situation is very different. God treats people as individuals. This is the special thrust of Chapter 18, and it is a great truth. A person does not need to miss out on eternal life merely because he or she grows up in a nonbelieving family or because he or she is part of a disobedient group or nation. One can be wicked in a righteous world or righteous in a wicked world. One can be lost among many who are saved or saved among many who are lost. In contrast to the way that God may cause the rise and fall of nations and groups in human history and thus judge the corporate affairs of this world, when the time comes that God judges the lives of all people at the end of the age, He will treat each person as an individual. No one will be punished for anyone else's sin; no one will gain eternal life on the coattails of someone else's favor with God.

Thus we as individuals have not yet been judged by God. But we as members of nations and other corporate groups are being judged all the time, as God shows or does not show favor to the groups to which we belong. God controls the ebb and flow of history, judging peoples and movements in the process. But our *personal* judgment is yet to come.

OBJECTIONS OVERRULED

18:19 "Yet you say, 'Why should the son not bear the guilt of the father?' Because the son has done what is lawful and right, and has kept all My statutes and observed them, he shall surely live.

20 "The soul who sins shall die. The son shall not bear the guilt of the father, nor the father bear the guilt of the son. The righteousness of the righteous shall be upon himself, and the wickedness of the wicked shall be upon himself.

21 "But if a wicked man turns from all his sins which he has committed, keeps all My statutes, and does what is lawful and right, he shall surely live; he shall not die.

22 "None of the transgressions which he has committed shall be remembered against him; because of the righteousness which he has done, he shall live.

23 "Do I have any pleasure at all that the wicked should die?" says the Lord GOD, "and not that he should turn from his ways and live?

24 "But when a righteous man turns away from his righteousness and commits iniquity, and does according to all the abominations that the wicked *man* does, shall he live? All the righteousness which he has done shall not be remembered; because of the unfaithfulness of which he is guilty and the sin which he has committed, because of them he shall die.

25 "Yet you say, 'The way of the Lord is not fair.' Hear now, O house of Israel, is it not My way which is fair, and your ways which are not fair?

26 "When a righteous *man* turns away from his righteousness, commits iniquity, and dies in it, it is because of the iniquity which he has done that he dies.

27 "Again, when a wicked *man* turns away from the wickedness which he committed, and does what is lawful and right, he preserves himself alive.

28 "Because he considers and turns away from all the transgressions which he committed, he shall surely live; he shall not die.

29 "Yet the house of Israel says, 'The way of the Lord is not fair.' O house of Israel, is it not My ways which are fair, and your ways which are not fair?

30 "Therefore I will judge you, O house of Israel, every one according to his ways," says the Lord GOD. "Repent, and turn from all your transgressions, so that iniquity will not be your ruin.

31 "Cast away from you all the transgressions which you have committed, and get yourselves a new heart and a new spirit. For why should you die, O house of Israel?

32 "For I have no pleasure in the death of one who dies," says the Lord GOD. "Therefore turn and live!"

Ezek. 18:19–32

In this passage, God continues to speak directly to Ezekiel's contemporaries in exile in Babylon in the early 580s. Corrupted by a combination of ancient Near Eastern fatalism and what they thought was reasonable, empirical observation about the nature of life, Ezekiel's contemporaries were not inclined to believe the doctrine of individual responsibility so carefully and repeatedly stated in the preceding verses. They may even have had an objection to it on principle, in the sense that they may have held to the popular notion that a child was to a considerable degree a continuation of his parent, both genetically (i.e., as the parent's "seed," Hebrew *zera'*) and psychologically (thus the use of *bānāh*, "build," "create" in the Old Testament to indicate "carrying on the family name and traditions"; see also Ruth 4:10). At any rate, they certainly did not believe that individual responsibility was the way that life worked and, therefore, did not tend to think that it was the way that the creator of life, God, worked either. As a result, if their minds were going to be changed, they needed to hear what they had not been accustomed to hearing and to hear it very clearly and completely.

Three facts needed careful explanation: (1) God judges the lives of individuals according to their *own* obedience to Him; (2) God is little concerned with what an individual was before his or her conversion and greatly concerned with what an individual has become *after* conversion; and (3) that it is possible to convert either from sin to righteousness or from righteousness to sin. To teach this to the Israelites in exile and, by extension, to all who would later hear or read these words, God adopts a dialogical teaching style in which He both asks and answers questions about individual responsibility and conversion.

This is an effective strategy. Good teaching does not merely present the truth neutrally, it argues for it. And part of careful argumentation may be the consideration of objections, actual or potential, to that which has been presented. Imagine a speaker addressing an audience on a controversial topic. After the speaker has made his point, several people from the audience raise objections or ask questions aimed at challenging what the speaker has proposed. If the speaker has good answers at the ready, the audience will be convinced, and the speaker will have persuaded them of the validity of his argument. But imagine, further, that long after the meeting is over, someone comes up with what seems to be a good objection to what the speaker had to say, and the speaker is meanwhile long gone from the meeting. What then? If no one who understood fully the speaker's point of view can offer a convincing response to the recently raised objection, it may turn out that the speaker may no longer be believed. The new objection will have cast doubt into everyone's mind, doubt for which an answer is not available in the absence of the original speaker.

How can we avoid this? The well-prepared, expert speaker may often head off such a problem by raising objections to his or her own presentation. In other words, it is not necessary for someone in the *audience* to raise the objections. The speaker cannot always depend on the audience to be aware of all the issues connected with the presentation or to come up with all possible objections fast enough, or at least before the meeting comes to a close. What the speaker must do, then, is anticipate objections that might at any time enter the mind of the audience. If there *might* be objections, the speaker can do a great deal to gain acceptance for his or her point by anticipating those objections and addressing them immediately. That way no one will have the experience of coming up with objections after there is no longer any opportunity to receive a satisfying answer, thus remaining in doubt about the accuracy of what has been presented.

This is just the sort of thing that God does in Ezek. 18:19–32 in relation to His audience's possible objections to the principle of individual responsibility and to the genuine opportunity for conversion.

God is the speaker here, and His audience is the people of Judah in the early sixth century B.C., specifically those in exile in Mesopotamia with Ezekiel. It is important to appreciate the fact that many or most of these people believed that individual responsibility was not the way that life worked and, by analogy, was not the way that God would handle the judgment of humans. They observed that when it came to both families and societies as a whole, one generation could indeed cause another generation to suffer for its errors.

What they saw were the sorts of things that we, too, can observe routinely in life. Parents who neglect or abuse their children can cause their children great pain and suffering, thus causing the younger generation to suffer from the sins of the older. Parents who practice any sort of sin as a way of life can so influence their children as they are growing up to do the same thing, thus, the second generation ends up reflecting the values and practices of the first and, in effect, inherits the guilt that goes along with it. For example, a high percentage of those persons who beat their spouses were raised in families where the same thing occurred between their own parents. When they grow old enough to imitate the behavior of their parents, they do. Thus one generation seems to get the next generation into sin.

Outside the family, on a grander scale, similar things happen. One generation of a nation builds enmity against another nation's comparable generation, but their children are those who are called to arms to fight each other. The young generation suffers and dies for the hostility of the older generation. Or one generation spends in a profligate manner the resources of its nation, perhaps accruing a substantial national debt in the process, and another generation must live with the deprivations produced by that spending and the burden of paying for that debt.

It can also happen that one generation sets a moral and ethical tone for its society by the practices it allows and the laws it passes, and the moral climate inherited by the next generation greatly affects how the people of that next generation get along with one another, the extent that they will engage in or tolerate crime, etc. And, of course, the most serious legacy of all is the spiritual legacy that one generation leaves to another. If one generation fails to remain faithful to God, no longer obeying His Word, it may leave to the next generation a disastrously dangerous precedent of disobedience. The next generation will disobey on its own, not of necessity, but easily following a pattern put in place by its predecessors that makes that disobedience all the more likely.

The Israelites of Ezekiel's day observed all of these sorts of influences of one generation on another, and they concluded that this meant that the children really did suffer for the sins of the parents. But they were not entirely correct. Each new generation does not *have* to do what the prior generation did. Each new person may choose not to follow in the ways of his or her parents. Habit is not necessity. Similarity is not causality. Individuals and the generations they are part of have a free will; they are responsible for their actions. This is the point that God wants to be sure that those who use the proverb mentioned in 18:2 will understand.

Fortunately, every generation has the opportunity to make up its own mind about the offer of God to turn to Him and live (v. 32). Thus every generation suffers for its own sins and not for the sins of the preceding generation, and every individual likewise. So generations do have an influence on their successors but do not control what their successors do.

God's words in verse 19 make this clear. Anyone who keeps God's statutes will live. And as verse 20 confirms, anyone who does not will die. The individual, and the individual generation, bears his or her own iniquity. This is God's fair plan. Repentance can lead the sinner to full forgiveness of his or her sins (vv. 21–22) because God has no interest in seeing the wicked die in their sins (v. 22). There is no need for anyone to live under condemnation for past sins if he or she is truly repentant and converted (cf. Rom. 8:1–17). But the awesome corollary is also true. If a person chooses *negative* conversion, from righteousness to wickedness, that person becomes a sinner and receives his or her proper reward—death. In effect, the end, not the beginning, is what determines the overall measurement by God of a person's life. Thus, as most people instinctively understand, it's not where you start out that determines your judgment, but where you end up.

Suppose, for sake of illustration, that you are going to be judged one evening at a gathering of some sort on how neatly and cleanly (not expensively) you are dressed. It doesn't really matter if you were dirty, grimy, and unkempt during the afternoon, wearing your oldest, most wrinkled work clothes. Since then, if you've showered and put on neat, clean clothes, now, at the gathering, you are neat and clean. You will be judged favorably. However, suppose you were absolutely neat and clean all day, but on the way to the gathering you stopped briefly to mud wrestle an alligator. *Now* you are dirty and messy, and those doing the judging are not going to be very favorable to you. Your protest, "But until just before I got here I was neat and clean!" is going to fall on deaf ears. Such a point must be appreciated if the gospel is to have its power. At the end of a person's life, when he or she concludes this temporary earthly journey, is when one *must* be right with God. Of course, it is very desirable to be right with God as early as possible in life—and very dangerous to assume that one will happen to have either the time or the will at the end of one's life to convert to God from sin. It is the end product of a person's life that makes the real difference, that is the "bottom line" of a life's evaluation (Matt. 10:22; 22:13; Mark 4:1–20). Many sins are covered by conversion to righteousness. Many good deeds are obscured by conversion away from it.

Anticipating another objection, that this principle of individual responsibility somehow isn't fair, God quotes what people might well say to Him (v. 25), that is, *"The way of the Lord is not fair."* God then through His prophet again patiently explains His just position: the convert to sin from righteousness has become a sinner and ought to be punished (v. 26) just as the convert from sin to righteousness ought to escape punishment (vv. 27–28).

A final objection (v. 29), using the same wording as the prior objection (v. 25), is met with both a clear warning and an invitation. The warning is that a final judgment will take place, with everyone's faithfulness to God's commands judged on its own merits (v. 30). The invitation is to repentance, to avoid the inevitable tragic results of sin. What people need is a new heart and a new spirit (v. 31), which are the characteristics of the converted individual, the person who can live forever with the Lord and not die. Heart (Hebrew, *lēb*) may also be translated "mind," for it refers precisely to a person's thinking and attitudes. "Spirit" (Hebrew, *rûaḥ*) has a wide range of meanings in translation but often refers, as here, to a person's way of thinking and living (cf. Hos. 4:13).

The passage ends with another statement of the divine will—that God does not enjoy in any way the death of a sinner—and another invitation to repentance so that eternal life might be the result. Again the assumption of the language is that the first death (normal human death) is not the issue, but the second (eternal death). The "death of one who dies" is the second death (Rev. 20:6, 14; cf. Rom. 6:23), eternal death. The invitation to "return and live" holds the promise of eternal life, not a relatively longer life on earth. As the Scripture frequently specifies (e.g., Job 21:7–13; Rom. 14:8; Phil. 1:21; James 4:15), the length of one's life on this earth has no necessary relationship to one's personal righteousness or wickedness. When God speaks of life and death relative to judgment, it is *eternal* life and *eternal* death that are in focus. Hebrew, *ḥāyāh*, normally translated "live" or "life" has a kind of rich ambiguity to it. It can mean simply the life of any person or animal that exists on the earth, or it can refer to eternal life, of both different duration and different quality than we yet know.

CHAPTER TEN

Lamentable Leadership

Ezekiel 19:1–14

Ezekiel 19 contains a compound lament, a musical dirge sung by the prophet at the inspiration of God, whose subject is the royal leadership during Judah's tragic final days of degeneration toward destruction. The subject matter chapter may be outlined as follows:

v. 1   Introduction: Command to lament
vv. 2–4   Lament for King Jehoahaz
vv. 5–9   Lament for King Jehoiakin [or King Zedekiah]
vv. 10–14a   Lament for King Zedekiah
v. 14b   Conclusion: Command to lament

Interestingly, Ezekiel's lament is composed in a way that blends this subject matter into a lovely allegorical poem that has a first section (vv. 2–9) somewhat longer than the second section (vv. 10–14), much in the manner of the sonnet, the European poetic style involving fourteen lines of poetry with a shift of focus or emphasis after the eighth line. Ezekiel shifts focus after verse 9 by moving from the metaphorical portrayal of Israel (specifically Judah at this time, since northern Israel was already in captivity by Ezekiel's day) as a lioness to Israel as a vine. What is not so certain is whether or not he moves from an allegorical portrayal of Jehoahaz and Jehoiachin of Judah in verses 2–9 to Zedekiah in verses 10–14a or whether already in verses 5–9 Zedekiah is symbolically described. On this question see the discussion below.

Sad songs of the type that we find here in Ezekiel 19 are known in Hebrew by the name *qînah*, which means "funeral dirge" or "funerary lament." Such songs were sung in ancient Israel to honor or commemorate persons who had died, and they may well have been sung at or soon after the funerals of such persons. In this sense they are like elegies (nostalgic poems expressing sorrow for one who is dead) and eulogies (speeches in praise of someone's contributions). From David's famous lament (*qînah*) over Saul and Jonathan in 2 Sam. 1:19–27 and similar lengthy laments in the Old Testament, we can distinguish four elements that normally go together to make up a *qînah*:

1. Summons/instruction to mourn
2. Direct address to the departed
3. Description of the tragedy (how greatly the loss is felt)
4. Retrospective praise of the qualities of the departed

The *qînah* of Ezekiel 19 certainly has all of these elements and thus qualifies as a classic lament of a type well attested in the Scripture.

Many scholars have made much of the fact that *qînah* poems have a certain supposedly "lilting" or "elegiac" metrical style (usually referred to by counting the Hebrew word groups to obtain a "3/2" meter). However, since such notable songs as the Twenty-third Psalm, which is obviously not a lament, also have this 3/2 Hebrew word-grouping pattern, such a categorization cannot be considered reliable. Nevertheless, like the laments in the Book of Lamentations, Ezekiel's lament does have a pattern sometimes associated with laments, as evidenced by the way that the syllables are distributed throughout the poetic couplets in the Hebrew, and this reinforces the fact that Ezekiel intended that his audience should see his poem as a sad song about the last kings of the dynasty of David in Judah. The implications of such a song are discussed below.

THE LIONESS AND HER CUBS

19:1 "Moreover take up a lamentation for the princes of Israel,
    2 "and say:

      'What *is* your mother? A lioness:
      She lay down among the lions;
      Among the young lions she nourished her
        cubs.

3 She brought up one of her cubs,
   And he became a young lion;
   He learned to catch prey,
   And he devoured men.

4 The nations also heard of him;
   He was trapped in their pit,
   And they brought him with chains to the land
      of Egypt.

5 "When she saw that she waited, *that* her hope
      was lost,
   She took another of her cubs *and* made him a
      young lion.

6 He roved among the lions,
   And became a young lion;
   He learned to catch prey;
   He devoured men.

7 He knew their desolate places,
   And laid waste their cities;
   The land with its fullness was desolated
   By the noise of his roaring.

8 Then the nations set against him from the
      provinces on every side,
   And spread their net over him;
   He was trapped in their pit.

9 They put him in a cage with chains,
   And brought him to the king of Babylon;
   They brought him in nets,
   That his voice should no longer be heard on
      the mountains of Israel.'"

Ezek. 19:1–9

The first part of Ezekiel's compound lament is the command to lament itself (v. 1). Ezekiel is told to sing a lament ("take up," Hebrew, *śā*ʾ, indicates singing here) for Israel's princes (Hebrew, *neśîʾîm*). Ezekiel tends to avoid the word "king" (Hebrew, *melek*) in favor of the word "prince," and he also, like most of the prophets, is inspired to keep reminding his audience that Judah is still part of Israel. Even though Judah and Israel had split politically as the result of a civil war that began in 931 B.C. and was never resolved, from God's point of view they together were still one entity, Israel, and their future would be a common glorious one under God's prince, a united nation ruled by an all-powerful Messiah descended from David (see Ezek. 37:14ff.). Thus the "princes of Israel," mentioned in this chapter metaphorically as lions, are in fact Judean kings.

Since Ezekiel's prophecies are generally datable, it is likely that this section of the book continues to reflect revelations received by the prophet around 592 and 591 B.C., when one of the characters mentioned, Zedekiah (in verses 5–9, perhaps, and definitely in the vine allegory of verses 10–14), was still king. At any rate, verses 2–4 clearly summarize the career of Jehoahaz II, who had ruled in 609 B.C. for only about three months (2 Kings 23:21).

As Ezekiel began this funeral dirge for his audience, they would recognize immediately by the tune and the tone that it was a lament, even if he did not repeat to them the words of his command to sing the lament as he received them in verse 1. Then as he sang the words, they would realize that it was intended not to refer to one of the exiles in their own midst who had died recently, but to Judean kings whose history they knew well. Comparing kings to lions would not have seemed strange to Ezekiel's audience, by the way. God is compared to a lion in Amos 1:2, and King Saul to a gazelle in the Hebrew of 2 Sam. 1:19, etc.

Verse 2 does not literally refer to Queen Hamutal, Jehoahaz's mother (2 Kings 23:21), but figuratively to the nation of Israel, the "mother" who had produced this king. Verse 3 continues the allegory describing how the king came to power and was potentially a great king ("he devoured men" is wording describing a lion to be feared). But this lion was trapped by "the nations," Hebrew, goyyîm, referring to the Egyptians and their allies as pagan foreigners, not to all the nations of the ancient world. This sums up how Jehoahaz, who was not obedient to the Lord's covenant, was captured and exiled to Egypt, where he eventually died (2 Kings 23:21–34), by Pharaoh Necho (610–595 B.C.). Necho led Egypt in a campaign of conquest in Palestine and Syria to reestablish Egypt's once great empire, and he wanted Jehoahaz out of the way so that he could install on the throne of Judah his own puppet king, Jehoiakim (609–598 B.C.; 2 Kings 23:34–24:7).

Ezekiel skips over the reign of Jehoiakim since he was not exiled. The prophet's inspired purpose is clearly to emphasize past and future exiles of kings in this allegorical lament. With verse 5 the allegory begins again, as it were, with the story of another king. The same sorts of things are said about this king in verse 6 as were said about Jehoahaz in verse 3, and the audience may already have suspected that Ezekiel was referring to Jehoiachin, who reigned for three months in 598 B.C. before being taken into exile by the Babylonians (2 Kings 24:8–16). It is also possible that they understood the lament to be talking about Zedekiah (598–587 B.C.) who was still king and still reigning in Jerusalem at the time they were hearing the lament (592/91 B.C.). If the latter is the case, they would have realized that the lament was in part a *prediction* of Zedekiah's downfall, just as verses 10–14 surely are. Since Zedekiah and Jehoahaz had the same mother, Hamutal (2 Kings 24:18), the mention of a "mother" in verses 2, 3, and 5 might have helped them make this connection.

It is most likely, however, that Jehoiachin is *not* left out here in favor of Zedekiah, and that he is indeed the king whom Ezekiel intends to be understood behind the images of verses 5–9. After all, it was Jehoiachin who was in power when Ezekiel and his audience were taken prisoner and brought into exile, and it was Jehoiachin who was considered by them the last legitimate king of Judah. Even 2 Kings ends by paying attention to Jehoiachin's fate in exile (2 Kings 25:27–30) since he was, in effect, the king of the exiles. Jehoiachin had great potential and was impressive (v. 7), but foreigners (Babylonians this time) captured him (v. 8) and brought him into exile, in Babylon (v. 9) so that *"his voice should no longer be heard,"* that is, he could no longer command his people as king.

THE VINE

19:10   'Your mother *was* like a vine in your bloodline,
            Planted by the waters,
            Fruitful and full of branches
            Because of many waters.
      11 She had strong branches for scepters of rulers.
            She towered in stature above the thick
               branches,
            And was seen in her height amid the dense
               foliage.
      12 But she was plucked up in fury,
            She was cast down to the ground,
            And the east wind dried her fruit.

> Her strong branches were broken and
>   withered;
> The fire consumed them.
> 13 And now she *is* planted in the wilderness,
>   In a dry and thirsty land.
> 14 Fire has come out from a rod of her branches
>   *And* devoured her fruit,
>   So that she has no strong branch—a scepter
>   for ruling.'
> This *is* a lamentation, and has become a
> lamentation.
>
> *Ezek. 19:10–14*

Now the focus of the allegorical lament is fixed not just on one of the kings, but also on the nation of Judah as a whole, with the role of its final puppet king, Zedekiah, being described as one of the factors in the whole nation's exile. Here, then, the lament becomes definitely predictive. Ezekiel's compatriots in exile in 592/91 may well have still hoped for some sort of rescue for their nation, a turn of events that might even provide a means for them to be brought back from Babylon and resettled in their homeland of Judah. The idea that Jerusalem would fall once for all to the Babylonians and that remaining Judeans would be exiled for many years was, however, what Ezekiel had been preaching right along, as the preceding chapters of the book display. This is also what the lament reiterates. Jehoiachin had surrendered in 598 B.C. after a brief Babylonian siege of the city so that the city and many of the population would be spared, even though Ezekiel and others had been deported along with the king. But now was coming a complete collapse and surrender, with the end of the nation as an independent member of the commonwealth of nations now in sight.

In verse 10 "your mother" (Israel, or more specifically Judah) is compared metaphorically to a lush, richly watered vine. Many rulers (v. 11), that is, kings of the Davidic dynasty—twenty-two in all from David's day to Zedekiah's day—came from Judah, but that vine (Judah) according to the lament has been violently uprooted and thrown to the ground (exiled and debased as a nation), dried up in the east (where Babylon was) and largely burned (v. 12). This is, of course, what happened to a vine in ancient times when it no longer bore fruit, since "grapewood" is hardly useful for much

169

except firewood (cf. John 15:6). What remains of the vine has been planted in a "dry and thirsty land" (v. 13, again referring to Babylon, especially the parts the Judeans were exiled to).

What is the immediate cause for this disastrous end to a once great nation? Verse 14 points out, somewhat cryptically, that "fire" from "a rod of her branches" is what burned the vine so badly that it could no longer provide "a strong branch—a scepter for ruling." The "branch" surely refers to any future king, and thus the point of the verse is that the "fire" brought an end to Israel's monarchy. Verses 2–9 spoke of the end of the reigns of two kings; verses 10–14 speak of the end of the reigns of all the kings. If this is the case, it is almost certain that the "fire" of verse 14 is Zedekiah himself.

Fire in the ancient world was always viewed as destructive, which it surely is. The fact that fire can reduce wood to merely a bit of ash from which the wood can never again be reconstituted was rightly impressive to ancient people, and thus fire in the Bible is routinely a symbol of annihilation (e.g., Gen. 19:24; Jer. 50:32; Amos 1:4, 7, 10, 12, 14; 2:2, 5; 7:4; Matt. 25:41; Rev. 20:14; etc.). It was Zedekiah whose leadership as a rebellious and godless king ruined Judah at the end of its history (2 Kings 24:18–25:7, esp. 24:20). This does not mean that Judah would not have been exiled without Zedekiah's evil. It does mean, however, that without Zedekiah's evil the inevitable destruction of the nation and deportation of its citizenry might have been delayed, as it was in days of the righteous Josiah (2 Kings 22:19–20). Judah's fate had long ago been decided (Deut. 4:21–31). The actions of its latter kings merely sped up the timing (2 Kings 23:26–27).

Zedekiah's rebellion against the Babylonians sometime in the late 590s (2 Kings 24:20) was the immediate cause of the nation's collapse. As a puppet king (2 Kings 24:17) Zedekiah had brought a sort of temporary stability to things in Judah, though at the price of heavy taxes and tribute paid to the Babylonians year after year. Undoubtedly in part to get out from under this burden, the king must have foolishly listened to advisers of poor judgment, who read the signs of the times wrongly, for his attempt to rebel never had a chance, and his own life and that of the nation ended disastrously with the siege of Jerusalem, the defeat of the Judeans, large-scale death and destruction, and a massive exile of people (2 Kings 25:1–21).

All happened just as Ezekiel predicted. For even though the verbs in Ezek. 19:10–14 are in the past tense, the lament is still a prediction. The prophets were allowed to see the future and report back to the present on what they *had seen* in the future. Thus they often employ the past tense when describing what has not yet taken place. So Ezekiel's final lament is futuristic, and his audience could only tremble at its implications for their own continuing miserable fate as captives in a hostile foreign land.

CHAPTER ELEVEN

Idolatry, Past and Future

Ezekiel 20:1–21:7

In the world of the Old Testament, everyone worshiped by using idols. It was unthinkable not to. Idols were thought to be absolutely necessary for proper worship in the same way that wings are thought necessary for an airplane today. The practice of idolatry was based on what is sometimes called "sympathetic magic," that is, the ability to influence reality by manipulating an image of that reality. Voodoo dolls are based on this concept. The doll maker creates a doll that is supposed to be in some way like a certain individual that someone wants to harm. When a pin is stuck into the doll, the person whom the doll represents is supposed to experience pain or illness. Though we have no knowledge that people in Ezekiel's day practiced *exactly* the same sort of thing that voodoo brings to mind, we know from many incantation texts of the time that they certainly believed essentially the same sort of thing.

They believed that an *image* of something really captured some of the *essence* of that thing. People in primitive cultures today who are afraid to have their pictures taken for fear that the camera will "capture their soul" have the same sort of notion about how images capture essences. Ancient people believed that if they made an image (idol) of a god, no matter how crudely it may have been fashioned and no matter how partially it may have represented the god, it nevertheless captured its essence. Therefore, with idols they could guarantee that the gods would be with them, right in their presence, taking note of their offerings and automatically hearing their prayers.

Idolatry thus seemed the only sensible way to worship. Would someone try to talk in a normal voice to a person on the other side of a mountain? Of course not. That would be stupid. Would someone try to worship a god without being sure that the god were present by means of an idol? Of course not. That, too, would be stupid, thought the ancients. And so they thought that the orthodox Israelite approach to the worship of Yahweh without using idols was stupid. The whole ancient world thought this way, and that made it very difficult for those few Israelites at any given time who actually were trying to be faithful to the Lord's covenant law. It's always hard to go against the prevailing norms and universally held beliefs of one's culture. It was hard for Israelites to say that God is a spirit and must be worshiped without idols of any sort, when everyone else thought just the opposite. It's hard to grow up thinking one way about reality (i.e., that idolatry is *necessary* to reaching a god) and convert to another way of thinking about reality (that idolatry will *prevent* you from reaching God).

Ezek. 20:1–44 describes Israel's history of idolatry—not just their past history from the standpoint of Ezekiel but also their future idolatry in exile, in a time still ahead of the prophet. Idolatry kept Israel from God's favor and blessing, so it was always seriously condemned by the prophets. What the passages within 20:1–44 demonstrate is that idolatry was not something Israel had flirted with now and again, but instead was a way of life to which the people were so attached that only the miraculous grace of God could provide rescue from it and its penalty. So it is with sin in general. We get in a rut of sinning so deep and long that our human nature offers no hope of rescue (Rom. 7:5–24). Sin is, in effect, addictive. Without God's grace (Ezek. 20:44) there is no hope for the sinner.

ABOMINATIONS OF THE FATHERS

20:1 It came to pass in the seventh year, in the fifth *month*, on the tenth *day* of the month, *that* certain of the elders of Israel came to inquire of the LORD, and sat before me.

2 Then the word of the LORD came to me, saying,

3 "Son of man, speak to the elders of Israel, and say to them, 'Thus says the Lord GOD: "Have you come to inquire of Me? *As* I live," says the Lord GOD, "I will not be inquired of by you."'

173

4 "Will you judge them, son of man, will you judge *them*? Then make known to them the abominations of their fathers.

5 "Say to them, 'Thus says the Lord GOD: "On the day when I chose Israel and raised My hand in an oath to the descendants of the house of Jacob, and made Myself known to them in the land of Egypt, I raised My hand in an oath to them, saying, 'I *am* the LORD your God.'

6 "On that day I raised My hand in an oath to them, to bring them out of the land of Egypt into a land that I had searched out for them, 'flowing with milk and honey,' the glory of all lands.

7 "Then I said to them, 'Each of you, throw away the abominations which are before his eyes, and do not defile yourselves with the idols of Egypt. I *am* the LORD your God.'

8 "But they rebelled against Me and would not obey Me. They did not all cast away the abominations which were before their eyes, nor did they forsake the idols of Egypt. Then I said, 'I will pour out My fury on them and fulfill My anger against them in the midst of the land of Egypt.'"

Ezek. 20:1–8

In verse 1 Ezekiel provides a precise date for the events of this passage. It was the seventh year (of their exile, i.e., 591 B.C.), the fifth month (i.e., the month of Ab, about July–August, since the new year was considered to begin in the spring in those days), and the tenth of the month. Thus we can tell that about a year had passed from the time of the last dated prophecy of Ezekiel (8:1). All that took place between 8:1 and 20:1 may be dated in that year.

The statement *"certain of the elders of Israel"* can also be translated "some elders of Israel" (i.e., some of the leaders of the exiled community). Therefore we should not infer that this group was a kind of delegation sent to Ezekiel by all the exiles. Rather, it was probably an ad hoc group sharing a common important question that they wished Ezekiel to answer for them by means of a revelation from God (*"to inquire of the Lord"*). In Old Testament times the Holy Spirit "fell upon" or was "in" selected individuals, such as prophets, but was hardly generally available to believers as in our own day. Accordingly, believers

174

in general often did not think of themselves as having direct access to God's guidance, approaching instead prophets through whom God could provide guidance to them. Ezekiel does not bother to tell us exactly what they were inquiring about. They might have wanted to know if Zedekiah would succeed in his rebellion against the Babylonians, or if their own conditions in Babylonian captivity would improve, or the like. At any rate, they *"sat before"* him, which means that they took their places to wait while he prayed for a revelation from God to answer their question(s).

Instead of such an answer, Ezekiel received from God (v. 2) a revelation that was critical of the elders and, by implication, the people they represented, the Judean Israelites in exile. God refused to go along with their desire, to *"be inquired of"* by them (v. 3). Rather, He had a word of judgment that they needed to hear, and asked Ezekiel emphatically if he was willing to deliver this word of judgment to his fellow exiles (v. 4). Ezekiel would have found the task of criticizing his friends and fellow sufferers in exile just as difficult as you or I would find it difficult to have to stand up in the midst of a community group to which we had been invited to speak on some noncontroversial topic and instead warn the audience sternly that God was about to judge them for their sins! Thus God asks him twice to be sure he is willing to do this task. The task is to *"make known to them the abominations of their fathers."* By implication this means that they, too, have a share in the abomination that is about to be described.

With verse 5 God begins to rehearse the history of His covenant bond to Israel. His national promises ("oaths") began in one sense with the promises to Abraham in Genesis 12, but were heard directly by his corporate people first in Moses' preaching to the Israelites in bondage in Egypt (Exodus 1ff.). The repetition of the phrase *"raised My hand in an oath"* in verses 5 and 6 reinforces the fact that God had committed Himself by divine solemn promise to choose His people, to rescue them from their misery in Egypt, and to settle them in the good land of Canaan, here called the *"glory of all lands"* to emphasize its being the land to which even the exiles should still look as the place where God will bless them. Keeping alive their desire to return from exile was one of God's concerns for Israel through Ezekiel (cf. 37:1–14) and other prophets of this time (e.g., Jeremiah 33).

In Egypt before the exodus the Israelites were hardly devoted, faithful, trusting servants of the Lord waiting longingly for the promises of old to be fulfilled. As the centuries had gone by they had become fully accommodated to their surroundings and had gradually adopted the idolatrous beliefs and worship practices that prevailed in Egypt and everywhere else. These beliefs and practices were so ingrained that it was necessary for the Israelites to be given strict laws against them once they—and the many non-Israelites who joined them in the exodus (Exod. 12:38)—got to Mount Sinai (Exod. 20:3–6, 23). Thereafter, they found it hard to keep such laws, as evidenced for example by the golden bull incident that occurred while they were still at Mount Sinai (Exodus 32) and the idolatrous incident at Baal-Peor as the people were about to embark on the conquest (Numbers 25). In Joshua's day, too (Josh. 24:14), and thereafter (Judg. 2:10–19), idolatry was a constant temptation for the Israelites, a temptation to which they usually yielded readily. The *"idols of Egypt"* (v. 7) were Israel's idols, too, and the fact that they could never seem to shake off their *"abominations which were before their eyes,"* that is, their idolatry (v. 8), meant that they were in danger of receiving the punishments of the Sinai covenant, including death and exile (Lev. 26:16–39; Deut. 28:64–68).

The statement at the end of verse 8 that God had considered punishing the Israelites for their idolatry in Egypt while they were yet resident there (*"I will pour out My fury on them . . . in the midst of the land of Egypt"*) does not quote anything contained in the Book of Exodus itself. Such passages as Exod. 5:19–21 and 6:9, however, make it clear that considerable resistance existed among the Israelites in Egypt to the whole idea of going along with Moses in exiting from Egypt, as the attempts at rebellion along the way confirm. In other words, the Israelites were very close to being left in Egypt as slaves forever, except for the mercy of God, of which verses 9ff. speak.

We will discuss below some of the selfish attractions of idolatry. Always idolatry involves disobedience to God's covenant, however, and this is what is central to verses 1–8. God's old covenant carried with it obligations on the part of His people. To refrain from idolatry, no matter how attractive idolatry may have seemed, was one of those obligations. Yet Israel found it hard to obey. There are similarities in this to our own situation under the new covenant. Were it not for the righteousness of Christ, our frequent disobedience would have long ago disqualified any of us from God's favor. Our tendency to sin is a part of our nature, and no knowledge or procedure can make us pure enough to escape it in our own strength. Without Christ, God had determined to pour out His fury and anger on *us*, too. And like the Israelites in Egypt, we would have deserved it.

DISOBEDIENCE IN THE WILDERNESS

20:9 "But I acted for My name's sake, that it should not be profaned before the Gentiles among whom they *were*, in whose sight I had made Myself known to them, to bring them out of the land of Egypt.

10 "Therefore I made them go out of the land of Egypt and brought them into the wilderness.

11 "And I gave them My statutes and showed them My judgments, 'which, *if* a man does, he shall live by them.'

12 "Moreover I also gave them My Sabbaths, to be a sign between them and Me, that they might know that I *am* the LORD who sanctifies them.

13 "Yet the house of Israel rebelled against Me in the wilderness; they did not walk in My statutes; they despised My judgments, 'which, *if* a man does, he shall live by them;' and they greatly defiled My Sabbaths. Then I said I would pour out My fury on them in the wilderness, to consume them.

14 "But I acted for My name's sake, that it should not be profaned before the Gentiles, in whose sight I had brought them out.

15 "So I also raised My hand in an oath to them in the wilderness, that I would not bring them into the land which I had given *them*, 'flowing with milk and honey,' the glory of all lands,

16 "because they despised My judgments and did not walk in My statutes, but profaned My Sabbaths; for their heart went after their idols.

17 "Nevertheless My eye spared them from destruction. I did not make an end of them in the wilderness.

18 "But I said to their children in the wilderness, 'Do not walk in the statutes of your fathers, nor

observe their judgments, nor defile yourselves with their idols.

19 'I *am* the LORD your God: Walk in My statutes, keep My judgments, and do them;

20 'hallow My Sabbaths, and they will be a sign between Me and you, that you may know that I *am* the LORD your God.'

21 "Notwithstanding, the children rebelled against Me; they did not walk in My statutes, and were not careful to observe My judgments, 'which, *if* a man does, he shall live by them'; but they profaned My Sabbaths. Then I said I would pour out My fury on them and fulfill My anger against them in the wilderness.

22 "Nevertheless I withdrew My hand and acted for My name's sake, that it should not be profaned in the sight of the Gentiles, in whose sight I had brought them out.

23 "Also I raised My hand in an oath to those in the wilderness, that I would scatter them among the Gentiles and disperse them throughout the countries,

24 "because they had not executed My judgments, but had despised My statutes, profaned My Sabbaths, and their eyes were fixed on their fathers' idols.

25 "Therefore I also gave them up to statutes *that were* not good, and judgments by which they could not live;

26 "and I pronounced them unclean because of their ritual gifts, in that they caused all their first-born to pass through *the fire,* that I might make them desolate and that they might know that I am the LORD."

Ezek. 20:9–26

Here is a story of grace and forgiveness. Through Ezekiel God reviews for the elders of the Judean captives in Babylon part of the long history of His goodness to His people in spite of their repeated rebellion against Him. He gives; they ignore. He forgives; they continue to sin. He blesses; they defile.

The story is not told to make the elders feel bad or to "rub in" their inadequacy as a people of God. It is told to get them to repent, to turn from their current disobedience. Particularly appropriate is the attention paid to Israel's wanderings as a nation in the Sinai Peninsula after their miraculous deliverance from Egypt. That, after all, was an era in which the people were without a homeland, living impermanently, looking forward to getting "back" to Canaan according to the promises of God. Ezekiel's audience could hardly miss the similarities to their own circumstances in Babylon. Even if they had not yet heard from the prophet the sort of encouraging predictions he would soon be making to them about their eventual return to Canaan from exile (e.g., chap. 37), they would be aware that some of the prophets who had told the unpleasant truth about the fall of Judah before the exile of 598 B.C., especially Isaiah and Jeremiah, had also promised a return from exile and had also frequently mentioned the wilderness wanderings in their oracles (e.g., Hos. 2:3, 16, 17; Isa. 10:26; 11:16; Jer. 2:2-6).

In this passage there are three reminders of Israel's rebellion and God's forbearance:

vv. 9-12   In Egypt [continuing from v. 7] and at Mount Sinai
vv. 13-20   In the wilderness [the first generation]
vv. 20-26   In the wilderness again [the second generation]

These reminders are organized chronologically and geographically, according to the story of Israel's exodus and wanderings in the Sinai Peninsula as told in Exodus and Numbers.

Reminder Number 1: In Egypt and at Mount Sinai (vv. 9-12). God did not punish the Israelites by leaving them to die in slavery in Egypt, though that was what they deserved. Instead, He gave them help they did not deserve, *"for My name's sake"* (v. 9). Here we see an aspect of the gospel in the Old Testament. God acts so that He Himself is glorified, not so that human beings can get what they have coming to them. He has determined that He will have a people whom He will rescue from death and who will bear witness to Him in the world. In the old age this people was Israel; in the new age it is the church. To leave His people without rescue is to invite nonbelievers from all the nations of the world to scoff at God's power or even His existence. Accordingly, He saved Israel from Egypt and brought them into the wilderness (v. 10) as a witness to the world. He also blessed them with His law (v. 11), which is always viewed in the Bible as a positive gift from God (contrary to the usual misreading of Galatians, for example), and with His Sabbaths (v. 12). The Sabbath was a *"sign"* in the sense of a regular weekly reminder of both God's goodness (it protected the Israelites from the seven-day week that characterized the exploitation of slavery in the ancient world) and of His demands upon Israel (they had to honor Him properly by not working or making anyone else work on that day). The Sabbath was *not* a time of worship in ancient Israel in the same sense that the three major festivals each year were times of full worship (see Exod. 23:10–17, Lev. 23). Keeping the Sabbath was one way that Israel proved it was faithful to the Lord.

Reminder Number 2: In the wilderness [the first generation] (vv. 13–20). The behavior of the nation in the early years of the wilderness wanderings was no better than it had been in Egypt. The people rebelled against the laws they had received at Mount Sinai. An especially evident form of that rebellion was the failure to keep the Sabbath (cf. Num. 15:32–36), which as Ezekiel uses it here is not the most serious of sins, but a paradigm for the many sins of rebellion against God. For the people to defile His Sabbaths was to show themselves ungrateful to God for all He had done for them and to express their hostility toward His lordship.

So once again it would have been entirely appropriate for God to destroy His people where they were (v. 13) without bringing any of them into the promised land, and this He considered doing. But once again He decided against that course of action so that the peoples of the nations might not wrongly conclude that He had no power to save (v. 14). However, God did punish that first generation of Israelites in the wilderness—the same group that had left Egypt with Moses. They were denied the right to enter Canaan, as He declared (v. 15, "lifted My hand in an oath," cf. Num. 14:12, 21–23), and instead were condemned to wander in the wilderness until the original exodus generation had died off. The special reason for this punishment is given in verse 16: *"their heart went after idols."* Now the text makes it clear how they "defiled" the Sabbaths. Whereas the Sinai covenant called for three special times of worship yearly, the Israelites found that entirely inadequate. They had grown up in Egypt thinking in terms of idolatry, which prized frequency of worship and easy access to worship altars. Among the many characteristics that gave idolatry its appeal was the "vain repetition" factor. The more you sacrificed to a god, the more you won his favor. The more often you sacrificed to a God the more obligated he was to help you. Therefore, sacrificing every week, on the Sabbath, was far preferable to the infrequent worship of the system Yahweh, Israel's God, desired.

Even so, God did not destroy the nation as a whole (v. 17) but warned the new generation, those born as children in the wilderness to the original exodus generation (v. 18) that they, in contrast to the failed obedience of their parents, should obey God's laws (v. 19) and keep his Sabbaths (v. 20). This would include staying away from idolatry, so tempting as the activity was on one's "day off" each week.

Reminder Number 3: In the wilderness [the second generation] (vv. 21–26). The people of Israel were forced to remain in the wilderness for forty years while the original exodus generation gradually died away leaving a new generation to enter into the promised land. That new generation was for the most part born in the wilderness, although it included some of the original group from Egypt, people like Joshua and Caleb, who had remained faithful even while most of the others had not (Num. 14:6–9). The new generation was given every chance to obey the Lord and to enjoy His constant protection and favor. They, too, however, showed themselves unfaithful, doing the same sorts of things that their parents had been condemned for (v. 21). Accordingly, God's anger was poured out against them (see Num. 25:3–9), again because of idolatry and all that it entailed. A major incident of idolatry committed by the second wilderness generation was that which occurred at Baal-Peor in Moab. There, the Israelites turned virtually en masse to Baal worship and to the ritual sex that accompanied it (Num. 25:1–3, 6–9, 14–18).

Ritual sex was another great attraction of idolatry. Most of the ancient Near Easterners believed that all things that came into being were *born* into being. This was a major tenet of their belief system. They believed that not only animals were born, but also plants. (This is the reason that they "sowed their field with two kind of seed," i.e., male and female seed as they thought of it; see Lev. 19:19.) What was born into being started, they believed, with sex on the part of the gods—specifically Baal and Asherah, the god and goddess of fertility according to the Canaanites. They also thought that if a person bringing an offering to Baal and/or Asherah would have ritual sex with a prostitute at the shrine as part of worship (!) this would help stimulate the divine powers of nature to have sex, and thus more animals and crops would be born, and the agriculture would flourish. Outlandish as this sounds to us, it was the pinnacle of theology among the Canaanites—and was what the Israelites readily accepted at Baal-Peor.

We can see, then, that all during the period of the wilderness wanderings, idolatry was a constant temptation to the people of Israel, just as Ezekiel portrays it in Chapter 20. For such disobedience God had every right to destroy Israel, since His covenant with them provided the death penalty for disobedience (Leviticus 26; Deuteronomy 28). Instead, however, He once again showed His people mercy for the sake of their being a light to the Gentiles (v. 22). But He did make it known to them early on that the penalty they as a nation would eventually pay for their rebellion, including idolatry (v. 24), would be exile from the promised land (v. 23; see Deut. 4:26–27). One of the ways that God punishes sin is to abandon people in it, so that they suffer its consequences. This is the theme of Deut. 4:28 (idolaters are into forced idolatry in exile) and Rom. 1:21–27 (God allows sin to degenerate into yet worse sin; note that Romans 1 describes *idolatry* as the sin that often leads to the other sins). God let the Israelites make up their own wrong beliefs and practices (*"statutes that were not good, and judgments by which they could not live,"* v. 25), in effect abandoning them to the ways of death.

Among the most disgusting of the idolatrous practices that developed among the Israelites was child sacrifice (v. 26). A sacrifice as understood by Israel's pagan neighbors was a way of giving desirable things to the gods. Humans were supposed to feed the gods by cooking food for them. (The smoke would send the food up to the gods.) And if you could send food via smoke to the gods, how about sending them servants that way? How about really impressing a god with your dedication and sincerity by sending that god something more precious to you than anything else—your own firstborn child? Thinking themselves likely to gain the lifetime favor of the gods in this way, the Israelites borrowed child sacrifice, too, from their neighbors and began killing their firstborn infants and burning them on altars as a means of sending them to the false gods they were worshiping. It is evident that such people really wanted the gods to love them and were willing to "give their all" to gain such love. But all they were doing was playing into the hands of Satan (1 Cor. 10:20). How could such worshipers then be "clean" in the worship of

Yahweh? How could they escape His making them "desolate," that is, imposing on them the curses of desolation predicted for the nation if it would rebel against Him (e.g., Lev. 26:31–35; Deut. 28:51; 29:23)?

If they had to learn the hard way that He was the Lord, then He would make them learn it the hard way (v. 26)! *"I am the Lord"* is a reference to the covenant language that clarifies, as it were, who's boss. Yahweh (the Lord) was the sovereign in the covenant relationship. Israel was His vassal, or servant. They had to do what He commanded, or they would suffer the consequences. We must learn from this. Our relationship to the Lord, if we are committed Christians, is no longer a voluntary one. We do what we are told. We are not on our own—we are "bought with a price" (1 Cor. 6:19–20) like a slave who belongs to a master. Our master is one who knows what is best for us. He makes the decisions. When we think we know better than He what is right, we guarantee His disfavor.

DISOBEDIENCE IN CANAAN

20:27 "Therefore, son of man, speak to the house of Israel, and say to them, 'Thus says the Lord GOD: "In this too your fathers have blasphemed Me, by being unfaithful to Me.

28 "When I brought them into the land *concerning* which I had raised My hand in an oath to give them, and they saw all the high hills and all the thick trees, there they offered their sacrifices and provoked Me with their offerings. There they also sent up their sweet aroma and poured out their drink offerings.

29 "Then I said to them, 'What *is* this high place to which you go?' So its name is called Bamah to this day."'

30 "Therefore say to the house of Israel, 'Thus says the Lord GOD: "Are you defiling yourselves in the manner of your fathers, and committing harlotry according to their abominations?

31 "For when you offer your gifts and make your sons pass through the fire, you defile yourselves with all your idols, even to this day. So shall I be inquired of by you, O house of Israel? *As* I live," says the Lord GOD, "I will not be inquired of by you.

> 32 "What you have in your mind shall never be,
> when you say, 'We will be like the Gentiles, like the
> families in other countries, serving wood and stone.'"
> *Ezek. 20:27–32*

The one place that should have inspired in every Israelite heart a passion for faithfulness to the Lord was Canaan. Here was the land of the promises to the patriarchs. Here was the land of milk and honey, grain and wine, longed for during the centuries of slavery in Egypt. When the days of the wandering in the wilderness were fulfilled and the people began the conquest of the promised land under Joshua (about 1400 B.C.), the rewards of obedience should have been obvious, and the will to keep the Lord's covenant should have been stronger than ever. Yahweh had kept His part of the bargain. He had, "on eagles' wings" (Exod. 19:4), brought them from Egypt, protected them from their enemies, and given them victory over all their foes in Canaan (Josh. 24:8–13). They now occupied a territory granted them by divine grace, a former gang of slaves having the honor to inhabit "the glory of all lands" (Ezek. 20:6, 15). Now they would surely be willing to fulfill God's expectation that they would be His "kingdom of priests and a holy nation" (Exod. 19:6)!

Instead, tragically, they could hardly wait to copy the Canaanites. One of the appealing characteristics of Canaanite idolatry was its convenience. Like the barber shop signs that used to say "Four Barbers—No Waiting" the motto of Canaanite religion might have been "Countless Shrines—No Waiting." Idolatry, with its concept that the essence of the gods could be "captured" for one's own advantage, meant that wherever you had an idol you had a god willing and able to accept your sacrifice. Why travel to the only tabernacle, and later, after Solomon's day, to the only temple? Why not worship the gods—including Yahweh—wherever there was a bit of a hill and a tree for shade (there being thousands of each in Canaan)? Years ago I saw a sign outside a church that gave somewhat the same impression. It read: "Come worship with us in air-conditioned comfort." Such an offer has a certain appeal, but little relationship to the self-sacrificial denial that is an integral part of biblical religion.

In verse 27 the Lord commands Ezekiel to tell not only the elders of the captive Israelites but to the people in general (*"the house of Israel"*) that they are descended from blasphemers. Blasphemy (Hebrew, *giddēf*) is taunting or reviling God. It may be done orally or by one's actions. In that the forefathers of the Israelites were almost immediately unfaithful to God in Canaan, they reviled Him.

The Israelites were supposed to worship God by offering Him sacrifices and by burning incense to Him. Such actions were completely proper (Leviticus 1–7; 16; Exodus 30, 35). But they could not be done just anywhere. God had commanded the Israelites through Moses that all their worship was to take place at a central sanctuary (Deuteronomy 12), that is, wherever the tabernacle was located prior to the construction of the temple and thereafter at the temple in Jerusalem. Thus to offer sacrifices at *"all the high hills and all the thick trees"* (v. 28) was to disobey God purely and simply, no matter how well intentioned the offerings themselves might have been.

In verse 29 God utters a catchy Hebrew saying (*"What is this high place to which you go?"*) that has the sounds of the Hebrew word *bamah*, "high place" or "shrine," in it more than once. The *bamah*s were where Israel found it convenient to worship and therefore defied Yahweh, while also going on to defile themselves with "harlotry." This term (Hebrew, *zānāh*) is one of Ezekiel's common ways of describing Israel's unfaithfulness. In marriage, unfaithfulness in the extreme would be not merely adultery, but prostitution—professional adultery. In terms of the symbolism of Israel's marriage to Yahweh, Israel was indeed a prostitute—a "pro" at unfaithfulness (v. 30). Their idolatrous sacrifices, including child sacrifice (probably often enough to Yahweh in addition to Baal), disqualified them from being accepted by God and therefore from receiving His helpful revelatory word (cf. v. 3). They wanted to "be like the Gentiles," "like the clans of the [world's] countries" [rather than "like the families *in* other countries"] just as they had always tended to desire. But God had other plans for His people. Their selfish unfaithfulness was not in charge of their destiny. He was.

The attractions of worldliness are, of course, nothing new. Even the religious worldliness of Ezekiel's contemporaries has its modern parallels. It can be spotted by its conspicuous materialism, its greed, its loosened concern for biblical standards, its self-interest, and its convenience to the worshiper. Such a distortion of true religion, whether it claims to be Christian or not and whether or not it has a large following or plenty of media access, is still a distortion—not the real thing. Its very flashiness, an aspect that makes it so attractive to some, is evidence of its falseness. It self-servingly worships power and success, not the true God.

A NEW EXODUS: PURGING AND ACCEPTANCE

20:33 *"As* I live," says the Lord GOD, "surely with a mighty hand, with an outstretched arm, and with fury poured out, I will rule over you.

34 "I will bring you out from the peoples and gather you out of the countries where you are scattered, with a mighty hand, with an outstretched arm, and with fury poured out.

35 "And I will bring you into the wilderness of the peoples, and there I will plead My case with you face to face.

36 "Just as I pleaded My case with your fathers in the wilderness of the land of Egypt, so I will plead My case with you," says the Lord GOD.

37 "I will make you pass under the rod, and I will bring you into the bond of the covenant;

38 "I will purge the rebels from among you, and those who transgress against Me; I will bring them out of the country where they dwell, but they shall not enter the land of Israel. Then you will know that I *am* the LORD.

39 "As for you, O house of Israel," thus says the Lord GOD: "Go, serve every one of you his idols—and hereafter—if you will not obey Me; but profane My holy name no more with your gifts and your idols.

40 "For on My holy mountain, on the mountain height of Israel," says the Lord GOD, "there all the house of Israel, all of them in the land, shall serve Me; there I will accept them, and there I will require your offerings and the firstfruits of your sacrifices, together with all your holy things.

41 "I will accept you as a sweet aroma when I bring you out from the peoples and gather you out of the countries where you have been scattered; and I will be hallowed in you before the Gentiles.

42 "Then you shall know that I *am* the LORD, when I bring you into the land of Israel, into the country *for* which I raised My hand in an oath to give to your fathers.

43 "And there you shall remember your ways and all your doings with which you were defiled; and you shall loathe yourselves in your own sight because of all the evils that you have committed.

44 "Then you shall know that I *am* the LORD, when I have dealt with you for My name's sake, not according to your wicked ways nor according to your corrupt doings, O house of Israel," says the Lord GOD.'"

Ezek. 20:33–44

Ezekiel has finished reciting to the elders of the exiles their history of idolatry, but God has still more to say to them through His prophet on this occasion. It concerns what will come in the future, after their time of exile is over, and it makes regular allusions to the time of the exodus and wandering in the wilderness that have just been covered in terms of the Israelites' tendency to idolatry in their past.

Israel became a nation in the first place by means of a divinely controlled process. That process took place over a forty-year period (ca. 1440–1400 B.C.) and included the nation's rescue from bondage in Egypt, their reception of God's covenant at Mount Sinai, the purging of the unfaithful during the wandering in the wilderness, and the conquest of Canaan, thus fulfilling the promises to the patriarchs.

The prophets often were inspired to look back upon that process as a symbolic model for the restoration of Israel from the Babylonian exile. In the present passage Ezekiel conveys from God to his audience a similar symbolic model for the gathering of the Israelites from Mesopotamia (and elsewhere) and their return to the promised land. This "new exodus" motif also has a particular emphasis on the fact that Israel will not go through the process again and remain unstable in its commitment to the Lord and enamored of idolatry as the people of the first exodus did. Instead, *this* time God will by His own power see to it that His people will be pure in their faith. He will purge them so that He might also be able to accept them, not by lowering His standards, but in a manner precisely consistent with His high standards for them.

This promise of resettling a purified Israel in Palestine following the Babylonian captivity is called the *restoration*. It is predicted here by God not at all for the first time, but rather is repeated just as it had been repeated by virtually all the orthodox prophets who preceded Ezekiel. The prophets preached the restoration of Israel on the basis of its original statement in the Mosaic covenant, in such places as Deut. 4:27–31; 30:1–10; and Lev. 26:40–45. There, through Moses, God had promised the first and second wilderness generations—and all generations after them—that in spite of the destruction and deportation of Israel that would inevitably result from their sin, He would nevertheless not allow His people to be exterminated totally. Instead, He would always retain a remnant, whom He would one day restore to truer prosperity and fidelity to Him than the nation had ever known. This is what verses 33–44 describe.

In verses 33–34 God again repeats the solemn oath wording of verse 3 ("As I live") and recalls with the phrases "with a mighty hand, with an outstretched arm" the language used in Exod. 6:6 to describe His power against Egypt and its pharaoh (cf. Deut. 4:34; 5:15; 7:19; 9:29; 11:2; 26:8). That same great power will rescue Israel again, this time from the various locations where the Northerners had been exiled (in 722 B.C., by the Assyrians; see 2 Kings 17), where the Southerners had been exiled (in 598, when Ezekiel was deported), and where they would yet be exiled (in the great exile of 586, still to come). In verses 35–36, the "wilderness of the peoples" (better translated "nations"), that is, a symbolic representation of all the areas the returning exiles would have to cross through to get back to Judah (Isa. 40:3–5, 9–10), replaces the original "wilderness of Egypt" of the Book of Numbers.

Verse 37 reflects the ancient shepherd's method of counting in sheep as they pass under his staff held over the doorway of the sheepfold. God will "count in" His people as they come back from wherever they, like lost sheep, have been scattered, to the safety of His covenant bond. But those who because of their continuing sin don't belong, like sheep not His own kept out of the sheepfold, He will keep out of the promised land (v. 38).

The middle of verse 39 should read: "hereafter, you will obey Me or else! But you will profane My holy name no more." The time will come when once again at Jerusalem's Mount Zion ("My holy mountain") Israelites will properly, not idolatrously, worship the Lord (v. 40) and will themselves become a pleasing sacrifice ("sweet aroma") to the Lord (v. 41). God will show the Gentiles, before whom He is determined that His glory not be dishonored (vv. 9, 14, 22) that His people really obey Him in holiness ("I will be hallowed in you," v. 41). The miraculous restoration of Israel to Canaan (v. 42) will help Israel to appreciate their covenant responsibility to Yahweh ("know that I am the Lord," cf. vv. 5, 19, 38), and the memory of their shameful idolatry in exile will help them keep pure in obedience to the Lord's covenant (v. 43). This latter remark may be something of a rebuke to the elders to whom Ezekiel was relaying this word from God, since they did not seem to have arrived at his house particularly ashamed of the idolatry widely practiced by them and their fellow Israelites (v. 32).

Blessings and curses are "earned" differently according to the Law. The curses of the Mosaic covenant are meted out as punishment for sins. They are deserved. But the restoration blessings are not meted out as rewards for good works. They cannot be deserved. The favor of God cannot be earned by humans. It is His gift to them. Accordingly, God reminds the people in verse 44 that the favor He will shower upon them in the restoration will come not in any way because of their history of behavior toward Him, but precisely *in spite of* their long record of corruption. This is exactly how God has always dealt with people, and it is certainly a welcome fact, for otherwise none of us would ever have had a chance to be accepted by God. He redeemed Israel in the first instance from slavery in Egypt and in the second instance from exile in Babylon and elsewhere, not by reason of their works but by reason of His grace. He redeems all who turn to Him in faith now, not by reason of anything they can do to impress Him, but directly in spite of all they may have done to make Him furious. He does this "for his name's sake"—that He might be glorified among us, as well He should be. And we should recognize in this miraculous grace a power every bit as awesome as the power with which He delivered His people in the past. As the end-times subjects of His greatest rescue, we must be sure that God also "rules over" us (v. 33) and that it is obvious by our faithfulness to Him that we know that He is the Lord (v. 44).

FOREST FIRE AND SWORD:
A PARABLE AND ITS MEANING

20:45 Furthermore the word of the LORD came to me, saying,

46 "Son of man, set your face toward the south; preach against the south and prophesy against the forest land, the South,

47 "and say to the forest of the South, 'Hear the word of the LORD! Thus says the Lord GOD: "Behold, I will kindle a fire in you, and it shall devour every green tree and every dry tree in you; the blazing flame shall not be quenched, and all faces from the south to the north shall be scorched by it.

48 "All flesh shall see that I, the LORD, have kindled it; it shall not be quenched."'"

49 Then I said, "Ah, Lord GOD! They say of me, 'Does he not speak parables?'"

21:1 And the word of the LORD came to me, saying,

2 "Son of man, set your face toward Jerusalem, preach against the holy places, and prophesy against the land of Israel;

3 "and say to the land of Israel, 'Thus says the LORD: "Behold, I am against you, and I will draw My sword out of its sheath and cut off both righteous and wicked from you.

4 "Because I will cut off both righteous and wicked from you, therefore My sword shall go out of its sheath against all flesh from south to north,

5 "that all flesh may know that I, the LORD, have drawn My sword out of its sheath; it shall not return anymore."'

6 "Sigh therefore, son of man, with a breaking heart, and sigh with bitterness before their eyes.

7 "And it shall be when they say to you, 'Why are you sighing?' that you shall answer, 'Because of the news; when it comes, every heart will melt, all hands will be feeble, every spirit will faint, and all knees will be weak as water. Behold, it is coming and shall be brought to pass,' says the Lord GOD."

Ezek. 20:45–21:7

This section of Ezekiel's prophecies contains a two-part oracle composed, first, of an initial revelation of an allegory (not strictly "parable," v. 49) in 20:45–49—the point of which was not comprehensible to Ezekiel's audience, and perhaps to Ezekiel himself—and second, its explanation in 21:1–7.

The main points of the passage may be outlined as follows:

Forest Fire Allegory (20:45–49)
    Command to preach against southern forest (20:45–46)
    Prediction of forest fire affecting everyone (v. 47)
    Identification of the Lord as the source of the fire (v. 48)
Warfare "Sword" Explanation (20:1–7)
    Command to preach against Jerusalem (21:1–2)
    Prediction of warfare ("sword") affecting everyone (vv. 3–4)
    Identification of the Lord as the source of the warfare (v. 5)
Response of Prophet and People (vv. 6–7)
    Ezekiel to sigh/moan (i.e., agonize, v. 6)
    People to agonize (v. 7)

Most of the time that a prophet received a revelation from the Lord, he or she understood its meaning and its implications. Indeed, it can well be held that there is no prophecy anywhere in the Bible whose meaning was intended to be incomprehensible. We may have trouble appreciating a few passages here and there because of our limited knowledge of the original language, or text, or context, but in principle we do not believe that anything in biblical prophecy was intended to be obscure to the believer.

But that is not to say that all prophecies were meant to be *immediately* comprehensible to everyone in a prophet's audience. One kind of prophecy that is *not* understandable without clues to its interpretation is the allegory. In an allegory the various major figures (people or things) stand for something else—their real meaning is not in themselves but in that to which they refer. Unless you have some idea of what they refer to, you don't have any way to get the point of the allegory. In Chapter 19, God told Ezekiel immediately what the major figures of the allegory referred to (the lion cubs were kings of Israel according to 19:1; the lioness "mother" was the nation of Israel according to 19:2, etc.).

191

In Ezek. 20:45–49, however, God gives no clue in His revelation to the prophet as to what the figures of the allegory represent. Ezekiel faithfully preached the allegory to the people, as he was commanded, but at the time he may not have understood its point himself. At any rate, the audience certainly didn't get it. They accused him of speaking "parables" (also translatable as "allegories," since the Hebrew *mashal* can refer to virtually any figure of speech). By this they apparently meant that his prophecy was too obscure or complicated for them to understand, just as Jesus' speaking in parables to people not willing to seek the kingdom of God was dismissed as purposeful obscuring of the message (Matt. 13:10).

In response to his appeal to God about the people's accusation (v. 49) Ezekiel then receives a second, supplementary revelation (21:1–7) in which he (and his audience) learns what the allegory really meant because the figures of the allegory are now defined clearly ("fire" = war, "south" = Judah, etc.). He is also told to undertake a simple kind of enactment prophecy (going around sighing) so that the people in exile with him will be vividly warned that the news of the fall of Judah will greatly demoralize them.

"The word of the Lord came to me" introduces new sections of prophecy, so from this wording in 20:45 we know that a new revelation has begun. In verse 46 three different Hebrew words (*têmān, derôm, negeb*), all meaning "south," are used to indicate the location of the coming allegorical forest fire described in verse 47. From Babylon, conquering armies followed the Fertile Crescent roads moving northwest, then west, then due south by the time they were invading Israel (Judah)—so "south" is the direction they faced as they attacked Judah. Their face, like Ezekiel's face here (cf. 4:3, 7), symbolizes the face of the Lord. The Babylonians will not do their terrible deed of destruction on their own authority; they will be mere pawns in God's hands, accomplishing His punishment on Israel.

That "every green tree and dry tree" will be burned and that every "face from north to south" will be scorched (v. 49) are symbols of what 21:4 explains: both righteous (green tree) and wicked (dry tree) will be killed or exiled by the Babylonians, throughout the entire land of Israel (north and south). The words "it shall not be quenched" (v. 48) express the same notion as "My sword . . . [to] its sheath . . . shall not return anymore" (21:5), that is, that God will not bring upon His people merely a *partial* conquest and exile this time, as was the case in 598 when Ezekiel was exiled. This time, God will finish the job completely through His agents, the Babylonians.

Again it is clear that religious infidelity, including idolatry, would be a major cause of the unleashing of God's wrath, since in verse 2 God specifically directs Ezekiel's preaching against Jerusalem (the site of the temple) and "the holy places" (various shrines and worship centers, all of them illegal according to the Mosaic Law [Deut 12]; cf. Amos 5:5–6; Hos. 4:15).

The "fire" and "sword" in this passage both symbolize divine judgment. "Fire is routinely a means of divine punishment in the Bible (Gen. 14:23–28; Deut. 28:24; 32:22; Rev. 20:15). "Sword" is a standard way of indicating "warfare," the actual means by which God decimated His nation in 586 B.C. in the events predicted in the present passage.

Ezekiel was to make quite a display of sighing (probably, more precisely, "groaning") in public so as to arouse the curiosity of his fellow exiles, who would ask the question predicted in 21:7. The answer was to be: "You will be discouraged and defeated in spirit—demoralized—when you find out that your homeland has been destroyed, Jerusalem razed, and the rest of your countrymen exiled. You'll groan for real then, like I'm making myself groan now."

There's a lot of bad news for Judah and Judeans in the Book of Ezekiel. God wants the exiles, to whom Ezekiel has especially been appointed a prophet, to be sure that they do not misunderstand His causing Judah to suffer its extinction as an independent nation. It must not happen that they miss what's going on, foolishly hoping that the present hard times were temporary and that Judah's fortunes would rise again soon. So through an allegory, its explanation, and a little bit of "acting" Ezekiel makes a deadly serious point. God will not be disobeyed forever. Sin has its inevitable consequences, and God is determined to enforce His covenant against those who sin against him. For Judah as a nation, it was too late now to repent. Only individuals could do that—and even the righteous individuals were going to be swept up in the bad events that were coming. Their eternal life might be secure personally, but their lives on earth had no hope of being spared from the brutality of the Babylonian invasion.

Likewise, Christians cannot assume that the righteous are to be protected from general disaster. All in Christ are safe from "the wrath to come." But by no means are all in Christ safe from the results of their wicked cultures. Warfare started by the wicked may kill many of the righteous. Disease started by perversion may spread to the innocent. Neglect of the poor hurts the righteous and the evil alike. The extermination of a nation for its sin may mean that the good minority has to die along with the bad majority. We thus hope in the Lord, as Ezekiel did, not for all things to go well in this life, but to be able to do all things faithfully so that we honor God in both bad times and good and recognize His sovereign right to punish groups, such as nations, in this world (cf. chap. 18).

CHAPTER TWELVE

The Sword

Ezekiel 21:8–32

All of the prophetic oracles in Ezekiel 21 are organized around the theme of "the sword," which, as we have seen already, is a way of saying "warfare." This manner of grouping separate oracles in a single location is called "catchword" ordering because it links one section to another by key vocabulary rather than by chronology. Thus the four sections of Chapter 21 may have been composed at different times and in an order different from that in which they now appear in the book. This does not necessarily mean that they were inspired at *widely* differing times, but perhaps within a year or two of each other rather than one right after the other.

There are a total of four "sword" passages in the chapter, as follows:

1. Explanation of the forest fire allegory (vv. 1–7)
2. God's sharp, polished sword of punishment (vv. 8–17)
3. The sword of the king of Babylon (vv. 18–27)
4. A sword against the nation of Ammon (vv. 28–32)

We have already commented on the first of these. The second and third do not so much introduce themes that are new to the Book of Ezekiel as they express expectations of God's judgment using new imagery and vocabulary. The fourth is noteworthy in part because it concludes the chapter with what is called "an oracle against a foreign nation," in this case Israel's old foe, Ammon. As such it is the first of the oracles against foreign nations in the book. Later (chaps. 25–32), the book contains a long string of such oracles, but this one is the earliest and is uniquely isolated in its present location, apparently because the catchword "sword" was taken to be a more significant factor in grouping Ezekiel's oracles in this instance than was the category (foreign nation oracle).

GOD'S SHARP, POLISHED SWORD OF PUNISHMENT

21:8 Again the word of the LORD came to me, saying,
   9 "Son of man, prophesy and say, 'Thus says the LORD!' Say:

> 'A sword, a sword is sharpened
> And also polished!
> 10 Sharpened to make a dreadful slaughter,
> Polished to flash like lightning!
> Should we then make mirth?
> It despises the scepter of My son,
> *As it does* all wood.
> 11 And He has given it to be polished,
> That it may be handled;
> This sword is sharpened, and it is polished
> To be given into the hand of the slayer.'
>
> 12 "Cry and wail, son of man;
> For it will be against My people,
> Against all the princes of Israel.
> Terrors including the sword will be against
>   My people;
> Therefore strike *your* thigh.
>
> 13 "Because *it is* a testing,
> And what if *the sword* despises even the
>   scepter?
> *The scepter* shall be no *more,*"

says the Lord GOD.

> 14 "You therefore, son of man, prophesy,
> And strike *your* hands together.
> The third time let the sword do double *damage.*
> It *is* the sword *that* slays,
> The sword that slays the great *men,*
> That enters their private chambers.
> 15 I have set the point of the sword against all
>   their gates,
> That the heart may melt and many may
>   stumble.

Ah! *It is* made bright;
It is grasped for slaughter:

16 "Swords at the ready!
Thrust right!
Set your blade!
Thrust left—
Wherever your edge is ordered!
17 "I also will beat My fists together,
And I will cause My fury to rest;
I, the LORD, have spoken."

Ezek. 21:8-17

"The Battle Hymn of the Republic" contains some words that express Christian hope in God's judgment against the forces of evil in a manner not gentle but decidedly combative:

Mine eyes have seen the glory of the coming of the
Lord,
He is trampling out the vintage where the grapes of
wrath are stored;
He has loosed the fateful lightning of His terrible
swift sword . . .

Likewise, Ezekiel's prophecy of God's sword is filled with violent descriptions and solemn language so that by its bluntness it might shock his audience into paying attention to what their complacency had been causing them to avoid thinking about: the ravages of war were coming soon, and many people would lose their lives.

Because of the considerable amount of language in the passage related to motion, it is quite possible that this prophecy was enacted as well as spoken. That is, Ezekiel may have done a "sword dance" while delivering this oracle, slashing the air, stabbing and swirling with a sword in his hand, as a dramatic reinforcement of the message he was imparting from God to the exiles. Additionally, it is possible that he sang this prophecy, judging from the poetic format and from the fact that ancient poetry was usually musical poetry and ancient prophets were almost always singers (cf. Exod. 15:1, 21; Judg. 5:1; 1 Sam. 10:5; Isa. 5:1-7).

We note that the sword in this passage takes on, as it were, a life of its own. Though it is actually only an object in the hand of the

197

prophet, it becomes in this song a thing unto itself, so that the focus of the passage is predominantly on the sword and only by implication on the one who holds it in the enactment prophecy—Ezekiel—and on the one whom Ezekiel represents—God.

Several verses in this passage contain difficult Hebrew; thus their interpretation is not completely certain. The end of verse 10 (*"It despises the scepter of My son, As it does all wood"*) is particularly strange in the Hebrew, and the translation rendered simply attempts to make sense of some of the Hebrew words as they stand in one Medieval text. It should not be taken as messianic or as even a trustworthy rendering of the original wording, which may have been largely lost through miscopying. However, the general point of this song is *not* hard to understand, fortunately: warfare is coming on Judah, and it will result in widespread bloodshed for the nation.

Verses 8–9a identify the passage as a separate, new oracle ("Again," however, is interpretive and does not reflect the Hebrew, which says simply, "The word of the Lord came to me"). It was given apparently verbatim to Ezekiel, who is repeating the song just as he heard it by inspiration. In verses 9–11 "polished" is a synonym for "sharpened." In other words, the sword is to be deadly sharp, not necessarily ceremonially pretty. The "lightning" of verse 10 refers to the glint of the shiny razorlike edge that will cut its deadly swath through those to be punished. The "slayer" is not identified in the passage, but it is clearly the enemy personified, in actual fact the Babylonian army.

Ezekiel, called here as elsewhere in the book "son of man" (v. 12), is commanded to wail just as he was to "sigh" in verse 6 as part of or perhaps a kind of intermission to the sword dance and song. Until this point in the passage it is possible to imagine some of Ezekiel's audience still wondering exactly whom the sword was intended to punish. But now they are told overtly: *"it will be against My people, Against all the princes of Israel."* Furthermore, the sword, that is, warfare, is only one of the "terrors" that God will be unleashing against Judah. Like any of the predictions of doom based on the Pentateuchal blessings and curses of Leviticus 26 and Deuteronomy 28–32, this passage intends that the hearer/reader should assume that "all these curses will come upon you and overtake you" (Deut. 28:15) as the point intended by the mention of any one or more of them (cf. Deut. 28:45, 61).

"Therefore strike your thigh" (v. 12) has somewhat the same meaning as would "Therefore beat your chest" or "Therefore hold your head in your hands." It is a way of telling the prophet to act out his distress visibly. Verse 13, again very hard to understand in the Hebrew, cannot be reliably translated into English, and the attempts in the various English versions are all guesses as to the real meaning. Verse 14, however, contains a clear command for the prophet to indicate how Judah will be greatly (doubly) punished, by clapping his hands twice and again brandishing the sword. "Double" punishment (cf. Isa. 40:2) reflects the standard multiple punishment type of curse predicted in the Mosaic Law (Lev. 26:21, 24). No one will be exempt from the slaughter of the enemy invasion of the land—not the wealthy in their protected houses (*"private chambers,"* v. 14) nor any of the Judean cities, no matter how well fortified (*"against all their gates,"* v. 15).

Fear (*"that the heart may melt"*) and helplessness (*"and many may stumble"*) are types of punishments also predicted by the Mosaic covenant sanctions (e.g., Deut. 28:65; Lev. 28:29). Their presence here in verse 15 intensifies the picture of misery caused by the coming conquest of Canaan.

With verses 16 and 17 the dance and song come to a close, again emphasizing the awful, unstoppable power of the sword (as the prophet jabs it right and left) and then of God's control of the whole process. Israel's Lord will clap His hands in heaven (a better rendering than "beat My fists together") and will be satisfied that His wrath has been carried out by the Babylonians (*"will cause my fury to rest"*).

Such a picture of brutal slaughter represents the reality that Ezekiel's contemporaries must learn to accept as the fate of their country and their fellow citizens. Their own exile several years before in 598 B.C. had been accomplished after a relatively bloodless siege of Jerusalem and quick surrender by the young king now also in exile (2 Kings 24:10-17). What was ahead for those who remained in Judah and Jerusalem was to be far worse. Yet the truth was painful, and the people's tendency to reject it required Ezekiel again and again to come back to them with various kinds of reminders that God's covenant guaranteed violent destruction for His nation if they did not keep His Law.

At least some of the problem that Ezekiel's audience had in accepting such a gloomy picture of the future can be traced to the natural religious tendency to think of God as kindly and thus not really capable of punishing people decisively. Why would God destroy His own beloved people in whom He had invested such time and effort since He brought them out of Egypt centuries before? Some of the problem lay also in people's natural, routine optimism. It is hard to imagine the country in which one grew up and enjoyed life in the past actually coming to an end, never again to be an independent nation, never again to have its own government and laws and economy and stable traditions. "Somehow, surely, we'll get through all this," thought the Judeans—both in exile and back in Judah. But it was not to be. God can be trusted to keep His promises. If He says that the punishment of those who reject Him is death, He means it. Wishful thinking will not change a thing.

THE SWORD OF THE KING OF BABYLON

21:18 The word of the LORD came to me again, saying:

19 "And son of man, appoint for yourself two ways for the sword of the king of Babylon to go; both of them shall go from the same land. Make a sign; put *it* at the head of the road to the city.

20 "Appoint a road for the sword to go to Rabbah of the Ammonites, and to Judah, into fortified Jerusalem.

21 "For the king of Babylon stands at the parting of the road, at the fork of the two roads, to use divination: he shakes the arrows, he consults the images, he looks at the liver.

22 "In his right hand is the divination for Jerusalem: to set up battering rams, to call for a slaughter, to lift the voice with shouting, to set battering rams against the gates, to heap up a *siege* mound, and to build a wall.

23 "And it will be to them like a false divination in the eyes of those who have sworn oaths with them; but he will bring their iniquity to remembrance, that they may be taken.

24 "Therefore thus says the Lord GOD: 'Because you have made your iniquity to be remembered, in that your transgressions are uncovered, so that in all your

doings your sins appear—because you have come to remembrance, you shall be taken in hand.

25 'Now to you, O profane, wicked prince of Israel, whose day has come, whose iniquity *shall* end,
26 'thus says the Lord GOD:

"Remove the turban, and take off the crown;
Nothing *shall remain* the same.
Exalt the humble, and humble the exalted.
27 Overthrown, overthrown,
I will make it overthrown!
It shall be no *longer*,
Until He comes whose right it is,
And I will give it to *Him*."'"

Ezek. 21:18–27

Another enactment prophecy now follows, continuing the use of the key vocabulary word of Chapter 21, "sword," and continuing also the theme of the imminent destruction of Judah and Jerusalem. It begins just as the previous passage did. It does not conclude sharply at verse 27 but passes easily into the Ammonite oracle of verses 28–32, which functions as a response to questions about the fate of Ammon raised by verse 20.

In the present oracle Ezekiel pretends to be the king of Babylon (Nebuchadnezzar, though he is not mentioned by name here) deciding at a northern crossroads (presumably in Syria) whether to direct his army to the east and attack Rabbah of the Ammonites or to direct them to the west and attack Jerusalem of Judah. He employs the various pagan techniques for decision making, and the supposed portents indicate that it is Jerusalem that he should go after. Jerusalem and Rabbah were roughly the same distance from certain crossroads points in Syria, so the choice between them was a logical one to make. Ezekiel then adds that the king's actions were really controlled by God, who is using the Babylonians as His instruments to punish a very guilty Judah. Finally, the end of the nation is portrayed by the possibly poetic imperative to the king of Judah (Zedekiah), called here as usual in Ezekiel the "prince," who must remove his royal crown, thus indicating Judah's loss of the kingship (i.e., its status as a nation) until a time in the future when a rightful king (i.e., the Messiah) will wear it again.

Verse 19 describes what Ezekiel had to do to set the visual scene for his enactment prophecy: create a semblance of a crossroads, complete with signs pointing to the roads leading west to Jerusalem and east to Rabbah (modern Amman, Jordan). The Hebrew text of verse 19 is very difficult but probably does not mean that Ezekiel was to place this pretend crossroads "at the head of the road to the city," that is, at the entrance to the exiles' town of Tel-Abib. Verse 20 suggests that Ezekiel used a sword to symbolize the army of the king of Babylon (rather than merely pointing with the sword as the king might do). "Fortified Jerusalem" emphasizes the fact that Jerusalem, in the time since the last siege in 598 B.C., had under the direction of Zedekiah, turned away from submission to Babylon and begun elaborate works of reinforcement so as to be able to withstand a siege. The exiles may have held hope that a well-prepared, heavily fortified Jerusalem could hold out this time, but their hope was obviously in vain.

The Babylonians relied enormously on divination—mechanical means of learning the will of the gods—as verse 21 suggests. Many of their divination texts survive on clay tablets, and these show that an elaborate system of rules of interpretation for various techniques of divination had been devised within their religion. The Hebrew words behind the translation "to use divination" in verse 21 may also be understood to mean "to cast lots," so that four objects used for divination are described in the verse: lots, arrows, images, and livers.

Lots were essentially dice either thrown on a surface or pulled out of a bag. What came "up" or was pulled out indicated a course of action, according to whatever the person seeking guidance had prayed that the values marked on the lots would stand for. Arrows were marked with options and placed in a quiver, out of which one would be drawn indicating a decision by the gods. These first two procedures were very much like drawing lots from a hat. "Images" were consulted in a way that we do not really understand, although some form of selection among various images (the Hebrew word is *teraphîm*, small idols or cult objects) must have been employed. Livers were examined by sacrificing an animal and examining the patterns of lines and swirls found on the animal's liver, according to standards established for each kind of pattern. The king himself might do some of the divination, although examination of livers (hepatoscopy) was normally the province of priestly specialists.

The "king's right hand" pulled the lot representing Jerusalem out of the bag (a description standing for the results of *all* the divination undertaken by the Babylonians), and therefore the battle plan will be formulated with Jerusalem as the target. No sigh of relief can be heard from Ezekiel's audience—and perhaps just the opposite, groans at hearing which choice the king would make. Verse 22 then goes on to describe how the enemy will mount the attack against Jerusalem. He will employ all the standard siege techniques of the day, including battering rams (for the wooden doors, the weakest part but also the most heavily defended part of the city), "siege mounds" (earthen ramps built up against the city wall in preparation for scaling it) and "walls" (better understood as siege works, i.e., various kinds of strong wooden and/or stone structures behind which the enemy could work, safe from the defenders' arrows, while building closer and closer to the city wall).

Verse 23, difficult in the Hebrew, may indicate something about how the Judahites will not believe that the king of Babylon would choose to attack them since they had in 598 B.C. sworn loyalty to him (an oath since broken; see 2 Chron. 36:13). It also seems to reflect either the king's or God's exposure of their sin (i.e., rebellion against the king or history of sin against the Lord). At any rate, verse 24 certainly places the ultimate blame on Israel's sins against the Lord, constant and severe so as to be unforgettable and unforgivable. There was nothing they could do to keep from being taken captive ("taken in hand").

King Zedekiah (598–586 B.C.), Judah's final king, is the "profane, wicked prince of Israel" of verse 25. His days are soon to be over, and he will have the kingship stripped from him, as symbolized by his loss of the royal turban and crown (v. 26; cf. 2 Kings 25:1–7). A major upheaval, a reversal of the status quo will take place when Jerusalem falls (*"Nothing shall remain the same. Exalt the humble, and humble the exalted,"* v. 26). In the Hebrew of verse 27, "overthrown" (better translated as "rubble" or "ruin," Hebrew, *ʿawwāh*) is repeated three times in a row, without any intervening words. This triple pattern is the ultimate Hebrew superlative (cf. "Holy, holy, holy" in Isa. 6:3 and "temple of the Lord, temple of the Lord, temple of the Lord" in Jer. 7:4), here emphasizing how completely Jerusalem will be destroyed (cf. 2 Kings 25:8–17; 2 Chron. 36:19). Verse 27 concludes with the prediction that the kingship will be restored only when Israel's rightful king is given the crown by God Himself. This true king, further portrayed by Ezekiel in Chapter 37ff., is the Davidic Messiah, not merely another Judean monarch. The hiatus of kingship after the fall of Jerusalem is a standard prophetic prediction (cf. Hos. 3:4–5) based on the Mosaic covenant curse of the captivity of the king (Deut. 28:36).

A SWORD AGAINST THE NATION OF AMMON

21:28 "And you, son of man, prophesy and say, 'Thus says the Lord GOD concerning the Ammonites and concerning their reproach,' and say:
'A sword, a sword *is* drawn,
Polished for slaughter,
For consuming, for flashing—
29 While they see false visions for you,
While they divine a lie to you,
To bring you on the necks of the wicked, the slain
Whose day has come,
Whose iniquity *shall* end.

30 'Return *it* to its sheath.
I will judge you
In the place where you were created,
In the land of your nativity.
31 I will pour out My indignation on you;
I will blow against you with the fire of My wrath,
And deliver you into the hands of brutal men
who are skillful to destroy.
32 You shall be fuel for the fire;
Your blood shall be in the midst of the land.
You shall not be remembered,
For I the LORD have spoken.'"
Ezek. 21:28–32

But what about the Ammonites? Many in Ezekiel's audience would surely be thinking about how Judah and Jerusalem would fare relative to other nations. Was the Babylonian invasion to touch them as well? Ezekiel's earlier words had shown the king of Babylon deciding by divination between an attack on Jerusalem and an attack on Ammon's capital, Rabbah. Did Ammon get off scot-free while Jerusalem suffered the ignominy of defeat and exile?

Thus this brief oracle against Ammon, of the type classified generally as an oracle against a foreign nation, addresses a specific question: what will happen to the enemies of Babylon? But it also addresses another, more general question: what will happen to Israel's enemies? Will the future hold promise for them while it holds distress for Israel? Most of the prophets are inspired to concern themselves with this question; in one way or another they all have something to say about God's judgment against those who have opposed His people over the years. The present oracle therefore begins to answer this concern, as Ezekiel 25–32 will do at length.

Oracles against foreign nations are an aspect of God's covenantal restoration promises to Israel (centrally located in Lev. 26:40–45 and Deut. 30:1–10). The reason for them is fairly simple: Israel's foes must decrease if Israel is to increase. The promise of power over enemies is a reversal of the curses of subjugation by enemies, as Deut. 30:7 says: "The Lord your God will put all these curses on your enemies." Such oracles, then, gave great reassurance to righteous Israelites that no matter how severe their own circumstances might be at the moment, the time was coming when the nation—in whatever future generation it might occur—would experience deliverance from exile and oppression and exaltation to God's favor and blessing. From the point of view of orthodox Israelites, the oracles against foreign nations were oracles of hope.

The oracle begins with rather typical wording commanding Ezekiel to speak what God has for the Israelites in exile to know about Ammon's future. Note that no Ammonites themselves would likely ever hear Ezekiel say these words. "Their reproach" (better translated "their insults") refers to the delight the Ammonites have always taken at any of Israel's misfortunes. On the history of Israelite-Ammonite hostility, see Deut. 23:3–6; Judg. 3:13; 10:6; 11; 1 Sam. 11:1–11; 12:12; 14:47; 2 Chron. 20:1–30; etc.

The vocabulary of verse 28b parallels closely that of verses 9–11, while verse 29 talks partly of divination. This time the focus of the oracle is on the false predictions of Ammonite diviners and prophets of success as opposed to the failure in war that will in fact produce great slaughter in Ammon. It is useless for the Ammonites to fight, so they are told to "return" their sword "to its sheath" in preparation for the Lord's judgment, which cannot be resisted (v. 30). Ammon will be judged in its own land (*In the place where you were created, in the land of your nativity*"), that is, it will be invaded and conquered, not merely defeated in some military campaign on foreign soil. The "fire" of the Lord's "wrath" reflects the covenant curse predictions of fire as symbolic of divine judgment (e.g., Deut. 28:24; 32:22) as before in Ezekiel and other prophets. "Brutal men skillful to destroy" are, of course, the Babylonian armies of conquest.

Ammon's eradication is the subject of three metaphors in verse 32: being burned up, having their blood shed, and not being remembered. Thus, in contrast to the fate of Israel, which will be decimated and exiled, destroyed as an independent nation but not wiped out, with a promised future of hope, the Ammonites can look forward only to annihilation.

"For I the Lord have spoken" ends this little prophecy against Ammon, and its full force can be appreciated in hindsight. The Lord's word is certain to be kept. The Babylonian king had many superstitious devices for prediction of the future, as did the Ammonites. Heterodox Israelites had any number of false prophets to whom they could listen. But those who knew and trusted in the Lord alone had the true word. Ammon faded from world history just as this oracle predicts. Israel, for a while in the form of an ethnic nation and now in the form of the church (Gal. 3:29), has not only not faded but has increased miraculously just as God promised. Oblivion was the fate of the one; eternal glory the promise of God to the other.

CHAPTER THIRTEEN

Jerusalem the Bloody

Ezekiel 22:1–31

"Jerusalem the Golden" was a popular song in Israel during the 1967 Seven-Day War. That war brought control of all of the city into the hands of the Israelis, something that had been a political and military goal of most Zionists for years.

"Jerusalem the Bloody" is Ezekiel's inspired chapter from around 590 B.C. or slightly later predicting the loss of biblical Jerusalem. The city will not be occupied or controlled by the Judeans, but just the opposite—it will be captured and its population deported so that it will lie destroyed and abandoned, as a result of the disgusting injustices that its inhabitants routinely committed within its walls.

There are three sections to the chapter:

- A Catalog of Israel's Bloody Sins (vv. 1–16)
- The Furnace as a Symbol of Jerusalem's Fate (vv. 17–22)
- The Complicity of Societal Leaders and People in Sin (vv. 23–31)

It is difficult to tell whether these three sections were originally preached independently and then grouped together on the basis of their common theme (the wickedness of Jerusalem just prior to its fall) or whether they may have been intended from the outset to be a unit, preached on a single occasion. It does not matter which of these options we choose, since our ability to appreciate and learn from the inspired final format of the chapter remains high in either case.

A CATALOG OF SINS

22:1 Moreover the word of the LORD came to me, saying,

2 "Now, son of man, will you judge, will you judge the bloody city? Yes, show her all her abominations!

3 "Then say, 'Thus says the Lord GOD: "The city sheds blood in her own midst, that her time may come; and she makes idols within herself to defile herself.

4 "You have become guilty by the blood which you have shed, and have defiled yourself with the idols which you have made. You have caused your days to draw near, and have come to *the end of* your years; therefore I have made you a reproach to the nations, and a mockery to all countries.

5 "*Those* near and *those* far from you will mock you as infamous *and* full of tumult.

6 "Look, the princes of Israel: each one has used his power to shed blood in you.

7 "In you they have made light of father and mother; in your midst they have oppressed the stranger; in you they have mistreated the fatherless and the widow.

8 "You have despised My holy things and profaned My Sabbaths.

9 "In you are men who slander to cause bloodshed; in you are those who eat on the mountains; in your midst they commit lewdness.

10 "In you men uncover their fathers' nakedness; in you they violate women who are set apart during their impurity.

11 "One commits abomination with his neighbor's wife; another lewdly defiles his daughter-in-law; and another in you violates his sister, his father's daughter.

12 "In you they take bribes to shed blood; you take usury and increase; you have made profit from your neighbors by extortion, and have forgotten Me," says the Lord GOD.

13 "Behold, therefore, I beat My fists at the dishonest profit which you have made, and at the bloodshed which has been in your midst.

14 "Can your heart endure, or can your hands remain strong, in the days when I shall deal with you? I, the LORD, have spoken, and will do *it*.

15 "I will scatter you among the nations, disperse

you throughout the countries, and remove your filthiness completely from you.
16 "You shall defile yourself in the sight of the nations; then you shall know that I *am* the LORD.""'
Ezek. 22:1-16

Seven times in this prophecy the words "blood" or "bloodshed"
(Hebrew, *dām* and *dāmîm*) occur as characterizing the crimes against
God's covenant that had been occurring routinely in Jerusalem.
These words have a special idiomatic meaning in Hebrew that their
usual translation does not entirely convey in English. They connote
"harm" or "hurt," and that is what much of verses 1–16 is about: the
harm or hurt done by people in power in Jerusalem (and by implication elsewhere in Judah) to those who have no power, such as the
poor, the sick, the uneducated, etc. By extension, "blood" and "bloodshed" also come to mean in Hebrew anything "violent" or just simply
"vile," even if it does not actually involve causing *physical* harm to
another person.

The list of sins that Ezekiel has been inspired to include here is
perhaps the longest such list anywhere in the Bible. Moving from
the general to the more specific and from the religious to the secular,
it covers a wide range of societal and personal abominations. It was
not the practice in Old Testament times to cite laws in legal cases,
even though legal cases were decided on the basis of laws well
known to all. Ezekiel therefore does not cite verbatim the various
laws from the Pentateuch that were broken by the practices ongoing
in Jerusalem, but those laws were nevertheless well available to
those who wanted to keep them, and thus the disobedience of Jerusalem's citizenry was completely without excuse.

The basic format of verses 1–16 is essentially legal-covenantal;
that is, it centers around the citation of evidence that God's
covenant people (specifically, the holy city) have broken His
covenant, and then describes briefly and clearly the punishment
(exile) that will result. Jerusalem is addressed throughout in the
second person feminine singular (cities, like the Hebrew word for
city, 'îr, are usually feminine in Hebrew). This direct address gives
the passage the overtone of a court scene in which the defendant is
being found guilty by a judge. The passage begins as if Ezekiel is to
be the judge (v. 2; cf. 20:4 and 23:36), but in fact the "I" and "My" of

the passage are quickly seen to be the Lord, who is, of course, Jerusalem's real judge—Ezekiel being merely His spokesperson, who like a prosecuting attorney lists the evidence of wrongdoing on the part of the defendant.

Verse 1 begins in standard Ezekiel fashion with a wording that is identical to the verses that introduce sections of the preceding chapter (21:1, 8, 18) and to the wording of verses 17 and 23 in the present chapter. Thus "Moreover" is not warranted here. Ezekiel receives in verse 2 the repeated, therefore stressed, command to "judge" Jerusalem, "showing" (making known to her, confronting her with) her abominations, that is, those things she has done that are offensive to God. This refers to the general, overall pattern of sins prevailing in the city. It does not imply that the entire city did such things together or that all citizens did them. Biblical punishments for corporate sins presume that some of the innocent would have to suffer along with the guilty (see Ezekiel 18).

"Sheds blood in her own midst" (v. 3) connotes internal violence/ crime rather than warfare or capital punishment or any such conceivably legitimate violence. *"That her time may come"* indicates expectation of the end of Jerusalem in the same way that one's "time" in modern English idiom can refer to the time when one will die. Idolatry, virtually the most blatant means of breaking God's Law, was also a routine practice in the bloody city (cf. Ezekiel 8). Verse 4's prediction of *reproach* and *mockery* is a way of talking about conquest and exile. These fates are what will cause other nations, even distant ones (v. 5), to dismiss Israel as a nothing, a nation of the past but not the present. Jerusalem's past kings, some of whom are alluded to opaquely in Chapter 19 and here called "princes," were leaders in the city's vile practices, again here called "bloodshed." It is important to note that the complicity of the national leadership was virtually always essential for full-blown waywardness to flourish.

Verses 7–12 list many sins of the population (who are now in view rather than merely the kings) including: dishonoring parents (failing to care for them in their old age, a violation of the Fifth Commandment, carrying the penalty of exile: cf. Exod. 20:12); mistreating resident aliens (cf. Lev. 19:33) and orphans and widows (Exod. 22:22); violating the Sabbath (v. 8; cf. Exod. 20:8–11); slander (v. 9; cf. Lev. 19:16); eating on mountains (i.e., eating sacrifices at various high places instead of at the only authorized location, the temple; cf. Deut. 12:5–18); lewdness (Leviticus 18); uncovering parents' nakedness and violating women during their period (Lev. 18:7–8, 19, respectively); adultery and incest (v. 11; cf. Exod. 20:14 and Lev. 18:6ff.); and bribery, usury, and extortion (Lev. 6:1–5 and Exod. 22:25). All these sins, standing as they do as samples of the many more that were actually done in Jerusalem, mean that the people *"have forgotten Me"* (v. 12), an idiomatic way of saying "have rejected My covenant" (cf. Deut. 4:23).

Verse 6 begins with the Hebrew *hinnēh*, "Behold" (translated here "Look"), and verse 13 starts with the same word. The one introduces the catalog of sins; the other introduces the judgment sentence of God against those who committed them. God will, with a gesture indicating scorn and rebuke—clapping His hands together ("beat My fists") as one would do to get someone to stop doing something objectionable—put a stop to Jerusalem's sins. How? By overcoming the city's own stubbornness (v. 14) and exiling its population; that is, purification by deportation (v. 15). Let the wicked city be exposed *"in the sight of the nations"* (v. 16; a standard metaphor for exile)! Then God's sovereignty over them will be evident, and they will *"know that I am the Lord"* (v. 16).

In Zeph. 3:1–13 God sounds a similar warning to Jerusalem. For the many sins of its inhabitants, particularly the misuse and abuse of others for personal pleasure or gain, Jerusalem will be depopulated and exiled, so that a new people may one day come to live in her. Her new population will consist of people of faith who respond to the Lord's call back from exile, people who are pure, instead of "rebellious and defiled." We must realize that Jerusalem deserved exactly what it got. There was nothing arbitrary or capricious in the Lord's actions against "the place where He caused His name to dwell (Deuteronomy 12; 1 Kings 8:29). Sin must be punished. That is the way that God has ordered things. And nothing can prevent the punishment of sin. It can be transferred, but it cannot be overlooked. To Christ our sins were transferred because of our faith in Him, but they were hardly overlooked—they were punished severely on the cross. Jerusalem's sins were committed by a people who were, for the most part, not faithful. Having rejected the Lord, they were themselves ripe to be rejected.

IN THE FURNACE

22:17 The word of the LORD came to me, saying,

18 "Son of man, the house of Israel has become dross to Me; they *are* all bronze, tin, iron, and lead, in the midst of a furnace; they have become dross from silver.

19 "Therefore thus says the Lord GOD: 'Because you have all become dross, therefore behold, I will gather you into the midst of Jerusalem.

20 'As *men* gather silver, bronze, iron, lead, and tin into the midst of a furnace, to blow fire on it, to melt *it;* so I will gather *you* in My anger and in My fury, and I will leave *you there* and melt you.

21 'Yes, I will gather you and blow on you with the fire of My wrath, and you shall be melted in its midst.

22 'As silver is melted in the midst of a furnace, so shall you be melted in its midst; then you shall know that I, the LORD, have poured out My fury on you.'"

Ezek. 22:17–22

There are three major aspects to punishment for sin: retribution, correction, and purification. Retribution is giving back or paying back what is deserved by someone who has done wrong. The desire that a person or group simply should not be able to get away with doing evil is answered by retribution. Retributive justice is a part of God's plan; He punishes evil first because it is evil, even before whatever other purposes He may have in punishing. Correction is the process of preventing a person or group from committing a sin again. It addresses the general tendency more than the particular original action, with the understanding that a sin once committed might be repeated, or that a sin once committed may lead to the willingness to commit others. Punishment can be part of the process of correction.

Finally, punishment can involve purification. Purification is analogous to correction but goes somewhat beyond it. Purification is the removal of the factor or faction that was responsible for a crime in the first place. To purify a person or group from the opportunity to sin, however, may require some fairly drastic action, such as getting rid of something or someone. Perhaps it is necessary to destroy

212

something that made the sin possible. Perhaps it is even necessary to destroy within a group the people who habitually were committing the sin that requires punishing. In Israel's case, it was necessary to destroy the headquarters city (Jerusalem) and most of the population of the nation in order to bring about the purification that God desired.

Comparing His covenant people to metal ore needing purification and His punishments (conquest, exile, and their accompanying destruction) to a metal refining furnace, God reveals through His prophet a way of thinking about the disasters that were coming on Israel in the near future. The language of verses 17–22 is metaphorical; the message is symbolic of a fearsome reality soon to envelop the nation.

A number of other passages in the prophetical books also use the image of a refiner's furnace to speak of God's process of purification (Isa. 1:22–25; 48:10; Jer. 6:27–30; 9:7; Zech. 13:0; Mal. 3:2–4). Most of these, however, emphasize at least in part the positive value of the furnace: it produces a pure end product that is much better than the impure beginning product, getting rid of undesirable by-products in the process. Ezek. 22:17–22, however, puts much more attention on the uselessness of the by-products: Israel being like junk metals of little value to the refiner who is seeking pure silver as the product of His furnace. From the point of view of the overall message of the book, God's refining Israel by fire will indeed produce a purified people to serve Him in the last days, and that concept is undoubtedly present here if only implicitly. The overt focus of the present passage, however, is on the worthlessness of the nation, needing and deserving to be burned away—punished in retribution as well as drastic purification because there is little redeeming value in them.

After a standard introduction (v. 17 and "Son of Man" in v. 18), the Lord identifies His current relationship to Israel. Their sins have made them like the undesirable by-products in a refining furnace. The refiner wants silver; the other metals are of no interest to him (v. 18). This is a way of saying that Israel did not measure up to the Lord's standards. They are only a disappointing imitation of the high-quality product for which He sought.

Since the nation is thus inferior to what it should have been, He will gather them *into the midst of Jerusalem* (v. 19). This is a way of predicting the swelling of Jerusalem with refugees once the invasion had begun. The great walled city of Zion was the place where everyone who could do so gathered as a last hope for refuge after the Babylonians had captured all the rest of the countryside of Judah. Here Jerusalem is likened to the furnace into which a refiner puts metals to heat them until the by-products melt away. By this analogy, silver per se is no longer the focus; the focus has been transferred to the process by which various metals, whatever they might be, are melted in a furnace in the course of refining. God will make the people's stay in the city under siege as "hot" for them as a smelting furnace is hot for the metals in it. Enduring the siege of Jerusalem will be a terrible thing (vv. 20–21). This description echoes the lengthy descriptions of the misery of being besieged by foreign enemies as divine punishment (Deut. 28:52–57). There the horrors of fear, starvation, burning thirst, cannibalism, and other distresses are held before the people as a warning of what would come to Israel if it did not keep God's Law. Now, through Ezekiel, God is telling the people that He is about to do just the sort of thing He had predicted.

In a refiner's furnace bellows were used to blow extra air on the fire so as to make it super hot. Likewise, the fire of God's wrath would soon enough blow on the inhabitants of Jerusalem, a metaphorical picture of the terrors of the deadly siege to come (v. 21). The people's inability to resist God's wrath is the subject, then, of verse 22, and the melting of silver is once again the image used to symbolize the process that the people of Israel are about to go through. Silver is what Israel should have been (cf. v. 18) and perhaps, implicitly, what it once was but is no longer. By "heating" the people in the midst of the "furnace" of besieged Jerusalem, God will destroy them.

Once again Ezekiel has given us a vivid prediction of the fall of Judah and Jerusalem, the main theme of Chapters 1–24. Once again the judgment of God on His people as a result of their sins is described, so that the false hopes and deluded complacency of those in Ezekiel's circle of fellow exiles would be firmly checked. Dashing hopes about Jerusalem in the 590s and 580s was a painful but necessary part of the prophet's ministry. Of course, sometimes what a prophet must do is raise hopes. When Jerusalem fell after a long and costly siege, the tendency to lose hope was then plenty strong enough in the survivors, and it became necessary to console them— increase their hope instead of countering it (chaps. 35–37). But, depending on the circumstance, there can be such a thing as too much hope just as well as too little, and false hope is perhaps always of the "too much" variety. God's people need no false hope. They need to avoid fooling themselves about God's kindliness and softness on sin. He does punish. He insists on retributive justice. He does not overlook sin.

When hope is needed, God is its giver. When false hopes must be dashed, He is no less faithful, no less true.

FIVE CLASSES OF CORRUPTION

22:23 And the word of the LORD came to me, saying,

24 "Son of man, say to her: 'You *are* a land that is not cleansed or rained on in the day of indignation.'

25 "The conspiracy of her prophets in her midst is like a roaring lion tearing the prey; they have devoured people; they have taken treasure and precious things; they have made many widows in her midst.

26 "Her priests have violated My law and profaned My holy things; they have not distinguished between the holy and unholy, nor have they made known *the difference* between the unclean and the clean; and they have hidden their eyes from My Sabbaths, so that I am profaned among them.

27 "Her princes in her midst *are* like wolves tearing the prey, to shed blood, to destroy people, and to get dishonest gain.

28 "Her prophets plastered them with untempered *mortar*, seeing false visions, and divining lies for them, saying, 'Thus says the Lord GOD,' when the LORD had not spoken.

29 "The people of the land have used oppressions, committed robbery, and mistreated the poor and needy; and they wrongfully oppress the stranger.

30 "So I sought for a man among them who would make a wall, and stand in the gap before Me on behalf of the land, that I should not destroy it; but I found no one.

31 "Therefore I have poured out My indignation on them; I have consumed them with the fire of My

wrath; and I have recompensed their deeds on their
own heads," says the Lord GOD.

Ezek. 22:23–31

Often the prophets are inspired to compose attacks on the leadership of Israelite society. The reason for this phenomenon is clear
enough: the nation could never have become sufficiently corrupt to
merit the outpouring of God's destructive wrath unless the societal
leadership had helped the process along.

All societies have leaders. The categories of leadership may vary
somewhat from people to people, and the relative influence of one
kind of leadership or another may change with the generations. But
large groups of people do not just coalesce into a nation. They respond to the call of leaders—however chosen or appointed—to join
together. And they remain together and act together, to whatever
extent they are in fact unified, not because their minds automatically
work in harmony, but because they are willing to heed the words
and examples of those among them who stand out as leaders. Following leaders is a natural human tendency. It can result in much good
or much evil, depending on the qualities of the leaders.

In the Israel of Bible times, at least eight kinds of leaders had significant influence in the society: kings, government officials
(including military leaders), priests, prophets, prominent landholders
(frequently but not always called "people of the land" in the Old Testament), clan chieftains, the wealthy, and wise men. Of this group,
five are mentioned in the present passage: kings (v. 25; "prophets" is not the original wording—see below), priests (v. 26), officials
(v. 27, called "princes" here), prophets (v. 28), and prominent landholders ("people of the land," v. 29). Such a collusion of five major
groups of societal leaders had to be overwhelming in its influence for
evil in Israel. These groups, with all their cumulative clout, were responsible for the degeneration of Israelite values and the general dis-
regard for God's covenant law that prevailed in Ezekiel's time.

Following a standard introduction (vv. 23–24a), Ezekiel is commanded to address Israel as a land devoid of God's blessing and instead doomed to undergo His wrath. The Septuagint's reading,
"watered or rained on" rather than "cleansed or rained on," reflects
even more strongly the point of verse 24: in relatively dry Palestine
rain meant blessing—it would be hard for anyone to imagine too

216

much of it since they were all so used to so little of it. The withhold-
ing of rain, then, is a curse from the Lord (cf. Lev. 26:19; 28:22–24),
and it is what Judah may expect to experience on the "day of indignation," that is, the day when Yahweh brings Judah to an end. Drought,
like any of the curse types, stands for all of the others. They all individually and collectively mean "disaster."

Who has led astray the Lord's covenant people? First to be mentioned are the kings. While the reading of "prophets" is based on
the Masoretic text (Hebrew *nebi›im*), the reading "princes" (Hebrew
nesi›im), Ezekiel's standard word for kings, is indicated in the Septuagint (prophets are covered in v. 28). Israel's kings have, in the
process of making themselves rich, gouged and impoverished people, even to the point of causing the death of many (*"they have made
many widows in her midst,"* v. 25). Some kings, of course, put people
to death to get what they wanted from them (cf. 1 Kings
2:25, 34, 46; 21:1–14). But what may be referred to here is probably
the more common result of excessive taxation imposed by the king.
The king eventually foreclosed on those unable to pay, putting
heads of households in debtors' prisons where they died, leaving
their wives widowed.

The nation's sin was also partly the responsibility of the priests
(v. 26). It was their covenantal obligation to keep the nation pure in
worship and general behavior by teaching the people what the Law
required, including holy living (as defined, for example, in Leviticus
19–25) and proper ceremony (including prevention of improper
worship and other "unclean" practices as defined, e.g., in Leviticus
11–15 and Numbers 19), and to maintain obedience to the laws that
protected people from exploitation, such as the Sabbath law.

Government officials (v. 27) were supposed to protect people, the
first function of government being the establishment of fair order for
all (cf. Romans 13). When officials used their power—including the
power to collect taxes and fines and to make rulings in property
disputes—to make money for themselves at the expense of others,
they incurred the Lord's wrath.

False prophets outnumbered true prophets during most of Israel's
history (cf. 1 Kings 18:22; Jer. 23:9–40), and true prophets were
often suppressed because their message was one of judgment rather
than complacency (e.g., Amos 2:12; 7:10–17). Thus verse 28 says
that the prophets "whitewash" (*"plastered them with untempered*

mortar," v. 28) the sins of the various leaders, instead of condemning them as they ought.

The "people of the land" (i.e., prominent landowners, Hebrew *'am
ha'āreṣ*) act comparably to the kings and officials. They use their
money, power, and influence to get richer and more powerful at the
expense of the poor and needy—the little people of the nation (v.
29). Their methods included lending at high interest rates to people
desperate for money to survive, selling some of them into slavery to
retire their debts, forcing people into serf labor conditions to pay
back indebtedness, selling inferior quality food and merchandise to
people too poor and hungry to bargain for anything better, and so
forth (cf. Amos 2:6–8; 5:11; 8:5–6).

Imagining a city wall as an object lesson, the Lord wishes for
someone whose righteous behavior would make him or her a "wall
builder" against Judah's destruction—a bulwark against its sins
(v. 30). But there was no one. Such a statement is hyperbole, purposeful exaggeration for effect. It hardly means that no one at all in
Jerusalem in the early 580s was righteous. Indeed, Ezekiel's fellow
orthodox prophet Jeremiah was in the city at that time faithfully
preaching the word of the Lord, and friends of his (such as Baruch)
were helping disseminate it. It means rather that there were so few
among the people who were righteous that the net effect was as if
no one at all cared about God's Will.

Therefore God's judgment was underway (v. 31). What they deserved they would get. His long-predicted punishments would now
be unleashed. The language is technically past tense (the so-called
prophetic perfect, indicating that the future had already been determined), but the full effect was yet to be felt. It would be consuming,
however, when it came.

All groups, all professions have a role in keeping a society good. If
even *one* class will resist firmly the tendency to slide toward corruption, dishonesty, exploitation, and immorality that is natural in all
human cultures, there will be the possibility of reform and renewal.
But if they all give in, there is very little likelihood that isolated
voices calling for repentance will be heard or taken seriously. The
responsibility for obedience to God is not something, therefore, that
can be delegated to others or assigned to a particular leadership class
while the rest of us do nothing. If government fails, we must not. If

church leadership fails, we must not. If prominent citizens allow immorality to continue unchecked, we must nevertheless resist. God was not looking for everyone to be perfect in Judah (v. 30). He was looking for some—enough to make a difference—to do His Will. The few should therefore always do their best to influence the many and never give up doing what is right simply because they are outnumbered. The few should also not forget that God reserves the right to punish the many and that all may have to be caught up in and endure the effects of that punishment.

CHAPTER FOURTEEN

Two Nymphomaniac Sister Cities

Ezekiel 23:1–49

This chapter contains the most graphic language in the Bible in reference to sexual imagery. For that reason it requires extreme care in teaching and preaching. Indeed, in Jewish tradition this chapter was among the last to be taught to young men studying for the rabbinate because of its potential to offend.

This potential to offend is, of course, its very point. The chapter is an allegory about the offensive disobedience of the Northern Kingdom (Israel) and the Southern Kingdom (Judah), with regard to their lack of trust in the Lord and their willingness to seek peace, security, and religion from the great international powers of the day, Assyria and Babylon. Behind the allegory is the common metaphorical language of ancient international treaties and of Israelite prophets that likened unfaithfulness to the Lord to adultery and, more commonly, prostitution (Hebrew, *zānāh*, vv. 3, 7, 8, etc.). Israel—either North or South or both—could be imagined as the wife of the Lord, cheating on Him with other gods and/or nations by her political and religious infidelity. To a considerable extent Chapter 23 follows and complements Chapter 16, although it does not seem to be the case that these two chapters are merely parts of what was once a single long allegory. More likely, at various times and perhaps even for various audiences, two separate but comparable prophecies were delivered about Israel's history.

It is important to appreciate the fact that God expected His people to depend on Him alone for their political security among the nations as well as for their worship. He was their national God as well as the personal God of each Israelite. They were forbidden to try to obtain by diplomacy what He had promised to give them if they would have faith in Him. Thus, just as they were not to depend in any way on other gods, so they were not to depend in any way on other nations. The prophets frequently attacked the tendency in both north and south to try to find stability, prestige, security or strength by alliances with other nations (e.g., Hos. 7:8–12; Isa. 30:1–5; Jer. 42:18–22). Unfortunately, the temptations were irresistible to Israel. What others had, she wanted. What others did, she copied.

The allegory is an easy one to follow (as compared to, e.g., chap. 19) because the figures are clearly identified throughout. It must be remembered that Samaria and Jerusalem (v. 4) were not merely major cities but *capital* cities of the Northern and Southern kingdoms respectively, and thus the decisions and actions of those capital cities controlled and represented the nations they governed. Capitals are often virtually identified with their nations in both Bible and modern times. The fact that cities are often called "daughter" in the poetic language of the Old Testament (e.g., Ps. 9:14; Lam. 1:6; Mic. 4:8) may also have been a factor in the language used in the allegory.

There are five major sections to the chapter, as follows:

Introduction (vv. 1–4)
Oholah's Story (vv. 6–10)
Oholibah's Story (vv. 11–21)
Judgment on Oholibah (vv. 22–35)
Judgment on Both Sisters (vv. 36–49)

For convenience we have combined the first two sections (vv. 1–10) in our analysis.

INTRODUCTION AND OHOLAH'S (SAMARIA'S) STORY

23:1 The word of the LORD came again to me, saying:

2 "Son of man, there were two women,
The daughters of one mother.
3 They committed harlotry in Egypt,
They committed harlotry in their youth;
Their breasts were there embraced,
Their virgin bosom was there pressed.
4 Their names: Oholah the elder and Oholibah
her sister;

They were Mine,
And they bore sons and daughters.
As for their names,
Samaria *is* Oholah, and Jerusalem *is* Oholibah.

5 "Oholah played the harlot even though she
      was Mine;
   And she lusted for her lovers, the neighboring
      Assyrians,
6 *Who were* clothed in purple,
   Captains and rulers,
   All of them desirable young men,
   Horsemen riding on horses.
7 Thus she committed her harlotry with them,
   All of them choice men of Assyria;
   And with all for whom she lusted,
   With all their idols, she defiled herself.
8 She has never given up her harlotry *brought*
      from Egypt,
   For in her youth they had lain with her,
   Pressed her virgin bosom,
   And poured out their immorality upon her.

9 "Therefore I have delivered her
   Into the hand of her lovers,
   Into the hand of the Assyrians,
   For whom she lusted.
10 They uncovered her nakedness,
   Took away her sons and daughters,
   And slew her with the sword;
   She became a byword among women,
   For they had executed judgment on her."

Ezek. 23:1–10

Infidelity in marriage was taken very seriously in ancient Israel. Adultery and prostitution were both odious to God and punishable by death, as several passages in Leviticus (19:29; 20:10; 21:9) and Deuteronomy (22:21–22; 23:17) indicate. The story of this chapter is about two adulteresses/prostitutes who betray God Himself, their symbolic husband, and whose guilt is thus unquestionably deserving of ultimate punishment.

The allegory of the sister cities begins by emphasizing their long history of promiscuity and identifying them as Samaria and

Jerusalem. Then the story of Samaria is told first, Oholah (Samaria) being the elder sister in the story. Historically, Jerusalem was founded by not later than 4000 B.C., according to carbon-14 dating, while Samaria was built more than three millennia later by the Israelite king, Omri (885–880 B.C.; 1 Kings 16:21–28). Thus Jerusalem was much older than Samaria. But as Samaria "died" first (destroyed by the Assyrians in 722 B.C. as opposed to Jerusalem's "death" at the hands of the Babylonians in 586 B.C.) and because Samaria embraced full idolatry and international dependencies far earlier than Jerusalem, it is treated in the story as if it were "older."

From the point of view of Ezekiel's audience, Samaria was a city of the past, destroyed about 133 years earlier. Jerusalem, on the other hand, was still standing, still magnificent, still hoping to withstand the Babylonians. Accordingly, the allegory rather quickly completes its review of Samaria's "life," including her judgment, in six verses (vv. 5–10) before turning in far more detail (vv. 11–35, i.e., twenty-five verses) to the city that held the real interest of Ezekiel's contemporaries, Jerusalem.

"*Daughters of one mother*" (v. 2) underlines Israel and Judah's common origin as a unified nation. Prostitution ("harlotry") in Egypt and "*their youth*" (v. 3) refers to the nation's lack of faithfulness during its idolatrous years in Egypt and the wilderness of the Sinai Peninsula as described in Exodus and Numbers particularly (cf. Ezek. 20:5–21). They were "*Mine,*" that is, the nations belonged to the Lord, presumably as His wives (v. 4). Neither Ezekiel nor anyone in his audience would have assumed that this imagery of the Lord's two wives meant that God favored polygamy. Polygamy was never outlawed in Bible times, and they would have known many men who had more than one wife (as Jacob, their ancestor had). The allegory simply makes use of that familiarity with polygamy to symbolize the history of a divided nation. "*Sons and daughters*" (v. 4) are the towns, cities, and populations that increased in number as God blessed His people in the promised land.

Oholah means "tent" and Oholibah means "my tent within her." Both names may have some overtones of the tabernacle where God "met" with His people in the wilderness, but both are also typical sorts of Hebrew names, useful for the story.

Verses 5–7 allude to (Northern) Israel's relationship with Assyria, whose wealth, culture, styles, and religion immensely impressed

223

Israelites and whom they copied heavily (cf. 1 Kings 15:19; Hos. 7:8–13; Zeph. 1:8; Isaiah 39). Israel was continuing her habits learned in Egypt (v. 8), habits that were never really abandoned.

"Therefore" in verse 9 introduces God's sentence of judgment (cf. Hos. 2:6, 9, 14). What Israel (Samaria) loved, she will get—but in a way she didn't want. She was trying to "live with" the Assyrians, and now she will live with them—in their own land, as their slaves in exile and as corpses in the graves their conquest created. Their "judgment" was the defeat and destruction imposed on them by Assyria (v. 10).

OHOLIBAH'S STORY

23:11 "Now although her sister Oholibah saw *this,* she became more corrupt in her lust than she, and in her harlotry more corrupt than her sister's harlotry.

12 "She lusted for the neighboring Assyrians,
Captains and rulers,
Clothed most gorgeously,
Horsemen riding on horses,
All of them desirable young men.
13 Then I saw that she was defiled;
Both *took* the same way.
14 But she increased her harlotry;
She looked at men portrayed on the wall,
Images of Chaldeans portrayed in vermilion,
15 Girded with belts around their waists,
Flowing turbans on their heads,
All of them looking like captains,
In the manner of the Babylonians of Chaldea,
The land of their nativity.
16 As soon as her eyes saw them,
She lusted for them
And sent messengers to them in Chaldea.

17 "Then the Babylonians came to her, into the
bed of love,
And they defiled her with their immorality;
So she was defiled by them, and alienated
herself from them.
18 She revealed her harlotry and uncovered her
nakedness.

Then I alienated Myself from her,
As I had alienated Myself from her sister.

19 "Yet she multiplied her harlotry
In calling to remembrance the days of her
youth,
When she had played the harlot in the land of
Egypt.
20 For she lusted for her paramours,
Whose flesh *is like* the flesh of donkeys,
And whose issue *is like* the issue of horses.
21 Thus you called to remembrance the lewdness
of your youth,
When the Egyptians pressed your bosom
Because of your youthful breasts."

Ezek. 23:11–21

Most people are proud of their native country. There is a natural tendency for people to look upon and identify with their own nation's history as a positive one, remembering the greatness of the past and—perhaps conveniently—forgetting those eras and actions that should bring shame. Few nations have a history free of guilt, but few people dwell on those aspects of their national story that are not so positive.

We can therefore imagine the Israelites in exile thinking this same way. Undoubtedly they saw the bright past—the conquest of Canaan, the international greatness of Israel under David and Solomon, the territorial expansions and military victories under kings like Jeroboam II in the North (793–753 B.C.) and Josiah in the South (640–609 B.C.), and so on. Their thinking probably did not dwell on the sorry story of the unresolved, ongoing North-South civil war after the death of Solomon or the increasing social injustice and class stratifications of the era of the kingship in both North and South, or the way that both Israel and Judah had been manipulated by the superpowers of the day, Assyria, Babylon, and Egypt.

Since Ezekiel's fellow exiles in Tel-Abib were Judeans, they would take pride in the fact that the Davidic dynasty still ruled in Judah in the person of Zedekiah, that any power attacking Judah would have to contend with a well-fortified Jerusalem, and that their continuity of traditions with the past was intact, since unlike now-destroyed

Samaria, their nation was still going strong, still enjoying the well-deserved (of course) blessing of the Lord.

All this was wrong. Judah was odious to the Lord. Jerusalem was a disgusting city. They should have been abjectly ashamed of themselves rather than proud—praying for forgiveness rather than congratulating themselves on their fine lineage. Thus when the allegory of Chapter 23 gets around to the story of Oholibah/Jerusalem, it gives no encouragement at all to the audience. The character they identify with is even worse than the character they've just been hearing about (Oholah, i.e., Samaria).

Verses 11–13 draw our attention to the fact that Jerusalem was even more enamored of Assyrian beliefs and power than Samaria had been. Of course, it was Assyria who destroyed Samaria in 722 B.C. and nearly finished off Jerusalem in 701 B.C. (2 Kings 18). But Assyria was impressive in spite of its role as conqueror and oppressor. Compared to Assyria's wealth and military might, Judah looked puny. Her jealous fascination with a greater nation is thus portrayed here as the lust of a young woman for dashing, handsome men.

With verse 14 the focus of Jerusalem's attention turns to the "Chaldeans," another name for the Babylonians. This reflects the fall of the Assyrian Empire to Babylon in 611–605 B.C. After 605, Babylon was the superpower to admire, and the Judeans wasted no time in shifting their awe. The mention in verse 14 of pictures of Babylonian military men on *the wall* stems from the fact that much visual art of Bible times was painted and/or carved on walls. Where exactly in Jerusalem such wall paintings might have existed (such as the palace?) is not known, if the expression is to be taken literally instead of figuratively (cf., however, chap. 8, where temple wall sculptures and paintings were worshiped). *"Messengers . . . to . . . Chaldea"* (v. 16) refers to various attempts to align Judah with Babylon, including the tragic military campaign of good King Josiah against Assyria's ally and Babylon's enemy, Egypt, in 609 B.C. in which Josiah lost his life (2 Kings 23:29–30). This pro-Babylonian sacrificial action on Judah's part produced no lasting gratitude from Babylon, and soon enough Babylon's empire threatened Judah, and Judah "was alienated from them," and thus from God (v. 18).

Right to the end, however (vv. 19–21)—and the end was very near, now, in the months approaching 586 B.C. when Jerusalem would fall—Jerusalem kept tying to solve her own problems by international diplomacy, making deals with Babylon, or Egypt, or whomever (2 Kings 23:29–24:20). These frantic attempts at arrangements to keep the nation free and independent all ended in failure, but nevertheless raised false hopes. Besides, Judah could not have made peace with Babylon or Egypt in her last days except by promising these powers great concessions in return—huge taxes, large numbers of Judeans to serve in the Babylonian or Egyptian armies, and payments of products and services to an extent that would have impoverished the land. Jerusalem's problem was that it sought help from nations (v. 20) and followed their ways as she had tended to do from her earliest days (v. 21), instead of depending on the Lord alone and following His laws. Ignoring the Law and the prophets (e.g., Isaiah 2; Jeremiah 3), she went her own way and earned God's judgment as described in the next portion of the chapter.

JUDGMENT ON OHOLIBAH

23:22 "Therefore, Oholibah, thus says the Lord GOD:

'Behold, I will stir up your lovers against you,
From whom you have alienated yourself,
And I will bring them against you from every
    side:
23 The Babylonians,
All the Chaldeans,
Pekod, Shoa, Koa,
All the Assyrians with them,
All of them desirable young men,
Governors and rulers,
Captains and men of renown,
All of them riding on horses.
24 And they shall come against you
With chariots, wagons, and war-horses,
With a horde of people.
They shall array against you
Buckler, shield, and helmet all around.

'I will delegate judgment to them,
And they shall judge you according to their
    judgments.

227

25 I will set My jealousy against you,
And they shall deal furiously with you;
They shall remove your nose and your ears,
And your remnant shall fall by the sword;
They shall take your sons and your daughters,
And your remnant shall be devoured by fire.
26 They shall also strip you of your clothes
And take away your beautiful jewelry.

27 'Thus I will make you cease your lewdness
    and your harlotry
Brought from the land of Egypt,
So that you will not lift your eyes to them,
Nor remember Egypt anymore.'

28 "For thus says the Lord GOD: 'Surely I will deliver you into the hand of those you hate, into the
hand *of those* from whom you alienated yourself.
29 They will deal hatefully with you, take away all
you have worked for, and leave you naked and bare.
The nakedness of your harlotry shall be uncovered,
both your lewdness and your harlotry.
30 'I will do these *things* to you because you have
gone as a harlot after the Gentiles, because you
have become defiled by their idols.
31 'You have walked in the way of your sister;
therefore I will put her cup in your hand.'

32 "Thus says the Lord GOD:

'You shall drink of your sister's cup,
The deep and wide one;
You shall be laughed to scorn
And held in derision;
It contains much.
33 You will be filled with drunkenness and sorrow,
The cup of horror and desolation,
The cup of your sister Samaria.
34 You shall drink and drain it,
You shall break its shards,
And tear at your own breasts;
For I have spoken,'
Says the Lord GOD.

35 "Therefore thus says the Lord GOD:

'Because you have forgotten Me and cast Me
    behind your back,
Therefore you shall bear the *penalty*
Of your lewdness and your harlotry.'"
                                        Ezek. 23:22–35

In the previous part of the allegory Oholibah/Jerusalem had been unable to restrain herself from taking lovers (depending on foreign nations for political security and religion). Now God will give her what she wanted, but not in the way that she wanted it. Previously she went after lovers. Now He will cause her lovers to come to her— but as rapists, not as paramours.

By foreign invasion and conquest—the very thing that Judah's cozying up to Assyria, Babylon, and Egypt had been designed to avoid—God would teach Judah a hard lesson. It was the same thing He had done to Samaria a century and a half earlier, yet Jerusalem had not learned from it. She was still imitating her "older" sister's "prostitution" and would have to be forcibly prevented from it. Thus the pain that Oholah had borne, Oholibah would now experience in even greater measure. The destruction and exile of the North in 722 B.C., awful as it was, would be surpassed by the destruction and exile of the South in 586 B.C.

"Therefore" (Hebrew, *lākēn,* v. 22) is legal language, a standard way of introducing the judgment sentence in a prophetic passage dealing with God's judgment for breaking His Law. The lovers Judah came to hate (*"from whom you have alienated yourself"*) will serve as God's instruments of punishment. In verse 23, the Babylonians and Chaldeans are two names for the same nation. Pekod, Shoa, and Koa were Aramean tribes, small nations east of the Tigris that were now part of the Babylonian Empire and whose populations presumably served in considerable numbers in the Babylonian army. Ezekiel sometimes mentions such obscure, distant lands and peoples in order to convey to Israel the idea that "the whole world" is or will be against them (cf. chaps. 38 and 39). In the conquering Babylonian army will also be Assyrians—the group that conquered Samaria— when the foe takes Jerusalem captive. The enemies' harsh "justice" will constitute God's delegated judgment (v. 24). It will include mutilation (*"They shall remove* [cut off] *your nose and your ears"*), death (*"your remnant shall fall by the sword"*), enslavement (*"They shall take*

229

your sons and your daughters"), and the burning of the city (*"devoured by fire,"* v. 25). Nothing of her former glory, symbolized here by clothes and jewelry, will be left, and thereby Jerusalem will learn not to think about "Egypt"—her idolatrous, dependent origins—any more (vv. 26–27).

Delivered to her enemies (exiled, v. 28), Jerusalem will be "naked." Hebrew *gālāh* means either "naked" or "exiled/exposed," and thus it and its synonyms are used often in the prophets as metaphors for exile, as here in verse 29. Judah's harlotry (promiscuous unfaithfulness, v. 30) requires that she drink from Samaria's "cup," that is, her same fate (v. 31). The short cup poem that follows (vv. 32–34) is a type of taunt song or mocking song (cf. Isa. 37:22–29; Ezek. 29:3–5) used to "rub in" the reality of Judah's coming fate. Indeed, near the end of the song, the people's coming misery is described in the symbolism of the cup's breaking into pieces and lacerating (tearing up, rather than "tearing at") Oholibah's breasts. Everything she has done will backfire on her. Her sins will produce not pleasure, only hurt. She should have loved the Lord only (v. 35), but having rejected Him and gone into prostitution, she will, having been tried for harlotry and found guilty, be punished to the full extent of the Law.

JUDGMENT ON BOTH SISTERS

23:36 The LORD also said to me: "Son of man, will you judge Oholah and Oholibah? Then declare to them their abominations.

37 "For they have committed adultery, and blood *is* on their hands. They have committed adultery with their idols, and even sacrificed their sons whom they bore to Me, passing them through *the fire,* to devour *them.*

38 "Moreover they have done this to Me: They have defiled My sanctuary on the same day and profaned My Sabbaths.

39 "For after they had slain their children for their idols, on the same day they came into My sanctuary to profane it; and indeed thus they have done in the midst of My house.

40 "Furthermore you sent for men to come from afar, to whom a messenger *was* sent; and there they came. And you washed yourself for them, painted your eyes, and adorned yourself with ornaments.

41 "You sat on a stately couch, with a table prepared before it, on which you had set My incense and My oil.

42 "The sound of a carefree multitude *was* with her, and Sabeans *were* brought from the wilderness with men of the common sort, who put bracelets on their wrists and beautiful crowns on their heads.

43 "Then I said concerning *her who had grown* old in adulteries, 'Will they commit harlotry with her now, and she *with them?*'

44 "Yet they went in to her, as men go in to a woman who plays the harlot; thus they went in to Oholah and Oholibah, the lewd women.

45 "But righteous men will judge them after the manner of adulteresses, and after the manner of women who shed blood, because they *are* adulteresses, and blood *is* on their hands.

46 "For thus says the Lord GOD: 'Bring up an assembly against them, give them up to trouble and plunder.

47 'The assembly shall stone them with stones and execute them with their swords; they shall slay their sons and their daughters, and burn their houses with fire.

48 'Thus I will cause lewdness to cease from the land, that all women may be taught not to practice your lewdness.

49 'They shall repay you for your lewdness, and you shall pay for your idolatrous sins. Then you shall know that I *am* the Lord GOD.'"

Ezek. 23:36–49

This final section of the allegory of the two sister cities expands upon what has been covered before and also goes on to describe the calculated, stubborn, incorrigible infidelity of the two nations and their final destruction.

While prostitution (harlotry) is still mentioned in the passage (vv. 43–44), the term "adultery" (Hebrew, *nā'ap*) is even more prominent, and thus the well-known penalty for adultery, stoning, is described in verse 47. Prostitution by an unmarried woman would still be a crime. But prostitution by a married woman is also *adultery on her part against her husband*, and this situation is analogous to what Israel had done to the Lord. She was not an unattached, loose-living nation. She was the Lord's bride. Her unfaithfulness grieved Him directly and incurred His wrath.

This final section of the chapter, then, brings us to the point in the story when the sisters are imagined still to be practicing their prostitution after countless encounters with lovers willing to use them, still trying to attract lovers who will pay for their favors, and fully guilty—many times over—of the death they deserve.

In one sense, the allegory saves the worst for last. It specifies that Israel's idolatry included child sacrifice (v. 37) and the desecration of the temple (v. 38), charges not yet mentioned in the chapter. Moreover, it stresses the extent to which Israel—North and South—had aggressively sought the services of foreign nations (vv. 40–44) rather than merely acceding to diplomatic overtures from them.

On the challenge to Ezekiel to pronounce God's judgment against His wayward people (v. 36), see 22:2. Samaria and Jerusalem were not only idolaters but violent ones (v. 37). In both places child sacrifice—viewed in those days as the ultimate act of self-denying worship of a god or goddess—had been practiced. This involved killing and then burning (*"passing them through the fire"*) infants and young children as a gift to the gods, that is, the shedding of the *"blood"* that was now *"on their hands."*

The defiling of God's sanctuary (v. 38) is already well documented in Ezekiel 8 with regard to Jerusalem and those who worshiped there during the reign of Zedekiah (598–587 B.C.). It was a practice with a long history behind it (cf. 2 Kings 23:4–14). Samaria, by reason of its practice of worship at the illegal sanctuary of Bethel, automatically defiled God's true sanctuary (e.g., 1 Kings 12:25–24). Because holy days included child sacrifice and worship that was idolatrous, the Lord's Sabbaths were also profaned in both the North and the South (vv. 38–39; cf. 2 Kings 21:2–7).

Verses 40–44 depict symbolically Israel's history of self-destructive international diplomacy, like a prostitute sending out invitations and making herself attractive to men (cf. Jer. 4:30; 2 Kings 9:30). In verse 41 *"My incense and My oil"* symbolizes the blessings of God being used wrongly—incense and oil being the prostitute's toiletries which she used to make herself attractive to her lovers even though they had been obtained with her husband's money. In verse 42 "Sabeans" reflects a Hebrew original (from the root *sb'*) better rendered "drunks"—that is, drunken, dirty tent dwellers, caravaneers (*"from the wilderness"*), and other lowlife (*"men of the common sort"*). These brought jewelry as payment for their illicit sex. Although the prostitute is "worn out" or "old" (Hebrew, *bālāh*, v. 43) lovers still want her (nations still see Israel as a valuable conquest).

The evidence is complete, Samaria and Jerusalem are obviously guilty, and now the judgment sentence can be pronounced (vv. 45–49). Adultery and murder (v. 45) deserve the penalties stated in the Mosaic Law: death. *"Trouble* (better understood as "terror") *and plunder"* (v. 46) are words particularly associated with conquest by an enemy, and thus are standard types of covenant punishments (on terror, cf. Lev. 26:16–17, Deut. 28:66–67, 32:25; on plunder, cf. Deut. 28:31). On stoning (v. 47) as a penalty for both idolatry, child sacrifice, and adultery, cf. Deut. 13:10; 17:5; 22:21, 24; and Lev. 20:2. Israel will be made an example of (v. 48) so that later generations and other nations (*"other women,"* v. 48) will not copy her. The Lord's covenant will thus be enforced (*"They will know that I am the Lord God"*).

Chapter 23 was preached by Ezekiel to correct an illusion, the idea that Israel deserved to continue to enjoy the favor of God. This illustrates an interesting human phenomenon: the tendency to believe better of ourselves than is warranted. Surveys consistently show that most people have a rather high view of themselves. The vast majority of high school students, for example, routinely indicate in response to the question "Are your more or less popular than average?" that they are more popular than average. Clearly, everybody cannot be more popular than average, but just as clearly, everybody can *feel* that he or she is.

The Israelites shared that human tendency to think themselves pretty good and thus undoubtedly acceptable to God. Many in Ezekiel's audience were surely offended by the allegory of Chapter 23, and not merely because of its graphic language. They would have been annoyed to hear the prophet condemning them and their history in such strong terms. After all, anything Israel—whether North or South, Samaria or Jerusalem—might have done wrong, other nations had done more wrong. Why shouldn't the Lord continue to love His people? Even if they committed some idolatry, didn't the rest of the nations all worship idolatrously? And if Israel had now and again captured some territory from its neighbors, would that be worth even mentioning compared to the huge conquests of the imperialist nations of the day, or even of most of Israel's own immediate neighbor states? And why should the Lord be so put out by a little international diplomacy? Wasn't it just plain good stewardship of national political and economic resources to take care to see that the nation would not allow itself to be pushed around in the community of nations?

In their own eyes they weren't wrong. In God's eyes, they were not only wrong, but completely disgusting! They were His special covenant people blessed with all sorts of advantages and opportunities to be a light to the nations. Instead they had completely forgotten Him (v. 35). They were His bride sworn to love only Him. Instead, they cheated on Him constantly. To themselves, they seemed attractive. To Him, they were lewd. So no matter what they thought of themselves, God knew what they were and what they deserved.

CHAPTER FIFTEEN

The Cooking Pot

Ezekiel 24:1–14

SYMBOL OF THE COOKING POT

24:1 Again, in the ninth year, in the tenth month, on the tenth *day* of the month, the word of the LORD came to me, saying,

2 "Son of man, write down the name of the day, this very day—the king of Babylon started his siege against Jerusalem this very day.

3 "And utter a parable to the rebellious house, and say to them, 'Thus says the Lord GOD:

"Put on a pot, set *it* on,
And also pour water into it.
4 Gather pieces *of meat* in it,
Every good piece,
The thigh and the shoulder.
Fill *it* with choice cuts;
5 Take the choice of the flock.
Also pile *fuel* bones under it,
Make it boil well,
And let the cuts simmer in it."

6 'Therefore thus says the Lord GOD:

"Woe to the bloody city,
To the pot whose scum *is* in it,
And whose scum is not gone from it!
Bring it out piece by piece,
On which no lot has fallen.
7 For her blood is in her midst;
She set it on top of a rock;
She did not pour it on the ground,
To cover it with dust.

8 That it may raise up fury and take vengeance,
I have set her blood on top of a rock,
That it may not be covered."

9 'Therefore thus says the Lord GOD:

"Woe to the bloody city!
I too will make the pyre great.

10 Heap on the wood,
Kindle the fire;
Cook the meat well,
Mix in the spices,
And let the cuts be burned up.

11 "Then set the pot empty on the coals,
That it may become hot and its bronze may
    burn,
That its filthiness may be melted in it,
That its scum may be consumed.

12 She has grown weary with lies,
And her great scum has not gone from her.
Let her scum *be* in the fire!

13 In your filthiness *is* lewdness.
Because I have cleansed you, and you were not
    cleansed,
You will not be cleansed of your filthiness
    anymore,
Till I have caused My fury to rest upon you.

14 I, the LORD, have spoken *it*;
It shall come to pass, and I will do *it*;
I will not hold back,
Nor will I spare,
Nor will I relent;
According to your ways
And according to your deeds
They will judge you,"
Says the Lord GOD.'"

Ezek. 24:1–14

Ezek. 11:3 quoted a saying popular in Jerusalem in the years after the first Judean exile of 598 B.C. and before the great exile of 586 B.C.: "This is the pot and we are the meat." Although the translation here is inconsistent with previous passages (the Hebrew *sîr* is rendered as "cauldron" in chap. 11 and as "pot" here), the connection between the

236

two passages is evident in the original. In 11:3 the people cited a "parable" that gave them comfort: they were the choice meat intended for the pot (Jerusalem), as opposed to the discarded by-products (those taken into exile). Now Ezekiel will utter a "parable" based upon the same sort of imagery, once again (cf. 11:11) condemning rather than reassuring Jerusalem.

Here in Chapter 24 the cooking pot imagery again envisions Jerusalem as the pot and its population as the meat. But God has turned the people's saying 180 degrees around. They are now described as meat to be left in the pot until it burns away, not meat that "belongs" where it is (the nondeported people who have taken over in Jerusalem following 598 B.C.) as opposed to the cull that is thrown away (i.e., the exiles like Ezekiel who have been deported from Jerusalem). The pot of Chapter 24 is not the protective environment metaphorically connoted by the people's saying; it is the place of destruction. In effect, if they are the "meat," then God is the "heat." Relentlessly He will apply His heat to them until they are burned away.

Verses 3b–5 contain the initial directions for an enactment prophecy, suggesting that Ezekiel, in some public place, put a pot over wood and boiled meat in it for a long time. Verses 10–11 then contain the second set of instructions, that is, to cook the meat until only scum was left and then to put the scummy pot directly on the hot coals so as to burn the scum to ashes. These ashes could then be shaken out, leaving a clean pot again—much in the way that a self-cleaning oven simply uses intense heat to char the scum on the oven walls into ash that is then easily swept out of the oven. Those who watched Ezekiel do all this would naturally ask what he was doing (as they had learned to do over the years of his many enactment prophecies) and would then hear the words of verses 6–9 and 12–14 as explanation of the symbolic meaning of his actions.

In the previous twenty-three chapters the main theme of the preaching that God commanded Ezekiel to undertake was the coming fall of Jerusalem. The previous twelve chapters often dealt with objections that might be raised to God's allowing this to happen. Now the end has begun. The Babylonians have laid siege to Jerusalem, and it is only a matter of time until the city is in their hands.

In 24:1–2, *"the ninth year . . . tenth month . . . tenth day"* (cf. 2 Kings 25:1; Jer. 52:4) computes to 15 January 588 B.C., the famous date for the beginning of the siege of Jerusalem, a date that later was included among the annual days of fasting and mourning observed by the exiles (Zech. 8:19). The "rebellious house" (v. 3, i.e., the Israelites, especially the exiled Judeans) will hear one more condemnation of their rebellion and prediction of their punishment via a "parable" (allegory).

Ezekiel must prepare to boil "choice cuts" (vv. 3a–4) to symbolize the chosen people still in the city. He must put plenty of wood under it (Hebrew, 'ēṣîm, wood, rather than 'amāṣîm, "bones," a copy error, as "wood" in v. 10 confirms). Thus a hot, long-burning fire can cook ("simmer") the meat to a residue (v. 5). The symbolic action is prelude to a woe oracle (vv. 6–9, 12–14) in which the death of Jerusalem is predicted. Jerusalem is called "the bloody city" (v. 6) just as the oppressive, imperialistic, pagan Nineveh was in Nah. 3:1. "Bring it out piece by piece" (v. 6) seems to anticipate the forced depopulation of the city after the siege has ended.

The bloody city has shed blood that still cries out for retribution ("on top of a rock," i.e., not sunk into the ground, vv. 7–8; cf. Gen. 4:10). In other words, Jerusalem's crimes cannot go unpunished, cannot be hidden (cf. Hos. 7:1–2). Since conquerors in ancient times routinely burned captured enemy cities (Josh. 6:24; 8:28; cf. Amos 1:4, 7, 10, 12, etc.), this is what Jerusalem, too, can expect (v. 9) from its conqueror, the Lord, through the agency of His servants, the Babylonians.

In verses 10–11 Ezekiel receives instructions to burn the scummy pot clean of its filth, by heating the pot ("bronze") directly over the coals. This foreshadows Jerusalem's punishment (vv. 12–13): the city scummy with lies (a synecdoche for all its disobedience) will have its sinfulness burned away and will be purged as the Babylonians empty the city of its population and set fire to it. This will be the means of God's imposing His fury (vv. 13–14) from which He will not relent. Jerusalem will thus get what it deserves, just as Ezekiel has been preaching for two dozen chapters. "They" (the city's deeds) "will judge you" is a way of saying exactly that.

A cooking pot is a common thing, and cooking meat in a pot is a simple matter. There is nothing complicated or extraordinary in Ezekiel's enactment prophecy. Likewise there was nothing really complex or extraordinary in what God was doing to Jerusalem. He was going to punish it in accordance with His covenant promises to punish His people if they sinned against Him. The people of Judah crammed into the closed-up city now surrounded by the Babylonians undoubtedly thought otherwise. Their emotions and plans were probably quite complex, involving all sorts of popular misconceptions about God's mercy and love, fueled by the encouraging preaching of the many false prophets in the city. Most of them must have thought that they were quite extraordinary, as their "we are the meat" boast (cf. 11:3) suggested. They were, after all, in the only city in all of Syria-Palestine that had successfully held out against the Assyrians 113 years earlier (2 Kings 18:17–19:36). They were, moreover, inside the city God had specially chosen (Deut. 12:5, 11) and where David had been promised a "son to rule forever" (2 Sam. 11–16). But they misunderstood their own importance and their wishful thinking blinded them to their coming fate. Misapplying the promises of God, they conveniently ignored their own sin and thought themselves essential to God's plans. Little did they realize how odious they had become in God's eyes. They who were once choice meat had become scum.

CHAPTER SIXTEEN

Ezekiel's Wife Dies

Ezekiel 24:15–27

THE PROPHET'S WIFE DIES

24:15 Also the word of the LORD came to me, saying,

16 "Son of man, behold, I take away from you the desire of your eyes with one stroke; yet you shall neither mourn nor weep, nor shall your tears run down.

17 "Sigh in silence, make no mourning for the dead; bind your turban on your head, and put your sandals on your feet; do not cover *your* lips, and do not eat man's bread *of sorrow.*"

18 So I spoke to the people in the morning, and at evening my wife died; and the next morning I did as I was commanded.

19 And the people said to me, "Will you not tell us what these *things signify* to us, that you behave so?"

20 Then I answered them, "The word of the LORD came to me, saying,

21 'Speak to the house of Israel, "Thus says the Lord GOD: 'Behold, I will profane My sanctuary, your arrogant boast, the desire of your eyes, the delight of your soul; and your sons and daughters whom you left behind shall fall by the sword.

22 'And you shall do as I have done; you shall not cover *your* lips nor eat man's bread *of sorrow.*

23 'Your turbans shall be on your heads and your sandals on your feet; you shall neither mourn nor weep, but you shall pine away in your iniquities and mourn with one another.

24 'Thus Ezekiel is a sign to you; according to all

that he has done you shall do; and when this comes,
you shall know that I *am* the Lord GOD.'"

25 'And you, son of man—*will it* not *be* in the day
when I take from them their stronghold, their joy and
their glory, the desire of their eyes, and that on which
they set their minds, their sons and their daughters:

26 'on that day one who escapes will come to you
to let *you* hear *it* with *your* ears;

27 'on that day your mouth will be opened to him
who has escaped; you shall speak and no longer be
mute. Thus you will be a sign to them, and they shall
know that I *am* the LORD.'"

Ezek. 24:15-27

Of all the things that Israelite prophets were called by God to do,
one of the hardest and saddest tasks was assigned to Ezekiel: he had
to incorporate his wife's death and his time of mourning for her into
an enactment prophecy.

By no means did this signify that God was insensitive to Ezekiel's
grief. Just the opposite is true. God's own grief at having to punish
His people and reject the sanctuary where they worshiped Him
would have been a mirror for Ezekiel's actions, and the Israelites'
grief at being driven from the home they loved was parallel to it as
well. Here, however, God's grief is not actually mentioned—the focus is limited exclusively to the grief of Ezekiel and the coming grief
of the people of Israel.

The passage has a simple structure which may be outlined as
follows:

- Command to Ezekiel not to mourn publicly (vv. 15–17)
- Ezekiel complies and people wonder why (vv. 18–19)
- Explanation: Jerusalem will "die," too (vv. 20–24)
- Command to Ezekiel to speak freely once Jerusalem has fallen
  (vv. 25–27)

After a standard introduction signifying the beginning of a new
section of prophecy (v. 15), Ezekiel hears that his wife is about to die.
It is possible that she had been sick for some time, but it is also possible that she contracted an illness suddenly. God, however, knew that
she was dying and informed Ezekiel that He would *"take away"* the

"desire of your eyes." It is, of course God who "takes away" in death. ("The Lord gives, and the Lord takes away. Blessed be the name of the Lord.") Noteworthy here is the reference to Ezekiel's personal emotion in the simple phrase "the desire of your eyes." Most prophetical books say nothing about their author's emotions or personal life, and Ezekiel is of this type. Indeed, here alone in the book do we learn that Ezekiel was married. He probably also had children, but these are not mentioned either since it is not the purpose of the book to provide biography about its human author. God knew that Ezekiel loved his wife and also that Ezekiel loved Him. He could thus count on the prophet to obey His command not to mourn her death publicly so that the divine message about Jerusalem would be understood by those to whom Ezekiel preached.

Five of the typical actions of ancient Israelite mourning are alluded to in verse 17: sighing (cf. Mal. 2:13; Isa. 24:7), removing one's turban (cf. Isa. 61:10; Ezekiel, a priest, routinely wore a turban; cf. Exod. 39:28), removing one's sandals (cf. 2 Sam. 15:30), covering one's lips (cf. Mic. 3:7), and eating special mourning bread (cf. Hos. 9:4). Note that nothing in the Old Testament commands that such mourning practices occur—they were simply practices that developed in Israelite culture as a means of showing grief at personal loss.

Verse 18 seems to indicate that Ezekiel, on the basis of God's sure word, foretold his wife's death on the morning of the day she died. It may also mean, however, that he preached or taught that morning as if nothing was amiss, even though he knew that his wife would die, as part of the process of obeying God and not indicating publicly his grief. When people noticed that he was not mourning for his wife (v. 19), they naturally asked him why, and this provided opportunity, as planned, for him to give the prophetic word God wanted the people to hear (vv. 20 ff.). Israel's delight, Jerusalem (called *"My sanctuary"* but signifying the city and not merely the temple; cf. Exod. 15:17; Isa. 63:18) will be "profaned," that is, ruined and made unsuitable. God's destruction of the people's sanctuary is one of the types of covenant punishments predicted at Mount Sinai (Lev. 26:31) for national disobedience. It was now occurring.

But why did God not want the Israelites to mourn the fall of Jerusalem? Why did He tell them to do just as Ezekiel had done, undertaking to display no outward signs of their grieving (vv. 22–23)? Some commentators have speculated that what God was saying to them was a sort of cynical command: "Go ahead—don't mourn. You're all so selfish that you don't care enough about what is happening to Jerusalem to mourn its passing." In other words, the command not to mourn was a critical exposure of the people's callousness in sin. Others have concluded that the prohibition of mourning was based on the severity of the event. The fall of Jerusalem ended Israel's history as an independent nation and introduced the exile, the long-predicted and long-feared (by righteous people) rejection of the nation by its God. This was such a horrendous event—indeed the nation's greatest disaster by far—that any form of ritual public mourning would be embarrassingly inadequate to reflect the magnitude of the tragedy and, thus, no mourning at all would be preferable. A third option, however, is more likely. Mourning was not appropriate in cases of capital punishment. When God commanded that someone was to die for his crimes, it was not expected that people would regret carrying out the punishment by mourning the dead. Many passages in the Pentateuch call for capital punishment (e.g., Exodus 21; Leviticus 20, 24; Numbers 35; Deuteronomy 24), but none demand mourning for the person executed for his crimes.

Thus while Ezekiel had every right to mourn for his wife whose life God had not ended in wrath, the Israelites had no right to mourn for Jerusalem whose existence was being symbolically brought to an end most certainly in wrath. Ezekiel's wife died of illness. Jerusalem died because of its sins against God. Ezekiel had a right to mourn his undeserved personal loss but did not. The Israelites had no right to mourn for their well-deserved national loss and could not (v. 24).

The final three verses of this section (vv. 25–27) bring to a conclusion a long, hard period in Ezekiel's ministry. The time is now late 597 B.C., and the fall of Jerusalem in the first month of 586 B.C. is not far away. His public ministry had begun about six years prior in 593 B.C. (1:2), and during those six years he had not been allowed to speak freely with people about anything he wanted to say. In other words, he had been forbidden by God to engage in small talk or routine conversation, his speech instead being dedicated to speaking God's words exclusively (3:26).

But now that era has ended, and when Ezekiel soon learns, as he and others surely will from one of the survivors (v. 26), that Jerusalem has fallen, he will be freed from his imposed silence to speak conversationally with the survivor (v. 27). Again, this will be a kind of enactment prophecy: Ezekiel's return to normal talking will be a signal that the six-year ministry of predicting doom is finished and a new ministry—which we will learn in subsequent chapters is a ministry of hope—will commence. Excessive silence on the part of an individual can signal many things, among them lack of joy or hope. That was part of its intent in 3:26. Now that joy and hope can return, Ezekiel can speak freely once again.

Obeying God's command not to mourn for his wife could not have been an easy thing for Ezekiel. Not to mourn dead relatives was almost surely considered the equivalent of an insult by the ancient Israelites. His beloved was dead, and he was showing no sadness. The one who had loved, supported, and cared for him for years was suddenly taken from him, and he couldn't show her the final respect that was considered fitting evidence of love and gratitude.

Nevertheless neither Ezekiel nor any of his countrymen could afford to concentrate on their individual, personal interests at this time. A much greater matter was at hand, a great turning point in history: the end of the covenant people in the promised land and the destruction of Jerusalem, God's chosen city. People had to come to their senses and leave behind less significant things. The work of God was what they needed to focus on, and they needed to follow Ezekiel's example not to let anything intervene to keep them from that. Jesus, in a somewhat similar context where paying attention to God's plan needed to be elevated above otherwise legitimate personal concerns said "Let the dead bury their dead" (Matt. 8:22). This wasn't cruel, insensitive advice. It was necessary. Our personal concerns must not keep us from responding to God's direction. What's happening in His kingdom doesn't wait for us to get around to doing something about it. What He has ordained in history can't depend upon our deciding whether it is convenient for us to pay attention to it.

Oracles against Foreign Nations

Ezekiel 25:1–32:32

CHAPTER SEVENTEEN

Four Bad Neighbors

Ezekiel 25:1–17

A second major division of the book begins at this point. The first twenty-four chapters were concerned primarily with prophecies about the fall of Jerusalem. Now come eight chapters (25–32) of oracles against foreign nations, of which the brief oracle against the Ammonites at the end of Chapter 21 was an early sample.

In Chapters 25–32 we encounter oracles against sixteen nations, all of whom in one way or another had incurred God's wrath, and all of whom therefore receive in these chapters a prediction of God's judgment against them. The nations are:

> Ammon (25:1–7)
> Moab (25:8–11)
> Edom (25:11–14; 32:29)
> Philistia (25:15–17)
> Tyre (26:1–28:19)
> Sidon (28:20–24)
> Egypt (29:1–32:21; 32:31–32)
> Ethiopia [Nubia] (30:4–9)
> Libya (30:4–9)
> Lydia (30:4–9)
> "All the mingled people" [Arabia] (30:4–9)
> Chub (30:4–9)
> Assyria (32:22–23)
> Elam (33:24–26)
> Meshech (33:26–28)
> Tubal (33:26–28)

247

It is noteworthy that one major nation is not mentioned in these chapters: Babylon. This is not because Babylon was good in God's eyes in contrast to the others. It is rather that a common denominator among the oracles against foreign nations in Chapters 25–32 is that Babylon will conquer them all. Judah, in other words, was hardly the only nation that was to feel the destructive might of the invading Babylonian armies. The entire Fertile Crescent was to fall—or already had fallen—to the Babylonian onslaught. These chapters thus give us, geographically speaking, a broad, wide-angle view of the massive influence of the Neo-Babylonian Empire and its impact on the ancient biblical world.

Some of these sixteen nations are mentioned only in passing (e.g., four of Egypt's allies are listed in 30:5), while others are prominently addressed (especially Tyre in chaps. 26–28 and Egypt in chaps. 29–32). The amount of space dedicated to each nation does not necessarily correspond to its importance in the ancient Near East of the sixth century B.C. Rather, by concentrating at length on two nations, mentioning at more-average length several others, and touching only briefly on yet others, this section of prophecies gives a realistic *overall* impression of both thoroughness and variety. In one way or another, all the nations will fall to Babylon, and none—large or small—will escape the general upheaval that God is bringing about along with the fall of Judah.

The oracles in Chapter 25 have similar styles and formats, each beginning with the simple "messenger speech" introduction: "Thus says the Lord God" (Hebrew, *kōh ʾāmar ʾadōnay yahweh*, vv. 3, 8, 12, 15). Each also cites crimes of attitude and/or action against the Lord and/or His people (beginning with "because") and announces punishments (beginning with "therefore"). In the Hebrew, each ends with "Then you shall know that I am the Lord," or in the case of Edom the slightly different "Then they shall know My vengeance." These are most of the medium-sized oracles of Chapters 25–32. Hereafter lengthy oracles will predominate.

AMMON

25:1 The word of the LORD came to me, saying,
    2 "Son of man, set your face against the Ammonites, and prophesy against them.

3 "Say to the Ammonites, 'Hear the word of the Lord GOD! Thus says the Lord GOD: "Because you said, 'Aha!' against My sanctuary when it was profaned, and against the land of Israel when it was desolate, and against the house of Judah when they went into captivity,

4 "indeed, therefore, I will deliver you as a possession to the men of the East, and they shall set their encampments among you and make their dwellings among you; they shall eat your fruit, and they shall drink your milk.

5 "And I will make Rabbah a stable for camels and Ammon a resting place for flocks. Then you shall know that I *am* the LORD.'

6 'For thus says the Lord GOD: "Because you clapped *your* hands, stamped your feet, and rejoiced in heart with all your disdain for the land of Israel,

7 "indeed, therefore, I will stretch out My hand against you, and give you as plunder to the nations; I will cut you off from the peoples, and I will cause you to perish from the countries; I will destroy you, and you shall know that I *am* the LORD."'"

Ezek. 25:1–7

The Ammonites are perhaps mentioned first in this section of oracles against foreign nations because the only previous such oracle was also about Ammon (21:28–32). At any rate, nothing we know about the Ammonites would suggest that they are mentioned first because of their prominence or the severity of their enmity to Israel or the like.

The Ammonites occupied the territory east of the Jabbok River, on the fringe of the Arabian desert. They had a long history of enmity to Israel, starting with their support for hiring the false prophet Balaam against Israel (Deut. 23:3–6). They were one of the oppressors in the days of the Judges (Judg. 3:13; 10:6–11:33) and Saul (1 Samuel 11). David fought them (2 Samuel 10, 12), and in the days of Jehoshaphat they attacked Judah (2 Chronicles 20). Ammonite enmity against Israel continued through the days of Jehoiakim (609–598 B.C.; 2 Kings 24:2), that is, into Ezekiel's day.

Oracles against foreign nations usually include direct address to the nation by God, mention of an arrogant attitude and/or action (often against Israel) that the nation has displayed, and prediction of doom. The present oracle has these elements exactly.

After the typical introduction (v. 1), Ezekiel is told to *"set"* his *"face against"* (i.e., show clear opposition to) the Ammonites (v. 2) and to condemn their delight at the fall of Jerusalem (*"My sanctuary"*), the desolation of Judah (*"the land"*), and the exile of the Judeans (*"the house of Judah"*) in verse 3. Their *"Aha!"* (v. 3) was the virtual equivalent of our modern "Oh boy," "Wow," or "Hooray." In verse 6, clapping and stamping are actions accompanying rejoicing over the misfortune of God's people. The Ammonites, long enemies of Israel and Judah, were certainly taking pleasure in seeing Judah's final downfall in 586 B.C.

The Ammonites' punishment for such opposition to God's people is predicted in verses 4, 5, and 7. They will be conquered and oppressed by their enemies, a standard covenant punishment (cf. Lev. 26:16–17; Deut. 28:31, 33, 43, etc.). In this case their enemies will be the desert-dwelling Arabs (*"men of the East,"* v. 4). Population decimation is depicted by a common sort of motif: the capital and the nation will be turned into animal sites (i.e., where humans live no more; cf. Deut. 28:62; Zeph. 2:15).

It is important to note that although the Ammonites were rejoicing at Judah's demise, there is nothing about Judah's demise that was inherently wrong. It's not that Judah shouldn't have fallen to the Babylonians. On the contrary, it *had* to fall—that was the decision of the Lord, and His punishments are just. The outcome the Ammonites sought was right, but *they* had no right to seek it. They should have been looking to quit their own sins, not delighting in watching another nation get punished for *its* sins.

Oracles against foreign nations are always implicitly oracles of encouragement for God's people. Suppression of Israel's enemies meant support for Israel (see also the discussion on 21:28–32). So even at a time when all seemed hopeless from a human point of view, God was already offering hope to His defeated, exiled people. Comprehensively revealing the coming doom of Israel's foes through the prophet Ezekiel, God was opening the way for His people to begin to expect their deliverance and eventual exaltation.

A similar situation pertains with regard to God's defeat of the principalities and powers that oppose His church and attempt to defeat His people still. When they are entirely subdued and destroyed, believers will no longer have to fear their influence and be sidetracked from glorifying God by their influence. Therefore the Bible gives hope to God's people by scenes of destruction that are not in themselves perhaps pleasant to contemplate (such as the gruesome burning of Satan and the false prophet in Rev. 20:10) but which are necessary precursors to lasting freedom and bliss for the righteous.

MOAB

25:8 'Thus says the Lord GOD: "Because Moab and Seir say, 'Look! The house of Judah is like all the nations,'

9 "therefore, behold, I will clear the territory of Moab of cities, of the cities on its frontier, the glory of the country, Beth Jeshimoth, Baal Meon, and Kirjathaim.

10 "To the men of the East I will give it as a possession, together with the Ammonites, that the Ammonites may not be remembered among the nations.

11 "And I will execute judgments upon Moab, and they shall know that I am the LORD."'

Ezek. 25:8–11

In this brief oracle against Moab we note the lack of direct address to the nation—although its words are quoted in verse 8—but otherwise it follows a format and content similar to the oracle against Ammon immediately preceding. Moab had been dominated politically and militarily by Israel and Judah throughout much of its history, and undoubtedly its people roared with approval at the fall of Jerusalem to the Babylonian armies. Thus they could exult that *"Judah is like all the nations,"* subject to Babylonian control, beaten, no longer in a position to give Moab any trouble (v. 8). Their sin is thus in arrogantly thinking that Yahweh was unable to deliver His people. As a result, their great cities will fall (v. 9), and they, like the Ammonites, will be invaded and occupied by desert Arabs (v. 10). The fate of Moab and Ammon, so long linked in Bible history (cf. Gen. 19:30–38) will once again be remarkably similar. Verse 11 concludes the oracle by predicting unspecified judgments against Moab in the manner of the general punishments predicted against Israel in the Mosaic covenant (e.g., Deut. 31:17, 21; 32:23).

EDOM

25:12 'Thus says the Lord GOD: "Because of what Edom did against the house of Judah by taking vengeance, and has greatly offended by avenging itself on them,"

13 'therefore thus says the Lord GOD: "I will also stretch out My hand against Edom, cut off man and beast from it, and make it desolate from Teman; Dedan shall fall by the sword.

14 "I will lay My vengeance on Edom by the hand of My people Israel, that they may do in Edom according to My anger and according to My fury; and they shall know My vengeance," says the Lord GOD.'

Ezek. 25:12–14

Edom, west and south of the Dead Sea, was a small nation that had steadily been Israel's enemy since the time of the hostility between Jacob and Esau, from whom Israel and Edom were descended (Genesis 25). Verse 12 mentions Edom's taking vengeance against Judah, the details of which are more precisely known from the Book of Obadiah. After the siege of Jerusalem began, Judah was no longer in a position to keep Edomite raiders from attacking southern Judean cities and towns. Edom quickly took advantage of the situation to annex Judean territory to itself. Moreover, Edomites attacked Judeans fleeing the Babylonians after the invasion of Judah in 588 B.C. (Obadiah 14).

Edom's punishment will be in line with that of Ammon and Moab: desolation, population decimation, and destruction of its major cities in war (v. 13). Particular stress is paid to the Lord's vengeance against Edom in verse 14. This is not petty vengeance but the exercise of the Sovereign's responsibility to take action against His vassal's enemies (Hebrew, *nāqam*). In this case, what is predicted is a vengeance *"by the hand of My people Israel,"* in the manner also described in Obadiah (vv. 17–21). That is, Judah would in the future retake not only the territory it had lost to the Edomites in 588–586 B.C. but would in fact dominate all of Edom once again. Then Edom would know what God calls here *"My anger . . . My fury . . . My vengeance."*

PHILISTIA

25:15 'Thus says the Lord GOD: "Because the Philistines dealt vengefully and took vengeance with a spiteful heart, to destroy because of the old hatred,"

16 'therefore thus says the Lord GOD: "I will stretch out My hand against the Philistines, and I will cut off the Cherethites and destroy the remnant of the seacoast.

17 "I will execute great vengeance on them with furious rebukes; and they shall know that I *am* the LORD, when I lay My vengeance upon them."'

Ezek. 25:15–17

The Philistines were a people originally from the Greek coasts and islands of the Aegean Sea who after a failed attempt to settle in Egypt concentrated their population along the Mediterranean coast of Palestine. They became Israel's main enemy during the days of the Judges, and their military successes against Israel were so great that by the time Saul and Jonathan fell in battle against them (1 Samuel 31) they were threatening to take virtually all of Israel's territory and become the new tenants of the promised land. David subdued them completely, but their hostility to Israel never abated, and they looked for any chance to break free from the subjugation they had endured so long. The Babylonian invasion of 588 B.C. provided just the moment for them to deal vengefully and take vengeance *"with a spiteful heart"* (v. 15).

Accordingly, God promises that He will simply cut them off from their former homeland (v. 16) and take *"great vengeance"* (*"furious rebukes"*) on Philistia. This prophecy, like all the others, certainly came true. We find virtually no record of Philistine civilization after the time of the Maccabees (the second century B.C.) in Palestine, even though it was the Philistines who gave their name to the region (Philistine = Palestine).

CHAPTER EIGHTEEN

The Fall of Tyre and Sidon

Ezekiel 26:1–28:26

Tyre and Sidon were city-states on the coast of Phoenicia (modern Lebanon) that had become prominent among the nations of the Fertile Crescent during the centuries prior to Ezekiel's lifetime. Sidon was less powerful and wealthy than Tyre, so it receives much less attention in the prophetic oracles against foreign nations. Here in Ezekiel it is mentioned in a relatively short oracle (28:20–24) in contrast to Tyre, which is the center of attention for the bulk of three chapters.

First, as far as we know, Israel never fought a war with either Tyre or Sidon, and contact between these small nations and Israel was often quite cordial, as evidenced by the account of how King Hiram of Tyre helped Solomon build the temple in Jerusalem (1 Kings 5, 7). However, there were good reasons for God's inspiring Ezekiel to condemn these peoples. First, both Tyre and Sidon to some extent either occupied or controlled by their influence part of the true promised land. According to the boundaries identified in the Book of Joshua, the northwest sector of the land granted to Israel in fulfillment of the original promises to Abraham included territory that by Ezekiel's day was in the hands of Tyre and Sidon (i.e., in the district allotted to Asher; cf. Josh. 19:28–29). Thus Tyre and Sidon continued to be oppressors of the promised land in Ezekiel's day just as they had been since the very beginning of the conquest under Joshua some eight hundred years before.

Second, while military conflict had not occurred between Israel and these coastal states, economic conflict had. The shipping industry in the Mediterranean had increased in influence to the point that shipping nations like Tyre and Sidon were economic crossroads, reaping enormous profits from international sea trade, to the consternation of much poorer nations such as Judah.

Third, there was the sheer prosperity and independence of Tyre and Sidon to consider. If God had promised His people that He would prosper them, how could it be that they were bleeding from Babylonian-inflicted wounds while Tyre and Sidon were sleek and fat? How could it represent any fulfillment of God's choice of Israel to have the people of Judah plodding in chains eastward to captivity in Babylon while major Phoenician coastal city-states enjoyed a higher lifestyle?

Fourth, as Joel 3:5 tells us, Tyre and Sidon profited from the conquest of Judah by the Babylonians and possibly the earlier conquests of the Assyrians and Egyptians as well. This may have happened in one or more of three ways: direct Phoenician plundering of northern Israelite territory while the Israelites were too occupied with Mesopotamian armies to respond (cf. Obadiah 13); profiteering from Babylonian, Assyrian, or Egyptian defeats of Israel and Judah by buying plundered goods at bargain prices; supplying conquering armies with goods and services paid for by plunder from Israel.

Finally, there was the matter of the slave trade. Ezekiel's prophecies against Tyre and Sidon do not mention this explicitly, but we know from Joel 3:6 that Tyre and Sidon had become the Mediterranean's paramount slave-trading nations, buying masses of slaves taken in the Babylonian onslaught and reselling them far away from home in places such as Greece.

Thus even though from the perspective of Ezekiel's contemporaries and undoubtedly in their own eyes the Tyrians and Sidonians were sitting pretty, they nevertheless were well deserving of judgment from God's perspective.

The future—including God's judgment on these nations—was known to God, who was assuring not just Ezekiel's contemporaries but future readers of the prophecy of His sovereignty over all nations and His judgment against those whose practices made them His enemies and thus the enemies of His people. They must decrease so that Israel might increase—that was basic to the promise of restoration (cf. the comments on Ezek. 21:28–32).

Six blocks of prophecy are contained in these three chapters. In outline they are:

1. Tyre's coming desolation (26:1–21)
2. Tyre like an ocean-going ship (27:1–36)

255

The first block, Chapter 26, contains two subsections: verses 1–14, where Tyre is portrayed as a bare rock, and verses 15–21, where its great plunge is a terrible thing to behold. The second block, Ezekiel 27, is a compound poetry-prose-poetry allegory with several subsections. The sixth block, Ezek. 28:25–26, is a very short prophecy of the restoration of Israel, which in spite of its brevity is like a center-piece for all the oracles against foreign nations in Chapters 25–32. After all, the main point of such oracles is that they reassure Israel that its foes will eventually be abased and Israel eventually be restored to greatness in God's plan. So a little "reminder" like 28:25–26 keeps the reader of the book aware that while nearly all the oracles in the immediate context are about other nations, the real audience for all of them is discouraged Israelites who need to be reassured about what God is doing and will do among all the nations of the world on behalf of His own.

TYRE, A BARE ROCK

26:1 And it came to pass in the eleventh year, on the first *day* of the month, *that* the word of the LORD came to me, saying,

2 "Son of man, because Tyre has said against Jerusalem, 'Aha! She is broken who *was* the gateway of the peoples; now she is turned over to me; I shall be filled; she is laid waste.'

3 "Therefore thus says the Lord GOD: 'Behold, I *am* against you, O Tyre, and will cause many nations to come up against you, as the sea causes its waves to come up.

4 'And they shall destroy the walls of Tyre and break down her towers; I will also scrape her dust from her, and make her like the top of a rock.

5 'It shall be *a place for* spreading nets in the midst of the sea, for I have spoken,' says the Lord GOD; 'it shall become plunder for the nations.

256

6 'Also her daughter *villages* which *are* in the fields shall be slain by the sword. Then they shall know that I am the LORD.'

7 "For thus says the Lord GOD: 'Behold, I will bring against Tyre from the north Nebuchadnezzar king of Babylon, king of kings, with horses, with chariots, and with horsemen, and an army with many people.

8 'He will slay with the sword your daughter *villages* in the fields; he will heap up a siege mound against you, build a wall against you, and raise a defense against you.

9 'He will direct his battering rams against your walls, and with his axes he will break down your towers.

10 'Because of the abundance of his horses, their dust will cover you; your walls will shake at the noise of the horsemen, the wagons, and the chariots, when he enters your gates, as men enter a city that has been breached.

11 'With the hooves of his horses he will trample all your streets; he will slay your people by the sword, and your strong pillars will fall to the ground.

12 'They will plunder your riches and pillage your merchandise; they will break down your walls and destroy your pleasant houses; they will lay your stones, your timber, and your soil in the midst of the water.

13 'I will put an end to the sound of your songs, and the sound of your harps shall be heard no more.

14 'I will make you like the top of a rock; you shall be *a place for* spreading nets, and you shall never be rebuilt, for I the LORD have spoken,' says the Lord GOD.

15 "Thus says the Lord GOD to Tyre: 'Will the coastlands not shake at the sound of your fall, when the wounded cry, when slaughter is made in the midst of you?

16 'Then all the princes of the sea will come down from their thrones, lay aside their robes, and take off their embroidered garments; they will clothe themselves with trembling; they will sit on the ground, tremble *every* moment, and be astonished at you.

17 'And they will take up a lamentation for you,
and say to you:

> "How you have perished,
> O one inhabited by seafaring men,
> O renowned city,
> Who was strong at sea,
> She and her inhabitants,
> Who caused their terror *to be* on all her
>   inhabitants!

18 Now the coastlands tremble on the day of your
>   fall;
> Yes, the coastlands by the sea are troubled at
>   your departure."'

19 "For thus says the Lord GOD: 'When I make you a
desolate city, like cities that are not inhabited, when I
bring the deep upon you, and great waters cover you,
20 'then I will bring you down with those who descend into the Pit, to the people of old, and I will make
you dwell in the lowest part of the earth, in places desolate from antiquity, with those who go down to the
Pit, so that you may never be inhabited; and I shall
establish glory in the land of the living.
21 'I will make you a terror, and you *shall be* no
more; though you are sought for, you will never be
found again,' says the Lord GOD."

Ezek. 26:1–21

The city of Tyre was partly built on the edge of the Mediterranean
Sea and partly on a coastal island about a mile long and a half mile
wide. The island part, for which the city was most famous and which
is the main focus of the current prophecy, was linked to the Phoenician mainland by a causeway built by Hiram I, father of the Hiram
who helped Solomon build the temple. Surrounded by the sea, it was
easily defensible against invasion. Tyre's location also made it a natural port and trading city. By the time the prophets wrote (760 B.C.
and thereafter), Tyre, only a hundred miles from Jerusalem, was the
preeminent center of sea trade, and its citizens were famous as seafarers (Isa. 23:8; Ezek. 26:17; 27:32). Tyre not only shipped the wares
of other nations around the Mediterranean world, it also manufac-
tured its own beautiful glasswares and dyes that sold for fine profits

abroad. As the most powerful city on the Phoenician coast, Tyre dominated not only other coastal cities, but the Phoenician inland areas as well. Tyre's name in Canaanite/Hebrew is ṣûr, which means simply "rock." In this prophecy, God declares that the island city will return to its original state, a bare rock in the sea.

The chapter may be outlined as follows:

1. Date and introduction (vv. 1–2)
2. Tyre to be conquered by many nations (vv. 3–6)
3. The destruction to be wrought by the Babylonians (vv. 7–14)
4. Lament over Tyre's great fall (vv. 15–18)
5. Tyre in the pit of hell (vv. 19–21)

After the introduction, each of the four succeeding sections begins with *"Thus says the Lord God."* *"For"* (Hebrew kî) is added at the beginning of sections 3 and 5. Thus the chapter as a whole reflects a clear, simple pattern in the Hebrew demarcating the subsections of the prophecy.

The eleventh year (like all of the book's dates, figured from 598 B.C. when Ezekiel and his fellow Israelites went into exile) was 587–586 B.C. The month is not specified in verse 1 but was probably the eleventh month, that is, just a few weeks after the fall of Jerusalem. If there was ever a need for the exiles to hear some encouragement, this was the time. Their hopes and dreams that Jerusalem would hold out against the foe were now dashed. They finally had to agree that Ezekiel had been right all along. His words had been harsh against Judah and Jerusalem, and many now may have been all the more discouraged for he had not yet said much that was positive about Israel's future. A prophecy against Tyre would, of course, be very encouraging, for the reasons we have outlined above.

Verse 2 depicts the delight that must indeed have filled Tyre. Jerusalem, once an economic and political rival and head of a nation that traditionally claimed Tyre's territories as its own, was now destroyed. Tyre, which had always escaped conquest in the past because it was so easy to defend, could say *"I shall be filled; she [Jerusalem] is laid waste."*

Tyre, however, was about to be besieged, too—and by a large force from many nations (v. 3). This, of course, would be the Babylonian-led army, with its many ethnic groups from various conquered territories pressed into service (cf. v. 7). Tyre will eventually be reduced, in the hyperbolic language of prophecy, to a bare rock (v. 4), good for little but a place from which to fish, its great wealth taken by others (v. 5). Tyre's suburbs on the mainland (called in the Hebrew idiom "daughters") will fall as well (v. 6).

Nebuchadnezzar, Jerusalem's conqueror, will also be Tyre's conqueror (v. 7). He will come *from the north,* that is, from Syria, as virtually all conquerors came into Palestine (cf. the discussion on Ezekiel 38–39). Using all the siege techniques of warfare in that era (vv. 8–9), the Babylonians would eventually prevail and enter the city (v. 10) to kill and to destroy (v. 11). Conquering armies gained their pay partly by being free to plunder whatever they could carry off, and the prophecy thus predicts the plundering and destruction of Tyre by the soldiers present at its fall. Soldiers were also demolitionists, since part of their task was to prevent further opposition, so they could be expected to throw much of Tyre into the sea (v. 12). Thus the sound of songs and harps would be heard no more in Tyre (v. 13)—a standard ancient way of describing the curse of desolation (e.g., Isa. 24:8; cf. Lev. 26:31, 33). Verse 14 repeats and thus reinforces the severity of the destruction that Tyre could expect. *"Shall never be rebuilt"* might be better translated "will not be built-up again," that is, "will not go back to its former state," and does not imply that the island of Tyre would never again have any buildings or inhabitants at all.

Verse 15 looks toward the reaction of others to the inevitable fall of Tyre. The Hebrew is ambiguous and can be understood to describe either the shaking of the land all along the Mediterranean coast, or the frightened quaking of the inhabitants of all the coastal regions, or both. After all, if the most influential and defensible of the cities of the Mediterranean world falls, all the kings of the other nations hoping to hold out against Babylon will know that they are "sunk" themselves when they see what has happened at Tyre (v. 16).

The prophecy imagines these kings lamenting Tyre's fall (v. 17). It was the practice in the ancient world for people to lament their dead in song, so this concept is not far-fetched (cf. Ezekiel 19, 27, etc.). The brief lament itself (vv. 17–18) typically addresses dead Tyre in the second person, extols its past greatness, and bemoans the extent of its tragic demise.

Then the prophecy reverts to a concluding direct quotation of the Lord speaking to Tyre, in which its future is likened to drowning

(v. 19) and to death in hell (v. 20). The *"Pit"* is the actual term used, a common synonym in the Old Testament for hell as the place of death ("the next world" in a general, unspecified sense) rather than necessarily as a place of torment (cf. 31:14; 32:17–32). Tyre's death and consignment to the Pit will result in *"glory in the land of the living"* (v. 20), a way of saying that the absence of this arrogant, slave-trading nation will be a divine blessing to the earth. Verse 21 sums up: The rocky spot where Tyre once was will be a horrible thing to behold (*"a terror"*), the city itself now nonexistent, nowhere to be found. This, again, is the language of the curses of desolation, well known from both the Mosaic covenant curses of Leviticus 26 and Deuteronomy 28–32 and from the other Old Testament prophets.

Shortly after Ezekiel relayed to his audience these words from the Lord, the Babylonian siege of the fortress of Tyre began. It lasted thirteen years, from 586–573 B.C., and reduced Tyre's status enormously. Centuries later (332 B.C.), Alexander the Great built a causeway a half mile long and 200 feet wide from the mainland to the well-defended island and took the city after seven months. Thereafter, Tyre was only modestly populated and much less influential. It always had some population, as it does today, and the purposeful hyperbole of the prophecy should not be misunderstood literalistically to imply that Tyre would never have habitation after Ezekiel's time. The point, rather, is that God would judge and punish this state, so powerful and successful from a worldly standpoint, because it is the plan of God that eventually all nations will be humbled before Him and that His people alone will enjoy His permanent blessing. This plan, still in effect, should both warn and comfort all who fear God.

TYRE, THE SHIP

27:1 The word of the LORD came again to me, saying,
    2 "Now, son of man, take up a lamentation for Tyre,
    3 "and say to Tyre, 'You who are situated at the entrance of the sea, merchant of the peoples on many coastlands, thus says the Lord GOD:

"O Tyre, you have said,
'I *am* perfect in beauty.'

4 Your borders *are* in the midst of the seas.
Your builders have perfected your beauty.
5 They made all *your* planks of fir trees from
  Senir;
  They took a cedar from Lebanon to make you
  a mast.
6 *Of* oaks from Bashan they made your oars;
  The company of Ashurites have inlaid your
  planks
  With ivory from the coasts of Cyprus.
7 Fine embroidered linen from Egypt was what
  you spread for your sail;
  Blue and purple from the coasts of Elishah was
  what covered you.

8 "Inhabitants of Sidon and Arvad were your
  oarsmen;
  Your wise men, O Tyre, were in you;
  They became your pilots.
9 Elders of Gebal and its wise men
  Were in you to caulk your seams;
  All the ships of the sea
  And their oarsmen were in you
  To market your merchandise.

10 "Those from Persia, Lydia, and Libya
  Were in your army as men of war;
  They hung shield and helmet in you;
  They gave splendor to you.
11 Men of Arvad with your army *were* on your
  walls *all* around,
  And the men of Gammad were in your towers;
  They hung their shields on your walls *all*
  around;
  They made your beauty perfect.

12 "Tarshish *was* your merchant because of your
many luxury goods. They gave you silver, iron, tin,
and lead for your goods.
13 "Javan, Tubal, and Meshech *were* your traders.
They bartered human lives and vessels of bronze for
your merchandise.
14 "Those from the house of Togarmah traded for
your wares and horses, steeds, and mules.

262

15 "The men of Dedan *were* your traders; many isles *were* the market of your hand. They brought you ivory tusks and ebony as payment.

16 "Syria *was* your merchant because of the abundance of goods you made. They gave you for your wares emeralds, purple, embroidery, fine linen, corals, and rubies.

17 "Judah and the land of Israel *were* your traders. They traded for your merchandise wheat of Minnith, millet, honey, oil, and balm.

18 "Damascus *was* your merchant because of the abundance of goods you made, because of your many luxury items, with the wine of Helbon and with white wool.

19 "Dan and Javan paid for your wares, traversing back and forth. Wrought iron, cassia, and cane were among your merchandise.

20 "Dedan *was* your merchant in saddlecloths for riding.

21 "Arabia and all the princes of Kedar *were* your regular merchants. They traded with you in lambs, rams, and goats.

22 "The merchants of Sheba and Raamah *were* your merchants. They traded for your wares the choicest spices, all kinds of precious stones, and gold.

23 "Haran, Canneh, Eden, the merchants of Sheba, Assyria, *and* Chilmad *were* your merchants.

24 "These *were* your merchants in choice items—in purple clothes, in embroidered garments, in chests of multicolored apparel, in sturdy woven cords, which were in your marketplace.

25 "The ships of Tarshish were carriers of your
merchandise.
You were filled and very glorious in the midst
of the seas.

26 Your oarsmen brought you into many waters,
But the east wind broke you in the midst of
the seas.

27 "Your riches, wares, and merchandise,
Your mariners and pilots,
Your caulkers and merchandisers,

All your men of war who *are* in you,
And the entire company which *is* in your midst,
Will fall into the midst of the seas on the day
    of your ruin.
28 The common-land will shake at the sound of
    the cry of your pilots.

29 "All who handle the oar,
The mariners,
All the pilots of the sea
Will come down from their ships *and* stand on
    the shore.
30 They will make their voice heard because of
    you;
They will cry bitterly and cast dust on their
    heads;
They will roll about in ashes;
31 They will shave themselves completely bald
    because of you,
Gird themselves with sackcloth,
And weep for you
With bitterness of heart *and* bitter wailing.
32 In their wailing for you
They will take up a lamentation,
And lament for you:
'What *city is* like Tyre,
Destroyed in the midst of the sea?

33 'When your wares went out by sea,
You satisfied many people;
You enriched the kings of the earth
With your many luxury goods and your
    merchandise.
34 But you are broken by the seas in the depths
    of the waters;
Your merchandise and the entire company will
    fall in your midst.
35 All the inhabitants of the isles will be
    astonished at you;
Their kings will be greatly afraid,
And *their* countenance will be troubled.
36 The merchants among the peoples will hiss at
    you;

You will become a horror, and *be* no more
   forever.'"'"

Ezek. 27:1-36

This is one of the most elegant and extensive of the prophetic laments in the Bible. Like other oracles against foreign nations in lament form, it employs the four lament characteristics of (1) direct address to the deceased, (2) description of the deceased's past greatness, (3) call to others to take notice and mourn, and (4) expression of the extent of the tragedy involved. Tyre is, of course, not deceased yet; the lament is proleptic, a predictive dirge that the audience would imagine being sung after Tyre's demise.

This lament is largely allegorical throughout. Tyre is imagined to be a great ocean-going ship, or "ship of Tarshish" (Hebrew *taršîš* means basically "open sea" or "deep sea"). To visitors to Tyre, the splendid city out in the water would certainly have been easy to compare to a ship heading out to sea, riding the waves, carrying expensive wares to distant coasts.

The chapter may be outlined as follows:

1. Command to Ezekiel to lament Tyre (vv. 1–3a)
2. Poetic description of ship and crew (vv. 3b–11)
3. Prose geography of trading destinations (vv. 12–24)
4. Poetic description of shipwreck and mourning (vv. 25–36)

The introduction to the chapter (v. 1) is typical, and the initial command (v. 2) is simple, containing Ezekiel's usual designation "son of man" (meaning "human"). Verse 3a contains the essence of the remainder of the chapter in its three aspects: (1) the direct address, signaling the coming fall of Tyre, since direct address in laments is most frequently aimed at the deceased; (2) Tyre's ocean location, on which the chapter plays extensively; (3) the mention of "merchant," foreshadowing the extensive list of trading partners in verses 12–24.

Verse 3b begins the direct address in the poetic section with Tyre's boastfulness. The arrogance of Israel's enemies is a common theme in prophetic oracles against foreign nations. In verse 4, *"borders"* may also be translated "territory" or "domain," with the point that Tyre's range of influence was the Mediterranean world. The second half of verse 4 begins the description of Tyre as a great ship, impressive to the eye, as if built partly with wood from Senir (Mount Hermon), Lebanon (v. 5), Bashan (southeastern Palestine), and Cyprus (v. 6), all known for their forests of great trees. Most of ancient Syria-Palestine had virtually no large tree growth, so the description of trees from these special regions is understandable.

The idea of highly prized Egyptian linen as sail cloth and lovely dyed fabrics from Elishah (the non-Phoenician part of Cyprus) as deck awnings (v. 7) reflects the imagistic nature of the lament, combining as it does the concept of great wealth with that of a sea-going city. The crew are imagined as from Tyre itself (*"pilots"* could be read simply as *"sailors"*), the southern coastal city of Sidon, and the northern Phoenician coastal city-island of Arvad. This suggests Tyre's extensive control of the entire Phoenician region. Verse 9 includes also in the imaginary crew people from Gebal (Byblos), another great ancient Phoenician coastal city.

Verse 10 mentions people of lands as distant as Persia (east of Mesopotamia), Lydia (in Anatolia), and Lybia (west of Egypt in North Africa) serving as mercenary soldiers in Tyre's army. To this verse 11 adds Arvad, Helech (Cilicia; rendered here as *"your army"*), and Gammad (location uncertain) as additional examples of sources of warriors. Note that verses 10 and 11 provide a transition from the ship allegory to a more straightforward description of Tyre as a city on land: Tyre an impressive sight, of *"beauty perfect."*

With verse 12 begins the geographic catalog of places with which the Tyrians carried on trade and whose wealth thus flowed through and to Tyre as the great merchant city took its cut from its shipping and trading businesses. Both coastal and landlocked places are mentioned, since Tyre was a hub for caravans arriving by land and transferring to ship and vice versa. The cities and territories mentioned are listed in a geographical order from the west (Tarshish, v. 12, here referring probably to Sardinia, was a name held by several places, the ancient equivalent of modern *"Portland"*) to the east (the Mesopotamian regions mentioned in v. 23). For the less-known places mentioned in verses 12–23 the following explanations may be helpful: Javan (v. 13) was part of Greece, while Tubal and Meshech were territories in Asia Minor (modern Turkey). Togarmah (v. 14) is now Armenia. The eastern Mediterranean island of Rhodes should be understood here (as it is recorded in the best manuscripts), instead of Dedan in verse 15. In verse 19 the text is difficult, and Dan and Javan are probably not place names but words signifying types of merchandise. Dedan (v. 20), Kedar (v. 21), Sheba, and Raamah (v. 22) were Arabian regions; the regions listed in verse 23 are mostly northern Mesopotamian, in what is today Iraq.

The particular materials mentioned as being traded were characteristic of their respective geographical areas as far as we know, but hardly limited to them. Thus it would be incorrect to assume, for example, that the products mentioned in connection with Israel and Judah in verse 17 are the only ones, or even the dominant ones, that were exported in Old Testament times. The point is rather that through Tyre moved the varied, splendid products of dozens of nations, so that it was an economic crossroads of unparalleled prestige.

But Tyre was not invulnerable. Any ship can be sunk by the Master of the seas. So verses 25–36, now again in poetic form, bring the lengthy allegory to a close with their portrayal of Tyre's coming destruction as if it were shipwrecked. Verse 25a (*"The ships of Tarshish were carriers of your merchandise"*) both concludes the geographic catalog of verses 12–24 and reintroduces the ship metaphor of verses 25b and following. Verses 25b and 26 describe the great ship of Tyre as being heavily loaded (read *"filled with heavy cargo"* for *"filled and very glorious"*), rowed away from its dock to the open sea (*"many waters"*), and then broken up by a storm. The storm comes from the east, of course, signifying the Babylonians who were to be Tyre's conquerors.

Verses 27 and 28 complete the description of the shipwreck, emphasizing the loss of Tyre's inhabitants. Reaction to the loss constitutes the remainder of the chapter. Seafarers will come for the "funeral" and will mourn, via the usual ancient Near Eastern practices of wailing, dirtying oneself with dust and ashes, shaving one's head, donning sackcloth, and singing the funeral song of lamentation (vv. 29–32). The mourners' lament song (vv. 32–36) echoes what Ezekiel's poem has been saying already: Tyre was once incomparably great but has now fallen into the sea, with loss of its inhabitants producing a massive reaction. That reaction has, however, two previously unmentioned aspects (vv. 35–36): first, that the rulers of other nations will realize that if Tyre could fall to the Babylonians, so can they; and second, that Tyre's former competitors, that is, *"the merchants among the peoples,"* that is, the nations, will be only too glad to see its demise.

What is the point of such a long poem in the Bible? Certainly it is not to teach us principles about how to lament, or how to identify the factors that contribute to the rise and fall of trading nations, or the like. No, the point is really profoundly simple: God controls the destinies of the world's nations. Because this is so, people of true faith everywhere in all ages have been able to endure the hardships of war and conquest, economic misery and political oppression, and other national trials and disasters, knowing that what nations choose to do is not what determines human destiny. No matter how evil one nation may be to another or to its own citizens, God will ultimately destroy those earthly states hostile to Him and will redeem His people into a heavenly kingdom. This basic confidence in the Lord's sovereignty over human history is the common denominator of many biblical passages, and so important, if simple, a truth that it must never be taken lightly. Without this confidence, world events can easily be misinterpreted to imply the absence or weakness of God, and the hopelessness of those who trust in Him. Just the opposite is, fortunately, the case.

DOWNFALL OF TYRE'S KING

28:1 The word of the LORD came to me again, saying,
2 "Son of man, say to the prince of Tyre, 'Thus says the Lord GOD:

"Because your heart *is* lifted up,
And you say, 'I *am* a god,
I sit *in* the seat of gods,
In the midst of the seas,'
Yet you *are* a man, and not a god,
Though you set your heart as the heart of a god
3 (Behold, you *are* wiser than Daniel!
There is no secret that can be hidden from you!
4 With your wisdom and your understanding
You have gained riches for yourself,
And gathered gold and silver into your
treasuries;
5 By your great wisdom in trade you have
increased your riches,
And your heart is lifted up because of your
riches),"

268

6 'Therefore thus says the Lord GOD:

"Because you have set your heart as the heart
    of a god,
7 Behold, therefore, I will bring strangers
    against you,
The most terrible of the nations;
And they shall draw their swords against the
    beauty of your wisdom,
And defile your splendor.
8 They shall throw you down into the Pit,
And you shall die the death of the slain
In the midst of the seas.

9 "Will you still say before him who slays you,
    'I *am* a god'?
But you *shall be* a man, and not a god,
In the hand of him who slays you.
10 You shall die the death of the uncircumcised
By the hand of aliens;
For I have spoken," says the Lord GOD.'"

Ezek. 28:1–10

The prior two chapters predicted the downfall of the city of Tyre. This poetic oracle predicts the downfall of the city's king. The ancient world was monarchical—virtually all governments were led by kings whose authority was nearly absolute. There were no legislatures, no elections, no judicial checks and balances against the power of a human sovereign in his own land. When a king became so unpopular that he no longer enjoyed the people's support, there were usually only two options open to those who disliked him: tolerate him or kill him. Thus in Israel the transition from king to king was often accomplished by assassination (e.g., 2 Kings 15:10, 15–16, 25; cf. Hos. 7:7; 8:4).

Here we see portrayed, then, something that ancient people knew very well: the forcible death of a king. But it is not Tyre's population that will bring this about. It is God. From all we can reconstruct, the people of Tyre loved their king. He was the centerpiece of Tyre's policies, the leader of this most successful of city-states. He symbolized their own prestige in the world, and they identified their own values and expectations with his. We must therefore appreciate the fact that this prophecy against Tyre's king is also a prophecy against the city of Tyre and its population corporately.

After an introduction by now well recognized as standard (v. 1), Ezekiel (typically, "son of man") is instructed to prophesy against Tyre's ruler (Hebrew *nāgîd*), *"prince,"* a term used routinely in the book for "king" (v. 2). In Ezekiel's day the king of Tyre was Ittobaal II, whose name meant "Baal is with him." He was one of a long line of rulers of Tyre whose names included reference to the weather-fertility god Baal. The Tyrians were historically in the Mesopotamian-Syrian religious tradition in which a king was considered appointed to the throne by a god or gods, but was not himself considered a deity. This contrasted with the Egyptian religious tradition, in which the king (Pharaoh) was considered divine.

What then does verse 2 mean when it speaks of Ittobaal's saying *"I am a god"*? There are two possibilities. One is that the people of Tyre, under the growing influence of the religion of Egypt—with whom they traded routinely and whose culture was influential on theirs—may have begun to adopt some of the features of divine kingship in their religion. The other is that Ezekiel is simply highlighting Ittobaal's arrogance metaphorically by portraying him as one with far too high an opinion of himself, somewhat like saying, "Well, look who thinks he's God almighty!" The latter possibility is the more likely one, especially in light of verse 3's similarly boastful comparison of the king to the traditional great wise man of the ancient Near East, Danel (here spelled Daniel). This person was not the Daniel we know about from the book of the same name, but a legendary figure known to us from the literature of the nation of Ugarit (cf. 14:14).

In verses 4 and 5, Ittobaal is further portrayed as having developed an exaggerated opinion of his abilities as the leader of a city state that had prospered enormously. His attitude was, unfortunately, not unlike that of some Christian leaders, who have inferred from the temporary fiscal success of their "ministries" that the hand of God was especially upon them in blessing—when in fact all that occurred was the selfish building of a personal financial empire. At any rate, verses 6 and 7, beginning with Hebrew *lākēn* (*"therefore"*), the standard prophetic introduction to a divine judgment sentence, introduce the Tyrian king's punishment from God: defeat and death from Tyre's enemy (Babylon, called *"The most terrible of the nations,"* as also in 30:11; 31:12; 32:12).

"Pit" (Hebrew *šahat*) is a standard term in the Old Testament for hell as the place of death, and the arrogant king's death is predicted right in his city of Tyre (*"In the midst of the seas"*). He will hardly be able to boast to the Babylonians that he is a god (v. 9) because he is (rather than *"shall be"*) merely a man. As an uncircumcised Phoenician, the king of Tyre would die outside of the Lord's covenant (v. 10) and thus under God's judgment. His exploitation of Israel and other nations would thus be avenged.

When Tyre finally succumbed to the thirteen-year Babylonian siege in 572 B.C., Tyre's dominance over Phoenician national life was also ended. Phoenicia split into enclaves of limited regional influence, never again to be united as a powerful economic-political bloc as it was under Tyre's leadership. Because no contemporary record of Tyre's fall in 572 B.C. exists, it is impossible to know any details of the fate of Ittobaal II. It is hard to imagine that he was not tortured and/or executed after such a long siege (cf. 2 Kings 25:7), dying in humiliation and misery as opposed to the splendor and prestige he had once enjoyed.

Wisdom, as the Bible defines it, is the ability to make right choices. Even ungodly people may make some correct choices, especially of the sort that are to their own advantage. Skillful manipulation and calculation, combined with determination and even courage, can propel a sinful person to worldly success—or even a "worldly" believer to worldly success. Such success is not of God, however, and should not be either attributed to or blamed on Him. Those who attribute financial success to the blessings of the Lord miss completely the impact of a prophecy like Ezek. 28:1–10. "Success" may be the result of evil, and envy of it can be foolish in the extreme.

LAMENT OVER TYRE'S KING

28:11 Moreover the word of the LORD came to me, saying,
12 "Son of man, take up a lamentation for the king of Tyre, and say to him, 'Thus says the Lord GOD:

"You *were* the seal of perfection,
Full of wisdom and perfect in beauty.
13 You were in Eden, the garden of God;
Every precious stone *was* your covering:

The sardius, topaz, and diamond,
Beryl, onyx, and jasper,
Sapphire, turquoise, and emerald with gold.
The workmanship of your timbrels and pipes
Was prepared for you on the day you were
    created.

14 "You *were* the anointed cherub who covers;
I established you;
You were on the holy mountain of God;
You walked back and forth in the midst of
    fiery stones.
15 You *were* perfect in your ways from the day
    you were created,
Till iniquity was found in you.

16 "By the abundance of your trading
You became filled with violence within,
And you sinned;
Therefore I cast you as a profane thing
Out of the mountain of God;
And I destroyed you, O covering cherub,
From the midst of the fiery stones.

17 "Your heart was lifted up because of your
    beauty;
You corrupted your wisdom for the sake of
    your splendor;
I cast you to the ground,
I laid you before kings,
That they might gaze at you.

18 "You defiled your sanctuaries
By the multitude of your iniquities,
By the iniquity of your trading;
Therefore I brought fire from your midst;
It devoured you,
And I turned you to ashes upon the earth
In the sight of all who saw you.
19 All who knew you among the peoples are
    astonished at you;
You have become a horror,
And *shall be* no more forever."'"

                                        Ezek. 28:11–19

The lament God inspires Ezekiel to sing over the king of Tyre contains a series of metaphorical references to the story of the Garden of Eden and to the Mountain of God. The king is compared to a guardian angel at the mountain and, in a way, to Adam himself in the garden. The comparisons are not exact, but imagistic—overtones and general allusions rather than straight one-for-one correspondences to the garden story. The allusions to the mountain of God (e.g., vv. 14, 16) reflect a poetic theme in the Old Testament in which the mountain represents God's abode.

Central to the lament is the idea of a great fall from an idyllic existence. That, after all, is partly what the Garden of Eden story is all about. The lament contains the usual components: direct address to the dead, eulogy of the dead, a call to mourning, and an expression of the magnitude of the loss to the survivors.

After a standard introduction to a lament (vv. 11–12a), Ezekiel begins the direct address eulogy with praise of the king's (soon-to-be former) perfection, wisdom, and beauty. This is not a literal description of the king of Tyre. It is figurative, like verses 2–4 in the prior passage. This is a kind of so-you-think-you're-so-great? way of speaking. The king's splendor in Tyre (and he must have been very rich) is compared in verse 13 to living in an Eden bedecked with jewels and surrounded by the sound of lovely musical instruments (if we carry through the implication of the translation here, we might conclude "your settings and mountings were prepared for you . . ." or the like). Ancient kings, of course, did have jeweled outfits and enjoyed special palace music (on the latter cf. 1 Sam. 16:14–23). Verse 14 shifts the scene to where the king is compared to a guardian angel (cherub), that is, the fiery mountain of God (like Sinai; cf. Exod. 19:18), where the king was like an unharmable supernatural being. Again, all this is hyperbole, nonliteral exaggeration for effect.

After "perfection," however, the king fell in sin (v. 15). This reminds one of the story of Adam. It is used here because it fits, in a certain exaggerated way, the typical lament tendency to describe the extent of the fall of the one being eulogized. Verse 16 then links the king's trading success with "violence" (also translatable as "oppression" or "exploitation"), since Tyre made its money partly in plundered goods and slaves (see the discussion of chaps. 26–28). Thus God's judgment came upon Tyre's king, here again likened to a guardian angel at God's holy mountain. The king's great arrogance must lead to his great fall (v. 17) and the stunned reaction of his survivors (cf. also v. 19).

Tyre's king then dies by fire from his midst, perhaps suggesting that his own greed is the thing that killed him. Fire is often a symbol of divine wrath (e.g., Amos 1:4, 7, 10, etc.). This "fire" will devour the king as a public spectacle (v. 18), producing a reaction of horror (v. 19). Tyre's great fall to the Babylonians after its long siege certainly became one of the most famous stories of national defeat in ancient times, judging from its telling by Josephus in his *Contra Apionem*.

It is especially instructive to note the emphasis placed in the lament on the way that the king's "trading" is linked with his arrogance and iniquity (vv. 16 and 18). God's intent through Ezekiel is not to suggest to us that all business is bad, but the way Tyre's king did business was evil. His problem was greed, and that is one of the reasons for the involvement of Garden-of-Eden overtones in the lament. What Adam and Eve were tempted to try to get was equality with God (Gen. 3:4). That is exactly what Tyre's king wanted, too. Whatever he personally may have thought of himself, the passage makes it clear that his actions were those of a person seeking such wealth and power as to be his own god. Personal power, dominance of others, conspicuous wealth—these are goals that corrupt people, no matter what their origins.

PESTILENCE IN SIDON

28:20 Then the word of the LORD came to me, saying,
   21 "Son of man, set your face toward Sidon, and
prophesy against her,
   22 "and say, 'Thus says the Lord GOD:

"Behold, I *am* against you, O Sidon;
I will be glorified in your midst;
And they shall know that I *am* the LORD,
When I execute judgments in her and am
   hallowed in her.
   23 For I will send pestilence upon her,
And blood in her streets;

> The wounded shall be judged in her midst
> By the sword against her on every side;
> Then they shall know that I *am* the LORD."'"
> 24 "And there shall no longer be a pricking brier
> or a painful thorn for the house of Israel from
> among all *who are* around them, who despise them.
> Then they shall know that I *am* the Lord GOD.'
>
> *Ezek. 28:20–24*

Ezekiel's audience knew that Sidon was the "second city" to Tyre in those days, a city of significant influence if not the leading city in Phoenicia. It was useful for them to hear that the prophecies against Phoenicia were not limited to Tyre. Sidon, too, would come under God's judgment. Ezekiel was thus told to *"set [his] face . . . against"* (cf. 4:3; 25:2, etc.) Sidon as well.

His prophecy about Sidon is a poem followed by a prose summation. It begins (v. 22) by proclaiming general judgment against Sidon so that the Lord may be glorified (more on this below). It continues (v. 23) with a prediction of "pestilence" followed immediately by description of the ravages of war, reminiscent of the Mosaic curse predictions of war in Deut. 32:24–25. There, too, pestilence and bloodshed are linked, because it was the expectation that disease would run rampant in a city under siege, so close and unsanitary were the conditions of large numbers of people trapped inside a besieged city.

The result of the subjugation of Sidon by its enemies (the Babylonians) will be what the prose summation reports (v. 24): relief for Israel from its enemies. This, again, is the abiding value of all prophecies against foreign nations in the prophetical books: Israel increases as its enemies decrease. The church, heir to all such promises (Gal. 3:29), can take hope in this guarantee that in due time those who oppose the people of the Lord will be abased, and the Lord's people exalted forever. Note as well that three times in this short passage *"they shall know that I am the Lord"* serves as a concluding statement (vv. 22, 23, 24). Ultimately, the purpose of the Lord's vindication of His people against their foes is not found in their glorification, but in His. He will receive honor and recognition, and His power will be manifestly proved to all who now doubt. The briers and thorns of the nations who contend against the Lord (v. 24; cf. Num. 33:55; Judg. 2:3) will have been once for all removed.

Israel's Return

28:25 'Thus says the Lord GOD: "When I have gathered the house of Israel from the peoples among whom they are scattered, and am hallowed in them in the sight of the Gentiles, then they will dwell in their own land which I gave to My servant Jacob.
26 "And they will dwell safely there, build houses, and plant vineyards; yes, they will dwell securely, when I execute judgments on all those around them who despise them. Then they shall know that I *am* the LORD their God."'

Ezek. 28:25–26

The long section of Tyre and Sidon prophecies draws to a close with just a little reminder of a major event in human history: the coming restoration of the people of God. All prophetic predictions of blessing presuppose the prior exile of Israel. For Ezekiel's audience, return from exile was hard to believe. They knew firsthand the miseries of captivity in a foreign land, and they could see no deliverance on the horizon for themselves. Anyone, indeed, surveying the political landscape in the early 580s when Babylon was preeminent in the known world and Israel had been crushed and annexed to the Babylonian Empire would have come to the same conclusion.

God, on the other hand, knew "the end from the beginning" and knew what He was planning to do for His people. Thus He announces in verse 26 that Israel would return from captivity in fulfillment of the ancient promises of Leviticus 26 and Deuteronomy 4 and 30, would rise to greatness, and would dwell securely again in the promised land. This blessed series of events would follow necessarily upon the subjugation of the nations that opposed Israel, as verse 27 states, and as the immediate context (oracles against foreign nations) reminds us. Once again, the ultimate result would be God's glorification, as this time not merely the foreign nations but Israel itself would *know that I am the Lord.*

From our point of view the important factor to keep in mind is that "Israel" in biblical prophecy is the true Israel, not ethnic Israel (cf. Gal. 3:29; Rom. 2:28–29; 9:6). It is those who believe the gospel,

276

not those who are of a given genetic lineage. We therefore take heart from this promise of restoration, since it applies to us as well as to those who truly believed from among the ancient Israelites. The house of Israel will indeed one day dwell securely in the promised land. That's where we are headed forever (cf. Heb. 11:13–16; 12:22–24).

CHAPTER NINETEEN

Go Down, Pharaoh

Ezekiel 29:1–32:32

The second large block of oracles against foreign nations concentrates on Egypt. Four chapters—one-twelfth of the book—are devoted to this subject. Part of the reason for this was historical immediacy: Egypt was a superpower that was an enemy of Babylon, and God was going to use Babylon to defeat the Egyptians. In fact, after the Babylonians got through with them, Egypt was never again a power in the ancient world. These were, then, the last days for Egypt just as they were for Tyre, and God carefully explained this through Ezekiel's prophecies so that his audience and all readers of the Scripture thereafter could be encouraged to trust the sovereign Lord of history.

There was, however, a second factor. Israel's history was determined, from a human point of view, by what the more powerful nations did or didn't do. Israel had been a minor military and political power in the ancient Near East and after 586 B.C. was no power at all. Thus *any* advance in Israel's national fortunes was tied to corresponding developments in the national fortunes of the greater nations. Unless the Egyptians, who had taken every opportunity over the years to control the land of Canaan, were weak, Israel could have no freedom. So God now announces that His people will no longer need to worry about the "Egyptian factor" that had been so prominent in their national history over the centuries. This factor was about to be eliminated.

There are seven separate passages of prophecy in this section of the book:

1. Pharaoh caught and Egypt desolate (29:1–16)
2. Egypt to be plundered by Babylon (29:17–21)

Each is dated except for 30:1–19, which may have been preached at a time so close to that of 29:17–21 that it is given no separate date. The dates extend from the tenth year of the exile of Jehoiachin (588 B.C.) to the twenty-seventh year (571 B.C.), although most are between the tenth and the twelfth years (588–586 B.C.).

PHARAOH CAUGHT, EGYPT CUT OFF

29:1 In the tenth year, in the tenth *month,* on the twelfth *day* of the month, the word of the LORD came to me, saying,
2 "Son of man, set your face against Pharaoh king of Egypt, and prophesy against him, and against all Egypt.
3 "Speak, and say, 'Thus says the Lord GOD:

"Behold, I *am* against you,
O Pharaoh king of Egypt,
O great monster who lies in the midst of his
    rivers,
Who has said, 'My River *is* my own;
I have made *it* for myself.'
4 But I will put hooks in your jaws,
And cause the fish of your rivers to stick to
    your scales;
I will bring you up out of the midst of your
    rivers,
And all the fish in your rivers will stick to
    your scales.
5 I will leave you in the wilderness,
You and all the fish of your rivers;
You shall fall on the open field;
You shall not be picked up or gathered.
I have given you as food
To the beasts of the field
And to the birds of the heavens.

6 "Then all the inhabitants of Egypt
Shall know that I *am* the LORD,
Because they have been a staff of reed to the
     house of Israel.
7 When they took hold of you with the hand,
You broke and tore all their shoulders;
When they leaned on you,
You broke and made all their backs quiver.'

8 'Therefore thus says the Lord GOD: "Surely I
will bring a sword upon you and cut off from you
man and beast.

9 "And the land of Egypt shall become desolate and
waste; then they will know that I *am* the LORD, because
he said, 'The River *is* mine, and I have made *it.'*

10 "Indeed, therefore, I *am* against you and
against your rivers, and I will make the land of
Egypt utterly waste and desolate, from Migdol *to*
Syene, as far as the border of Ethiopia.

11 "Neither foot of man shall pass through it nor
foot of beast pass through it, and it shall be
uninhabited forty years.

12 "I will make the land of Egypt desolate in the
midst of the countries *that are* desolate; and among
the cities *that are* laid waste, her cities shall be
desolate forty years; and I will scatter the Egyptians
among the nations and disperse them throughout the
countries."

13 'Yet, thus says the Lord GOD: "At the end of
forty years I will gather the Egyptians from the
peoples among whom they were scattered.

14 "I will bring back the captives of Egypt and
cause them to return to the land of Pathros, to the
land of their origin, and there they shall be a lowly
kingdom.

15 "It shall be the lowliest of kingdoms; it shall
never again exalt itself above the nations, for I will
diminish them so that they will not rule over the
nations anymore.

16 "No longer shall it be the confidence of the
house of Israel, but will remind them of *their*

> iniquity when they turned to follow them. Then
> they shall know that I *am* the Lord GOD."'"
>
> *Ezek. 29:1–16*

Ezekiel and his fellow Judeans had been in captivity for nearly eleven years. It was January 587 B.C., and Jerusalem had long been under siege (cf. 24:1). Those in exile who believed the word of the Lord through Ezekiel knew that the holy city's situation was hopeless. Thus some comfort could be taken in the fact that a great power like Egypt would suffer the same fate as the tiny nation of Judah was now facing.

There is little in Egypt that does not depend upon the Nile for sustenance. Rainfall is minimal, and all agriculture and most plant and animal life needs the river to live. This section of the book involves the Nile, then, as the centerpiece of the land of Egypt. The poetic part of the passage, verses 3–7, portrays Pharaoh as a fish caught in the Nile and thrown onto the land as food for animals. The prose section (vv. 8–16) predicts Egypt's desolation, since the Nile is under God's control (v. 9) and cannot bring abundance if God does not let it. Also prominent in the pose section is a foreshadowing of Egypt's captivity and later restoration—again paralleling that of Judah and thus a kind of a consolation for Ezekiel's audience.

This prophecy came to Ezekiel a full year after the siege of Jerusalem had begun (thus in 587 B.C.) and is the earliest of the oracles against Egypt recorded in the book. It prophesied doom for both Pharaoh as an individual ruler and Egypt as a nation (v. 2). In a manner typical of oracles against foreign nations, Pharaoh is described as boastful, to the extent even of claiming to have created the Nile (v. 3). Although both the Pharaoh and the Nile were thought divine by the Egyptians, the idea of his creating the Nile is a purposeful stylistic exaggeration in the manner of 28:2, etc. Here Pharaoh is metaphorically compared to a huge fish (the ancients called whales, giant sharks, giant squids, etc. "monsters") caught—with all the other Nile fish stuck to it—on Yahweh's fishing line (v. 4). Birds and other animals will eat up their dead, the dry carcasses that the Lord leaves out on the land (*"the open field,"* v. 5).

Again, the intended result is that Egypt should know the power of the Lord, expressed in the typical wording *"shall know that I am the*

Lord" (v. 6). Over the centuries, Israel had repeatedly sought military and/or economic help from Egypt against the advice of God (cf. Deut. 17:16; 2 Kings 3:1; 10:28; Isa. 30:1-3, etc.). Egyptian help had never done any real good against other foes such as Assyria and Babylon, so leaning on the metaphorical reed "staff" of the land known for its reeds was bound to get Israel hurt (vv. 6-7).

The prose section begins (v. 8) with a typically worded (cf. Exod. 11:5; Jer. 7:20; Zeph. 1:3) prediction of desolation. It is the "sword" (warfare) that will produce the coming great loss. Then God will have shown the Egyptians who made the Nile (v. 9; cf. v. 3)! When God attacks Egypt's precious rivers, that is, the Nile, its tributaries, and the delta outlets, Egypt will indeed become a wasteland (v. 10) from north (Migdol was a delta city) to south (Syene [modern Aswan] is at the border with Nubia [here called Ethiopia, now known as Sudan]). Verses 11-13 indicate a forty-year desolation and captivity for the Egyptians before their return from (Babylonian) exile. Again, this paralleling of Egypt's coming fate with that of Judah was a means of encouraging God's people. "Forty" (Hebrew, *'arbā'îm*) is often a general term for quantity, like English "dozens," and thus Egypt could expect a long exile, too. When the Egyptians returned, however, in contrast to the Judeans, they could not expect a happy restoration under the abundant blessing of the Lord. Instead, back in Pathros (the poorer upper, or southern, half of Egypt, far away from the Israelites whom they could never harm again), they would become only an obscure nation without military or political influence (vv. 14-15), their fate serving as a reminder to the Israelites of the Lord's power and the dangers of sin against Him (v. 16).

These prophecies all came about. Egypt's exile, though little more than a token captivity of slaves taken in battle by the Babylonians, did last from 586 until 539 B.C. when Cyrus, the Persian conqueror of Babylon, allowed captive people to return to their homelands. After the Babylonian defeat, Egypt was never again a power to be reckoned with, but instead suffered repeated conquests and was subjugated to other powers, including the Persians, Greeks, and Ptolemies. The nation declined to the status of an obscure entity in the ancient world. God's promises are true. Their fulfillment had only begun in Ezekiel's day, and few of his contemporaries would live to see all that he spoke concerning the fate of Egypt, Israel's onetime oppressor and frequent useless ally. But it all happened eventually, just as all else that the

Lord has caused His prophets to speak has happened or will happen. His promises are true.

EGYPT PAYS BABYLON'S WAGES

29:17 And it came to pass in the twenty-seventh year, in the first *month*, on the first *day* of the month, that the word of the LORD came to me, saying,

18 "Son of man, Nebuchadnezzar king of Babylon caused his army to labor strenuously against Tyre; every head *was* made bald, and every shoulder rubbed raw; yet neither he nor his army received wages from Tyre, for the labor which they expended on it.

19 "Therefore thus says the Lord GOD: 'Surely I will give the land of Egypt to Nebuchadnezzar king of Babylon; he shall take away her wealth, carry off her spoil, and remove her pillage; and that will be the wages for his army.

20 'I have given him the land of Egypt *for* his labor, because they worked for Me,' says the Lord GOD.

21 'In that day I will cause the horn of the house of Israel to spring forth, and I will open your mouth to speak in their midst. Then they shall know that I *am* the LORD.'"

Ezek. 29:17–21

This prophecy, if it did not begin with a separate statement of the date Ezekiel received it from the Lord, might have been assumed to follow as part of the prior passage (29:1–16). It is a short and simple prediction about the defeat of Egypt by the Babylonians, and the resultant plundering of the wealth of Egypt, all in line with what has already been predicted for the land of the Nile. However, Ezekiel preached it more than sixteen years after he preached the oracle contained in 29:1–16, that is, in the spring of 571. It is the latest dated oracle in the book.

The passage concerns the coming plunder of Egypt. In ancient times armies were not paid as they are today. Soldiers might receive a small allowance along with their rations, but it would have been foolish to join an army just for the pittance paid as wage. Instead, a special incentive system made army life attractive and often exciting.

Soldiers successful in battle were allowed to take and keep anything they could lay hands on and carry away. Many battles took place at or near large cities or in prosperous lands where wealth was concentrated. Indeed, ancient wars of conquest were launched precisely so that the conquerors could acquire the wealth of other nations. After defeating an enemy, an army would dig into the spoils. Those fortunate enough to find gems, precious metals, or other great valuables among the possessions of their defeated foes might become instantly rich. Almost all could at least supplement their income handsomely.

Ezek. 29:17–21 describes the coming plunder of Egypt by Babylon, whose armies will get well paid at the expense of the people of Egypt. The defeated nation of Pharaoh would thus, in a roundabout way, have footed the bill for the Babylonian conquest.

This prophecy was needed so many years after the prior passage because at the time it was delivered (581 B.C.) many people must have come to the conclusion that Egypt was going to escape the Babylonian conquest—and they required a reminder that God's intention to punish Egypt via the Babylonians had not waned. It only seemed that way, since Babylon had not paid much attention to Egypt for several years after beginning the long siege of Tyre, which they indeed brought to its knees. The sacking of Tyre, however, hardly paid back the cost of a thirteen-year campaign. Tyre's wealth had, it is presumed, fled by ship and/or been exhausted paying for thirteen years of defense. When Tyre surrendered and paid tribute to Babylon, it was obvious that Babylon had gotten the worst of the deal, even though Tyre had been humiliated just as Ezekiel had prophesied.

After describing the timing of his revelation (v. 17), Ezekiel reports the frustration that the Babylonians endured in their siege of Tyre. The image of heads and shoulders rubbed raw is an idiomatic way to suggest hard physical labor over a long period of time (18). In the metaphor of the passage, the effort spent on Tyre has not been paid, so "wages" (plunder) were overdue to the Babylonian army. Plunder from Egypt would substitute for plunder from Tyre (v. 19). Indeed, just three years later (568/567 B.C.) the Babylonians did successfully invade Egypt. Our sources about this conquest are sparse, but Pharaoh Amasis II apparently had to pay huge sums to buy off the Babylonians, thus "paying the bill" left by Tyre.

But why should God care whether or not the Babylonian troops got their reward? The answer is very simple: they were doing the Lord's bidding. It was by His design that the conquest of the western lands (Syria, Palestine, Phoenicia, Egypt, etc.) had occurred (cf. Isa. 37:26; Hab. 1:6). So the divine controller of history used one evil nation's wealth to reward another evil nation's conquests against yet other evil nations—including Judah.

Yet evil nations are not those who will ultimately succeed (cf. Hab. 2:5–20). It is God's people who will inherit the earth, symbolized here by the *"horn of the house of Israel"* (v. 21). "Horn" (Hebrew, *qeren*) often stands for "power" or "authority" in the Old Testament, and the final verse of the passage predicts the restoration and aggrandizing of the influence of the people of God in the latter days. Ezekiel will also have some influence. He will speak God's word (he is the "you" here) among the Israelites as an encouragement to them even in the midst of their wounded state of exile. Thus Ezekiel's ministry must have gone on after 571 B.C. even though we cannot prove that by any dated oracles in the book. The people of God needed to know His greatness ("that I am the Lord"). Much of the rest of the book represents the encouraging words that the faithful prophet spoke to that end.

EGYPT AND HER ALLIES IN ANGUISH

30:1 The word of the LORD came to me again, saying,
2 "Son of man, prophesy and say, 'Thus says the Lord GOD:

"Wail, 'Woe to the day!'
3 For the day *is* near,
Even the day of the LORD *is* near;
It will be a day of clouds, the time of the
    Gentiles.
4 The sword shall come upon Egypt,
And great anguish shall be in Ethiopia,
When the slain fall in Egypt,
And they take away her wealth,
And her foundations are broken down.

5 "Ethiopia, Libya, Lydia, all the mingled people,
Chub, and the men of the lands who are allied, shall
fall with them by the sword."

6 'Thus says the LORD:

"Those who uphold Egypt shall fall,
And the pride of her power shall come down.
From Migdol *to* Syene
Those within her shall fall by the sword,"
Says the Lord GOD.

7 "They shall be desolate in the midst of the
    desolate countries,
And her cities shall be in the midst of the
    cities *that are* laid waste.
8 Then they will know that I *am* the LORD,
When I have set a fire in Egypt
And all her helpers are destroyed.
9 On that day messengers shall go forth from
    Me in ships
To make the careless Ethiopians afraid,
And great anguish shall come upon them,
As on the day of Egypt;
For indeed it is coming!"

10 'Thus says the Lord GOD:

"I will also make a multitude of Egypt to cease
By the hand of Nebuchadnezzar king of Babylon.
11 He and his people with him, the most terrible
    of the nations,
Shall be brought to destroy the land;
They shall draw their swords against Egypt,
And fill the land with the slain.
12 I will make the rivers dry,
And sell the land into the hand of the wicked;
I will make the land waste, and all that is in it,
By the hand of aliens.
I, the LORD, have spoken."

13 'Thus says the Lord GOD:

"I will also destroy the idols,
And cause the images to cease from Noph;
There shall no longer be princes from the land
    of Egypt;
I will put fear in the land of Egypt.
14 I will make Pathros desolate,
Set fire to Zoan,

286

And execute judgments in No.
15 I will pour My fury on Sin, the strength of
       Egypt;
   I will cut off the multitude of No,
16 And set a fire in Egypt;
   Sin shall have great pain,
   No shall be split open,
   And Noph *shall be in* distress daily.
17 The young men of Aven and Pi Beseth shall
       fall by the sword,
   And these *cities* shall go into captivity.
18 At Tehaphnehes the day shall also be darkened,
   When I break the yokes of Egypt there.
   And her arrogant strength shall cease in her;
   As for her, a cloud shall cover her,
   And her daughters shall go into captivity.
19 Thus I will execute judgments on Egypt,
   Then they shall know that I *am* the LORD."'"
                                            Ezek. 30:1-19

This is the only undated prophecy in the group against Egypt, and it is in some ways the most sweeping. Ranging through a number of states in North Africa that were, either loosely or closely, allies of Egypt and through most of the major cities in Egypt itself, the passage leaves the reader with the clear impression that the Babylonian conquest would devastate a once great region. It is important to realize that Egypt and its allies had been pretty much untouched by foreign invasion. Nothing in Africa could threaten them militarily, and aside from the short invasion of Egypt by Assyria in 664 B.C., the Asian powers had left Egypt alone for centuries.

This is a "Day of the Lord" passage (vv. 2-3). Such passages describe the Lord's coming to intervene decisively in human affairs in the same way that a truly great king was popularly thought in the ancient world to be able to complete a war in a single day. The Lord, the great King of kings, would one day act in judgment against His enemies and on behalf of His people, according to the Day-of-the-Lord concept. The Israelites found the idea of the Day of the Lord much to their liking, since it would represent devastation for their enemies. What they usually failed to realize, however, was that they, too, had become God's enemies and therefore would receive His

287

wrath rather than His rescue on the Day (Amos 5:18–20; Isa. 2:12–17; Zeph. 12:14–18; Joel 2:1–11; etc.). In the present passage, however, the emphasis, in keeping with the context, is strictly on foreign nations.

Most of verses 1–2 is introductory language quite standard in Ezekiel. Verses 2b–3 introduce the passage as a Day-of-the-Lord oracle and include the reminder common to virtually all such prophecies that the "Day" will be not bright but dark (thus full of "clouds") for the various nations on whom the Lord's wrath will fall. Egypt and Nubia (*"Ethiopia,"* v. 5, modern Sudan) will suffer war losses of people and wealth and will experience destruction.

Verse 5 brings Egypt's neighbor states, as well as its many ethnic groups (*"mingled people"*), into the coming anguish of war ("the sword"). Some of these nations are mentioned as well in the oracle against Tyre in Chapter 27. The allies will have no power against the Babylonians, and Egypt will be defeated from north to south (*"From Migdol to Syene,"* v. 6). Verses 7–9 describe the capture of Egyptian cities and their burning, as was standard in ancient warfare, with the terrifying news traveling by ship up the Nile to Nubia ("Ethiopia"). Nebuchadnezzar, Babylon's long-ruling emperor (605–562 B.C.) and his unstoppable army would be the agents of God's action against Egypt (vv. 10–11), and the devastation they would bring about is metaphorically compared to drying up Egypt's life-blood, its rivers (v. 12).

The final subsection of the passage, verses 13–19, contains a catalog of Egyptian cities somewhat in the manner of the catalog of places with whom Tyre traded (27:12–24). Various forms of misery characteristic of the Day of the Lord are mentioned here as what the cities of Egypt may expect. All of them are intended to apply to all of Egypt, although the style of the passage is to pair miseries with cities randomly, in a kind of literary collage. Idols will cease from Noph (Memphis, v. 13). This is a way of rejecting Egypt's religion (cf. Lev. 26:31). The royalty ("princes") will suffer, and the land will fear (cf. Deut. 28:66–67). In verse 14 desolation, fire, and "judgments" will come to Pathros (upper Egypt), Zoan (Tanis, in the eastern Nile Delta), and No (Thebes). Sin (Pelesium, on the Mediterranean coast) and No (Thebes) are both mentioned twice in verses 15–16 and linked with a variety of miseries characteristic of the wrath of God (cf. Leviticus 26; Deuteronomy 28–32). Memphis, first mentioned in the catalog in verse 13, is mentioned here again, completing a kind of concentric pattern of place names, thus giving the ancient hearer a feeling of extensive coverage.

Aven (Heliopolis; cf. Gen. 41:15) and Pi Beseth (Bubastis) were both important cities along the Nile, and with them the great threats of defeat in war and captivity are paired (v. 17). "Darkness" language is again used of the Day of the Lord in verse 18, and the city named here is Tahpanhes, the city on the Suez Canal route where Jeremiah stayed after leaving Judah (Jer. 43:7).

Thus "up and down and all around" Egypt, as it were, the wrath of God will be felt. One of His purposes is to reveal Himself as sovereign among humankind, to be glorified even in the sight of His foes. Such things constitute part of God's redemptive role in this world. The Egyptians, oppressors of the Israelites at many stages in their history, were defiant of the Lord, a deity whom they regarded as puny in relation to their "great" gods. As it had taken severe measures to teach the Egyptians that the Lord was supreme over them at the time of the exodus, so it would be necessary for them to suffer His wrath again so that they might recognize His sovereignty ("know that I am the Lord"). God's purpose in speaking all these oracles against foreign nations through Ezekiel was the same: to get the faith and confidence of the nations—especially Israel—away from their idols, who could not save, and toward Himself, who alone could.

PHARAOH'S BROKEN ARMS

30:20 And it came to pass in the eleventh year, in the first *month*, on the seventh *day* of the month, *that* the word of the LORD came to me, saying,

21 "Son of man, I have broken the arm of Pharaoh king of Egypt; and see, it has not been bandaged for healing, nor a splint put on to bind it, to make it strong enough to hold a sword.

22 "Therefore thus says the Lord GOD: 'Surely I *am* against Pharaoh king of Egypt, and will break his arms, both the strong one and the one that was broken; and I will make the sword fall out of his hand.

23 'I will scatter the Egyptians among the nations, and disperse them throughout the countries.

24 'I will strengthen the arms of the king of Babylon
and put My sword in his hand; but I will break
Pharaoh's arms, and he will groan before him with the
groanings of a mortally wounded *man*.

25 'Thus I will strengthen the arms of the king of
Babylon, but the arms of Pharaoh shall fall down;
they shall know that I *am* the LORD, when I put My
sword into the hand of the king of Babylon and he
stretches it out against the land of Egypt.

26 'I will scatter the Egyptians among the nations
and disperse them throughout the countries. Then
they shall know that I *am* the LORD.'"

Ezek. 30:20–26

Ezekiel dates this oracle to the beginning month of the ancient calendar (March–April) of his eleventh year of captivity, that is, 587 B.C.
It was thus revealed to him by God while the Babylonians were still
besieging Jerusalem, and many of the exiles must have clung to the
same sort of hope that their kinsmen in Jerusalem held: Egypt would
rescue Judah from Babylon. Jer. 37:5–11 tells us that there was a time,
late in 588 B.C., when the Egyptians actually distracted the Babylonians from Jerusalem so that the siege was lifted for a few weeks. The
Egyptians had sent out an army, at the request of King Zedekiah of
Judah, to rescue the beleaguered Judeans. But the Babylonians had
easily driven the Egyptians back to Egypt, just as Jeremiah had
prophesied, and then resumed the siege of Jerusalem once again,
never again to be dissuaded from taking the city (cf. Jer. 37:17; 38:2).

The Babylonian defeat of the Egyptian army sent to relieve Judah
was the metaphorical "broken arm" of Pharaoh referred to in
Ezek. 30:21. Ezekiel is told that the "arm" (Hebrew, *zeraʿ*, a typical
metonymy for "power" in the Old Testament) will not heal—Pharaoh
will not recoup after this loss in order to march back to Judah to help
the Israelites. Indeed, Pharaoh's other "arm" will be broken as well.
This was fulfilled in stages as Pharaoh Hophra (589–570 B.C.) was
defeated in a war he started with Lybia, was then demoted to co-
regent after a revolt against him in Egypt, and was finally assassi-
nated by people loyal to his rival co-regent, Ahmose, in accord with
the prediction of Jer. 44:30.

As a result, Egypt was helpless before the Babylonians, who were
soon enough to conquer Egypt, just as they had conquered Palestine,

and drive the Egyptians as refugees to other lands as well as taking some of them captive (v. 23). Babylon's power ("arms") would increase, but Egypt's would decrease (vv. 24–25). Egyptians would end up on the run or in captivity (v. 26). Again, the result would serve the Lord's end in displaying His sovereign power to the once-proud nation of Egypt (v. 26), so the verse ends with the familiar "Then they shall know that I am the Lord." God is in charge of history and of the events of nations. This passage represents an instance where He revealed to His prophet, and through His prophet to a wider audience, a particular way that His plan for shaping and moving history would take form. To the reader looking for God's purposes to be accomplished, the passage is another reassurance of the redemptive plan of God unfolding. To the ancient or modern skeptic, of course, it was just a matter of one nation losing to another in war. But the skeptic never has the true picture; God always does.

EGYPT CUT DOWN LIKE A GREAT TREE

31:1 Now it came to pass in the eleventh year, in the third *month*, on the first *day* of the month, *that the* word of the LORD came to me, saying,
2 "Son of man, say to Pharaoh king of Egypt and to his multitude:

'Whom are you like in your greatness?
3 Indeed Assyria *was* a cedar in Lebanon,
With fine branches that shaded the forest,
And of high stature;
And its top was among the thick boughs.
4 The waters made it grow;
Underground waters gave it height,
With their rivers running around the place
      where it was planted,
And sent out rivulets to all the trees of the field.

5 'Therefore its height was exalted above all the
      trees of the field;
Its boughs were multiplied,
And its branches became long because of the
      abundance of water,
As it sent them out.

291

6 All the birds of the heavens made their nests
    in its boughs;
Under its branches all the beasts of the field
    brought forth their young;
And in its shadow all great nations made their
    home.

7 'Thus it was beautiful in greatness and in the
    length of its branches,
Because its roots reached to abundant waters.
8 The cedars in the garden of God could not
    hide it;
The fir trees were not like its boughs,
And the chestnut trees were not like its
    branches;
No tree in the garden of God was like it in
    beauty.
9 I made it beautiful with a multitude of
    branches,
So that all the trees of Eden envied it,
That *were* in the garden of God.'

10 'Therefore thus says the Lord GOD: 'Because you have increased in height, and it set its top among the thick boughs, and its heart was lifted up in its height,

11 'therefore I will deliver it into the hand of the mighty one of the nations, and he shall surely deal with it; I have driven it out for its wickedness.

12 'And aliens, the most terrible of the nations, have cut it down and left it; its branches have fallen on the mountains and in all the valleys; its boughs lie broken by all the rivers of the land; and all the peoples of the earth have gone from under its shadow and left it.

13 'On its ruin will remain all the birds of
    the heavens,
And all the beasts of the field will come
    to its branches—

14 'So that no trees by the waters may ever again exalt themselves for their height, nor set their tops among the thick boughs, that no tree which drinks water may ever be high enough to reach up to them.

'For they have all been delivered to death,

To the depths of the earth,
Among the children of men who go down to the
Pit.'

15 "Thus says the Lord GOD: 'In the day when it
went down to hell, I caused mourning. I covered the
deep because of it. I restrained its rivers, and the great
waters were held back. I caused Lebanon to mourn for
it, and all the trees of the field wilted because of it.

16 'I made the nations shake at the sound of its fall,
when I cast it down to hell together with those who
descend into the Pit; and all the trees of Eden, the
choice and best of Lebanon, all that drink water, were
comforted in the depths of the earth.

17 'They also went down to hell with it, with those
slain by the sword; and *those who were* its *strong* arm
dwelt in its shadows among the nations.

18 'To which of the trees in Eden will you then
be likened in glory and greatness? Yet you shall be
brought down with the trees of Eden to the depths of
the earth; you shall lie in the midst of the uncircumcised, with *those* slain by the sword. This *is* Pharaoh
and all his multitude,' says the Lord GOD."

Ezek. 31:1-18

We come to another of Ezekiel's great allegories. This one is much
like a funerary lament allegory (cf. Ezekiel 27 and 32), although it is
not identified as a lament. Nevertheless it has the elements of direct
address to the nation about to be "dead" and an eulogy of its past
greatness, two of the four elements that constitute a lament (the
other two being the call to mourning and the evaluation of the loss
to the survivors). Mourning is mentioned in verse 15 and survivors
of a sort in verses 15–16, but the mood is not exactly that of a typical
lament. It is more a tragic allegory.

Egypt is, of course, the subject of the sad story, and Pharaoh and
the population are taken together as an entity in a manner somewhat
like that of Chapter 32, but not exactly paralleled in any other passage in this section of the book. The first nine verses of the chapter
are in poetry, and the rest is prose, with the possible exception of
verses 13–14b, which are either poetry or—more likely—somewhat
parallelistic prose. Overall, the chapter may be outlined as follows:

Poem comparing Egypt to a splendid great tree (vv. 2–9)
Prose description of the tree cut down by Babylon (vv. 10–14)
Prose description of the tree's fall to hell (vv. 15–18)

The chapter is dated to the first of May–June of the year 578 B.C., that is, just fifty-three days after the preceding passage. Jerusalem was once again under siege by Babylonian troops back from the defeat of the Egyptians (see the the discussion above on 30:21–22). Still, many may have held out hope that Egypt would mount an even stronger expedition against the Babylonians, or at least escape an actual conquest of its homeland, something the Palestinian nations had been unable to do.

On the use of a great tree to symbolize a great nation or population, cf. Ezekiel 17; 19:1–14; Daniel 4; Matt. 13:31–34.

Verses 1–2a give the date and identify the subject of the allegorical prophecy. The question *"Whom are you like in your greatness?"* (v. 2b) is a challenge to Egypt's arrogance, comparable to the challenge to Tyre in 28:3, 9 (cf. Isa. 37:23, 26). In verse 3 the allegory proceeds to identify the figure that will represent Egypt: a great tree of Lebanon, the richly forested region just north of Israel in ancient times. *"Assyria"* renders a Hebrew word (ʾaššūr) that may also be translated as "cypress." The latter is probably the better translation, since Assyria is not the symbol of Egypt in the allegory, whereas a great tree surely is. "Cypress" and "cedar" are thus used together in this verse to convey the idea of a great tree, the exact species of which is not told us. This is similar to the way that Egypt is described first as a lion and then immediately thereafter as a huge fish in 32:2—that is, Egypt is a big animal, the species left unidentified.

Verses 3–7 are merely poetic depictions of the greatness of the tree, thus reminding the hearer/reader of the greatness of Egypt, which was one of the superpowers of Old Testament times and a place where many nations traded and with whom they had political alliances. Then, in verses 8–9, the tree is praised as more impressive even than the trees of the Garden of Eden. It is important to understand that this is hyperbole—purposeful exaggeration to make a point. In the lament-style allegories found so frequently in Ezekiel, the greatness of a nation (whether real or merely selfishly imagined) is portrayed in high tones as a prelude to the description of the tragic fall. Here the poetic tone is ironic. What verses 3–8 describe is not reality as God sees it, but reality as Egypt sees it. It thinks itself the greatest of God's creations (v. 9). We know from Egyptian religious texts that the Egyptians did indeed think exactly that of themselves.

The Garden of Eden overtones continue somewhat in verses 10–14, much in the manner of Ezek. 28:13–19. In other words, what applied to Tyre could also apply to Egypt. After such pride must come a great fall. The human agent of the fall will be the *"mighty one of the nations"* (v. 11), that is, Babylon. Egypt will thus be "driven out" for its wickedness—like Adam and Eve were driven out for theirs (vv. 10–11). What is that "wickedness?" It is simply opposition to God's rule, proved in the case of these oracles against foreign nations by the nations' opposition to or oppression of God's people. In verse 12 the allegory moves on to the fallen, dead tree, now no longer a place to which people of the world pay much attention (i.e., Egypt will become a minor place). Wild animals will settle on the remains of the tree (v. 13), a standard biblical way of portraying the desolation of a place once inhabited by many people (cf. Isa. 13:19–22; Jer. 50:39–40; in the Pentateuch cf. Lev. 26:33–35; Deut. 29:23). Verse 14 stresses the purpose of Egypt's coming judgment: it is part of God's justice which condemns all those who exalt themselves against Him. All such must die.

In verses 15–18 the allegory moves on to imagine Egypt in hell (Hebrew, *šeʾōl*) with other nations or groups who died for their sins against God. This is not a literal picture of hell, but a figurative one, as an appreciation of the allegory requires. The first result of Egypt's death as a great nation, symbolized by the tree's fall, is worldwide mourning (v. 15). The nations would feel the loss of their counterpart—and would also fear lest the same thing happened to them. In the language of the allegory the worldwide mourning is indicated by a stoppage of the flow of the world's waters and a sympathetic wilting of the world's trees. Other "trees," already in hell, take some comfort in the fall of the "tree" of Egypt (v. 15), a tree whose fall scares and affects other nations on the earth (v. 16). Egypt's allies are in hell, too (v. 17, *"those who were its strong arm"*), in the allegory—they would not escape while Egypt suffered at the hand of the Babylonians just as Egypt would not escape while Palestine likewise suffered. Egypt's fall will be like that of of the Garden of Eden (which is imagined as being destroyed here after Adam and Eve

will join the *"uncircumcised"* (a way of referring to all those who
have rejected God) and *"those slain by the sword"* (those punished by
God through the intermediation of the Babylonians and others He
unleashed on evil nations, v. 18).

Some have thought that to be with the "uncircumcised" and those
"slain by the sword" was to be in the lowest part of hell, but there is
no certainty that that is what the allegory intends to imply. The language is figurative, and the communicator would make a mistake to
try to see in the allegory any teaching about the nature of hell or
degrees of final punishment, or any such thing. The purpose of the
allegory is to reassure the faithful among the exiles and all subsequent readers that God does not judge His own covenant people
without also having a plan to punish the rest of the world, and nations who oppose His will will surely get their deserved fate.

To the Judeans of Ezekiel's day Egypt was a giant and they were a
dwarf. They needed encouragement, especially at a time when their
little capital city—all that remained of their nation—was surrounded
by enemy troops while huge, prosperous Egypt enjoyed respect
among the nations of the world. But Egypt's time would come. It was
big, and it would fall hard.

A Lament for Pharaoh and Egypt

32:1 And it came to pass in the twelfth year, in the
twelfth *month*, on the first *day* of the month, *that*
the word of the LORD came to me, saying,
2 "Son of man, take up a lamentation for Pharaoh
king of Egypt, and say to him:

'You are like a young lion among the nations,
And you *are* like a monster in the seas,
Bursting forth in your rivers,
Troubling the waters with your feet,
And fouling their rivers.'

3 "Thus says the Lord GOD:

'I will therefore spread My net over you with
a company of many people,
And they will draw you up in My net.
4 Then I will leave you on the land;
I will cast you out on the open fields,

And cause to settle on you all the birds of the
heavens.
And with you I will fill the beasts of the
whole earth.
5 I will lay your flesh on the mountains,
And fill the valleys with your carcass.

6 'I will also water the land with the flow of
your blood,
Even to the mountains;
And the riverbeds will be full of you.
7 WhKn *I* put out your light,
I will cover the heavens, and make its stars
dark;
I will cover the sun with a cloud,
And the moon shall not give her light.
8 All the bright lights of the heavens I will make
dark over you,
And bring darkness upon your land,'
Says the Lord GOD.

9 'I will also trouble the hearts of many peoples,
when I bring your destruction among the nations,
into the countries which you have not known.
10 'Yes, I will make many peoples astonished at
you, and their kings shall be horribly afraid of you
when I brandish My sword before them; and they
shall tremble *every* moment, every man for his own
life, in the day of your fall.'
11 "For thus says the Lord GOD: 'The sword of the
king of Babylon shall come upon you.
12 'By the swords of the mighty warriors, all of
them the most terrible of the nations, I will cause
your multitude to fall.

'They shall plunder the pomp of Egypt,
And all its multitude shall be destroyed.
13 Also I will destroy all its animals
From beside its great waters;
The foot of man shall muddy them no more,
Nor shall the hooves of animals muddy them.
14 Then I will make their waters clear,
And make their rivers run like oil,'
Says the Lord GOD.

15 'When I make the land of Egypt desolate,
   And the country is destitute of all that once
      filled it,
   When I strike all who dwell in it,
   Then they shall know that I *am* the LORD.

16 'This *is* the lamentation
   With which they shall lament her;
   The daughters of the nations shall lament her;
   They shall lament for her, for Egypt,
   And for all her multitude,'
   Says the Lord GOD."

Ezek. 32:1–16

Ezekiel's oracles against foreign nations draw to a close with Chapter 32, which contains two laments on Egypt. Although 32:2 might seem to limit the first lament (vv. 1–16) to the Pharaoh, it is obvious from the contents that all of Egypt is the subject, even though Pharaoh is the one to whom the oracle is directly addressed. Verses 1–16 are comparable to 29:1–16, with which they share both imagery and vocabulary.

This lament has an unusual perspective in that it is spoken almost entirely predictively in the first person by God Himself, much in the manner of a judgment sentence or curse prediction. Most laments speak about and/or to the subject but not so strongly from the divine voice, and they are more retrospective. Nevertheless, the four lament elements are present: direct address to the (future) dead; eulogy of the dead (mainly v. 2 here); call to mourning (v. 16, prose conclusion); and evaluation of the loss to the survivors (vv. 9–10 especially).

The date of this oracle is the end of the twelfth year of the exile of King Jehoiachin (and Ezekiel), that is, late 586 B.C., just weeks after the news reached the exiles in Tel-Abib that Jerusalem had fallen to the Babylonians (cf. 33:21). Many must have been very disheartened, and surely Ezekiel himself would not have relished the news, even though it confirmed the accuracy of his preaching of the last dozen years. Perhaps now some in his potential audience would actually pay some attention, and another oracle against Egypt would be heard with more open ears. The fact of so many prophecies on the same subject should be a reminder to the modern communicator that the truth of a message is conveyed only when the audience

298

actually pays attention to it. Since audiences often change gradually and/or constantly, and people don't always pay attention the first time—or the next time—the communicator may have to repeat the message many times before some people really hear it.

The passage may be outlined as follows:

Introduction (vv. 1–2)
Description of Egypt's fall (vv. 2–8)
Description of people's reaction: horror (vv. 9–12a)
Egypt's desolation (vv. 12b–15)
Call to lament (v. 16)

Parts or all of verses 2b–15 may be poetry or stylized prose. Since lamentations were sung, we must assume that the passage is poetic, but its parallelism and meter are not always obvious.

After a simple and standard sort of introduction to the lament (vv. 1–2a), Pharaoh and Egypt together are imagined to be a large animal, called poetically both a lion and a huge fish (Hebrew, *tannîn*). The terms of description in verse 2 sound like what might be said of a crocodile (cf. Job 41), an animal quite appropriate to an oracle about Egypt, but still imaginarily giant in the context. Armies of the nations will catch this animal (Egypt) in a net (v. 3) and leave it on the dry land to die, bleeding everywhere—a great death indeed (vv. 3–6; cf. 29:3–5, which has similar vocabulary and imagery). Verses 7–8 contain the darkness language characteristic of prophecies of the Day of the Lord, already seen in Ezekiel in 30:3 and 30:18.

"If mighty Egypt can fall, what about us?" is the point of verses 9–10, which depict the fear Egypt's conquest by the Babylonians will engender in many other nations yet to feel Babylon's oppression. The Babylonian onslaught will indeed be destructive to Egypt (vv. 11–12). Desolation will be Egypt's fate (v. 13, suggested by the absence of man and beast; cf. 29:8; Jer. 33:10, 12; etc.). With no one around in the desolate land, the usually muddy Nile and its streams will run clear and fast (*"like oil,"* v. 14).

The desolation will be a reminder to refugees and exiles from Egypt, as well as more distant observers (any of these may be the "they" of v. 15), that the Lord is the one true God ("they shall know that I am the Lord"). Then *"the daughters of the nations"* will sing for Egypt this sad song (v. 16). Women were often the community singers of ancient times (cf. Exod. 15:20–21; 1 Sam. 18:6–7), and this verse imagines women all over the ancient world singing about Egypt's fall. In other words, it will become a famous national disaster hymned far and wide.

Once again the purpose of an oracle against a foreign nation is God's determination to reassure His people that they are not alone or forgotten in their sufferings and to assert the certainty that His own glory will eventually be recognized. Babylonian armies were merely His minions; Nebuchadnezzar himself was merely His lackey in the task. Egypt's coming fate—that of a once-great but now impotent nation—would remind all who thought about it of how God's will would be accomplished on the earth. We should be reminded of God's greatness, then, by Egypt's history. The fact that after Nebuchadnezzar finished with it, Egypt never again reclaimed its greatness should be an encouragement to all who trust in the Lord. If His promise was true in this case, will it not be true in all others?

THE NATIONS IN THE PIT

32:17 It came to pass also in the twelfth year, on the fifteenth *day* of the month, that the word of the LORD came to me, saying:

18 "Son of man, wail over the multitude of Egypt,
And cast them down to the depths of the earth,
Her and the daughters of the famous nations,
With those who go down to the Pit:
19 'Whom do you surpass in beauty?
Go down, be placed with the uncircumcised.'
20 "They shall fall in the midst of *those* slain by
the sword;
She is delivered to the sword,
Drawing her and all her multitudes.
21 The strong among the mighty
Shall speak to him out of the midst of hell
With those who help him:
'They have gone down,
They lie with the uncircumcised, slain by the
sword.'
22 "Assyria *is* there, and all her company,

300

With their graves all around her,
All of them slain, fallen by the sword.
23 Her graves are set in the recesses of the Pit,
And her company is all around her grave,
All of them slain, fallen by the sword,
Who caused terror in the land of the living.

24 "There *is* Elam and all her multitude,
All around her grave,
All of them slain, fallen by the sword,
Who have gone down uncircumcised to the
  lower parts of the earth,
Who caused their terror in the land of the
  living;
Now they bear their shame with those who go
  down to the Pit.
25 They have set her bed in the midst of the slain,
With all her multitude,
With her graves all around it,
All of them uncircumcised, slain by the sword;
Though their terror was caused
In the land of the living,
Yet they bear their shame
With those who go down to the Pit;
It was put in the midst of the slain.

26 "There *are* Meshech and Tubal and all their
  multitudes,
With all their graves around it,
All of them uncircumcised, slain by the sword,
Though they caused their terror in the land of
  the living.
27 They do not lie with the mighty
Who are fallen of the uncircumcised,
Who have gone down to hell with their
  weapons of war;
They have laid their swords under their heads,
But their iniquities will be on their bones,
Because of the terror of the mighty in the land
  of the living.
28 Yes, you shall be broken in the midst of the
  uncircumcised,
And lie with *those* slain by the sword.

29 "There *is* Edom,
   Her kings and all her princes,
   Who despite their might
   Are laid beside *those* slain by the sword;
   They shall lie with the uncircumcised,
   And with those who go down to the Pit.
30 There *are* the princes of the north,
   All of them, and all the Sidonians,
   Who have gone down with the slain
   In shame at the terror which they caused by
      their might;
   They lie uncircumcised with *those* slain by the
      sword,
   And bear their shame with those who go down
      to the Pit.

31 "Pharaoh will see them
   And be comforted over all his multitude,
   Pharaoh and all his army,
   Slain by the sword,"
   Says the Lord GOD.

32 "For I have caused My terror in the land of the
      living;
   And he shall be placed in the midst of the
      uncircumcised
   With *those* slain by the sword,
   Pharaoh and all his multitude,"
   Says the Lord GOD.

                                        Ezek. 32:17–32

This is the seventh and final passage in the group of oracles against Egypt (chaps. 29–32) and the concluding oracle in the book's collection of oracles against foreign nations (chaps. 25–32). It is dated by Ezekiel to the twelfth year, that is, late 586 B.C., probably also in the twelfth month (cf. 32:1), and thus just fourteen days later than the preceding prophecy. It is not the latest of the foreign nation oracles, since almost fifteen years later Ezekiel received another revelation about Egypt (29:17–21). It is, however, an appropriate oracle with which to conclude this major section of the book since it incorporates so many nations with such a wide geographical range and describes their final destruction in hell in such seeping terms. No one among Ezekiel's audience could fail to miss the implication: no matter how bleak things looked for the Israelites and for the exiled community on the Chebar Canal, the days were coming when those nations now in the spotlight would be in the dark Pit of hell, and God's people would be freed from the grip of international empires of conquest and the oppression they brought upon all in their path.

The fate of Babylon is, of course, not mentioned anywhere among these oracles against foreign nations. Babylon, for Ezekiel's audience, was the agent of God. Other prophets had already preached its eventual downfall; for the time being the Babylonians were the people God had chosen to punish the nations, and that was what Ezekiel's contemporaries needed to know.

This passage is a lament as well, since Ezekiel is told by God to *"wail over the multitude of Egypt"* (v. 18). It displays the four lament characteristics mentioned in connection with the previous passage. Here it is presented as poetry; other English translations (such as the NIV) treat it entirely as prose. If it is poetry, its poetic structure is certainly unusual. Perhaps Ezekiel is given the facts here in prose with the symbolic expectation that he would make up a song from them. Ezekiel, of course, reported faithfully just what God had inspired him to know. Any musical poem he might have made up based upon this revelation could have been his own work. These words, on the other hand, are from God.

It would be a mistake to try to learn about the nature of hell from this passage. The Bible teaches about hell elsewhere and only uses the idea of hell poetically in this passage. It mentions the "Pit" (Hebrew, *bōr*) and hell (Hebrew, *še'ōl*) but only in an imaginary scenario. In this hell various nations and their leaders are imagined as buried together in large groups, some nations in more shameful locations within hell than others. Pharaoh and his army (i.e., those whom the Babylonians will defeat) will lie in hell in one of the places imagined as reserved for armies beaten in battle, and the fact that so many other great empires of the past are also lying in similar circumstances will be a sort of consolation to the Egyptians. None of these details fits with what the Bible otherwise teaches about hell, and therefore they must be taken as a symbolic backdrop against which the point of the prophecy can be clearly seen: great earthly powers, no matter how ruthless and powerful, all eventually come to an end as God judges the affairs of the earth.

The passage may be outlined as follows:

1. Egypt lamented and welcomed to the Pit (vv. 17–21)
2. Assyria (vv. 22–23)
3. Elam (vv. 24–25)
4. Meshech and Tubal (vv. 26–28)
5. Edom (v. 29)
6. Phoenicia and Sidon (v. 30)
7. Recapitulation: Egypt has joined the others (vv. 31–32)

The introductory words (v. 17) are typical. In verse 18, the reference to *"her and the daughters of the famous nations"* is like the mention of *"the daughters of the nations"* in verse 16 at the end of the previous passage—it names others who will join Ezekiel in the lament over Egypt, not those who will go to hell along with Egypt.

Egypt is addressed directly in verse 19 in lament style, with the ironic question *"Whom do you surpass in beauty?"* as seen routinely in these laments. The concern of the passage then moves immediately to the fate of Egypt, which is to lose in war (to the Babylonians) and thus go to the place in hell reserved for slain armies. There (among many nations who rejected God, thus described as "uncircumcised," or outside of God's covenant blessing) Egypt will descend, welcomed as it were by *"the strong"* of hell, who are doorkeepers of a sort in this imagistic lament (vv. 19–21).

Who else is there? In verse 22 begins a litany of past great world powers who no longer are around on the earth. Assyria has its graves in one section, in the *"recesses of the Pit,"* that is, in a location not favored. Once a terror, Assyria is now a dead nation (vv. 22–23). The Assyrians were defeated by the Babylonians between 609 and 605 B.C., an event still vivid in the memory of most of Ezekiel's contemporaries. It was well known that Assyria simply ceased to exist as a nation, except as a region within the Babylonian Empire.

Elam is also in hell (vv. 24–25). Many of the same things are said of Elam that were said above of Assyria. Once great, both now lie slain, defeated militarily and confined in shame to hell. After the destruction of the Assyrian Empire, Elam, a nation to the east of the Tigris River, was annexed by the ancient Indo-European Iranian Empire and eventually became part of the Persian Empire. It was thus never again a nation in its own right.

Meshech and Tubal (vv. 26–28) are more distant powers. Meshech occupied a region in the Fertile Crescent southeast of the Black Sea. In conjunction with Tubal (about whom little is known), it was a former great Indo-European nation that had conquered what is now eastern Turkey, demolishing much of what was originally the Hittite Empire in the process. As people of an entirely different culture and language family, Meshech and Tubal were especially awesome to the Semitic Israelites. Nevertheless, they, too, were in hell when Pharaoh and the Egyptians got there. The Assyrians had wiped out their power in a long series of wars before themselves falling prey to the Babylonians.

Edom (v. 29) is the "standard" foreign nation mentioned in oracles against foreign nations in the prophetical books. Edom had such a long history of enmity to Israel, even though as a nation descended from Abraham and Isaac it was a "brother" nation, that it was routinely included in such contexts as a kind of synecdoche for any or all of the foreign peoples who had opposed the Lord's people over the years.

The *"princes of the north"* and *"the Sidonians"* (v. 30) apparently refer to the rulers of a variety of city-states in Phoenicia, north of Israel, as well as to Sidon, which after the defeat of Tyre by Babylon became the predominant Phoenician city and thus is mentioned by name here. Tyre, under siege at the time this oracle was received by Ezekiel, is not mentioned, possibly because Ezekiel had already devoted so much attention to it (chaps. 26–28) but perhaps also as a prediction of its coming ignominy in contrast to the growing influence of Sidon, its coastal neighbor to the south.

Verses 31–32 conclude the lament with a reminder that Egypt, too, will be there in hell along with all the other once-great, uncircumcised nations who were beaten by other nations in war. It will be a consolation of sorts for the Egyptians to know that they will have plenty of friends in hell—and that is not to be lost on the hearer/reader. It is a major point of the entire prophecy: all the once-great dominating powers, many of whom oppressed relatively tiny Israel, will be destroyed. They will not forever dominate the world scene. Their influence lasted only as long as God allowed it, and they did only what God permitted them to do, including killing one another off. When God decrees it, they take their turn in the Pit.

If this control of God over the events of nations through history could be understood, then it could be believed that God had the power to restore little Israel, who in Ezekiel's day stood shamed before the other nations of the world as a destroyed, deported, "dead" nation. That is what the exiled Israelites needed desperately to realize: God was running history, controlling the states of earth. The Babylonians were not in charge. God was. He would eventually shame the other nations, at whose hands Israel now felt ashamed, and make an end of the powers that had seemed to human eyes to have brought about Israel's end. The prophecies that follow in the remainder of the book build upon the certainty that God will restore His people and protect them from the greatest dangers the powers of the world can throw at them, bringing them to a glorious eternal end. Not only can He do it, but Ezekiel's prophecies against the nations show to the faithful a reassuring glimpse of the fact that it will indeed happen.

Hope and Danger in the Future

Ezekiel 33:1–39:29

CHAPTER TWENTY

Responsibility and Irresponsibility

Ezekiel 33:1–34:31

We come to a new section of Ezekiel. Chapters 1–24 concerned mainly the certainty and necessity of the fall of Judah and Jerusalem to Babylonian conquest. Chapters 25–33 contained oracles predicting the doom of a wide range of nations foreign to Judah and Jerusalem. Now, in Chapters 33–37, we are back, in a sense, to oracles that relate to the fall of Judah and Jerusalem. This time, however, the oracles are hopeful rather than judgmental. Now that the Lord has completed His plan for destruction of His former people, it is important that they have a clear understanding of what He has done and what will happen to them as a people—and also generally as individuals—in the future. The oracles are not all entirely reassuring to the Judeans, but they are basically positive, emphasizing the sovereignty of God, His fairness, and His good plans for the new Israel that He will create from the ruins of the old.

In Ezekiel 33–34 three passages that have to do with responsibility, or lack of it, are grouped together. Each passage points in some way to human irresponsibility and by contrast to God's justice. In the aftermath of the fall of Jerusalem, the exile community could no longer doubt that God's word through Ezekiel had been true all along. Now they needed to understand some important principles of God's action and to prepare themselves for their future as a people—if they were willing to take the responsibility to do so, that is.

ONCE MORE: INDIVIDUAL RESPONSIBILITY AND GOD'S FAIRNESS

33:1 Again the word of the LORD came to me, saying,
2 "Son of man, speak to the children of your

people, and say to them: 'When I bring the sword upon a land, and the people of the land take a man from their territory and make him their watchman,

3 'when he sees the sword coming upon the land, if he blows the trumpet and warns the people,

4 'then whoever hears the sound of the trumpet and does not take warning, if the sword comes and takes him away, his blood shall be on his *own* head.

5 'He heard the sound of the trumpet, but did not take warning; his blood shall be upon himself. But he who takes warning will save his life.

6 'But if the watchman sees the sword coming and does not blow the trumpet, and the people are not warned, and the sword comes and takes *any* person from among them, he is taken away in his iniquity; but his blood I will require at the watchman's hand.'

7 "So you, son of man: I have made you a watchman for the house of Israel; therefore you shall hear a word from My mouth and warn them for Me.

8 "When I say to the wicked, 'O wicked *man*, you shall surely die!" and you do not speak to warn the wicked from his way, that wicked *man* shall die in his iniquity; but his blood I will require at your hand.

9 "Nevertheless if you warn the wicked to turn from his way, and he does not turn from his way, he shall die in his iniquity; but you have delivered your soul.

10 "Therefore you, O son of man, say to the house of Israel: 'Thus you say, "If our transgressions and our sins *lie* upon us, and we pine away in them, how can we then live?"'

11 "Say to them: '*As* I live,' says the Lord GOD, 'I have no pleasure in the death of the wicked, but that the wicked turn from his way and live. Turn, turn from your evil ways! For why should you die, O house of Israel?'

12 "Therefore you, O son of man, say to the children of your people: 'The righteousness of the righteous man shall not deliver him in the day of his transgression; as for the wickedness of the wicked, he shall not fall because of it in the day that he turns

from his wickedness; nor shall the righteous be able to live because of *his righteousness* in the day that he sins.'

13 "When I say to the righteous *that* he shall surely live, but he trusts in his own righteousness and commits iniquity, none of his righteous works shall be remembered; but because of the iniquity that he has committed, he shall die.

14 "Again, when I say to the wicked, 'You shall surely die,' if he turns from his sin and does what is lawful and right,

15 "*if* the wicked restores the pledge, gives back what he has stolen, and walks in the statutes of life without committing iniquity, he shall surely live; he shall not die.

16 "None of his sins which he has committed shall be remembered against him; he has done what is lawful and right; he shall surely live.

17 "Yet the children of your people say, 'The way of the LORD is not fair.' But it is their way which is not fair!

18 "When the righteous turns from his righteousness and commits iniquity, he shall die because of it.

19 "But when the wicked turns from his wickedness and does what is lawful and right, he shall live because of it.

20 "Yet you say, 'The way of the LORD is not fair.' O house of Israel, I will judge every one of you according to his own ways."

Ezek. 33:1–20

The question of individual responsibility and God's fairness was raised in detail in Ezekiel 18. It is addressed in a somewhat different way here, but the point is the same: how God punishes and forgives is not unfair, but completely correct. It is what the Israelites have thought about punishment and forgiveness that is not correct.

The passage may be outlined as follows:

Responsibility of a watchman vis-à-vis his people (vv. 1–6)
Ezekiel's responsibility to his people like that of a watchman (vv. 7–11)

Sin can overcome a history of righteousness (vv. 12–13)
Righteousness can overcome a history of sin (vv. 14–16)
God's way is fair (vv. 17–20)

The wording of verse 1 is known to us by now as that of an introduction to a new individual prophecy. In verses 2–6 Ezekiel hears what he must pass on to his people. It is the principle, undoubtedly perfectly logical to them, that when people fail to listen to the warning of a watchman that enemy troops are approaching (i.e., "the sword" is coming), they must bear the consequences of their own irresponsible behavior. The watchman is responsible to warn; the people are responsible to act for themselves after that. No one in Ezekiel's audience of fellow captive Israelites would have doubted this principle, and it thus served to lead the way to the point of verses 7–9, that Ezekiel was God's "watchman," whose warnings were to be heeded—or else! Verses 1–9, then, constitute a kind of reaffirmation of Ezekiel's commission. They are addressed to him so that he will know his responsibility and as well to the people with the hope that they will realize theirs.

What, in fact, does God want from the Israelites? Repentance! What will it produce? Forgiveness! That is the message Ezekiel must preach and the people must hear, according to verses 10–11. It is a great message. Ezekiel 1–24 is full of warnings to the Israelites that their long history of disobedience to God's law, extending from the time they entered the promised land to the present, meant that they had to be punished. Those same chapters contain much to remind the people that the wages of sin is death and, therefore, the nation must die. So the pessimism of verse 10 (*"how can we then live?"*) was understandable from a human point of view. From the divine point of view, however, there was great hope. What Israel needed to do was to turn from its sin toward God—making Him Lord and thus accepting Him as Savior. For the rest of the book this invitation to turn to the Lord, obeying His word and receiving His deliverance, is a central theme.

But there was still a way of thinking that had to be changed. Ezekiel's fellow exiles remained committed to this old way of thinking: the idea that the past can't be overcome, that people never really become different just by taking a new direction in their lives (vv. 12–16). Such thinking is common today as well. When a person claims to have committed his or her life to Christ, many people are skeptical—especially if the person was well known to be a sinner. "Let's see how long this lasts," people say, because they find it hard to believe that anyone would really be able to change his or her basic personality. Of course, no one can succeed in such a change without divine help. That is what breaks the usual cycle and overcomes the routine pattern of failure in spite of good resolutions. The fact that a person in Christ is a new creation (2 Cor. 5:17) is really a dramatically important truth. An old creation, by nature, cannot significantly change from habits of sin. A new creation can! With God's help, people can be different. They can please Him. And *His* pleasure is that none should die (vv. 11, 15, 16) but that all should convert to Him and live.

Again (cf. 18:25) we read of a popular saying among Ezekiel's contemporaries: *"The way of the Lord is not fair"* (vv. 17, 20). This was not necessarily an anti-Yahwistic statement, as if the people were condemning Yahweh (the Lord) in comparison to other gods for being a generally or usually unfair god. Rather, it can also be translated "The way of the Lord is not equal," the sense being that some people get more than others from the Lord. Clearly, however, the popular saying was wrong on any account, since it implied that God shows favoritism. He does not. As verse 20 concludes, *"I will judge every one of you according to his own ways."* Of course, repentance and turning to God from sin is part of one's "ways." Such a decisive, life-changing action can redeem a life headed for death. And just as truly, but also tragically, turning from God to sin can pollute a life that had been heading toward abundant life, so that the result is death.

Again, as in Chapter 18, these references to life and death are not statements about the duration of this present life, but of eternal life—or death. A conversion even after a long life of evil in this world can produce eternal life with the Lord. What a promise to a people long debilitated by their sin! What a hope, indeed, guaranteed to everyone who hears the words of God and responds to them!

JERUSALEM'S DESOLATION AND THE PEOPLE'S IRRESPONSIBILITY

33:21 And it came to pass in the twelfth year of our captivity, in the tenth *month*, on the fifth *day* of the month, *that* one who had escaped from Jerusalem came to me and said, "The city has been captured!"

22 Now the hand of the LORD had been upon me the evening before the man came who had escaped. And He had opened my mouth; so when he came to me in the morning, my mouth was opened, and I was no longer mute.

23 Then the word of the LORD came to me, saying:

24 "Son of man, they who inhabit those ruins in the land of Israel are saying, 'Abraham was only one, and he inherited the land. But we *are* many; the land has been given to us as a possession.'

25 "Therefore say to them, 'Thus says the Lord GOD: "You eat *meat* with blood, you lift up your eyes toward your idols, and shed blood. Should you then possess the land?

26 "You rely on your sword, you commit abominations, and you defile one another's wives. Should you then possess the land?"'

27 "Say thus to them, 'Thus says the Lord GOD: "*As* I live, surely those who *are* in the ruins shall fall by the sword, and the one who *is* in the open field I will give to the beasts to be devoured, and those who *are* in the strongholds and caves shall die of the pestilence.

28 "For I will make the land most desolate, her arrogant strength shall cease, and the mountains of Israel shall be so desolate that no one will pass through.

29 "Then they shall know that I *am* the LORD, when I have made the land most desolate because of all their abominations which they have committed."'

30 "As for you, son of man, the children of your people are talking about you beside the walls and in the doors of the houses; and they speak to one another, everyone saying to his brother, 'Please come and hear what the word is that comes from the LORD.'

31 "So they come to you as people do, they sit before you *as* My people, and they hear your words, but they do not do them; for with their mouth they show much love, *but* their hearts pursue their *own* gain.

32 "Indeed you *are* to them as a very lovely song of one who has a pleasant voice and can play well on an

instrument; for they hear your words, but they do not do them.

33 "And when this comes to pass—surely it will come—then they will know that a prophet has been among them."

Ezek. 33:21–33

There are three subsections to this passage. In verses 21–22 Ezekiel receives word that Jerusalem has fallen and his divinely imposed, symbolic silence is lifted. In verses 23–29 he prophecies to those left in Judah who think they have a right to the promised land now that so many of their countrymen have been exiled. Then in verses 30–33 he hears a word about his own ministry—advising him not to be taken in by the fact that the people listen to him very attentively now that his prior messages have been confirmed by events.

A special emphasis of this section is that nothing has changed in terms of the people's relationship to God. Jerusalem has fallen, but the contrition and repentance that should have ensued are missing. The very things people were doing to bring on the great punishment that God had unleashed are still going on. The people's selfish irresponsibility continues.

Jerusalem fell at the beginning of 586 B.C. Months later, the news finally reached Ezekiel (v. 21). It took Ezra four months to travel from Mesopotamia to Jerusalem with a full retinue over well-maintained Persian roads in a time of peace (Ezra 7:9). A refugee who had waited in hiding, then dodged Babylonian troops, taking the back roads and relying on his wits to find his way to the Jewish exile community on the Chebar Canal off the Tigris River would have taken much longer—perhaps as many as eighteen months (as one way of computing the dates would suggest was the actual time lag between Jerusalem's fall and the date given here in 33:21). At any rate, Ezekiel and his fellow exiles now had official confirmation from an eyewitness of what the prophet had faithfully, and unpopularly, predicted for years. Jerusalem had indeed succumbed. The nation of Judah, the remainder state of Israel, was no more.

In 24:15–27 we learned that Ezekiel had lost his wife and been made unable to speak (either entirely or periodically) as a sign that the fall of Jerusalem was imminent. Chapters 25–32, the oracles against foreign nations, temporarily interrupt the chronological sequence of events between Chapters 24 and 33. But in fact, the last thing that Ezekiel was to expect from Chapter 24 was the arrival of a messenger who would tell him "the news" so that he could speak freely again (24:27). This has finally occurred, and Ezekiel will now resume his full schedule of preaching that had been curtailed symbolically for months (v. 22).

God describes to Ezekiel a new slogan that had become popular in Judah in the months since the fall of Jerusalem: *"Abraham was only one . . . But we are many . . ."* (vv. 23–24). It was much like the slogan that had sprung up among the survivors of the first great capitulation and exile of Jerusalem in 598 B.C. (the one that had sent Ezekiel to Babylon): "This city is the cauldron and we are the meat." In that event, those who survived and remained began to think of themselves as the rightful heirs of the city of David, entitled to take over the homes and farms of the hapless exiles. A dozen years later the same thing was happening again. Those who were so worthless to the Babylonians that they weren't taken captive (cf. 2 Kings 25:12) now seized the opportunity to take over fields and houses they had long coveted and occupied what they simplistically saw as their destiny: the land. They were left to control what Abraham had been promised. Shouldn't they, who after all numbered in the thousands, have a greater right to the land than Abraham, who was only one person? The argument was silly, of course, but it made a nice-sounding slogan.

The trouble was that they didn't deserve the land (vv. 25–26). Abraham had been faithful to God (Gen. 15:6; Rom. 4:3) and thus had been promised the land; these survivors were no more faithful than those who had gone into exile. Samples of their disobedience are given: eating blood (an idolatrous religious ritual thought to prolong life, forbidden in the Mosaic Law; cf. Lev. 17:12); idolatry (cf. Exod. 2:4–5); violence (Gen. 9:6; Exod. 20:13); and sexual immorality (Exod. 20:14; Lev. 18). It is interesting to note that this list compares closely with the basic prohibitions of Acts 15:29; what the people of Ezekiel's day were doing were those things later thought to be the most *basic* acts of disobedience to the spirit of the Law.

As a result of their sin, the survivors would experience the desolation of the land long-predicted as the outcome of the fall of Judah (vv. 27–29; cf. Lev. 26:31–35). They themselves would be prey to

316

further military action, that is, "the sword" (such as followed the as-sassination of Gedaliah by typically overconfident survivors; Jer. 40:7–43:13). Dangers from wild animals and disease (pestilence) are also typical Mosaic covenant punishment predictions (Lev. 26:22; Deut. 32:24; Deut. 28:21–22; etc.; cf. 2 Kings 17:25–26). The desolation Judah experienced in the decades after 586 was so severe (v. 28) that the remaining survivors as well as the exiled survivors suffered openly for their sins. A hard life in Judah was indeed what those returning from exile found when they arrived after the exile had ended (Ezra 4–5; Hag. 1:6).

In exile at Tel-Abib, however, Ezekiel suddenly enjoyed great popularity. Seven years of doom saying (see 1:2 for the date of his call to the prophetic office seven years earlier) had suddenly been vindicated. Here was a true prophet! He spoke the word of the Lord (v. 30). Unfortunately, the ability to recognize the truth does not automatically carry with it the willingness to obey. Everyone may have wanted to hear what Ezekiel had to say, but whether they would obey it was a very different matter—especially if it didn't bring them some kind of personal advantage or "gain" and required instead sacrifice or discipline (v. 31). To his audience he was an entertainer, like a musician with a good voice, but who *obeys* entertainers? Therefore further miseries ("this" of v. 33 refers to the desolations predicted for Judah in the prior verses) would take place before the people would really take to heart what Ezekiel was saying.

In our day there are a good many "news junkies"—people who watch, listen to, or read news broadcasts or publications of all kinds, preferring them to other forms of media entertainment. Indeed, in some forms of "tabloid newspapers" the distinction between fictional entertainment and news is not really made at all. Television "docudramas" are often thinly disguised fiction masquerading as reporting. News is big business. It is interesting, often provocative, and ultimately entertaining—even to people who have no intention whatever of doing anything about what they hear or read.

Moreover, there can be a morbid fascination to bad news. "If it bleeds, it leads" goes the popular rule of thumb in deciding what news should belong in the headlines. The grisly is sometimes the most attractive. That is the phenomenon that Ezekiel had to confront. He had a big audience for terrible news about Judah and Jerusalem and undoubtedly for his dire predictions for foreign nations. People would listen as long as they didn't have to do anything and could even enjoy what he preached as long as it didn't immediately represent pain or suffering for them. These people were hearers—avid hearers in fact—but they weren't doers. No Christian can afford to copy their example (James 1:22; 2:18–24).

IRRESPONSIBLE SHEPHERDS AND THE
TRUE SHEPHERD

34:1 And the word of the LORD came to me, saying,

2 "Son of man, prophesy against the shepherds of Israel, prophesy and say to them, 'Thus says the Lord GOD to the shepherds: "Woe to the shepherds of Israel who feed themselves! Should not the shepherds feed the flocks?

3 "You eat the fat and clothe yourselves with the wool; you slaughter the fatlings, *but* you do not feed the flock.

4 "The weak you have not strengthened, nor have you healed those who were sick, nor bound up the broken, nor brought back what was driven away, nor sought what was lost; but with force and cruelty you have ruled them.

5 "So they were scattered because *there was* no shepherd; and they became food for all the beasts of the field when they were scattered.

6 "My sheep wandered through all the mountains, and on every high hill; yes, My flock was scattered over the whole face of the earth, and no one was seeking or searching *for them.*"

7 'Therefore, you shepherds, hear the word of the LORD:

8 "*as* I live," says the Lord GOD, "surely because My flock became a prey, and My flock became food for every beast of the field, because *there was* no shepherd, nor did My shepherds search for My flock, but the shepherds fed themselves and did not feed My flock"—

9 'therefore, O shepherds, hear the word of the LORD!

10 'Thus says the Lord GOD: "Behold, I *am* against the shepherds, and I will require My flock at their hand; I will cause them to cease feeding the sheep, and the shepherds shall feed themselves no more; for I will deliver My flock from their mouths, that they may no longer be food for them."

11 'For thus says the Lord GOD: "Indeed I Myself will search for My sheep and seek them out.

12 "As a shepherd seeks out his flock on the day he is among his scattered sheep, so will I seek out My sheep and deliver them from all the places where they were scattered on a cloudy and dark day.

13 "And I will bring them out from the peoples and gather them from the countries, and will bring them to their own land; I will feed them on the mountains of Israel, in the valleys and in all the inhabited places of the country.

14 "I will feed them in good pasture, and their fold shall be on the high mountains of Israel. There they shall lie down in a good fold and feed in rich pasture on the mountains of Israel.

15 "I will feed My flock, and I will make them lie down," says the Lord GOD.

16 "I will seek what was lost and bring back what was driven away, bind up the broken and strengthen what was sick; but I will destroy the fat and the strong, and feed them in judgment."

17 'And *as for* you, O My flock, thus says the Lord GOD: "Behold, I shall judge between sheep and sheep, between rams and goats.

18 "*Is it* too little for you to have eaten up the good pasture, that you must tread down with your feet the residue of your pasture—and to have drunk of the clear waters, that you must foul the residue with your feet?

19 "And *as for* My flock, they eat what you have trampled with your feet, and they drink what you have fouled with your feet."

20 'Therefore thus says the Lord GOD to them: "Behold, I Myself will judge between the fat and the lean sheep.

21 "Because you have pushed with side and

shoulder, butted all the weak ones with your horns, and scattered them abroad,

22 "therefore I will save My flock, and they shall no longer be a prey; and I will judge between sheep and sheep.

23 "I will establish one shepherd over them, and he shall feed them—My servant David. He shall feed them and be their shepherd.

24 "And I, the LORD, will be their God, and My servant David a prince among them; I, the LORD, have spoken.

25 "I will make a covenant of peace with them, and cause wild beasts to cease from the land; and they will dwell safely in the wilderness and sleep in the woods.

26 "I will make them and the places all around My hill a blessing; and I will cause showers to come down in their season; there shall be showers of blessing.

27 "Then the trees of the field shall yield their fruit, and the earth shall yield her increase. They shall be safe in their land; and they shall know that I *am* the LORD, when I have broken the bands of their yoke and delivered them from the hand of those who enslaved them.

28 "And they shall no longer be a prey for the nations, nor shall beasts of the land devour them; but they shall dwell safely, and no one shall make *them* afraid.

29 "I will raise up for them a garden of renown, and they shall no longer be consumed with hunger in the land, nor bear the shame of the Gentiles anymore.

30 "Thus they shall know that I, the LORD their God, *am* with them, and they, the house of Israel, *are* My people," says the Lord GOD.'"

31 "You are My flock, the flock of My pasture; you *are* men, *and* I *am* your God," says the Lord GOD.

Ezek. 34:1–31

This chapter is a long, compound prophecy, but it was obviously received by Ezekiel as a unified word from the Lord. Its subsections are each worthy of exposition; together they form a most encouraging picture of the eventual future for a people whose past and present, as well as immediate future, leave much to be desired.

The chapter may come from the time soon after the fall of Jerusalem, but its date is not furnished, so we cannot be sure. It is a mistake to think that prophets spoke only harsh words about Israel before the exile and suddenly turned to hope once it had occurred. Rather, a mixture of punishment and promise characterizes the preaching of all the prophets, who convey faithfully the full sweep of God's revealed plan.

That plan is reflected in Ezekiel 34. First described in the Pentateuch (in such passages as Leviticus 26, Deuteronomy 4 and 28–32) and reflected by both the historical books and the prophets, it envisions: (1) Israel's increasing degeneracy and failure to keep God's covenant; (2) God's rejection, that is, punishment of His people by conquest and exile and the many miseries involved in those events; and (3) eventual restoration, not just to Israel's former state, but restoration of a newly created people to a far better relationship of true faithfulness to God. Chapter 34 follows this "plan" as its contents demonstrate:

- Israel's past failure under irresponsible shepherds (leaders) (vv. 1–10)
- God, the Good Shepherd, takes over (vv. 11–16)
- God judges His flock and puts His Messiah in charge (vv. 17–24)
- The resulting blessed new age of the covenant of peace (vv. 25–31)

The passage is yet another of Ezekiel's allegories. Throughout the Israelites are referred to as God's flock, and the special focus of the allegory is on the kingship (here "shepherds") in Israel. The history of the monarchy was not a proud one. Of forty-three kings from 1051 B.C. to 586 B.C., only David, Hezekiah, and Josiah were solidly, consistently loyal to God in their leadership of the nation. Eight or nine of the other forty did some good, while the majority were rascals. In order for the new age to come, one absolutely necessary development had to be the abolition of the monarchy as it had functioned historically and the establishment of a new kingship that would truly carry out the Lord's wishes. This passage, then, is antimonarchical—not in the sense of being against kingship per se, but in the sense of being a rejection of the kingship that Israel had known for so much of its history. A new age was coming. The old monarchy had to go. A new Davidic kingship would characterize the restoration.

In verses 1–2 it is evident that the problem with kings in the past is that they were selfish. In the allegory of the passage, they "fed themselves" as opposed to the flocks (the people of God). Living off the people's productivity and wealth (v. 3), they did not seek to help the nation, but rather ruled as despots for their own advantage (v. 4). The result (v. 5) was disaster for the "flock," Israel, which became scattered among the nations and prey to enemies (allegorically, scattered and unprotected as sheep, and prey for wild animals to whom sheep are vulnerable when the shepherd is irresponsible). Israel was then "lost" in exile with no "shepherds" (rulers) any more to seek them (v. 6). The shepherds were called to task by God, the owner of the flock who promised ("as I live," v. 8) as a result of the misbehavior of the shepherds (vv. 7–9) that He would remove them from their jobs, and who held them accountable for their corrupt leadership (v. 10). Thus the historical monarchy in Israel was rejected.

Now (vv. 11–16) the good shepherd, God, will take over. He is the owner of the flock, and He will find His own sheep, having fired the shepherds who botched the job and allowed the flock to be scattered and subject to danger (vv. 11–12). God will bring Israel back to its homeland from exile (v. 13) and will take care of them and see to it that they prosper, as sheep prosper with good places to eat and rest (vv. 13–15). It is useful to note that in Palestine most grazing land is on the hillsides, while most crop land is closer to the valleys. Thus the sheep are here depicted as living on the hills (although grazing sometimes in valleys, v. 13) since that is appropriate to the allegory. God will revive His people, now allegorically "lost" and "sick," while at the same time destroying their oppressors (who are surely the wicked kings who ruled Israel, as well as perhaps the foreign nations repeatedly excoriated in chaps. 25–32).

It is typical in Old Testament allegories for some of the metaphorical comparisons to shift from one figure to another. In this part of the allegory (vv. 17–24) the wicked kings and those associated with them in leading Israel away from righteousness are called "fat sheep" instead of "shepherds." The focus has also shifted slightly to the need

322

for God to judge both the good and the bad within Israel, according to the principle of individual responsibility introduced in Chapter 18 and repeated in Chapter 33. So the Israelites need to realize that not all of them will move on to the new age of blessing. To be born an Israelite will no longer mean being part of the covenant of God. As Paul reminds us in Rom. 2:28–29, being born a Jew cannot save; one must be a Jew "inwardly," that is, by making Christ Lord and Savior. Thus within ethnic Israel itself there would be a separation of righteous from unrighteous based on God's good and fair judgment and not on any automatic criterion.

God will judge among His people in a way that parallels how a shepherd judges among members of his flock, deciding which should be sold, slaughtered, etc. (v. 17). The selfish Israelites who have exploited their countrymen and ruined the nation (vv. 18–19) and thus grown fat at the expense of those they have oppressed (v. 20) and displaced (v. 21) will answer to God, whose interest is the protection of His people (v. 22). What will be the means of His fair and good rule? It will be the Davidic Messiah, described here as *My servant David"* (v. 23). He (this restoration-era David) will be both God's servant and the people's prince (v. 24). The designation "prince" (Hebrew, *nāśî'*), as we have already seen (e.g., 7:27; 12:10; 19:1; etc.), is Ezekiel's most common word for "king." This prophecy corresponds to what the prophets in general predicted for the new age they anticipated: a newly constituted righteous nation will live under the blessing and discipline of God's special, anointed king.

The final subsection of the passage (vv. 25–31) speaks of the blessings that will follow. God's *"covenant of peace"* (v. 25) is a way of saying that His new covenant will produce peace, including the elimination of the punishments associated previously with disobedience (33:27, etc.). Agricultural bounty is a standard way of symbolizing the benefits of the restoration age (vv. 26–27; cf. Deut. 30:9) as is rescue from captivity (v. 27; cf. Jer. 30:8). Return from captivity will mean safety from danger from nation or beast (v. 28) as well as abundance (v. 29) and independence (not bearing *"the shame of the Gentiles anymore"*; cf. Deut. 30:3–7).

Verse 30 contrasts with the many previous "they shall know . . ." endings to passages in the book, which tend to emphasize how Israel or foreign nations will feel the wrath of God and thus be forced to recognize His sovereignty. This, instead, is the language of promise: the true Israel will know that God is *with them,* their being His people and His being their God. This is vocabulary widely associated in the Old Testament with the establishment or reestablishment of the divine covenant (cf. Exod. 6:7; Jer. 7:23; Hos. 2:23; etc.). Verse 31 brings the allegory to a close, identifying Israel as God's flock (something so obvious it hardly needs to be mentioned, except for emphasis). The statement *"you are men"* is probably not original, based on its questionable presence in the early manuscripts. At any rate, it is a somewhat awkward statement that contributes nothing to the passage.

This is not a passage that teaches about the nature of human government in general or that enumerates the principles of leadership. Its concern instead is the historical plan of God, in which He exchanges one type of leadership for another over His people. The change is brought about by the need to resolve a conflict. That conflict involved the failure (predictable, to be sure; cf. Deut. 17:14–20) of Israel's kings as leaders and the firm plan of God that His people should be obedient to Him and should enjoy His blessing. With their bad leaders, the Israelites simply could not exercise the discipline and faith to obey God and receive His blessing. Their own natural tendency to sin was reinforced by the corrupt natural leadership of the kings, and they were, to boot, exploited by those whom they placed over them. This cycle needed breaking, and God accomplished it via the Babylonian conquest and exile. Israel and Judah were no more. They never again could become independent nations and, thus, never again would have kings—at least not of the type they had suffered under thus far.

What they would get, because God would see to it, was a new kind of king, a new David, who would be true to God and thus a true shepherd for the owner's flock. Therefore it is only in Christ, the one true son of David, that this prophecy is fulfilled. He is the one who provided for God's people—all who truly name Him as Lord—to have the great benefits of the restoration summarized by the images of peace and safety in this chapter. Some of those benefits have begun to come already, such as the peace that passes understanding (Phil. 4:7; cf. John 14:27). Many others await their full implementation in the Davidic king's second and final coming.

CHAPTER TWENTY-ONE

Mount Seir and the Mountains of Israel

Ezekiel 35:1–36:15

After the fall of Jerusalem in 586 B.C. the situation in Judah was bleak. There was no king, little effective government, no military, and considerable chaos (see Jer. 40:7–41:15). Edom—Judah's neighbor state to the southeast—took advantage of the situation, with Babylonian approval, to move in force to take over Judean territory. With its leadership and core population in exile and those left behind starving and exploited (cf. Lam. 5:4–5, 9), Judah was in no position to resist the Edomites or to hope for much in the future—from a human point of view, that is.

Through Ezekiel God encourages His people in this otherwise discouraging time. He assures them—once again—that Edom will not long be victorious, but will be crushed as a nation soon enough, and that Israel, now humiliated and near death, will enjoy future blessing on a scale and of a nature hardly comprehensible to those enduring the present sufferings.

Edom was a particularly mountainous country, as its alternate Old Testament name "Mount Seir" implies, but Israel was very mountainous as well. Contrasting the two hilly nations is an effective way of remembering their similarities (as "brother nations" historically) while at the same time emphasizing their very different futures in the plan of God.

DESOLATION FOR MOUNT SEIR
(A FINAL ORACLE AGAINST EDOM)

35:1 Moreover the word of the LORD came to me, saying,

2 "Son of man, set your face against Mount Seir and prophesy against it,

3 "and say to it, 'Thus says the Lord GOD:

"Behold, O Mount Seir, I *am* against you;
I will stretch out My hand against you,
And make you most desolate;
4 I shall lay your cities waste,
And you shall be desolate.
Then you shall know that I *am* the LORD.

5 "Because you have had an ancient hatred, and have shed *the blood of* the children of Israel by the power of the sword at the time of their calamity, *when* their iniquity *came to an* end,

6 "therefore, *as* I live," says the Lord GOD, "I will prepare you for blood, and blood shall pursue you; since you have not hated blood, therefore blood shall pursue you.

7 "Thus I will make Mount Seir most desolate, and cut off from it the one who leaves and the one who returns.

8 "And I will fill its mountains with the slain; on your hills and in your valleys and in all your ravines those who are slain by the sword shall fall.

9 "I will make you perpetually desolate, and your cities shall be uninhabited; then you shall know that I *am* the LORD.

10 "Because you have said, 'These two nations and these two countries shall be mine, and we will possess them,' although the LORD was there,

11 "therefore, *as* I live," says the Lord GOD, "I will do according to your anger and according to the envy which you showed in your hatred against them; and I will make Myself known among them when I judge you.

12 "Then you shall know that I *am* the LORD. I have heard all your blasphemies which you have spoken against the mountains of Israel, saying, 'They are desolate; they are given to us to consume.'

13 "Thus with your mouth you have boasted against Me and multiplied your words against Me; I have heard *them.*"

14 'Thus says the Lord GOD: "The whole earth will rejoice when I make you desolate.

15 "As you rejoiced because the inheritance of the house of Israel was desolate, so I will do to you; you shall be desolate, O Mount Seir, as well as all of Edom—all of it! Then they shall know that I *am* the LORD."'

Ezek. 35:1–15

Even though Ezekiel's oracles against foreign nations are grouped almost exclusively in Chapters 25–32, we have already seen that there are exceptions to this pattern, such as the oracle against Ammon in 21:28–32. This final oracle against Edom is a similar exception. It is located in a section of prophecy that is largely concerned with Israel's glorious future, not because there is anything about its style or content that makes it different from the other foreign nation oracles, but for two other reasons: (1) the immediate historical situation around 586 B.C. was one in which the recent— and ongoing—Edomite invasions of Judah constituted a major topic of interest; and (2) hope for Israel's future required a reversal of what existed at the moment. What better way to portray such a reversal than to contrast a nation now at its ascendancy (Edom) but heading for doom with a nation now at its nadir (Israel) but heading for a great new day?

It should be remembered that 35:1–15 is not an entirely separate oracle from what follows, but rather the first half of a compound Edom-Israel oracle that ends with 36:1–15. The present passage may be outlined as follows:

1. God declares that He is against Edom and will desolate it (vv. 1–4)
2. Edom will become desolate because of its historical hatred for Israel which has led to bloodshed (vv. 5–9)
3. Edom will become desolate because it has annexed Israelite land (vv. 10–15)

In each case the punishment is desolation. This certainly occurred as prophesied. Edom declined steadily under Babylonian, then Persian, then Greek, then Roman rule (in the latter empire as the region

327

of "Idumea"). Its former mountain strongholds are now merely deserted curiosities in southern Jordan.

The oracle begins with a straightforward command to prophesy against (*"set your face against"*) Mount Seir in verses 1–2, a rather standard opening style for such oracles (cf. 25:2; 29:2; etc.). Edom is here and throughout this oracle called by its main mountain range, Mount Seir, as in 25:8 (cf. Deut. 1:2; Isa. 21:11; etc.). In verses 3 and 4, taken here in English translation as poetry but more likely properly handled as prose, God announces His determination to lay Edom waste, that is, to destroy it as a nation as part of His plan to ensure that the world knows His power ("that I am the Lord").

The first reason for Edom's coming desolation, its murder of Israelites, is expounded beginning in verse 5. From a similar oracle against Edom from about the same time, in the Book of Obadiah, we know that Edomites slaughtered Judeans fleeing from the Babylonians at the time of the siege of Jerusalem in 588–586 B.C. (Obadiah 10, 14). Edomites, operating on the basis of their *"ancient hatred,"* going back to the conflicts of Jacob and Esau in Genesis 25–33, thus took advantage of God's punishment of Israel *"when their iniquity came to an end"* (v. 5), better rendered "when their punishment was at its worst." Since bloodshed characterized Edomite behavior toward Israelites, bloodshed will be their punishment (v. 6). Eventually no one will live in Edom anymore—neither survivors nor returnees from exile (v. 7). As a result of the great slaughter that will come on the Edomites (v. 8) their nation will be permanently devoid of human habitation (v. 9).

The *"two nations"* that the Edomites planned to possess were (northern) Israel and Judah (v. 10). Edom had big plans to move into and control the promised land God had set aside for His people Israel. By this time the original Israel had split into two separate political entities, Israel and Judah, who are the "two nations" identified in Edom's thinking. The point of verse 11 is that Edom's punishment will fit its crime. Edom's anger and envy will be recompensed by divine wrath and by the successes of the people it envied, Israel. God would thereby be honored and properly recognized not in Edom, which was headed for oblivion, but in Israel (*"known among them"*).

The Edomites welcomed the idea of desolation—Israel's rather than their own, that is (v. 12). Blasphemy is verbal insult of God, and that's what Edom did in its proclamations against Israel. Criticism of and boasting against Israel was automatically understood as criticism of and boasting against the Lord (v. 13). Edom, however, had little to boast about. Arrogance is especially objectionable when it is completely unfounded. We may dislike arrogance and self-assurance whenever we see them exhibited by someone, but we are particularly annoyed when someone who has no basis to boast does so. For example, a great athlete may brag and we may dislike it but nevertheless tolerate it since there is a basis in reality behind the boasting. But bragging about athletic ability from one who obviously has none can be, if not humorous, downright infuriating. What the Edomites failed to realize is that while they were boasting, everyone else was resenting it. Thus, the whole world would receive with glee the news of Edom's own downfall (v. 14), so despised were these despisers of Israel.

The first major part of the Edom-Israel oracle ends with a summation of what is coming for Edom: (1) they will get what they've been giving (rejoicing at the enemy's downfall); (2) they will be desolate; (3) the Lord's power will have been shown them ("they will know that I am the Lord").

THE MOUNTAINS OF ISRAEL

36:1 "And you, son of man, prophesy to the mountains of Israel, and say, 'O mountains of Israel, hear the word of the LORD!

2 'Thus says the Lord GOD: "Because the enemy has said of you, 'Aha! The ancient heights have become our possession,'"'

3 "therefore prophesy, and say, 'Thus says the Lord GOD: "Because they made *you* desolate and swallowed you up on every side, so that you became the possession of the rest of the nations, and you are taken up by the lips of talkers and slandered by the people"—

4 'therefore, O mountains of Israel, hear the word of the Lord GOD! Thus says the Lord GOD to the mountains, the hills, the rivers, the valleys, the desolate wastes, and the cities that have been forsaken, which became plunder and mockery to the rest of the nations all around—

5 'therefore thus says the Lord GOD: "Surely I have spoken in My burning jealousy against the rest of the nations and against all Edom, who gave My land to themselves as a possession, with whole-hearted joy *and* spiteful minds, in order to plunder its open country."'

6 "Therefore prophesy concerning the land of Israel, and say to the mountains, the hills, the rivers, and the valleys, 'Thus says the Lord GOD: "Behold, I have spoken in My jealousy and My fury, because you have borne the shame of the nations."

7 'Therefore thus says the Lord GOD: "I have raised My hand in an oath that surely the nations that *are* around you shall bear their own shame.

8 "But you, O mountains of Israel, you shall shoot forth your branches and yield your fruit to My people Israel, for they are about to come.

9 "For indeed I *am* for you, and I will turn to you, and you shall be tilled and sown.

10 "I will multiply men upon you, all the house of Israel, all of it; and the cities shall be inhabited and the ruins rebuilt.

11 "I will multiply upon you man and beast; and they shall increase and bear young; I will make you inhabited as in former times, and do better *for you* than at your beginnings. Then you shall know that I *am* the LORD.

12 "Yes, I will cause men to walk on you, My people Israel; they shall take possession of you, and you shall be their inheritance; no more shall you bereave them *of children.*"

13 'Thus says the Lord GOD: "Because they say to you, 'You devour men and bereave your nation *of children,*'

14 "therefore you shall devour men no more, nor bereave your nation anymore," says the Lord GOD.

15 "Nor will I let you hear the taunts of the nations anymore, nor bear the reproach of the peoples anymore, nor shall you cause your nation to stumble anymore," says the Lord GOD.'"

Ezek. 36:1–15

330

Now it is Israel's turn. The story on Edom has been told. What about those whose troubles the Edomites had been gloating over? What about that poor little southern Palestinian nation recently overrun by the Babylonians whose cities were in ruins and whose temple razed to bedrock? What about those tens of thousands of people exiled great distances from their previous homes, having to face an uncertain and difficult future trying to stay alive as impoverished strangers in a hostile foreign land?

Mount Seir was spoken to directly in Chapter 35. Now, in parallel fashion, Israel's mountains are addressed. This is a rhetorical device, a means of making a point. The real audience for this prophecy was all those who would hear it or read it once Ezekiel had proclaimed it. Another parallel between the Edom (35:1-15) and Israel (36:1-15) sections of this compound prophecy is the emphasis on desolation. Edom's desolation is yet to come. Israel's desolation is underway but will be entirely reversed when the promises for Israel contained here are fulfilled. Curses of desolation are major types of predictions of divine punishment in the Old Testament (e.g., Lev. 26:31-35; Deuteronomy 51; 29:23). Promises of repopulation on a grand scale are, in comparable fashion, characteristic of predictions of divine blessing (e.g., Deut. 30:5, 9). One nation, Edom, could expect to go from population to desolation. The other nation, Israel, could expect just the opposite.

The present passage has two main divisions:

1. The mountains are assured that Israel's enemies will be punished (vv. 1-7)
2. The mountains are assured that they will be wonderfully inhabited again (vv. 8-15)

Although this prophecy is not dated, it is reasonable to assume that it was delivered shortly after the fall of Jerusalem, that is, in the mid 580s (see also the remarks on date in connection with chap. 35). The style of the Hebrew sentences in verses 1-7 is sometimes thought unusual, and this has led some scholars to speculate that these verses were once poetic or that they have in some way been expanded or contracted from an originally different wording. In fact, the language is highly structured, with frequent use of "because" (Hebrew, ya‛an) and "therefore" (Hebrew, lākēn) to introduce divine predictions which come rapidly one after the other.

Verse 1 is standard in form for a prophecy to or against something or someone and is unusual only in the sense that it seems to our Western ears unusual for inanimate objects to be addressed directly. It is a well-known biblical phenomenon, however (cf. Ps. 24:7, 9; 87:3, 7). The boasting of the Edomites (v. 2), summarized here as in 35:10, links this part of the oracle with the part specifically about Edom in the prior chapter. Israel's demise was well known and indisputable. Its reputation as a nation could hardly be lower (v. 3). The land was at the present indeed a "forsaken" land and a subject of mockery for other nations who had once regarded Israel with at least a grudging respect (v. 4).

In verse 5 God reminds the mountains that He has already said plenty about the doom coming for the various nations that had made themselves enemies of His people (i.e., the foreign nation oracles in chaps. 25–32) and specifically to Edom, which was the one nation that had most severely exploited Israel's inability to fight back in the aftermath of the Babylonian conquest. The history of Edom's resentment and opposition to Israel was so long and substantial that it is no exaggeration at all for verse 5 to speak of the Edomites' *"wholehearted joy and spiteful minds"* in describing their delight at finally overcoming their great enemy. After yet another reference to the shame that Israel was at that time enduring (v. 6), and which Ezekiel's audience surely felt as well, God then promises a reversal (v. 7). The shame will shift from Israel to the other nations. God was planning to direct the course of history in such a way that the rankings of nations would eventually be very different. Those gloating in pride at Israel's embarrassment would soon enough look to the ground in consternation as their own fortunes turned radically for the worse.

At verse 8 the focus changes to the positive things ahead for Israel. Agricultural abundance will accompany the new age (in accord with the promises made already in the days of Moses; cf. Lev. 26:42; Deut. 30:9). God's presence (also a restoration blessing known from the Pentateuch, as in Lev. 26:42, 45; Deut. 4:29; 30:9) will bring about the fruitfulness of the land (v. 9) which in turn will allow for repopulation and rebuilding (v. 10). Fertility of people and animals (cf. Deut. 30:9) will outdo what the Israelites had known even during their best days of prosperity in the promised land prior to the exile (cf. Deut. 30:5), with the result so frequently cited in Ezekiel's oracles that deal with foreign nations: "they will know that I am the Lord" (will honor and recognize the greatness of God).

The mountains will once again be trod by Israelites, their desolation overcome (v. 12). Verses 13 and 14 quote a saying that may have been popular among the Judean exiles of Ezekiel's day (compare the popular sayings in 11:3; 18:2; etc.) or else is imagined to be something that the nations of the world were saying about Israel now that its people had been so decimated. It has a close parallel in the report of the preconquest Israelite scouts in Num. 13:32, who said of Canaan: "The land devours those living in it." Whatever its origin, the saying is a way of pointing out how relatively hard life in Israel had been. Israel did not have by any means the most fertile soil or the most hospitable climate. It was a land "flowing with milk and honey" in the sense of the beauty that was in the eye of its beholders, former slaves in Egypt who could see what a great gift their own land would be. It was, realistically, a hard land.

Nevertheless that would all eventually be done away with. Israel would be a great place to farm, an abundant place to enjoy the fruits of God's blessing. So great were the plans of God for His people that the result would be respect, not taunting, and honor, not reproach (v. 15). The mountains would not provide a hostile environment (causing "stumbling") but a happy one, sustaining God's people in their promised land.

From the perspective of the New Testament, these promises all apply to the church as the new Israel. How could such seemingly materialistic images have relevance for God's people who are not a single earthly nation farming in a single part of the world? The answer is that they apply literally but not literalistically. The church may take great comfort in the fulfillment of the sort of greatness, confidence, certainty of success, and ultimate victory over all its foes that such a compound oracle (i.e., 35:1–36:15) guarantees. Mere farming success would be a pittance if that were the actual total fulfillment of these chapters. America's farm belt so far outproduces anything ever grown in ancient or modern Israel that literalistic fulfillment of these promises would impoverish them. We may instead rejoice that God has had in mind for us things that the eye had not seen nor the ear heard (1 Cor. 2:9)—things that the present description of the abundance of the mountains of Israel is intended only to symbolize.

CHAPTER TWENTY-TWO

Renewal, Revival, Reunification

Ezekiel 36:16–37:28

In Ezekiel 34 the subject was Israel's leaders, past and future. In 35:1–36:15 it was the land of Israel, present and future. Now the focus is on Israel's people: past, present, and future. The issues of land and leadership, however, are hardly absent. Land, leadership, and people go together throughout the Book of Ezekiel and throughout the Old Testament as a whole. After all, what people can exist in any organized way without a leader or a place to live? Indeed, the church, the heir to the great promises of these chapters in Ezekiel, scattered though it is at present, looks forward to an eternal dwelling place in the presence of its head, Christ.

Three passages are included in this part of the book. They are:

1. Israel renewed as a people for God's holy name (36:16–38)
2. Israel revived as a people by God's word and Spirit (37:1–14)
3. Israel reunited as a people under the messianic king (37:15–28)

We have no way of knowing for certain the date of these passages. Ezekiel may well have received and preached them in the order that we find them here, perhaps soon after the fall of Jerusalem. On the other hand, they may have been preached at different times and grouped here thematically rather than chronologically, as we know other prophecies in the book have been grouped.

In terms of time, these passages look primarily to the future. They review the past and/or the present, but mainly as a prelude to revealing the glories that are to come. Here is great hope for a beaten, discouraged people. Here are words of energizing consolation for a faithful remnant in a wicked world.

RENEWAL

36:16 Moreover the word of the LORD came to me,
saying:

17 "Son of man, when the house of Israel dwelt in
their own land, they defiled it by their own ways and
deeds; to Me their way was like the uncleanness of a
woman in her customary impurity.

18 "Therefore I poured out My fury on them for
the blood they had shed on the land, and for their
idols *with which* they had defiled it.

19 "So I scattered them among the nations, and they
were dispersed throughout the countries; I judged
them according to their ways and their deeds.

20 "When they came to the nations, wherever they
went, they profaned My holy name—when they said
of them, 'These *are* the people of the LORD, *and* yet
they have gone out of His land.'

21 "But I had concern for My holy name, which
the house of Israel had profaned among the nations
wherever they went.

22 "Therefore say to the house of Israel, 'Thus says
the Lord GOD: "I do not do *this* for your sake, O house
of Israel, but for My holy name's sake, which you have
profaned among the nations wherever you went.

23 "And I will sanctify My great name, which has
been profaned among the nations, which you have
profaned in their midst; and the nations shall know
that I *am* the LORD," says the Lord GOD, "when I am
hallowed in you before their eyes.

24 "For I will take you from among the nations,
gather you out of all countries, and bring you into your
own land.

25 "Then I will sprinkle clean water on you, and you
shall be clean; I will cleanse you from all your filthiness and from all your idols.

26 "I will give you a new heart and put a new
spirit within you; I will take the heart of stone out of
your flesh and give you a heart of flesh.

27 "I will put My spirit within you and cause you
to walk in My statutes, and you will keep My judgments and do *them*.

28 "Then you shall dwell in the land that I gave to your fathers; you shall be My people, and I will be your God.

29 "I will deliver you from all your uncleannesses. I will call for the grain and multiply it, and bring no famine upon you.

30 "And I will multiply the fruit of your trees and the increase of your fields, so that you need never again bear the reproach of famine among the nations.

31 "Then you will remember your evil ways and your deeds that *were* not good; and you will loathe yourselves in your own sight, for your iniquities and your abominations.

32 "Not for your sake do I do *this*," says the Lord GOD, "let it be known to you. Be ashamed and confounded for your own ways, O house of Israel!"

33 'Thus says the Lord GOD: "On the day that I cleanse you from all your iniquities, I will also enable *you* to dwell in the cities, and the ruins shall be rebuilt.

34 "The desolate land shall be tilled instead of lying desolate in the sight of all who pass by.

35 "So they will say, 'This land that was desolate has become like the garden of Eden; and the wasted, desolate, and ruined cities *are now* fortified *and* inhabited.'

36 "Then the nations which are left all around you shall know that I, the LORD, have rebuilt the ruined places *and* planted what was desolate. I, the LORD, have spoken *it*, and I will do *it*."

37 'Thus says the Lord GOD: "I will also let the house of Israel inquire of Me to do this for them: I will increase their men like a flock.

38 "Like a flock *offered as* holy *sacrifices*, like the flock at Jerusalem on its feast days, so shall the ruined cities be filled with flocks of men. Then they shall now that I *am* the LORD."'"

Ezek. 36:16–38

Concern for reputation and appearances figures prominently in this passage. The reputation is that of the Lord, whose people are now in exile in various locations. It would seem to those in other nations, who associated Israel with their God, the Lord, that He must not be worth much if He couldn't protect His people from conquest and exile at the hands of the people of another god. They would not understand that the Lord's people were being punished. They would reason from their own theology, which did not involve the concept of covenant faithfulness and did not expect exile as a punishment for disobedience to the national god. They would then jump to the "natural" conclusion that the fate of a nation shows the relative power and greatness of its god.

The appearances were those of Israel as a people and its former land. Both looked to be in bad shape. Israel was scattered to the winds. Large numbers of the northern nation (Israelites) had been exiled by the Assyrians in 722 B.C. and replaced by people from other conquered territories (2 Kings 17:24-33). Large numbers of the southern nation (Judeans) had been deported at three different times (605, 598, 586 B.C.) by the Babylonians to many places, including North Africa (Jer. 41:17), eastern Iran (Neh. 1:1), and Europe (Joel 3:6). Back in Judah, the land was in ruins. The cities were burned and broken down, and the land not seized by the Edomites and others was returning to wilderness for lack of cultivation.

In response to this, God reassures those faithful to Him and His word that all will one day be very different. He will be glorified on the earth, and for the sake of His reputation ("Name," Hebrew, *šēm*) will rescue His people from exile, return them to Canaan, and renew their population.

The passage may be outlined as follows:

1. God's reputation questioned though the fault was Israel's (vv. 16-23)
2. God's renewal of His people to obedience (vv. 24-32)
3. Rebuilding and replanting (vv. 33-36)
4. Population increase (vv. 37-38)

After the book's most common sort of introduction to a prophetic passage (v. 16), Ezekiel hears God compare Israel's past sin to the impurity of a woman during her monthly period (v. 17). This is not an antifeminist statement but simply reflects the fact that all nonalimentary issues of bodily fluids defile a person according to the Mosaic Law (Leviticus 15), and women's monthly periods are the most common and obvious of such issues. In verse 18 two crimes are cited as examples—by no means as the totality—of what the Israelites had historically done: murder (bloodshed) and idolatry. The appropriate punishment, as predicted in the Law, was exile (v. 19). But exile, while a punishment well deserved, was also an invitation for scoffers from other peoples to conclude that Israel's God was a loser, unable to protect His people from their conquerors (v. 20). God's concern was worldwide, of course, because He is the world's only real God (v. 21), so Ezekiel was instructed to inform the Israelites in exile that God would bring them back to the promised land, not because they deserved it (no prophet ever says that the Israelites deserved anything except punishment) but because such an act would glorify Himself, making known His saving power to other peoples whom it was also His desire to save (vv. 22–23). In this way His name would be "sanctified" rather than "profaned," that is, held as holy rather than scoffed at.

The clear promise of a general return from exile is proclaimed in verse 24. But how can a holy God reward a notoriously unholy people in this way? Will the Lord simply bring them back to Canaan to sin again as they had always done? The answer contains a condition for the restoration of Israel that demonstrates that such a restoration is intended not for ethnic Israel but for a new people: they will be made pure by God's miraculous action (v. 25). Sprinkled with holy water symbolizing their acceptance by God for worship (cf. Numbers 19), they will also be given a new mind ("heart") and the indwelling of the Holy Spirit (vv. 26–27). This is, of course, the language of conversion. Change of mind is exactly what the New Testament term for repentance (Greek, *metanoia*) means; the new mind is the converted mind that will love and follow Christ and keep God's commands faithfully, as also predicted for the new covenant age by the prophet Jeremiah (31:33–34). The fact of the Spirit of God indwelling all who are converted is a dramatically different picture of people's relationship to the Spirit than that of the old covenant, in which the Spirit was *occasionally* given to *some* people, often temporarily (cf. 1 Sam. 16:14).

In the new covenant age, people and God will once again be united (v. 28; cf. 34:30; Hos. 2:23). Having turned to God and received the righteousness He alone offers (cf. Deut. 4:30), the new Israel will enjoy bounty and respect (vv. 29–30). They will also have a conscience about the past (*"loathe yourselves in your own sight"*), hating the sin, including idolatry, that characterized their previous era (v. 31). The Lord will bring this about. Israel won't be able to do it. They can only receive, not produce righteousness. Furthermore, God will accomplish this purification and renewal of His people for His own sake, not theirs. They don't deserve it in the slightest. A nation that has done almost nothing during its history to honor God hardly deserves honor in return. But a God who has determined that His glory and saving power should be known in the whole world is willing to redeem a people not otherwise worthy of redemption. For in so doing, He invites sinners everywhere to repent and turn to Him for rescue from their sin. In other words, Ezekiel's prophecy is making the point that God's control of Israel's history is not focused so much on Israel as it is on the world as a whole. Israel is an example to others—all others—of the power and mercy of God. Israel deserves only to be ashamed of itself (v. 32); God deserves to be honored everywhere, within and without ethnic Israel.

In verse 33 the theme emerges of rebuilding the cities and reworking the farms of the promised land. Again, we should be alert to the fact that this language applies not so much literalistically to the ancient nation of Israel as it does literally, by means of metaphorical comparison, to the church. For the prophets, material and agricultural abundance is a common way of looking forward to the new age of the Messiah. In the same way that Christians expect that heaven will be far more than a city with golden streets and jeweled gates, these prophecies expect much more of the eschatological age than nice houses and plenty to eat. But they express what cannot exactly be described in terms that are simple to appreciate. The result of the rebuilding and replanting described in verses 33–34 is, again, not reward for the new Israel but honor and glory to God (vv. 35–36). God's interest in this plan is an evangelistic one. People will see His accomplishments and glorify Him. Otherwise, they would remain hopelessly lost in their lack of knowledge of Him.

A final characteristic of the new covenant age, the vast increase of the people of God, is the subject of the concluding verses, verses 37–38. Ezekiel's audience learns that in the coming restoration era, God's people may ask Him to increase their number and He will gladly do so. The picture chosen to illustrate this is one that many in Ezekiel's audience would remember well from the days before their captivity. On the three great annual feast days (Passover, Pentecost, and Tabernacles) before the Babylonian conquest, Jerusalem's narrow streets had been choked with sheep and goats being brought to the temple for sacrifice in accordance with the law of Moses. The streets teemed with flocks. In the new age, it will be flocks of people. What is the point? It is that God wants Ezekiel's audience to know that ethnic Israel will no longer be the people of God under the new covenant. His plan is to increase His people vastly, so that it will be far greater in numbers. This is a theme of many of the prophetical predictions of the new age (cf. Gen. 22:17; Hos. 1:10) and a way of fulfilling God's interest that more than just the small numbers in ethnic Israel should know that "I am the Lord."

Throughout this passage then, "Israel" is used in two ways, just as it is in Romans 9–11 and other passages of Scripture. It sometimes refers strictly to the Old Testament people who lived in the promised land. But it can also designate that greater people from every tribe and nation who will comprise God's new people, the church, in fulfillment of the prophetic promises. Thus the references to renewal also have a broader focus than the merely materialistic restoration of ethnic Israel in the land of Canaan. They look metaphorically to an age in which a true relationship to God will put people on a much higher plane than houses and land can provide. We who know Christ are in that age. It has hardly come to its fullness yet, but it has started. Let us be sure that we help bring about the longed-for population increase of God's people by our faithful witness to Him, and let us also be sure that in every way we contribute to the whole world's knowing that He is the Lord.

REVIVAL

37:1 The hand of the LORD came upon me and brought me out in the Spirit of the LORD, and set me down in the midst of the valley; and it was full of bones.

2 Then He caused me to pass by them all around, and behold, there were very many in the open valley; and indeed they were very dry.

3 And He said to me, "Son of man, can these bones live?" So I answered, "O Lord GOD, You know."

4 Again He said to me, "Prophesy to these bones, and say to them, 'O dry bones, hear the word of the LORD!

5 'Thus says the Lord GOD to these bones: "Surely I will cause breath to enter into you, and you shall live.

6 "I will put sinews on you and bring flesh upon you, cover you with skin and put breath in you; and you shall live. Then you shall know that I *am* the LORD."'"

7 So I prophesied as I was commanded; and as I prophesied, there was a noise, and suddenly a rattling; and the bones came together, bone to bone.

8 Indeed, as I looked, the sinews and the flesh came upon them, and the skin covered them over; but *there was* no breath in them.

9 Also He said to me, "Prophesy to the breath, prophesy, son of man, and say to the breath, 'Thus says the Lord GOD: "Come from the four winds, O breath, and breathe on these slain, that they may live."'"

10 So I prophesied as He commanded me, and breath came into them, and they lived, and stood upon their feet, an exceedingly great army.

11 Then He said to me, "Son of man, these bones are the whole house of Israel. They indeed say, 'Our bones are dry, our hope is lost, and we ourselves are cut off!'

12 "Therefore prophesy and say to them, 'Thus says the Lord GOD: "Behold, O My people, I will open your graves and cause you to come up from your graves, and bring you into the land of Israel.

13 "Then you shall know that I *am* the LORD, when I have opened your graves, O My people, and brought you up from your graves.

14 "I will put My Spirit in you, and you shall live, and I will place you in your own land. Then you shall know that I, the LORD, have spoken *it* and performed *it*," says the LORD.'"

Ezek. 37:1–14

This passage contains the first vision report in the book since that of Chapter 11, in which Ezekiel was taken by God's Spirit to Jerusalem to observe the malfeasance of its leaders. The present prophecy reports on Ezekiel's spiritual transportation to see a visionary valley (or plain; Hebrew, *biqʿāh*) in which the skeletal remains of a fallen army slain long ago and never buried represent Israel in the years after the fall of Jerusalem. What he sees happen is a source of great hope for God's people, for he sees symbolized in the resurrection of the bones the revival of God's people.

The date of this visionary experience is probably the 580s, when hope for the restoration of Israel was, from a human point of view, at a low ebb. Israel was a defeated nation. It had been crushed militarily, its people had been separated from one another in exile, and it had suffered the inevitable result of its abandonment of the Lord. Alone, exhausted, discouraged, and impoverished, Israel was indeed as good as dead.

But God had other plans. The controller of history had something in mind for His people that they couldn't have imagined possible, especially since most of them retained little knowledge of the promises of the law of Moses that they would one day be brought back from exile by the mighty hand of God (e.g., Deut. 4:29–31; 30:1–10). It didn't matter, though, if they had forgotten. God had not and would accomplish His purposes for His glory by reviving Israel.

The passage has a simple structure:

1. Ezekiel visits the dry bones (vv. 1–2)
2. He receives the prophecy he is to proclaim to the bones (vv. 3–6)
3. He preaches and the bones are resurrected (vv. 7–10)
4. God explains how this symbolizes Israel's revival (vv. 1–14)

In order to understand fully the events in this passage and their symbolism it is important to know how burials were done in ancient Israel, as well as how the Israelites expected the resurrection of the dead to take place. With regard to burials, the dead were, in effect, buried twice. Here's how the process worked. When an individual died, his or her body was placed in a large family tomb, typically in a tomb cut out of rock, in one of the many chambers lining the walls of the tomb. This was not the final burial, but a kind of preliminary burial. Then the family of the deceased sealed up the tomb and left it alone, perhaps until such time as someone else in the family was buried. When the family reentered the tomb, they would find the body desiccated—dried up, with skin, flesh, and sinews gone—in other words, a skeleton. The skeleton was then taken from the wall chamber where it had resided and placed in a common bone coffin located typically in the middle of the tomb. This common coffin, called an ossuary, held the bones of many persons, sometimes dozens of people. The bones were often separated from their usual skeletal positions in order to make storage in the ossuary efficient. A rib cage might be placed next to a foot, and so on, allowing for the storage of the maximum number of bones in a single ossuary.

Only when bones were dry would they be moved to the ossuary. The purpose of the ossuary was to group everyone as a family awaiting the resurrection, which would take place in reverse order of the desiccation. That is, instead of beginning with a full body of flesh and ending with bones, the resurrection would begin with bones and end with a full body of flesh.

What Ezekiel saw when God's Spirit took him in his vision to the valley was the equivalent of a giant outdoor ossuary. Here were bones of people long dead, "buried" together like a huge family. They were, in fact, like the remains of a whole nation's army slain in battle with no one to gather their bones and give them a proper, final burial. When the bones came together and flesh was added to them, he saw the equivalent of what the Israelites expected the resurrection would entail. We should also note that this demonstrates that the Israelites believed in resurrection of the body as opposed to the mere immortality of the soul. The reason for their elaborate double burial practice was precisely their concern for resurrection. They wanted their remains (i.e., bones, the only part of any person's body that long "remains") carefully preserved so that when the resurrection came, they could participate in it. Resurrection then, was a revival of life starting with bones, and that's what this passage symbolizes for God's people.

Ezekiel reports that he had a spiritual experience that placed him in a valley or plain where he saw dry bones (v. 1). The language in verse 1 does not tell us whether he actually went physically to a place where God had caused thousands of skeletons to be gathered, or whether this was a visionary visit to a visionary place. The latter seems more likely, but the former is in no way impossible. He was required to inspect the bones (v. 2) as a means of learning that they were old, dry, cracked, etc., that is, the bones of people who had been dead for quite a while. (Ezekiel's audience could relate to this since they knew well the process of inspecting bones in the tombs to see if they were ready to move to the ossuary.) Verse 3 contains the question of importance, posed by God to the prophet: can these bones live? Ezekiel wisely says that God knows. The answer is, of course, yes—if God wills it.

Ezekiel then begins to understand how these bones and therefore how the nation that they symbolize could come back to life. There is, in effect, a two-part formula here for revival, the first ingredient of which is the preaching of the word of God (v. 4). "Prophesy" (Hebrew, *hinnābēʾ*) means essentially "preach God's word." In verse 5, the other part of the formula is revealed: the Spirit of God must be in the bones for them to live. Where is there any mention of the Spirit in verse 5? It is in the word rendered in most of the English translations as "breath." This word, *rûaḥ* in the Hebrew original, has three meanings in English, all of which are used in this passage. They are "breath," "wind," and "spirit." The passage cleverly works back and forth between these meanings—very effective in the Hebrew, but not obvious at all in the English unless the communicator takes the trouble to point it out to his or her audience. When Ezekiel first heard verse 5 spoken to him, he would have perhaps wondered which of the three meanings was intended for the Hebrew word *rûaḥ*. Later it became obvious (v. 14).

After receiving the word of God predicting their reception of breath/wind/spirit, the bones would begin the reversal process toward life (v. 6). Again, as so often in Ezekiel's prophecies, the purpose was so that God might be recognized as the only true and powerful deity ("know that I am the Lord"). When Ezekiel did what he was told to do, the bones, not yet held together by cartilage and muscle, began to rejoin (v. 7) and then to be fleshed out (v. 8). But they still lacked the breath/wind/spirit from God that they needed to live. So in verse 9 Ezekiel is told to prophecy to the *rûaḥ* to inhabit the dead bones. The reference to the *rûaḥ* (breath/wind/spirit) as coming from *"the four winds"* (*rûaḥ*, plural) not only heightens the emphasis of the passage as it moves inevitably toward the importance of Israel's having God's Spirit, but also alludes to God's universal sovereignty. He was not merely the God of one nation and land, as so many, even among the Israelites, thought, but was the only God, the God of all the earth. Filled with God's *rûaḥ*, the bones then came alive (v. 10).

The Israelites, whom the bones symbolized, thought themselves a dead people (v. 11). They had been so long dead that it was hard to imagine any life coming back into them. Many among them might now have realized that they were not only politically and socially no longer a people, but also religiously deceased—no longer united to their God. It didn't matter. God was going to bring His people back from the dead (v. 12). The metaphor of the passage shifts slightly at this point, because God's people are now described as "in the grave" rather than as slain on the field of battle and unburied. This is not a contradiction, but an enriching of the symbolism. It likens Israel's revival to the very concept of resurrection as held among the people of the day: graves opening up to allow resurrected people to come forth. The result, again, is true knowledge of God (v. 13). The revived nation will hardly be able to miss the fact that their God, the Lord, is the only real God. The return to their land from exile would also be a sign of God's power for all the world to see and acknowlededge (v. 14).

The physical return of Israelite exiles to the promised land began with the decree of Cyrus, the Persian conqueror of Babylon, in 539 B.C., only a few decades after Ezekiel preached hope to the exiles on the basis of this vision. No one in Ezekiel's day could have foreseen that event, however, without divine help. In the 580s, Babylon looked unbeatable. It had defeated or encircled every foe and forcibly resettled hundreds of thousands of exiles throughout its vast empire. Persia was hardly a cloud on the international political horizon in the 580s, and the idea that Persia would reverse the exile policy of its superpower predecessors, Assyria and Babylon, would have seemed ridiculous. Nonetheless, Israel did return to the promised land and reinhabit it beginning in 538 B.C.—never again as an independent nation and never with the level of blessings predicted by Ezekiel, because those predicted blessings, including resurrection, were meant to stand for something much greater than the recreation of one of the world's smaller nations. But the end of the exile and the beginning of an orthodox community of faith signaled the dawn of the new age, whose brightness could be seen only when Christ arrived, and whose fullness is yet to come.

It was the word of God and God's Spirit that made it all possible—and still does so.

REUNIFICATION

37:15 Again the word of the LORD came to me, saying,

16 "As for you, son of man, take a stick for yourself and write on it: 'For Judah and for the children of Israel, his companions.' Then take another stick and write on it, 'For Joseph, the stick of Ephraim, and *for* all the house of Israel, his companions.'

17 "Then join them one to another for yourself into one stick, and they will become one in your hand.

18 "And when the children of your people speak to you, saying, 'Will you not show us what you *mean* by these?'—

19 "say to them, 'Thus says the Lord GOD: "Surely I will take the stick of Joseph, which *is* in the hand of Ephraim, and the tribes of Israel, his companions; and I will join them with it, with the stick of Judah, and make them one stick, and they will be one in My hand."'

20 "And the sticks on which you write will be in your hand before their eyes.

21 "Then say to them, 'Thus says the Lord GOD: "Surely I will take the children of Israel from among the nations, wherever they have gone, and will gather them from every side and bring them into their own land;

22 "and I will make them one nation in the land, on the mountains of Israel; and one king shall be king over them all; they shall no longer be two nations, nor shall they ever be divided into two kingdoms again.

23 "They shall not defile themselves anymore with their idols, nor with their detestable things, nor with any of their transgressions; but I will deliver them from all their dwelling places in which they have sinned, and will cleanse them. Then they shall be My people, and I will be their God.

24 "David My servant *shall be* king over them, and they shall all have one shepherd; they shall also walk

in My judgments and observe My statutes, and do
them.

25 "Then they shall dwell in the land that I have
given to Jacob My servant, where your fathers dwelt;
and they shall dwell there, they, their children, and
their children's children, forever; and My servant
David *shall be* their prince forever.

26 "Moreover I will make a covenant of peace with
them, and it shall be an everlasting covenant with
them; I will establish them and multiply them, and I
will set My sanctuary in their midst forevermore.

27 "My tabernacle also shall be with them; indeed
I will be their God, and they shall be My people.

28 "The nations also will know that I, the LORD,
sanctify Israel, when My sanctuary is in their midst
forevermore."'"

Ezek. 37:15–28

The North and the South of Israel had not been unified politically
since the revolt of Jeroboam, after the death of Solomon in 931 B.C.,
nearly 350 years prior to this prophecy. Since 722, when the North
lost its political identity and was annexed by the Assyrians, and especially since 586, when Judah had also fallen, the idea of a reuni-
fied Israel of the sort that David and Solomon had ruled over in the
ninth century would have seemed ludicrous to any observer of international events in Ezekiel's day. It would be like suggesting today
that Spain would again become the world's dominant political and
military power or that Rome would again dominate Europe.

It must be said immediately that the North and South of Israel
never did reunite politically. They never again gained independence
and gradually submerged into the Persian, Greek, Seleucid, Roman,
Turkish, and other empires, respectively. Therefore if one looks for a
political fulfillment for this passage, it will not be found—and certainly not in the modern Jewish state that has taken the name Israel,
since in that state only 5 percent of the population is actively religious, and Christ, the true son of David, is more firmly rejected
there than almost anywhere else. However, if one carefully looks
at the passage's language, it becomes clear that this is a prediction of
the eschatological new age, and the reality it envisions goes far beyond mere political considerations of a this-worldly sort.

This is the first enactment prophecy in the book since Chapter 24, where Ezekiel records his having to refuse to engage in mourning rites for his dead wife as a sign of the coming captivity of Judah. It is a rather simple enactment, merely involving putting two sticks together. In all likelihood, Ezekiel simply held them together end to end in his hand with his fist closed over the two joined ends so that the two would look like one in his hand (v. 17). A few scholars have speculated that magic deception or a miracle was somehow involved, but nothing in the text suggests that.

This is also the most "Davidic" of Ezekiel's prophecies so far, in that it emphasizes the role of the new David as the messianic king through whom God's rule over His newly constituted people will take place. Indeed, in verse 24 there is considerable, though not unanimous, textual support for reading the word "king" (Hebrew, *melek*) instead of Ezekiel's more usual "prince" (Hebrew, *nāśîʾ*) as the title of the messianic ruler. This is not in itself a crucial issue but may indicate that the new David will, in fact, be worthy of the title "king" even though the kings of Israel and Judah were not.

The passage may be outlined as follows:

1. Command to use the sticks as an enactment prophecy (vv. 15–17)
2. Explanation: Reunification and purification (vv. 18–23)
3. Further explanation: messianic rule (vv. 24–25)
4. Further explanation: presence of God's sanctuary (vv. 26–28)

The two sticks Ezekiel must write on are to represent the two kingdoms of Israel and Judah (v. 16). Ezekiel routinely refers to Judah as "Israel," since he lived in a day when Northern Israel was long gone and Judah was all that was left of the original nation. He thus avoids "Israel" as a designation for just the Northern Kingdom. Here, then, the terms "Joseph" and "Ephraim" are used, just as in other prophetic books, as a designation for the North, and not as a means of showing special favor or attention for the lineage of Joseph, of which Ephraim was part. The heart of the North was within the tribal boundaries of the Joseph tribes, Ephraim and Manasseh, and the capital during the days of the North's independence was in Samaria, which is in the midst of Ephraim. In the cases of both sticks, the wording "and the Israelites/family of Israel associated with him" ["*his companions*"] is added to eliminate any misunderstanding: the whole nation descended from Jacob (and all those who adopted it as their nation during the exodus) is intended. Unifying these sticks is a means of illustrating something (v. 17) which people in Ezekiel's community in Tel-Abib would surely ask about (v. 18). The audience will learn that Ezekiel's hand represents the Lord's hand (v. 19) and the sticks they see joined represent unity (v. 20).

This leads to a straightforward prediction of return from exile (v. 21) to be followed by a permanent reunification of the nation (v. 22). Never again will it be broken apart like it was after Solomon's death. There will be a single people that will have a single king in the last days, as opposed to the historic experience of the two nations with separate kingships as Ezekiel and his audience were all very used to (v. 23). In exile, the Israelites were continuing to practice idolatry as Ezekiel himself had prophesied (14:1–11). They were hardly yet a pure people. Indeed, one of the ways that the Mosaic covenant predicts misery for disobedience is to paint the picture of Israelites exiled to foreign lands where being forced into idolatry would be a routine fate (Deut. 4:28; cf. Daniel 3). As prerequisite for restoration and reunification, purity would be necessary. God's true people cannot be a continuation of any sinful nation or group; they must be cleansed; and that is what verse 23 also predicts. The result will be a proper relationship of people and God, as also mentioned in 36:28, et al.

In verse 24, the full-blown concept of Davidic, messianic rule in the new age is introduced. The "servant" language (cf. Isaiah 49, 53, etc.) is characteristic of messianic prophecies and reflects in part the historical memory that no matter how great a scoundrel the first David may have been in terms of his personal morality, he was "a man after God's own heart" in terms of his complete avoidance of idolatry and polytheism and his steady belief in the Lord. David's faith contrasted with that of his predecessor Saul, one of whose children's names indicated Baal worship (Ish-baal, also known as Ish-bosheth) and Solomon, the king who first gave idolatry official sanction in Israel. The motif of the promised land appears naturally in verse 25 with the dual promise of occupation of the land forever instead of conditionally (cf. Exod. 20:12; Lev. 26:33; etc.) and the leadership of the Davidic prince, better known to most of us as the Messiah.

This will result in peace—not temporary but permanent, not accidental but imposed by the covenant of the authoritative God (v. 28). Then, as well, God's sanctuary or "holy place" will be with His people. Earlier in the book, the glory of God had departed from the temple in Jerusalem, leaving it defiled and useless as a sanctuary (chap. 10). What God has in mind is not the rebuilding of the old temple, at this time only a memory after the Babylonians had broken it down to bedrock, leaving not even its foundation remaining (Ezra 3), but a whole different temple, the subject of much of Chapters 40–48. It is compared to the "tabernacle" (Hebrew, *miqdāš*) in verse 27, the portable tent shrine of the wilderness and Judges eras, where Israel met with God and where He was in the midst of their camp (Numbers 1). This will result in God's being glorified in the world ("the nations will know"), which is the ultimate purpose of His actions in reuniting Israel around true faith in Him (v. 28).

This final verse typifies the heart of what God is promising through Ezekiel in these chapters of hope following the chapters of doom (chaps. 1–24) and oracles against foreign nations (chaps. 25–32). The new people will not be simply the old people blessed more. It will be a new Israel that will be obedient, cleansed from sin, and, for once, genuinely acceptable to be called the people of God.

Disunity, disobedience, corrupt national leadership, and multiple sanctuary polytheism—these things that would be overturned by divine action in the future were what Israel and Judah had known throughout most of their history. They had their roots in the past, in the rivalry of Jacob's children reported in Genesis, in the tendency to idolatry described in Exodus, in the warnings against the dangers of kingship in Deuteronomy, in the intertribal rivalries described in Judges, and so on. The point is that the Israelites had established a pattern. They were habituated to sin, just as all human institutions and people are. What they needed was a change of the nature and magnitude that they themselves could not possibly bring about by human effort. They needed the special grace of the Lord to help them, so that He would offer rescue, and they would need only to respond in faith. We know in retrospect that it was only the work of Christ that could provide for all that Ezekiel's audience was hearing in Chapter 37. Only in Him could the people of God be truly unified and obedient, and only His leadership was the sort that could show them the way to the eternal sanctuary of God.

CHAPTER TWENTY-THREE

Gog and the Restoration of Israel

Ezekiel 38:1–39:29

These two chapters constitute a separate and special section of oracles of the foreign nation sort but with apocalyptic-style modifications. Their ultimate purpose is to reassure the Israelites concerning their restoration—both their return to the land from exile and their long-term protection by God even against the greatest foe the world can hurl against them.

This prophecy against Gog and his assembled army is widely misinterpreted. Because the identity of Gog is debatable, and Gog comes out of the "north," many people who know little about how apocalyptic prophecy is properly interpreted have tried to equate Gog with some modern "northern" nation. Since the Communist Revolution in Russia in 1917, American antipathy for the Russians has made the Soviet Union the prime candidate for identification with Gog, especially because of the mention of "Rosh" in 39:3, since "Rosh" sounds something like the first syllable of "Russia" (although not in Russian or Hebrew). The communicator must help his or her audience to get beyond this misinterpretation, and a good starting place is one of the basic rules of interpreting Bible prophecy: no modern nation is mentioned in the Bible. This does not, of course, mean that modern times and characteristics are not mentioned in the Bible, but simply that the history of any particular modern nation is not a subject that God has chosen to cause to be incorporated into His Word.

There are two oracles against Gog here. Chapter 38 contains the first, and Chapter 39 the second. They are quite similar to one another, and both make the same essential point: a great power will one day threaten God's people, but God will protect His people from that power and deliver them forever. At the close of the second oracle, there is a final reminder to the exiles that God will bring them back to their land. In all, these chapters divide into seven subsections, each introduced by the clause: "Thus says the Lord God." They are:

1. Gog's army prepares to invade (38:3–9)
2. Gog's plan: to plunder peaceful Israel (38:10–13)
3. God is in control of Gog (38:14–16)
4. God overthrows Gog's army and is glorified (38:17–23)
5. Gog attacks, is destroyed, and his army buried (39:1–16)
6. Animals feast on Gog's slain; God is vindicated (39:17–24)
7. God's restoration of Israel, vindicating His name (39:25–29)

Again, we must remember that this is apocalyptic prophecy, which by its nature is highly figurative and symbolic. Too much attention to the particular details will throw the reader off from the real point: the victory of God over the forces of evil on behalf of His people. In the oracles against foreign nations of Chapter 25–32, the nations mentioned were all nations with which Judeans were well acquainted and who had some sort of contact on a more-or-less regular basis with the land of Israel. Now we read about the plan of God for the far distant nations of the earth, outside the Fertile Crescent and Israel's orbit of relationships, those whom the Israelites had no direct contact with and whose inclusion in attacking Israel is a way of symbolizing the great combined powers of evil threatening God's restored people. Thus what Ezekiel is talking about is what the Book of Revelation talks about in the depiction of the battle of Armageddon: a figurative description of the powers of darkness influencing the world to try to crush God's people and the sure and total victory of God against these forces, guaranteeing His people the peace He has promised them forever. Rev. 20:8, indeed, identifies Gog and Magog precisely as a figure for all the pagan foes of the Messiah.

GOG ATTACKS ISRAEL AND IS DESTROYED

38:1 Now the word of the LORD came to me, saying,
2 "Son of man, set your face against Gog, of the land of Magog, the prince of Rosh, Meshech, and Tubal, and prophesy against him,

3 "and say, 'Thus says the Lord GOD: "Behold, I *am* against you, O Gog, the prince of Rosh, Meshech, and Tubal.

4 "I will turn you around, put hooks into your jaws, and lead you out, with all your army, horses, and horsemen, all splendidly clothed, a great company *with* bucklers and shields, all of them handling swords.

5 "Persia, Ethiopia, and Libya are with them, all of them *with* shield and helmet;

6 "Gomer and all its troops; the house of Togarmah *from* the far north and all its troops—many people *are* with you.

7 "Prepare yourself and be ready, you and all your companies that are gathered about you; and be a guard for them.

8 "After many days you will be visited. In the latter years you will come into the land of those brought back from the sword *and* gathered from many people on the mountains of Israel, which had long been desolate; they were brought out of the nations, and now all of them dwell safely.

9 "You will ascend, coming like a storm, covering the land like a cloud, you and all your troops and many peoples with you."

10 'Thus says the Lord GOD: "On that day it shall come to pass *that* thoughts will arise in your mind, and you will make an evil plan:

11 "You will say, 'I will go up against a land of unwalled villages; I will go to a peaceful people, who dwell safely, all of them dwelling without walls, and having neither bars nor gates'—

12 "to take plunder and to take booty, to stretch out your hand against the waste places *that are again* inhabited, and against a people gathered from the nations, who have acquired livestock and goods, who dwell in the midst of the land.

13 "Sheba, Dedan, the merchants of Tarshish, and all their young lions will say to you, 'Have you come to take plunder? Have you gathered your army to take booty, to carry away silver and gold, to take away livestock and goods, to take great plunder?'"'

353

14 "Therefore, son of man, prophesy and say to Gog, 'Thus says the Lord GOD: "On that day when My people Israel dwell safely, will you not know *it?*

15 "Then you will come from your place out of the far north, you and many peoples with you, all of them riding on horses, a great company and a mighty army.

16 "You will come up against My people Israel like a cloud, to cover the land. It will be in the latter days that I will bring you against My land, so that the nations may know Me, when I am hallowed in you, O Gog, before their eyes."

17 'Thus says the Lord GOD: "Are *you* he of whom I have spoken in former days by My servants the prophets of Israel, who prophesied for years in those days that I would bring you against them?

18 "And it will come to pass at the same time, when Gog comes against the land of Israel," says the Lord GOD, "*that* My fury will show in My face.

19 "For in My jealousy *and* in the fire of My wrath I have spoken: 'Surely in that day there shall be a great earthquake in the land of Israel,

20 'so that the fish of the sea, the birds of the heavens, the beasts of the field, all creeping things that creep on the earth, and all men who *are* on the face of the earth shall shake at My presence. The mountains shall be thrown down, the steep places shall fall, and every wall shall fall to the ground.'

21 "I will call for a sword against Gog throughout all My mountains," says the Lord GOD. "Every man's sword will be against his brother.

22 "And I will bring him to judgment with pestilence and bloodshed; I will rain down on him, on his troops, and on the many peoples who *are* with him, flooding rain, great hailstones, fire, and brimstone.

23 "Thus I will magnify Myself and sanctify Myself, and I will be known in the eyes of many nations. Then they shall know that I *am* the LORD."'

Ezek. 38:1–23

In verses 1–2 Ezekiel is told by God to "set his face against Gog," standard language for the beginning of an oracle against a foreign nation (cf. 25:2; 29:2; etc.). Gog is called "the prince, the head of Meshech and Tubal" (*the prince of Rosh, Meshech, and Tubal*), the Hebrew *rōʾš*, meaning "head" rather than being a place name. Another way to render the Hebrew original is: "Gog, of the land of Magog, chief prince of Meshech and Tubal." Gog is also identified as "of the land of Magog," a place mentioned in Gen. 10:2 and 1 Chron. 1:5. We know nothing of this place, and Ezekiel's original audience probably didn't either, thinking of it as a distant, obscure land having the same sort of connotation that "Timbuktu" has to our ears. Meshech and Tubal were mentioned in the long list of Tyre's trading partners in 27:13 and are associated with the descendants of Japheth in Gen. 10:2 and 1 Chron. 1:5, just as Magog is.

Meshech and Tubal are also among those who are found in hell with Egypt in 32:26. Meshech must have had a reputation for being especially warlike, since Ps. 120:5–7 portrays it as a place one who loved war would choose to live. The people of Meshech are called the "Muski" in Assyrian documents and the "Moschoi" in Greek literature. We know quite a bit about their history: how they were an Indo-European people who migrated to what is now part of Armenia, southeast of the Black Sea, how they allied with the people of Tubal in the same region, fought often with the Assyrians, etc. We know, then, that Meshech has nothing whatever to do with "Moscow" or Tubal with "Tobolsk," but are simply distant, fierce, warlike nations that are mentioned in the Bible to signify the forces opposed to the Lord's people.

After proclaiming that He will oppose Gog and his coalition of northern powers (v. 3), the Lord then tells how He will control what Gog does in the same way that a fisherman controls a fish he has caught or a farmer controls an animal (on "hooks in jaws," cf. Isa. 37:29; Ezek. 29:4). The control of God will cause Gog to assemble an enormous and expert army, well equipped for battle (v. 4). In verses 5–6 we learn that this battle will shape up as a contest between a great range of distant nations and God's people. Persia was far to the east of Israel, across the Tigris River. Cush, or Nubia (translated *Ethiopia* here), was far to the south in Africa, and Libya was to the southwest in North Africa. Gomer (the "Gimirraia" of the Assyrians, also called the "Cimmerians") was from north of the Black Sea, that is, north even of Gog, and Togarma was where modern-day Armenia is located. So from all over the reaches of the known world, troops will join with Gog to attack little, restored Israel.

In verses 7–9 those many nations are told to get ready for the attack on Israel, a great force from regions virtually unknown, and are told that their attack will come in "the latter years," a synonym for "the last days." In other words, they will constitute an eschatological army at the end of human history, ready to fight a special battle different from those that have characterized every era in the past.

With verse 10 begins the second of the subsections, this one centering on how Gog's plan will be the plunder of Israel, taking away everything that the restored people have worked to build up after coming back to their previously desolated land (vv. 10–12). God will make Gog think this way (v. 10) as part of His divine plan for punishing the nations. There will be good reason to annihilate those opposed to the Lord, but even better reason to bring about that annihilation while at the same time delivering God's people from overwhelming odds. Verse 13 mentions Sheba and Dedan (southern Arabian caravan-trading nations) and Tarshish (any of a number of sites in mid and western Mediterranean coastal areas). These distant lands will of course be very interested in Gog's invasion of Israel because they hope to be able to buy the plundered goods for resale in the various areas with which they trade. *"Their young lions"* (v. 13) may be an illusion to their leaders but is more likely a simple copy error in the Hebrew for a similar word, better translated "their villages."

God's control of all that Gog does (even though Gog may not realize it) is outlined in verses 14–16. Gog will be aware of the restored, prosperous, but undefended Israel (v. 14), will mount an impressive coalition of troops from his location in the north, that is, the Black Sea region (v. 15), will attack Israel in the latter days in such great numbers that the army will appear like a cloud covering the earth—but nevertheless all is under God's control (v. 16).

Gog's actions will thus fulfill prophecies about the great battle of the last days (v. 17). These prophecies would include particularly that of Joel 2:19–25, where the "northern army" is God's great army sent against Israel (Joel 2:1–11) but also destroyed in the last battle. The result will be, as Joel 2:27 says, that God will be glorified and known before the world (as here in vv. 16 and 23). As verses 17–23 make clear, Gog will suffer for his sins. It should be noted that Gog will have been by no means innocent. God's control of his actions is not the same as God's control of all his tendencies, desires, and motives. God will have harnessed Gog's evil motives and his well-practiced skill at opposing God to lead him into a trap—not to cause him to sin. At any rate, God's fury against the powers of darkness whom Gog and his army represent in the prophecy will produce *a great earthquake* (v. 19) and worldwide cataclysmic destruction (v. 20). God will cause Gog's army to die in battle ("the sword") by bringing such a confusion on his troops that they will kill each other (cf. Lev. 26:37; Deut. 28:29), thus sparing God's people (v. 21). The covenant curses of pestilence (e.g., Deut. 32:24), bloodshed (e.g., Deut. 32:42), flood (Genesis 6), hail, fire, and brimstone (Deut. 29:23) will all be unleashed against Gog's forces (v. 22). Thereby God will have shown Himself supreme, superior to all the powers of darkness and evil, the only true God in all the world, and the nations will recognize it, however grudgingly (v. 23).

Deut. 28:49, from the days of the renewal of the Mosaic covenant in 1400 B.C., is another of the prophecies that Ezek. 38:17 alludes to. It says: "The Lord will bring a nation against you from afar, from the end of the earth, as swift as the eagle flies, a nation whose language you will not understand, a nation of fierce countenance which does not respect the elderly nor show favor to the young." In one sense, this kind of prophecy was fulfilled by both the Assyrian and the Babylonian invasions. In another sense, its ultimate fulfillment was to come only in the latter days, when, as the Book of Revelation describes it, all the powers opposed to God will be destroyed.

There is nothing at the moment that we can do to win that coming great final battle since God will do the fighting for His people in that day, but there is plenty that we can do in light of it. We can be on the right side—the side that will win rather than lose. We can enlist as many others as possible to be on the right side so that they too may also be rescued in that day. And we can be obedient to the only final Victor, so that He will be pleased with the faithfulness that He finds on the part of His people. We, after all, are part of the "Israel" of whom the passage speaks (Gal. 3:29).

GOG'S ATTACK RETOLD AND ISRAEL'S RESTORATION

39:1 "And you, son of man, prophesy against Gog, and say, 'Thus says the Lord GOD: "Behold, I *am* against you, O Gog, the chief prince of Rosh, Meshech, and Tubal;

2 "and I will turn you around and lead you on, bringing you up from the far north, and bring you against the mountains of Israel.

3 "Then I will knock the bow out of your left hand, and cause the arrows to fall out of your right hand.

4 "You shall fall upon the mountains of Israel, you and all your troops and the peoples who *are* with you; I will give you to birds of prey of every sort and *to* the beasts of the field to be devoured.

5 "You shall fall on the open field; for I have spoken," says the Lord GOD.

6 "And I will send fire on Magog and on those who live in security in the coastlands. Then they shall know that I *am* the LORD.

7 "So I will make My holy name known in the midst of My people Israel, and I will not *let them* profane My holy name anymore. Then the nations shall know that *I am* the LORD, the Holy One in Israel.

8 "Surely it is coming, and it shall be done," says the Lord GOD. "This *is* the day of which I have spoken.

9 "Then those who dwell in the cities of Israel will go out and set on fire and burn the weapons, both the shields and bucklers, the bows and arrows, the javelins and spears; and they will make fires with them for seven years.

10 "They will not take wood from the field nor cut down *any* from the forests, because they will make fires with the weapons; and they will plunder those who plundered them, and pillage those who pillaged them," says the Lord GOD.

11 "It will come to pass in that day *that* I will give Gog a burial place there in Israel, the valley of those who pass by east of the sea; and it will obstruct travelers, because there they will bury Gog and all

his multitude. Therefore they will call *it* the Valley of Hamon Gog.

12 "For seven months the house of Israel will be burying them, in order to cleanse the land.

13 "Indeed all the people of the land will be burying, and they will gain renown for it on the day that I am glorified," says the Lord GOD.

14 "They will set apart men regularly employed, with the help of a search party, to pass through the land and bury those bodies remaining on the ground, in order to cleanse it. At the end of seven months they will make a search.

15 "The search party will pass through the land; and *when anyone* sees a man's bone, he shall set up a marker by it, till the buriers have buried it in the Valley of Hamon Gog.

16 *"The* name of *the* city *will* also *be* Hamonah. Thus they shall cleanse the land."'

17 "And as for you, son of man, thus says the Lord GOD, 'Speak to every sort of bird and to every beast of the field:

"Assemble yourselves and come;
Gather together from all sides to My sacrificial
  meal
Which I am sacrificing for you,
A great sacrificial meal on the mountains of
  Israel,
That you may eat flesh and drink blood.
18 You shall eat the flesh of the mighty,
Drink the blood of the princes of the earth,
Of rams and lambs,
Of goats and bulls,
All of them fatlings of Bashan.
19 You shall eat fat till you are full,
And drink blood till you are drunk,
At My sacrificial meal
Which I am sacrificing for you.
20 You shall be filled at My table
With horses and riders,
With mighty men
And with all the men of war," says the Lord
  GOD.

359

21 "I will set My glory among the nations; all the nations shall see My judgment which I have executed, and My hand which I have laid on them.

22 "So the house of Israel shall know that I *am* the LORD their God from that day forward.

23 "The Gentiles shall know that the house of Israel went into captivity for their iniquity; because they were unfaithful to Me, therefore I hid My face from them. I gave them into the hand of their enemies, and they all fell by the sword.

24 "According to their uncleanness and according to their transgressions I have dealt with them, and hidden My face from them."'

25 "Therefore thus says the Lord GOD: 'Now I will bring back the captives of Jacob, and have mercy on the whole house of Israel; and I will be jealous for My holy name—

26 'after they have borne their shame, and all their unfaithfulness in which they were unfaithful to Me, when they dwelt safely in their *own* land and no one made *them* afraid.

27 'When I have brought them back from the peoples and gathered them out of their enemies' lands, and I am hallowed in them in the sight of many nations,

28 'then they shall know that I *am* the LORD their God, who sent them into captivity among the nations, but also brought them back to their land, and left none of them captive any longer.

29 'And I will not hide My face from them anymore; for I shall have poured out My Spirit on the house of Israel,' says the Lord GOD."

Ezek. 39:1–29

Chapter 39 retells the story of Gog's attack and defeat but with a slightly different emphasis from that of the prior chapter. Not much attention is given to the attack itself (merely vv. 1–2), whereas a great deal of space is devoted to describing the massive slaughter of Gog's forces. In a sense, then, Chapter 38 concentrates on the threat from the powers opposed to God and His people, while Chapter 39 concentrates more on the deliverance of God's people from that threat.

The end of the chapter dwells at length on Israel's restoration (vv. 21–29), especially on the immediate (pre-Gog) era of that restoration. Thus the chapter starts with the distant future but ends in the nearer future with the promise of return from captivity to the land of Canaan and the greater truths which that return points toward.

Verses 1–16 comprise the first subsection of the chapter, delineated by the standard phrase "Thus says the Lord God" that occurs at the beginning of each of the seven subsections in Chapters 38 and 39. Verses 1–2 are close in wording to vv. 3–4 of the preceding chapter and summarize Gog's attack, unwittingly under the influence of the Lord who is leading Gog's hordes to their well-deserved defeat. Gog won't stand a chance when the Lord goes to war against him (v. 3). This compares to the warnings to Israel that the Day of the Lord will find them unable to fight (e.g., Amos 2:14–16). Dead Gog and his slain army are then the subject of descriptions of their burial and their flesh being eaten by scavenging animals (vv. 4–20). For an army to fall on the open field (v. 5) means that it has been completely killed without survivors to carry the dead back home or even to bury the dead (cf. 37:1–14). In fact, God won't stop there. He will kill by means of divine fire (v. 6) all those who weren't part of the invading army but were allied with Gog. "Coastlands" (Hebrew, ʾiyyîm) may also be translated "distant lands," that is, the places from which Gog's multitude symbolically originates in these chapters.

God's renown, His recognition in all the earth will be, as so often stated in Ezekiel, the positive result of the defeat of Gog and destruction of his people (v. 7). These events are inevitable and are what the Lord has often spoken of through His prophets, including Ezekiel, as "the day" or "the Day of the Lord" (v. 8; cf., e.g., 32:7–10; 30:2, 3). The weaponry of the great eschatological army will provide all the firewood that the people of Israel will need for seven years, and the valuables taken as plunder from the slain will enrich the Israelites (vv. 9–10). In Old Testament times most shields were made of wood or oiled leather (cf. 2 Samuel 1:21), so it is not illogical that they too could be burned. This language is that of hyperbole—purposeful exaggeration for effect—and it gives a sense of how enormous Gog's army is, thus suggesting how large are the numbers of those opposed to God in the world as compared to those who seek to honor Him.

A description of the burial of the horde begins with v. 11. Again, the picture is hyperbolic, with a whole valley so filled with bodies that people will have to pick a different route to go to the Mediterranean. This valley will be named Hamon Gog, which means "Gog's Multitude." Such names were sometimes given to locations to commemorate an event so as to keep its lessons in peoples' consciousness (cf. Josh. 7:26). The burying process will take seven months (v. 12) in contrast to the usual immediate burial of the dead common in the arid climate of Palestine. Everyone will need to help in the worthy task of getting underground the evil of the earth (v. 13). Verses 14–15 extend the force of the hyperbole by describing the need for bone-spotting teams. The point emphasized is that Gog's huge army will be completely and permanently destroyed. The continuing stylized use of the number seven (v. 14) makes clear that a literalistic fulfillment is not what Ezekiel had in mind or what his audience would have assumed. They would recognize these words as a way of getting a point across about the ultimate victory of God over the forces of evil. A city will also be named after the burial event (v. 16). Hamonah means "multitude." Thus the land will be cleansed of the evil dead (dead bodies were unclean) so that holiness would again prevail in the promised land.

Inviting carrion-eating birds and other scavenging animals to come eat the flesh of Gog's army (vv. 17–20) is a graphic way of emphasizing Gog's demise. The term translated "sacrificial meal" (Hebrew, *zebah*) in verse 17 may also be rendered "slaughter." The picture of the Israelites getting firewood and valuables off the dead enemy army is here paralleled by the army's flesh providing food for many animals.

In verse 21 the focus begins to shift toward Israel's restoration and away from the death of the powers of darkness, although it is not until verse 25 that the seventh "Thus says the Lord God" appears. The recognition of God's sovereignty is once again stressed as the goal of these events in verses 21–22. Moreover, the vindication of God's reputation which appeared tarnished from the point of view of the pagans because His people were in the control of another (cf. 36:20–23) will take place (vv. 23–24). None will be able to doubt after all that has happened to Gog and Israel's deliverance from his conquest that God does just as He chooses and, therefore, that the Babylonian captivity was hardly a humiliation of the Lord.

The final of the seven subsections of the Gog and Israel story of Chapters 38–39 begins at verse 25. It deals with the present prospects of Ezekiel and his fellow exiles. What about their immediate future? The answer is that the exile will be only temporary, and the exiles will return to their homeland. God will vindicate His reputation (v. 25). Israel had gotten what it deserved for sinning against God while it was under His blessing and protection (v. 26) but now will return from exile to God's glory (v. 27). He will receive the honor He is due when this seemingly impossible event actually occurs (v. 28) and the restored people will be in right relationship with Him through the work of His Spirit (v. 29). This closing reference to the Spirit of God connects the whole passage to the emphasis in Chapters 36 and 37 on the Spirit and summarizes what Ezekiel's prophecies really look forward to.

Far beyond any mere material restoration and far beyond any mass human warfare stands the matter of belonging to God forever—eternal life. That is what the presence or *"face"* of God (v. 29) provides. Israel may come back to a land they had been forcibly removed from, but more importantly they will come back, once and for all, to the God they had abandoned and to the purity they could never on their own hope to maintain. The new "house of Israel" will be that transformed and recreated people so frequently predicted by the prophets. This people will be made up of all those who will enter into heaven with the King of kings, and whose final inheritance is not an earthly but a heavenly one (Heb. 9:15).

Vision of the New Temple and Land

Ezekiel 40:1–48:35

CHAPTER TWENTY-FOUR

A New House of Worship

Ezekiel 40:1–43:27

The final nine chapters of the book, 40–48, are a great vision of the future Jerusalem and Judah. This grand vision account, the longest in the Bible outside the Book of Revelation, contains lengthy descriptions of the physical characteristics of the holy city, its temple, the holy land, and related regulations for proper worship and membership in God's people. There are three sections to the vision:

1. New house of worship described (chaps. 40–43)
2. Nature and role of all who live in the New Jerusalem (chaps. 44–46)
3. Promised land and its tribal allotments (chaps. 47–48)

Hope is the focus of these last nine chapters—hope in spite of the depressing realities of captivity in Ezekiel's day, hope based upon the revealed plan of God to move His people into a new age of blessing and close relationship to Himself. The visions are not designed to encourage the Israelites to expect a restoration of the life they had enjoyed before their conquest and exile, but to anticipate a much better order of things, brought about supernaturally by the Lord and not capable of being spoiled by the selfish unfaithfulness that had wrecked Israel's relationship to the Lord again and again in the past.

There is much in these chapters that can seem tedious to the modern reader. Even though the long descriptions of Jerusalem, its temple, and its surrounding countryside are intended to be understood as symbolic of the important realities of the eschatological age which began to be fulfilled with the arrival of Christ, they are nevertheless so detailed and have such a dull "story line" that Ezekiel 40–48 has never been a very popular part of the Bible. Of course, had we lived in the Jerusalem of old and known the temple, city, and land like Ezekiel and his contemporaries knew it, we could have better appreciated the descriptions. So we must work to understand and evaluate what is happening in these chapters, and as communicators we must take pains to be sure that the real message of hope is highlighted in the midst of these detailed visions accounts.

In Ezekiel 40–43 hope centers around the Jerusalem temple. When the Babylonians destroyed Jerusalem in 586 B.C., they apparently razed to bedrock the temple Solomon had built, the place where the people of Israel had worshiped for centuries. They destroyed it so completely that not even its foundation was left (and thus a new foundation had to be laid, as described in Ezra 3). Ezekiel's contemporaries would have known of this total elimination of the holy place where they had once worshiped, as news from Jerusalem was brought to them by newly arriving exiles. For God to lead Ezekiel by means of a vision through the temple that was to come was a way, then, of reassuring the Israelites that while their beloved temple (called "the desire of your eyes" in 24:21) was gone, a far better one was eventually to be put in its place. A great hardship is bearable if one knows that after the hardship will come something superior to what existed before. That principle is a large part of the encouragement brought by these chapters.

THE OUTER COURT AND ITS GATES

40:1 In the twenty-fifth year of our captivity, at the beginning of the year, on the tenth *day* of the month, in the fourteenth year after the city was captured, on the very same day the hand of the LORD was upon me; and He took me there.

2 In the visions of God He took me into the land of Israel and set me on a very high mountain; on it toward the south *was* something like the structure of a city.

3 He took me there, and behold, *there was* a man whose appearance *was* like the appearance of bronze. He had a line of flax and a measuring rod in his hand, and he stood in the gateway.

4 And the man said to me, "Son of man, look with your eyes and hear with your ears, and fix your mind on everything I show you; for you *were* brought here so that I might show *them* to you. Declare to the house of Israel everything you see."

5 Now there was a wall all around the outside of the temple. In the man's hand was a measuring rod six cubits *long, each being a* cubit and a handbreadth; and he measured the width of the wall structure, one rod; and the height, one rod.

6 Then he went to the gateway which faced east; and he went up its stairs and measured the threshold of the gateway, *which was* one rod wide, and the other threshold *was* one rod wide.

7 Each gate chamber *was* one rod long and one rod wide; between the gate chambers *was a space of* five cubits; and the threshold of the gateway by the vestibule of the inside gate *was* one rod.

8 He also measured the vestibule of the inside gate, one rod.

9 Then he measured the vestibule of the gateway, eight cubits; and the gateposts, two cubits. The vestibule of the gate *was* on the inside.

10 In the eastern gateway *were* three gate chambers on one side and three on the other, the three *were* all the same size; also the gateposts were of the same size on this side and that side.

11 He measured the width of the entrance to the gateway, ten cubits; *and* the length of the gate, thirteen cubits.

12 *There was* a space in front of the gate chambers, one cubit *on this side* and one cubit on that side; the gate chambers *were* six cubits on this side and six cubits on that side.

13 Then he measured the gateway from the roof of *one* gate chamber to the roof of the other; the width *was* twenty-five cubits, as door faces door.

14 He measured the gateposts, sixty cubits high, and the court all around the gateway *extended* to the gatepost.

15 *From* the front of the entrance gate to the front of the vestibule of the inner gate *was* fifty cubits.

16 *There were* beveled window *frames* in the gate chambers and in their intervening archways on the inside of the gateway all around, and likewise in the vestibules. *There were* windows all around on the inside. And on each gatepost *were* palm trees.

17 Then he brought me into the outer court; and *there were* chambers and a pavement made all around the court; thirty chambers faced the pavement.

18 The pavement was by the side of the gateways, corresponding to the length of the gateways; *this was* the lower pavement.

19 Then he measured the width from the front of the lower gateway to the front of the inner court exterior, one hundred cubits toward the east and the north.

20 On the outer court was also a gateway facing north, and he measured its length and its width.

21 Its gate chambers, three on this side and three on that side, its gateposts and its archways, had the same measurements as the first gate; its length *was* fifty cubits and its width twenty-five cubits.

22 Its windows and those of its archways, and also its palm trees, *had* the same measurements as the gateway facing east; it was ascended by seven steps, and its archway *was* in front of it.

23 A gate of the inner court was opposite the northern gateway, just as the eastern *gateway;* and he measured from gateway to gateway, one hundred cubits.

24 After that he brought me toward the south, and there a gateway was facing south; and he measured its gateposts and archways according to these same measurements.

25 *There were* windows in it and in its archways all around like those windows; its length *was* fifty cubits and its width twenty-five cubits.

26 Seven steps led up to it, and its archway *was* in front of them; and it had palm trees on its gateposts, one on this side and one on that side.

27 *There was* also a gateway on the inner court, facing south; and he measured from gateway to gateway toward the south, one hundred cubits.

Ezek. 40:1–27

This portion of the vision may be subdivided into five sections, as follows:

1. Introduction: the angel, the measuring tools, and the command to Ezekiel (vv. 1–4)
2. The outer court's east gate (vv. 5–16)
3. Inside the outer court (vv. 17–19)
4. The outer court's north gate (vv. 20–23)
5. The outer court's south gate (vv. 24–27)

From verse 1 we learn that this visionary visit to Jerusalem took place in the year 573 B.C., when Jerusalem was in ruins, including the temple. Of course, what Ezekiel sees is not the Jerusalem of his day, but a future, visionary city whose features will symbolize the true religion of the restoration era to come. Jerusalem in Ezekiel's vision is not built on a low mountain, as Jerusalem historically has been. Instead, it is on a very high mountain (v. 2) because this is the eschatological city, the existence of which points to a new day in the plan of God (cf. Isa. 2:2). The "man" Ezekiel sees in verse 3 is an angel, described as bright in appearance as angels sometimes looked (e.g., Dan. 10:6; Rev. 1:15). Ezekiel was commissioned to note everything he was shown so that he might pass on accurately the encouraging vision to his audience (v. 4). The angel had with him two standard measuring devices: a six-cubit rod (i.e., ten and a half feet, the royal cubit of the Book of Ezekiel being twenty-one inches long) and a flax rope (of an unspecified length, for some of the longer measurements, v. 3).

The various measurements in verses 5–16 are intended to give us a picture of the size of the great wall surrounding the temple's outer court and the size and complexity of one of its gateways—the eastern one. The temple was not so much a building as an enclosure. The word "temple" is thus used two ways in the Scripture—sometimes to refer to the roofed building that was understood to symbolize the Lord's "house," but more often to refer to the large area surrounded by walls inside which people gathered to worship. It is important to note that people always worshiped outdoors in ancient Israel, in the courtyards that surrounded the temple building itself. Only priests were admitted to the temple building, for the purpose of bringing burning incense. Surrounding the temple

371

building were two courtyards. The nearest to the "house" was the "inner" court, and the larger one that mostly surrounded the inner one was called the "outer" court.

In this vision the outer court—and thus the whole temple complex—was surrounded by a wall ten and a half feet high and thick (v. 6). Leading through it on the east was a three-chambered gateway that had several compartments which, from above, made it look like a capital letter "E" and its mirror image. Each compartment was a guardhouse, so that anyone entering the outer court had to pass three sets of temple guards (v. 10). There were various windows through which approaching persons could be observed (v. 16). A special vestibule led directly to the actual outer courtyard (vv. 7–9, 15).

The outer courtyard itself is then described (vv. 17–19), with various chambers where worshipers could eat (worship in ancient Israel always involved a meal, made of the sacrificed food shared between worshiper and priest). The walking distance from the edge of this courtyard to the edge of the inner courtyard was 100 cubits, or about 175 feet. The enclosed area of the outer courtyard was thus shaped like a squared horseshoe around the inner courtyard, and was in total about 4 1/2 acres, providing room for tens of thousands of worshipers at once.

The northern gateway is mentioned rather briefly (vv. 20–23) and does not differ significantly from the eastern gateway just described. The same can be said for the southern gateway (vv. 24–27).

There is no western gateway, because that side of the temple complex is closed off to the worshipers. It is the side that had the temple building itself, and near the western wall was the holy of holies, the innermost room of the temple "house," where God's presence was most closely guarded. No general traffic could be allowed to enter the temple area from that side!

Why all this elaborate gate and guard structure? Why locate all the entrances as far away as possible from the holy of holies? The reason is the desire for *controlled access,* symbolizing the fact that God's people must be pure. Unbelievers will not be allowed to pollute God's house in the new age. Their access to worship will be firmly controlled, that is prevented. Those corrupted by sin will not be able to bring their corruption with them—they will be kept out. Only those who are pure before God by reason of the blood shed by His son will be eligible to enter this new temple. Ezekiel does not say all this yet, of course, but that is what his lengthy temple description is leading to. The visionary temple signifies both the true relationship to God enjoyed by His true church and the dwelling with God that heaven will provide. Neither of these is open to just anyone at all. So the visionary temple has gates and guards. But it also is a place where huge crowds can gather. Its size was enormous for Ezekiel's day, thus symbolizing the large number that will be part of the kingdom, those whose faith in Christ has made them worthy to worship in the Lord's house.

The Inner Court

40:28 Then he brought me to the inner court through the southern gateway; he measured the southern gateway according to these same measurements.

29 Also its gate chambers, its gateposts, and its archways *were* according to these same measurements; *there were* windows in it and in its archways all around; *it was* fifty cubits long and twenty-five cubits wide.

30 *There were* archways all around, twenty-five cubits long and five cubits wide.

31 Its archways faced the outer court, palm trees *were* on its gateposts, and going up to it *were* eight steps.

32 And he brought me into the inner court facing east; he measured the gateway according to these same measurements.

33 Also its gate chambers, its gateposts, and its archways *were* according to these same measurements; and *there were* windows in it and in its archways all around; *it was* fifty cubits long and twenty-five cubits wide.

34 Its archways faced the outer court, and palm trees *were* on its gateposts on this side and on that side; and going up to it *were* eight steps.

35 Then he brought me to the north gateway and measured *it* according to these same measurements—

36 also its gate chambers, its gateposts, and its archways. It had windows all around; its length *was* fifty cubits and its width twenty-five cubits.

37 Its gateposts faced the outer court, palm trees *were* on its gateposts on this side and on that side, and going up to it *were* eight steps.

38 *There was* a chamber and its entrance by the gateposts of the gateway, where they washed the burnt offering.

39 In the vestibule of the gateway *were* two tables on this side and two tables on that side, on which to slay the burnt offering, the sin offering, and the trespass offering.

40 At the outer side of the vestibule, as one goes up to the entrance of the northern gateway, *were* two tables; and on the other side of the vestibule of the gateway *were* two tables.

41 Four tables *were* on this side and four tables on that side, by the side of the gateway, eight tables on which they slaughtered *the sacrifices.*

42 *There were* also four tables of hewn stone for the burnt offering, one cubit and a half long, one cubit and a half wide, and one cubit high; on these they laid the instruments with which they slaughtered the burnt offering and the sacrifice.

43 Inside *were* hooks, a handbreadth wide, fastened all around; and the flesh of the sacrifices *was* on the tables.

44 Outside the inner gate *were* the chambers for the singers in the inner court, one facing south at the side of the northern gateway, and the other facing north at the side of the southern gateway.

45 Then he said to me, "This chamber which faces south *is* for the priests who have charge of the temple.

46 "The chamber which faces north *is* for the priests who have charge of the altar; these *are* the sons of Zadok, from the sons of Levi, who come near the LORD to minister to Him."

47 And he measured the court, one hundred cubits long and one hundred cubits wide, foursquare. The altar *was* in front of the temple.

48 Then he brought me to the vestibule of the temple and measured the doorposts of the vestibule, five cubits on this side and five cubits on that side; and

the width of the gateway was three cubits on this
side and three cubits on that side.

49 The length of the vestibule *was* twenty cubits,
and the width eleven cubits; and by the steps which
led up to it *there were* pillars by the doorposts, one on
this side and another on that side.

Ezek. 40:28-49

To a considerable degree, the inner court is a smaller version of
the vision of the outer court. It has similar gateways on the north,
south, and east, and has essentially the same squared-horseshoe
shape, albeit on a smaller scale. Its purpose is different, however.
The inner court was used by the priests in their assisting the worshipers, and it contained their workrooms, food preparation tables,
and implements.

This part of the vision may be outlined simply:

1. Gateways to the inner court (vv. 28–37)
2. The rooms where sacrifices were prepared (vv. 38–43)
3. The rooms for the priests (vv. 44–46)
4. The size of the inner court and the vestibule (vv. 47–49)

The section describing the gateways to the inner court (vv. 28–
37) makes no mention of a wall surrounding the inner court, but
such a wall is assumed by reason of the existence of the gateways.
The only difference between the three gateways to the inner court
and the three to the outer court already described is the location of
the vestibules. In the case of the inner gateways, the vestibules are
at the start of the gateway, that is, next to the outer court. As worshipers moved closer to the temple building itself, they went higher,
so verse 37b mentions the eight steps up from outer to inner court.
The temple building itself was the highest thing on ancient Mount
Zion and is also apparently the highest thing on the new Mount
Zion of Ezekiel's vision.

A main function of priests in Bible times was butchering meat for
sacrifice. For this butchering they needed workrooms, storage rooms,
meat tables, implement tables, etc., and these are seen in the inner
court where the actual sacrificing took place (vv. 38–43). The tables
for preparation of the meat may have been located in the vestibules,

but that is not clear in the original and is a detail not terribly important to the vision as a whole.

Around the edge of the inner court (*"outside the inner gate,"* v. 44) were places for the priests to gather, rest, robe, wait for their turn at work, etc. In much the same way that modern churches have staff offices, choir rooms, etc., the temple in Ezekiel's vision provided needed space for those who were in charge of the worship process throughout the temple in general (v. 45) as well as those who handled the sacrifices at the altar (v. 46). *"Chambers for the singers"* in verse 44 reflects a Hebrew word not supported by other ancient versions such as the Septuagint and is probably better translated simply "two chambers." The sons of Zadok were the only priests authorized to make sacrifices since Solomon's time, and all priests had to be members of the tribe of Levi (v. 46). Thus the temple was to be properly staffed according to the Law, in contrast to Israel's past corruption in worship (2 Kings 22–23; cf. 1 Kings 12:31; 2 Kings 17:7–23).

The dimensions of the inner court are given in verse 47, ten thousand cubits square (about three-fourths of an acre). The altar is right in the center, in front of the temple building; it was the focal point of daily worship. The vestibule of the temple building (v. 48), that is, the portico that was attached to it, was reached by climbing ten steps (mentioned in the Septuagint but omitted in the Hebrew). Its width was twelve cubits (v. 49) rather than eleven, again a copy error in the Hebrew which the Septuagint did not have (only a twelve-cubit width fits the other dimensions given.) We are now at the very sanctuary itself, which had three sections: vestibule (portico or porch), holy place (first inner chamber), and holy of holies (innermost chamber). The description of the sanctuary continues in Chapter 41.

In this passage, like the one that precedes it, there is an emphasis on controlled access, as indicated by the amount of attention once again paid to gateways. An additional emphasis may be discerned, however, and that is the emphasis on *equipment* (understood as furniture, tools, and room to work). This visionary temple will have in place all that is necessary to carry out proper sacrifice, which is the heart of worship. Such detail, tedious though it may seem to us, nevertheless is designed to encourage all who heard it that nothing had been left out of God's plan to restore His people to Himself in the future and to give them all they needed for their most important task in life—worshiping Him.

THE SANCTUARY

41:1 Then he brought me into the sanctuary and measured the doorposts, six cubits wide on one side and six cubits wide on the other side—the width of the tabernacle.

2 The width of the entryway *was* ten cubits, and the side walls of the entrance *were* five cubits on this side and five cubits on the other side; and he measured its length, forty cubits, and its width, twenty cubits.

3 Also he went inside and measured the doorposts, two cubits; and the entrance, six cubits *high*; and the width of the entrance, seven cubits.

4 He measured the length, twenty cubits; and the width, twenty cubits, beyond the sanctuary; and he said to me, "This *is* the Most Holy *Place.*"

5 Next, he measured the wall of the temple, six cubits. The width of each side chamber all around the temple *was* four cubits on every side.

6 The side chambers *were* in three stories, one above the other, thirty chambers in each story; they rested on ledges which *were* for the side chambers all around, that they might be supported, but not fastened to the wall of the temple.

7 As one went up from story to story, the side chambers became wider all around, because their supporting ledges in the wall of the temple ascended like steps; therefore the width of the structure increased as one went up *from* the lowest *story* to the highest by way of the middle one.

8 I also saw an elevation all around the temple; it was the foundation of the side chambers, a full rod, *that is*, six cubits *high*.

9 The thickness of the outer wall of the side chambers *was* five cubits, and so also the remaining terrace by the place of the side chambers of the temple.

10 And between *it and* the *wall* chambers was a width of twenty cubits all around the temple on every side.

11 The doors of the side chambers opened on the terrace, one door toward the north and another toward

the south; and the width of the terrace *was* five cubits all around.

12 The building that faced the separating courtyard at its western end *was* seventy cubits wide; the wall of the building *was* five cubits thick all around, and its length ninety cubits.

13 So he measured the temple, one hundred cubits long; and the separating courtyard with the building and its walls *was* one hundred cubits long;

14 also the width of the eastern face of the temple, including the separating courtyard, *was* one hundred cubits.

15 He measured the length of the building behind it, facing the separating courtyard, with its galleries on the one side and on the other side, one hundred cubits, as well as the inner temple and the porches of the court,

16 their doorposts and the beveled window frames. And the galleries all around their three stories opposite the threshold were paneled with wood from the ground to the windows—the windows were covered—

17 from the space above the door, even to the inner room, as well as outside, and on every wall all around, inside and outside, by measure.

18 And *it was* made with cherubim and palm trees, a palm tree between cherub and cherub. *Each* cherub had two faces,

19 so that the face of a man *was* toward a palm tree on one side, and the face of a young lion toward a palm tree on the other side; thus *it was* made throughout the temple all around.

20 From the floor to the space above the door, and on the wall of the sanctuary, cherubim and palm trees *were* carved.

21 The doorposts of the temple *were* square, *as was* the front of the sanctuary; their appearance was similar.

22 The altar *was* of wood, three cubits high, and its length two cubits. Its corners, its length, and its sides *were* of wood; and he said to me, "This *is* the table that *is* before the Lord."

378

23 The temple and the sanctuary had two doors.

24 The doors had two panels *apiece,* two folding panels: two *panels* for one door and two panels for the other door.

25 Cherubim and palm trees *were* carved on the doors of the temple just as they *were* carved on the walls. A wooden canopy *was* on the front of the vestibule outside.

26 *There were* beveled window *frames* and palm trees on one side and on the other, on the sides of the vestibule—also on the side chambers of the temple and on the canopies.

Ezek. 41:1-26

In this section of the vision, Ezekiel enters the temple building itself—the sanctuary—but not the holy of holies. To enter the holy of holies would have been forbidden him, as he was a mere priest. Only the high priest could enter that most holy room of the temple, and then only once a year for the purpose of sprinkling blood as a symbol of the blood atonement (Heb. 9:7).

His angelic guide takes careful measurements, as usual, so that Ezekiel will be able to report to his hearers/readers all the pertinent construction details. Ezekiel describes all that he sees from his vantage point in the holy place, and all of Chapter 41 is thus a straightforward description of the interior of the eschatological temple. The passage may be divided, however, somewhat artificially as follows:

1. The outer sanctuary: doors and overall width (vv. 1–2)
2. The inner sanctuary (holy of holies): dimensions (vv. 3–4)
3. The side storage chambers along the walls (vv. 5–11)
4. The large western-end storage building (v. 12)
5. Overall dimensions and design details (vv. 13–26)

Certain things about this temple building are worth noting carefully. The dimensions of the doors, for example, are interesting. The outer entranceway, leading onto the vestibule, is open (with no doors) and is fourteen cubits (24 1/2 feet) wide (40:48). The entranceway from the vestibule to the holy place, however, is only ten cubits wide (17 1/2 feet) and has doors (vv. 1–2). These doors, by the way, do not run *"the width of the tabernacle"* (v. 1), but are simply located "on each side," as the best ancient manuscripts read. Then the doors to the holy of holies are only six cubits (10½ feet) wide (v. 3). Thus, the closer one gets to the place where God's presence is especially symbolized, the narrower are the entrances. This again illustrates the principle of controlled access to God, which the temple design in part represents.

Another noteworthy feature is the storage chambers: ninety small ones lining the holy place and one large one on the western side around back from the holy of holies. It should be remembered that the temple was understood to be both (1) God's palace and (2) a place where the people, led by their priests, gathered to perform the rituals of worship. Storage chambers were needed for both functions. As the palace of God, the temple was the place where the Lord's treasures were kept. These included the money, precious metals, gems, and other valuables that represented the wealth of the nation. The nation was the Lord's and so the wealth was His and was stored in His house. This, of course, was the ideal—hardly carried out consistently in Old Testament times, as we know from the long history of disobedience chronicled in the Old Testament historical books. As the place of ritual worship, the temple also had on hand the precious implements of worship, such as cups, bowls, silverware, candlesticks, incense burners, etc., something like the table settings we have in our homes to put out for guests. The temple worshipers were, after all, the Lord's guests when they came to His house to sacrifice and eat. They brought *His* food from the tithe that He had temporarily entrusted to them; He offered them also His hospitality so that they dined, in effect, at His table.

Also, there is the interesting symmetry of the temple itself. Add up all the key measurements in the chapter, particularly verses 13–26, and you find that the temple building and its separating courtyards (as in v. 14) formed an area one hundred royal cubits (175 feet) square. This was no haphazard structure, built up as the years went by as many Canaanite and other Near Eastern temples undoubtedly were. This was the divinely given temple of the future, all in order, perfectly ready for God to dwell among His people and they to have access to Him.

Finally, note the beauty of it all. This building was decorated in a manner befitting its role as the symbolic earthly house of the one who is "altogether lovely." Wood paneling covered most of the interior (vv. 15–16)—and that in an area of the world where wood was incredibly expensive and not normally used in decorative architecture. Intricate carvings also adorned many surfaces (vv. 17–20), featuring palm tree designs that suggested the oasis atmosphere so delightful in the Near East, and cherub designs (essentially like double-faced winged sphinxes) that suggested the heavenly guardianship of the temple and its holy places (cf. also Ezekiel 1). Even the doors were double folding doors (hinged in the middle) so that they were of more elaborate than usual construction (v. 24). An elevated foundation support structure on the outside surrounded the whole building (v. 8), adding to its mass and stability, and protecting its lower, most accessible level, from unauthorized penetration (cf. 1 Kings 6:6).

It was a grand sight. For Ezekiel and his audience, in a day when no temple existed, it was also a guarantee of great things to come. Israel would be restored. They would one day worship again in the Lord's house. They would be guests at His divine sanctuary, a place more glorious than they had yet experienced. As the writer of Hebrews reminds us, the earthly temple, actual or visionary, was intended to function as a reflection of heavenly existence with the Lord (Heb. 9:23–25). So even in the detailed descriptions and measurements of Ezekiel's vision we can be reminded of the glories to come for all who belong to God—a temple not made with hands, eternal in the heavens, which we shall not merely visit in a vision, but shall dwell in forever.

ROOMS FOR THE PRIESTS AND OUTER TEMPLE DIMENSIONS

42:1 Then he brought me out into the outer court, by the way toward the north; and he brought me into the chamber which was opposite the separating courtyard, and which *was* opposite the building toward the north.

2 Facing the length, *which was* one hundred cubits (the width was fifty cubits), was the north door.

3 Opposite the inner court of twenty *cubits*, and opposite the pavement of the outer court, *was* gallery against gallery in three *stories*.

4 In front of the chambers, toward the inside, *was* a walk ten cubits wide, at a distance of one cubit; and their doors faced north.

5 Now the upper chambers *were* shorter, because the galleries took away *space* from them more than from the lower and middle stories of the building.

6 For they *were* in three *stories* and did not have pillars like the pillars of the courts; therefore *the upper level* was shortened more than the lower and middle levels from the ground up.

7 And a wall which *was* outside ran parallel to the chambers, at the front of the chambers, toward the outer court; its length *was* fifty cubits.

8 The length of the chambers toward the outer court *was* fifty cubits, whereas that facing the temple *was* one hundred cubits.

9 At the lower chambers *was* the entrance on the east side, as one goes into them from the outer court.

10 Also *there were* chambers in the thickness of the wall of the court toward the east, opposite the separating courtyard and opposite the building.

11 *There was* a walk in front of them also, and their appearance *was* like the chambers which *were* toward the north; they *were* as long and as wide as the others, and all their exits and entrances *were* according to plan.

12 And corresponding to the doors of the chambers that *were* facing south, as one enters them, *there was* a door in front of the walk, the way directly in front of the wall toward the east.

13 Then he said to me, "The north chambers *and* the south chambers, which *are* opposite the separating courtyard, *are* the holy chambers where the priests who approach the LORD shall eat the most holy offerings. There they shall lay the most holy offerings— the grain offering, the sin offering, and the trespass offering—for the place *is* holy.

14 "When the priests enter them, they shall not go out of the holy *chamber* into the outer court; but there they shall leave their garments in which they minister, for they *are* holy. They shall put on other

garments; then they may approach *that* which *is* for the people."

15 Now when he had finished measuring the inner temple, he brought me out through the gateway that faces toward the east, and measured it all around.

16 He measured the east side with the measuring rod, five hundred rods by the measuring rod all around.

17 He measured the north side, five hundred rods by the measuring rod all around.

18 He measured the south side, five hundred rods by the measuring rod.

19 He came around to the west side *and* measured five hundred rods by the measuring rod.

20 He measured it on the four sides; it had a wall all around, five hundred *cubits* long and five hundred wide, to separate the holy areas from the common.

Ezek. 42:1–20

This passage completes one part of the tour of the temple, namely the physical layout of the total enclosed area (courtyards and sanctuary building). It addresses two topics:

1. Priests' rooms in the outer court (vv. 1–14)
2. Total outer dimensions of the entire temple complex (vv. 15–20)

The outer court was, as we have noted, shaped like a square horseshoe, with the two ends of the horseshoe on the western end of the whole complex. At both of these ends of the outer court, large chambers for the use of priests were located. Even though these chambers were part of the outer courtyard, they were at the end of the whole complex where the temple building itself was located, and so their location was near the holy of holies. The two large priests' buildings were probably located on either side of the large storage room mentioned in 41:12.

The two buildings were mirror images of each other—one located on the northern end of the western wall, the other on the southern end of the same wall. Each building was really a double structure, with one half (the large room part) connected to the other half (the many-compartmented, three-story gallery) by a walkway (v. 4). Each higher floor was somewhat recessed, in a sort of terraced construction (vv. 5–6). Doors, surrounding walkways, etc. are also mentioned.

The priests' rooms are identified as having two particular functions: dining (v. 13) and changing clothes (v. 14). These, however, are not merely routine matters. The dining was the eating of the sacred portions from the food that had been prepared and sacrificed. Such a function made the place where the priests ate a holy place (v. 13) to be regarded seriously. In the same way in a modern church that the minister and the congregation both eat the communion elements, even though the meal is "at the Lord's table," so in Old Testament times the priests and the congregation ate the sacrificial meal after it had been cooked on the Lord's altar. The priests took a share, and the worshipers took the rest. The worshipers would take their part to one of the many chambers surrounding the outer courtyard (40:17) while the priests took theirs to one of the special rooms mentioned in this passage.

The other main function, changing clothes, was also a holy one. Priests wore special vestments when they served before the Lord's altar in the inner court, and they could not profane these clothes by wearing them outside the temple or for general mingling with the crowds in the outer courtyard. So they had to change from sacred to secular clothing after completing their tasks, and, accordingly, the special chambers were also wardrobe centers.

Verses 15–20 complete this part of the vision with their enumeration of the total outer dimensions of the entire temple area. It was five hundred cubits square, as the text of the Septuagint says (not 500 *rods* square as in the Hebrew text; that figure would not correspond to the dimensions given throughout chaps. 40–42). In other words, the whole complex was about eighteen acres in size. Interestingly, the temple complex that Herod built over several decades up to and during the time of Christ's ministry, that is, the temple complex mentioned in the New Testament, was more than thirty acres in size. This helps us appreciate the fact that size alone is hardly the main interest of the passage. Rather, even though this temple complex was bigger than that Solomon had built, its real importance was in its *function*. Here was the meeting point of God and His people, beautifully built and symmetrically designed, waiting for the restoration of the true

Israel. It provided a symbol of God's holiness and set aside places where holy activity could be carried out properly. That is the point of the passage.

GOD'S GLORY RETURNS TO THE TEMPLE

43:1 Afterward he brought me to the gate, the gate that faces toward the east.

2 And behold, the glory of the God of Israel came from the way of the east. His voice *was* like the sound of many waters; and the earth shone with His glory.

3 *It was* like the appearance of the vision which I saw—like the vision which I saw when I came to destroy the city. The visions *were* like the vision which I saw by the River Chebar; and I fell on my face.

4 And the glory of the LORD came into the temple by way of the gate which faces toward the east.

5 The Spirit lifted me up and brought me into the inner court; and behold, the glory of the LORD filled the temple.

6 Then I heard *Him* speaking to me from the temple, while a man stood beside me.

7 And He said to me, "Son of man, *this is* the place of My throne and the place of the soles of My feet, where I will dwell in the midst of the children of Israel forever. No more shall the house of Israel defile My holy name, they nor their kings, by their harlotry or with the carcasses of their kings on their high places.

8 "When they set their threshold by My threshold, and their doorpost by My doorpost, with a wall between them and Me, they defiled My holy name by the abominations which they committed; therefore I have consumed them in My anger.

9 "Now let them put their harlotry and the carcasses of their kings far away from Me, and I will dwell in their midst forever.

10 "Son of man, describe the temple to the house of Israel, that they may be ashamed of their iniquities; and let them measure the pattern.

11 "And if they are ashamed of all that they have done, make known to them the design of the temple and its arrangement, its exits and its entrances, its entire design and all its ordinances, all its forms and all its laws. Write *it* down in their sight, so that they may keep its whole design and all its ordinances, and perform them.

12 "This *is* the law of the temple: The whole area surrounding the mountaintop *is* most holy. Behold, this *is* the law of the temple."

Ezek. 43:1–12

The temple itself, as a piece of construction, was nothing without God's presence. A church is, of course, similar—just a building that people occupy, unless God is among those who gather there. Indeed, in the early church, no special buildings were yet available for worship, and the only "temple" that the true God had to dwell in was the group of believers themselves who knew Him as Lord and Savior in any given place (1 Cor. 3:16). This passage reflects the concept that only the Lord's presence makes the temple a true house of worship.

Ezekiel had witnessed, via a vision, the departure of the glory of the Lord from the old, now destroyed, Jerusalem temple (chap. 10). That departure took place in the sixth year of Ezekiel's captivity, or 592 B.C. (cf. 9:1). Now it was the twenty-fifth year (573 B.C.; cf. 40:1), almost two decades later. Of course, there was still no actual temple in Jerusalem. This was a vision about a temple to come, not a visionary view of a temple in existence. God's glory would need to return to the new temple before it would be a holy place.

The passage begins with the angelic guide's bringing Ezekiel to the eastern gate of the temple complex. That was the most important gate, since it led straight ahead through the other gates to the temple sanctuary building itself. In 10:18–19, the glory of the Lord was depicted as leaving in an eastward direction, from the temple building to the eastern gate. Now it is depicted as returning in the opposite direction, from the east toward the temple building on the western end of the complex (vv. 2, 4). Ezekiel reports that what he saw reminded him of his first visionary encounter with God's divine chariot (v. 3; cf. chap. 1). God again spoke directly to Ezekiel (vv. 6–7) as in Chapter 2, and what Ezekiel heard is the emphasis of the passage.

386

That emphasis concerns holiness—the importance of God's people being a pure, obedient people who can live in His presence. It is useful at this point to remember the biblical perspective that the presence of God kills the unrighteous but blesses the righteous. In particular, verses 7–9 allude to the long-established pre-exilic practice of burying Judean kings near the temple, in what would be the outer courtyard of the visionary temple. The Solomonic temple that Ezekiel had served at did not have an outer wall, and thus only in the most general sense could it be said to have an outer courtyard. It was quite popular for kings to be buried near the temple, and perhaps even between the temple and the palace (which Solomon built next to the temple; cf. 1 Kings 7:1–12). This practice of royal burials at or near the temple is alluded to repeatedly in the historical books (e.g., 2 Kings 14:20; 2 Chron. 21:20). These practices reflected the way that the kings of Israel in the past had manipulated the temple for their own purposes (cf. 2 Chron. 26:16–21) and had further defiled it with their paganism (2 Kings 23:4–12).

A new temple, pure, divine in construction, with restricted access and a proper priesthood, dedicated only to the Lord and not polluted by false religion or improper worship, was something that the Israelites of Ezekiel's day needed to have a "vision" of as well—and so His vision was to be communicated to them (v. 10) as a reminder not to repeat the sins of the past (v. 11) and to keep the temple area truly holy (v. 12).

An emphasis on holy living has its dangers—legalism, judgmentalism, and so on. But it is far more to be desired that the "easy believism" that pervades so much of contemporary Western Christian thinking. The Bible makes no excuses for holiness. It is absolutely required for access to the blessings of the Lord. Ezekiel's contemporaries, like us, needed to be reminded of that, and the vision of the return of the glory of the Lord to His temple served the purpose well.

THE ALTAR

43:13 "These are the measurements of the altar in cubits (the *cubit is* one cubit and a handbreadth): the base one cubit high and one cubit wide, with a rim all around its edge of one span. This *is* the height of the altar:

14 "from the base on the ground to the lower ledge, two cubits; the width of the ledge, one cubit; from the smaller ledge to the larger ledge, four cubits; and the width of the ledge, *one* cubit.

15 "The altar hearth *is* four cubits high, with four horns extending upward from the hearth.

16 "The altar hearth *is* twelve cubits long, twelve wide, square at its four corners;

17 "the ledge, fourteen *cubits* long and fourteen wide on its four sides, with a rim of half a cubit around it; its base, one cubit all around; and its steps face toward the east."

18 And He said to me, "Son of man, thus says the Lord GOD: 'These *are* the ordinances for the altar on the day when it is made, for sacrificing burnt offerings on it, and for sprinkling blood on it.

19 'You shall give a young bull for a sin offering to the priests, the Levites, who are of the seed of Zadok, who approach Me to minister to Me,' says the Lord GOD.

20 'You shall take some of its blood and put *it* on the four horns of the altar, on the four corners of the ledge, and on the rim around it; thus you shall cleanse it and make atonement for it.

21 'Then you shall also take the bull of the sin offering, and burn it in the appointed place of the temple, outside the sanctuary.

22 'On the second day you shall offer a kid of the goats without blemish for a sin offering; and they shall cleanse the altar, as they cleansed *it* with the bull.

23 'When you have finished cleansing *it*, you shall offer a young bull without blemish, and a ram from the flock without blemish.

24 'When you offer them before the LORD, the priests shall throw salt on them, and they will offer them up *as* a burnt offering to the LORD.

25 Every day for seven days you shall prepare a goat *for* a sin offering; they shall also prepare a young bull and a ram from the flock, both without blemish.

26 'Seven days they shall make atonement for the altar and purify it, and so consecrate *it*.

27 'When these days are over it shall be, on the eighth day and thereafter, that the priests shall offer you burnt offerings and your peace offerings on the altar; and I will accept you,' says the Lord GOD."

Ezek. 43:13–27

A sacred place is intended to be used. In other words, what good would a holy place, such as the temple, do for people if it were not somehow able to help them become more holy themselves? We now come to a series of passages that address the question of how the temple would be used. The prior descriptions, from 40:1 onward, showed an essentially unoccupied temple. With the altar description comes the first major "use" passage, a prescription for the priests, so that the passage has two interests:

1. The design of the future altar (vv. 13–17)
2. Rules for how the priests are to consecrate it (vv. 18–27)

This is still a part of the temple "tour," but it is clearly transitional, in that function (usefulness) has become important as opposed to mere design. Function will be the dominant concern of the chapters ahead, as opposed to mere physical description, although some of each is found in the remainder of the great vision of Chapters 40–48.

The altar design was fairly simple (vv. 13–17). It was a stone structure that had a ground-level base (also translatable as "bottom gutter") and three stages, the topmost of which was the hearth on which prepared meat was cooked by the priests. This hearth had at its four corners protrusions that we might call "ears" but which the Hebrew calls *qerānîm* or "horns." The basic purpose of the horns was to help hold firewood and meat on the otherwise flat altar. Each stage was narrower as the stages went higher, so that the appearance was that of what is known from the ancient Near East as a ziggurat or step pyramid. Of course, this was a frustum, or pyramid that ended part way up with a broad, flat hearth rather than continuing to a point. It was more than twelve feet high, so the hearth stage had to be reached by steps. These were on the eastern end, so that the priest who brought the offering up to the hearth, cooked it, and eventually took it down would always be facing the temple building itself, thus symbolically facing the Lord.

This altar does not yet exist. It is part of a vision that shows the future, not the present. In the vision, Ezekiel is told to note the ritual process that will one day make the altar, a mere stone structure, into a holy place of contact between God and His people. First, the blood of a bull is sprinkled on the altar (vv. 18–20), symbolizing the shedding of blood without which there is no forgiveness of sins (Heb. 9:22). Then the bull meat is burned entirely (not eaten by the priest and worshipers, as usual, but burned to a crisp) on the altar ("*the appointed place,*" v. 21). The same sort of thing is then done with a goat kid (v. 22), another young bull, and a ram (vv. 23–24), and so on for seven days (vv. 25–26). Then the altar will have been made pure, so that it can be used for routine sacrifices (v. 17), both burnt offerings (to atone for sin) and peace offerings (the regular or special tithing and offering of gifts to the Lord).

How does sprinkling blood and burning up the meat of some animals for a week make something holy? It doesn't—unless of course the Lord decides that that is the ritual He will accept from His people, in turn for which *He* will make the altar holy. This aspect of the process of holiness should not be missed here: the ritual is only a means of showing obedience and faith. People don't make anything holy—God is the source of all holiness. He imparts His holiness to people or things according to standards *He* establishes. In His mercy to Israel, He gave them an atonement system based on the shedding of blood and the sacrificing of animals. They had to accept His process on His terms, but they had a way to find peace with God, something that on their own they could never have achieved.

The vision of the new altar looks forward to a God-given means to make people holy; namely, the shedding of blood and sacrifice. How fortunate we are to be able to understand, in retrospect, what the vision of the altar really symbolized: the atoning sacrifice of Christ, who made Himself sin so that we would know no sin. He made us holy on God's terms according to God's standards.

CHAPTER TWENTY-FIVE

Prince, Priests, People, Procedures

Ezekiel 44:1–46:24

We now enter a section of the great vision that looks not so much toward the way that things will appear—although there is a considerable degree of that—but more to the way that things will be done. It describes worship procedures and how they apply to various persons in the temple and, to a small extent, in the city of Jerusalem. Throughout, there is a consistent emphasis on holiness. What Ezekiel sees is the holy future, as contrasted to the corrupt present he knew so well. The redeemed people of the future will be a worshiping people, and their worship must be properly done so that nothing compromises its holiness.

These chapters may be considered in several large blocks:

1. Admission to the temple: people and Levites (44:1–14)
2. Roles of the priests (44:15–31)
3. Distribution of the land and justice (45:1–12)
4. Offerings and holy days (45:13–25)
5. The prince and worship procedures (46:1–18)
6. Cooking and kitchens (46:19–24)

There are many individual topics within these sections, and scholars have grouped the sections, or the topics within them, in a variety of ways. In the Book of Ezekiel itself, all the sections and subsections are presented one after another as part of a harmonious, whole picture delineating the new age's proper worship and service of God.

ADMISSION TO THE TEMPLE: PEOPLE AND LEVITES

44:1 Then He brought me back to the outer gate of the sanctuary which faces toward the east, but it *was* shut.

2 And the LORD said to me, "This gate shall be shut; it shall not be opened, and no man shall enter by it, because the LORD God of Israel has entered by it; therefore it shall be shut.

3 *"As for* the prince, *because* he *is* the prince, he may sit in it to eat bread before the LORD; he shall enter by way of the vestibule of the gateway, and go out the same way."

4 Also He brought me by way of the north gate to the front of the temple; so I looked, and behold, the glory of the LORD filled the house of the LORD; and I fell on my face.

5 And the LORD said to me, "Son of man, mark well, see with your eyes and hear with your ears, all that I say to you concerning all the ordinances of the house of the LORD and all its laws. Mark well who may enter the house and all who go out from the sanctuary.

6 "Now say to the rebellious, to the house of Israel, 'Thus says the Lord GOD: "O house of Israel, let Us have no more of all your abominations.

7 "When you brought in foreigners, uncircumcised in heart and uncircumcised in flesh, to be in My sanctuary to defile it—My house—and when you offered My food, the fat and the blood, then they broke My covenant because of all your abominations.

8 "And you have not kept charge of My holy things, but you have set *others* to keep charge of My sanctuary for you."

9 'Thus says the Lord GOD: "No foreigner, uncircumcised in heart or uncircumcised in flesh, shall enter My sanctuary, including any foreigner who *is* among the children of Israel.

10 "And the Levites who went far from Me, when Israel went astray, who strayed away from Me after their idols, they shall bear their iniquity.

11 "Yet they shall be ministers in My sanctuary, *as* gatekeepers of the house and ministers of the house;

they shall slay the burnt offering and the sacrifice for the people, and they shall stand before them to minister to them.

12 "Because they ministered to them before their idols and caused the house of Israel to fall into iniquity, therefore I have raised My hand in an oath against them," says the Lord GOD, "that they shall bear their iniquity.

13 "And they shall not come near Me to minister to Me as priest, nor come near any of My holy things, nor into the Most Holy *Place;* but they shall bear their shame and their abominations which they have committed.

14 "Nevertheless I will make them keep charge of the temple, for all its work, and for all that has to be done in it."

Ezek. 44:1–14

Controlled access to the temple is once again the predominant theme of the passage, with the goal of teaching God's people the true nature of holiness and holy worship. It must be remembered that the history of access to the Jerusalem temple from the time that Solomon built it to the time of its destruction in 586 B.C. had not been a positive one. Violations of its holiness were common over the centuries, and Ezekiel had with his own visionary eyes seen the depths to which improper worship could go among the Israelites (chaps. 8 and 9).

At fault especially were three disparate groups: king, foreigners, and Levites (including most of the priests). These are the three that are mentioned in the present passage:

1. Prince's restriction (vv. 1–3)
2. Foreigners' restriction (vv. 4–9)
3. Levites' restriction (vv. 10–14)

Each of these three groups bore significant responsibility in corrupting the worship practices of the pre-exilic temple. The king, as the head of the nation and supervisor of worship, should have kept the temple pure. Foreigners should never have been admitted, since they were there simply as syncretists and not as true worshipers of the Lord. The Levites by all means should have upheld the restrictions against foreigners of the Mosaic law (e.g., Exod. 12:43; Lev. 22:25), which it was their job to teach to the people (Numbers 18; Deut. 27:14ff., etc.). Ezekiel's vision looks to a correction of the long history of abuse. In the eschatological temple, everything will be properly done, and access will once again be restricted to the true people of God.

Because the eastern gate was the route of the return of the Lord's glory to the temple (43:1–4), it was kept shut so that no common access by mere humans could defile its holiness (vv. 1–2). The prince (again, Ezekiel's standard word for king) could use the large rooms of this outer court gateway (cf. 40:6–16) for eating his portion of the sacrificial meals (v. 3), but he had to get into the gateway from the inside, that is, through the vestibule (40:9, 15) rather than from the outside, that is, through the gate doors. What is the point of this restriction? It is simply that the temple is now in the Lord's control and not the king's. The king has a small, special privilege—eating in the eastern gate—but not the sort of control of the temple that the Israelite kings once exercised (cf. 2 Chronicles 26). Thus is symbolized the principle of controlled access to holiness in the new age.

Verses 4–9 correct an abuse of the past: foreigners eating in the temple. All non-Israelites believed in a plurality of gods and goddesses and thought it sensible to worship various ones. They did this by making the rounds of the temples and offering sacrifices at many, eating their portions in the various temples where they were welcomed. No one would ever have been excluded from the temples of Baal, Asherah, Molech, Chemosh, Dagon, etc. Only Yahweh, Israel's God, was an exclusive God. Eventually, even those who controlled access to the Solomonic temple degenerated in their thinking to the point that nonbelievers were invited into the Lord's temple to worship there. Those who came under these conditions were not even considered nonbelievers, since they believed in Yahweh *along with* many other gods. Neither the Levites nor the citizenry at large nor the government were orthodox enough to keep the temple pure. Improper worship thus defiled the sanctuary (v. 7). That would never happen in the new age (v. 9).

The Levites, including many descended from Aaron, were directly responsible for temple purity. Yet they had badly carried out their duties over the years. They would not have opportunity in the new temple to corrupt it as they had in the old temple. During the pre-exilic era Levites of all sorts had not remained with the duties properly assigned to them, but they had sacrificed on the altar, had entered the holy place (and probably the holy of holies, too, since security was so lax), and—worst of all—had practiced idolatry (v. 12). In the temple to come they would, however, be restricted to their proper duties only (vv. 10–14). These included guarding the gates, slaughtering the animals brought for sacrifice (v. 11), and general supervision of temple activities outside the altar and temple building (v. 14).

All of this continues to symbolize the holiness of the new age, in which God's standards would be kept and His sanctity protected.

ROLES OF THE PRIESTS

44:15 "But the priests, the Levites, the sons of Zadok, who kept charge of My sanctuary when the children of Israel went astray from Me, they shall come near Me to minister to Me; and they shall stand before Me to offer to Me the fat and the blood," says the Lord GOD.

16 "They shall enter My sanctuary, and they shall come near My table to minister to Me, and they shall keep My charge.

17 "And it shall be, whenever they enter the gates of the inner court, that they shall put on linen garments; no wool shall come upon them while they minister within the gates of the inner court or within the house.

18 "They shall have linen turbans on their heads and linen trousers on their bodies; they shall not clothe themselves with *anything that causes* sweat.

19 "When they go out to the outer court, to the *outer* court to the people, they shall take off their garments in which they have ministered, leave them in the holy chambers, and put on other garments; and in their holy garments they shall not sanctify the people.

20 "They shall neither shave their heads, nor let their hair grow long; but they shall keep their hair well trimmed.

21 "No priest shall drink wine when he enters the inner court.

22 "They shall not take as wife a widow or a divorced woman, but take virgins of the descendants of the house of Israel, or widows of priests.

23 "And they shall teach My people *the difference* between the holy and the unholy, and cause them to discern between the unclean and the clean.

24 "In controversy they shall stand as judges, *and* judge it according to My judgments. They shall keep My laws and My statutes in all My appointed meetings, and they shall hallow My Sabbaths.

25 "They shall not defile *themselves* by coming near a dead person. Only for father or mother, for son or daughter, for brother or unmarried sister may they defile themselves.

26 "After he is cleansed, they shall count seven days for him.

27 "And on the day that he goes to the sanctuary to minister in the sanctuary, he must offer his sin offering in the inner court," says the Lord GOD.

28 "It shall be, in regard to their inheritance, *that* I *am* their inheritance. You shall give them no possession in Israel, for I *am* their possession.

29 "They shall eat the grain offering, the sin offering, and the trespass offering; every dedicated thing in Israel shall be theirs.

30 "The best of all firstfruits of any kind, and every sacrifice of any kind from all your sacrifices, shall be the priest's; also you shall give to the priest the first of your ground meal, to cause a blessing to rest on your house.

31 "The priests shall not eat anything, bird or beast, that died naturally or was torn *by wild beasts.*"

Ezek. 44:15–31

In verse 11 the Levites were said to "stand before [the people] to minister to them." In the present passage (v. 15) the priests are said to *"come near to Me to minister to Me."* This summarizes the difference between Levites and priests, as it properly should have been maintained under the Mosaic law during the era of the first temple and as it would be maintained in the visionary temple of Ezekiel. Since the days of Solomon, only those Levites descended from the Aaronic lineage through Zadok could serve as priests at the temple (1 Kings 4:2; 2 Chron. 31:10). Thus this family alone was the authorized priestly family (v. 15), suitable to offer *"the fat and the blood."* These two elements of the sacrificial animals were always burned and poured out, respectively, on the altar as symbolic gifts to the Lord (Exod. 24:5ff.; Lev. 3:14; 1 Sam. 2:15). The rest of the animal was cooked, either by roasting or boiling, and then shared by priests and worshipers.

All of the regulations detailed in verses 16–31 of the present passage may be found in Exodus or Leviticus in one location or another (cf. esp. Exodus 39; Leviticus 21–22). The avoidance of sweat by wearing cool linen (vv. 17–18) is consistent with the Levitical teaching the bodily issues of any kind are ritually unclean (Leviticus 12, 13, 18, etc.). This does not mean that there is something unholy about sweat in general or that hard work would make a person unclean. It means that God required sometimes arbitrary standards in order to symbolize graphically His holiness and purity, and dry skin stays cleaner than sweaty skin.

Several of the regulations repeated here from the Pentateuch emphasize the importance of not mingling the common with the secular. This does not mean that common, everyday things are bad in themselves. Rather, the usual, typical, routine, regular, common things of life do not point people to God and certainly do not emphasize the fact that *special* steps must be taken to cleanse people from sin. We do not overcome sin automatically. In this fallen world, we can be sure that human beings will never reach God's standards and will never receive His favor if they just continue doing what is typical and common. The route to God is a special route—and the restrictions on mingling the secular with the common helped the ancient Israelites, if they were willing to learn, to see exactly that.

This is of course what verse 23 says explicitly: the rituals and special standards imposed upon the priests are a kind of visual aid to teach the people that there is a difference between the holy and the unholy, the clean and the unclean. Such differences should have been observed all along in the pre-exilic temple. But since they were not,

Ezekiel is commanded to relay them again to his audience so that they can capture, through his report of the great vision, a glimpse of their need to do something out of the ordinary to have peace with God. We know what that is. It is decidedly not ritual purity—that was intended merely to point to something. It is obedient faith in God's Son, who alone provided the means for the cleansing from sin of all people who have ever lived. His priesthood, moreover, fulfills everything Ezekiel's vision expected of ideal priests—doing God's will perfectly and thus representing the needs of the people directly before Him.

DISTRIBUTION OF THE LAND AND JUSTICE

45:1 "Moreover, when you divide the land by lot into inheritance, you shall set apart a district for the LORD, a holy section of the land; its length *shall be* twenty-five thousand *cubits,* and the width ten thousand. It *shall be* holy throughout its territory all around.

2 "Of this there shall be a square plot for the sanctuary, five hundred by five hundred *rods,* with fifty cubits around it for an open space.

3 "So this is the district you shall measure: twenty-five thousand *cubits* long and ten thousand wide; in it shall be the sanctuary, the Most Holy *Place.*

4 "It shall be a holy *section* of the land, belonging to the priests, the ministers of the sanctuary, who come near to minister to the LORD; it shall be a place for their houses and a holy place for the sanctuary.

5 "*An area* twenty-five thousand *cubits* long and ten thousand wide shall belong to the Levites, the ministers of the temple; they shall have twenty chambers as a possession.

6 "You shall appoint as the property of the city *an area* five thousand *cubits* wide and twenty-five thousand long, adjacent to the district of the holy *section;* it shall belong to the whole house of Israel.

7 "The prince shall have *a section* on one side and the other of the holy district and the city's property; and bordering on the holy district and the city's property, extending westward on the west

side and eastward on the east side, the length *shall be* side by side with one of the *tribal* portions, from the west border to the east border.

8 "The land shall be his possession in Israel; and My princes shall no more oppress My people, but they shall give *the rest of* the land to the house of Israel, according to their tribes."

9 'Thus says the Lord GOD: "Enough, O princes of Israel! Remove violence and plundering, execute justice and righteousness, and stop dispossessing My people," says the Lord GOD.

10 "You shall have honest scales, an honest ephah, and an honest bath.

11 "The ephah and the bath shall be of the same measure, so that the bath contains one-tenth of a homer, and the ephah one-tenth of a homer; their measure shall be according to the homer.

12 "The shekel *shall be* twenty gerahs; twenty shekels, twenty-five shekels, *and* fifteen shekels shall be your mina."

Ezek. 45:1–12

Ownership of land is a very important factor in human society. Throughout history, the opportunity for each family to own land has been seen as a basic necessity for peace and happiness. Nations that have allowed a few people to control most of the land, reducing the majority of the population to mere hired workers on others' land, have typically been nations that have eventually experienced social unrest, including revolution. The Russian Revolution, the Chinese Revolution, many of the revolutions in Africa and Latin America, etc., have been fought over the right of people to have land of their own. Where societies have provided means for each family to have land of its own, at least potentially, social stability and civil peace have been the norm.

Israel was a nation settled on the premise that every family would have some land of its own to farm. God wanted His people to constitute a universally landed nation. The lengthy descriptions of land distribution in Joshua 12–21, unexciting reading in themselves, reflect the importance of democratically distributed access to the land. The promised land would be less than a land of promise if only a few people had opportunity to work land of their own. In other words, fair distribution of the land was a part of Israel's social justice. In Chapters 47–48 further attention is given to the distribution of the land among all the tribes. Here the focus is on the future city of Jerusalem.

In the passage the subject of land distribution leads naturally to the subject of social justice in general. The passage has two main concerns:

1. The city apportioned—temple, priests, Levites, prince, etc. (vv. 1–8)
2. The need for fair and just laws in general (vv. 9–12)

Imagine a rectangle of land stretching from the Mediterranean Sea on the west to the Jordan River on the east, that is, a broad strip of land cutting right through the midsection of the territory of Israel. Imagine that rectangle divided again into thirds. The middle third would then be further divided as follows, according to verses 1–4: a special holy section would be at the center of the middle third, set apart for the Lord, inhabited by the priests and containing the square temple plot described in Chapters 40–43. North of this holy center section, but still within the middle third of the broad rectangle, would be a section of land for the Levites (v. 5). Then south of the holy center section, still in the middle third of the broad rectangle, would be land designated for the city of Jerusalem (v. 6). It is useful to remember here that David captured the city of Jerusalem after the conquest and made it a separate administrative district (something like Washington, D.C.), so that the city did not belong to any of the tribal districts per se.

Then the prince, the messianic king of the new age foreseen in the vision, would have the remaining territory of the broad rectangle of land—both the eastern third, along the Jordan, and the western third, along the Mediterranean (vv. 7–8). With his own land, the prince would not need to gain wealth by imposing high taxes, forced labor, and other oppressive governmental conditions and controls on the rest of the population, as had so frequently been the experience in the past (e.g., 1 Kings 5:13; 12:4; 21:1–16; cf. Deut. 17:14–20).

Indeed, in the restoration age the king would never again do what the kings of the past had become notorious for; namely, oppressing the people (v. 9). Justice, as symbolized often in the Old Testament by proper weights and measures (v. 10–12; cf. Lev. 19:36; Prov. 16:11; Hos. 12:7; Amos 8:5), would be universalized. This sort of language was hardly new to Ezekiel or his audience. Its purpose was to call people back to what should have been the case all along, not to institute any new concepts of justice.

On the other hand, Jerusalem was a very different city in his vision from the historical Jerusalem before or after his day. The whole topography of the land was different, as 40:2 already suggested. Instead of the little city of a few hundred acres, the Jerusalem Ezekiel sees is enormous. This is further evidence that the vision's purpose is not to cause us to expect fulfillment of these predictions in a literalistic way, and certainly not in any way connected with the modern highly secular state of Israel. Rather, the vision's symbolic message is where we must look for real meaning. In the kingdom of God, all will be in order, all will be just, and God will be at the center. This is the encouragement of the passage for believers of all ages.

OFFERINGS AND HOLY DAYS

45:13 "This *is* the offering which you shall offer: you shall give one-sixth of an ephah from a homer of wheat, and one-sixth of an ephah from a homer of barley.

14 "The ordinance concerning oil, the bath of oil, *is* one-tenth of a bath from a kor. A kor *is* a homer or ten baths, for ten baths *are* a homer.

15 "And one lamb shall be given from a flock of two hundred, from the rich pastures of Israel. These shall be for grain offerings, burnt offerings, and peace offerings, to make atonement for them," says the Lord GOD.

16 "All the people of the land shall give this offering for the prince in Israel.

17 "Then it shall be the prince's part *to give* burnt offerings, grain offerings, and drink offerings, at the feasts, the New Moons, the Sabbaths, and at all the appointed seasons of the house of Israel. He shall prepare the sin offering, the grain offering, the burnt

offering, and the peace offerings to make atonement
for the house of Israel."

18 'Thus says the Lord GOD: "In the first *month,* on
the first *day* of the month, you shall take a young
bull without blemish and cleanse the sanctuary.

19 "The priest shall take some of the blood of the
sin offering and put *it* on the doorposts of the temple, on the four corners of the ledge of the altar, and
on the gateposts of the gate of the inner court.

20 "And so you shall do on the seventh *day* of the
month for everyone who has sinned unintentionally
or in ignorance. Thus you shall make atonement for
the temple.

21 "In the first *month,* on the fourteenth day of
the month, you shall observe the Passover, a feast of
seven days; unleavened bread shall be eaten.

22 "And on that day the prince shall prepare for
himself and for all the people of the land a bull *for* a
sin offering.

23 "On the seven days of the feast he shall prepare
a burnt offering to the LORD, seven bulls and seven
rams without blemish, daily for seven days, and a
kid of the goats daily *for* a sin offering.

24 "And he shall prepare a grain offering of one
ephah for each bull and one ephah for each ram, together with a hin of oil for each ephah.

25 "In the seventh *month,* on the fifteenth day of
the month, at the feast, he shall do likewise for seven
days, according to the sin offering, the burnt offering, the grain offering, and the oil."'

Ezek. 45:13–25

Social justice is never enough. People must be more than merely
right with each other. They must be right with God. Thus the chapter
goes on from concerns for land distribution and proper weights and
measures to prescriptions for keeping the system of offerings above
reproach and regular.

Ezekiel's vision does not include provisions for all of the offerings
and feasts. If it did, the vision would be much longer, as a perusal
of the offering and feast laws in chapter after chapter of the Book
of Leviticus makes clear. Instead, we have here a sampling of

regulations for offerings and feasts, suggestive rather than exhaustive, intended to give a flavor of the sacrificial calendar obediently kept in the restoration era.

Verses 13–15 describe offering amounts in varying ratios. One-sixth of an ephah from a homer is one-sixtieth of the total (v. 13; cf. v. 11), the fraction of one's wheat and barley harvest that has to be given to the prince. For oil offerings, the fraction is one-hundredth (v. 14); for lambs, one two-hundredth (v. 15). Grain, burnt, and peace offerings were among the several types of offerings that could be given (cf. Leviticus 1–7). But these were not tithes. They were special levies for the general offerings at the temple. These offerings would be handled by the prince (king) on behalf of the people to provide temple offerings daily, weekly, monthly, and seasonally (vv. 16–17). According to the Old Testament law, the people themselves were required to come to the temple only three times yearly (Exodus 23). They could not constantly be there, since they lived all over Israel, but they could come "seasonally" for the three great feasts of Passover (spring), Pentecost (summer), and Tabernacles (autumn). The king was responsible to see to it that the more frequent sacrifices (daily, etc.) were done properly. He was right on the scene in Jerusalem and could do what the entire population couldn't. This is an example of a right role for government—doing on everyone's behalf what they cannot conveniently or efficiently do for themselves.

Sacrifices and rituals for the new year's day ceremonial cleansing of the temple (vv. 18–19) and the repetition of it a week later (v. 20) are mentioned briefly, as are the seven days of Passover (which begins one week thereafter) as specific responsibilities of the king (vv. 21–24). The first month in the Israelite calendar was not, of course, January, but mid-March to mid-April, that is, the beginning of spring. The feast of Pentecost is not mentioned here in this quick overview (it was always the "third" in importance), and the autumn festival, Tabernacles, is mentioned only briefly (v. 25). The king clearly has an important, although limited role in the ritual services of the eschatological temple, making sure that the general, nationwide offerings and procedures are correctly done so that God's commands are obeyed.

And what is the point of it all? Very simply it is this: God comes first. The first money you make is God's. The best time you have is God's. The primary affection you have must be God's. Even the first of your "vacation" days—right after planting in the spring (Passover) or harvest in the autumn (Tabernacles) are God's. It is *not* biblical to think, as many do, that we set aside whatever tithe or percentage *we* choose for the Lord and keep the rest for ourselves. The Bible says that we set aside the first, best, and primary for God and only then keep the rest for ourselves. His is the best, ours is the rest.

THE PRINCE AND WORSHIP PROCEDURES

46:1 'Thus says the Lord GOD: "The gateway of the inner court that faces toward the east shall be shut the six working days; but on the Sabbath it shall be opened, and on the day of the New Moon it shall be opened.

2 "The prince shall enter by way of the vestibule of the gateway from the outside, and stand by the gatepost. The priests shall prepare his burnt offering and his peace offerings. He shall worship at the threshold of the gate. Then he shall go out, but the gate shall not be shut until evening.

3 "Likewise the people of the land shall worship at the entrance to this gateway before the LORD on the Sabbaths and the New Moons.

4 "The burnt offering that the prince offers to the LORD on the Sabbath day *shall be* six lambs without blemish, and a ram without blemish;

5 "and the grain offering *shall be one* ephah for a ram, and the grain offering for the lambs, as much as he wants to give, as well as a hin of oil with every ephah.

6 "On the day of the New Moon *it shall be* a young bull without blemish, six lambs, and a ram; they shall be without blemish.

7 "He shall prepare a grain offering of an ephah for a bull, an ephah for a ram, as much as he wants to give for the lambs, and a hin of oil with every ephah.

8 "When the prince enters, he shall go in by way of the vestibule of the gateway, and go out the same way.

9 "But when the people of the land come before the LORD on the appointed feast days, whoever enters

by way of the north gate to worship shall go out by way of the south gate; and whoever enters by way of the south gate shall go out by way of the north gate. He shall not return by way of the gate through which he came, but shall go out through the opposite gate.

10 "The prince shall then be in their midst. When they go in, he shall go in; and when they go out, he shall go out.

11 "At the festivals and the appointed feast days the grain offering shall be an ephah for a bull, an ephah for a ram, as much as he wants to give for the lambs, and a hin of oil with every ephah.

12 "Now when the prince makes a voluntary burnt offering or voluntary peace offering to the LORD, the gate that faces toward the east shall then be opened for him; and he shall prepare his burnt offering and his peace offerings as he did on the Sabbath day. Then he shall go out, and after he goes out the gate shall be shut.

13 "You shall daily make a burnt offering to the LORD *of* a lamb of the first year without blemish; you shall prepare it every morning.

14 "And you shall prepare a grain offering with it every morning, a sixth of an ephah, and a third of a hin of oil to moisten the fine flour. This grain offering is a perpetual ordinance, to be made regularly to the LORD.

15 "Thus they shall prepare the lamb, the grain offering, and the oil, *as* a regular burnt offering every morning.'

16 'Thus says the Lord GOD: "If the prince gives a gift *of some* of his inheritance to any of his sons, it shall belong to his sons; it is their possession by inheritance.

17 "But if he gives a gift of some of his inheritance to one of his servants, it shall be his until the year of liberty, after which it shall return to the prince. But his inheritance shall belong to his sons; it shall become theirs.

18 "Moreover the prince shall not take any of the people's inheritance by evicting them from their property; he shall provide an inheritance for his sons from

his own property, so that none of My people may be
scattered from his property."'"

Ezek. 46:1–18

This passage expands upon some of the topics in the prior passages, notably the role of the future-age prince (king) in worship and the need for the prince to refrain from any activity that would bring about inequity in reference to ownership of the land. It may be outlined as follows:

1. Sabbath and New Moon offerings (vv. 1–7)
2. Proper gate use by worshipers (vv. 8–10)
3. Other offerings and a further detail on gate use (vv. 11–15)
4. Rules for inheriting the king's property (vv. 16–18)

On the principle of controlled access to God's holiness, the important eastern gate leading from the outer court to the inner court would be kept closed except on Sabbaths and new moons (v. 1). The king can worship in that gateway, and the people in general at its entrance, able to see directly into the altar and the temple building, but neither the king nor anyone else who is not a Levite or priest can enter the inner courtyard under any circumstances (vv. 2–3). Such a limitation on the king shows that in Ezekiel's vision, the "prince" is not exactly the same as the Messiah (as verses 16–18 also confirm). Verses 4–7 detail the offerings appropriate to the Sabbaths and new moons, and verses 5 and 7 mention the grain and oil offerings that were to accompany them. This resulted in a balanced meal: meat and vegetables, the oil being used for breads of all sorts. These offerings are analogous to those the Pentateuch requires for the Sabbaths and new moons (e.g., Num. 28:9–15), expanded in quantity to reflect the fact that the vision foresees a greater and larger people of God than yet existed.

Verses 8–10 are in effect traffic directions. The crowds anticipated for the temple on holy days would be enormous. Ezekiel's audience could remember the crowds in the temple at worship from their own days in Jerusalem. So a traffic pattern was needed. One stream of worshipers would enter via the northern gate and exit via the southern gate, and the other stream would go the other way. The lines would pass each other neatly in the outer courtyard. This eliminated the potential confusion of people turning around to go out the way they came in and kept lines moving in and out of worship. The king is one of the crowd (v. 10), a humble worshiper under these conditions even though he has a slightly special entering and exiting route (v. 8).

Verses 11–15 again teach regularity in worship and proper proportions so that everything necessary for the worship of God is carried out. Special, voluntary offerings are handled basically like those given on the Sabbaths or new moons (v. 12). As always, there must be only the best for God: balanced meals of choice ingredients, faithfully provided according to the calendar of daily offerings (vv. 13–15).

We have already noted that in Chapter 45, and as well in Chapters 47–48, attention is paid to the important question of social justice via land distribution. This issue surfaces again here in verses 16–18, in connection with the king's lands. For social justice to prevail, it is not enough to distribute the land *once.* The land must *continue* to be distributed fairly in all succeeding generations. Threatening this fairness was the possibility that wealthy individuals could buy up land not belonging to their own families, or that people might will their land to persons not in their families. This could eventually result in family members being forced off their ancestral lands. Thus the Pentateuchal laws insisted that all lands stay within the families to which they were originally distributed by lot, no matter what. This practice was sometimes followed (as in Ruth 4) but was most often ignored in pre-exilic Israel, causing great social injustice (cf. Isa. 5:8). In the new age, even the king would have to abide by the regulations to keep his land within his family. Gifts of land to others would revert to the royal family at each year of jubilee (*"the year of liberty,"* v. 17), in accordance with Lev. 25:8–55.

The goal of these regulations is order and justice—order in worship so that things are done "decently and in order" and justice in the dispersion of land belonging to the king so that royal land never leaves the king's family. Because the great vision points to realities beyond its mere mechanistic descriptions, we understand that the ultimate value of these factors for us is that they help us to appreciate the fact that God desires to be worshiped rightly, with no lack of honor due Him, forever. And we also realize that the true government of God (the prince) is one that would never "scatter" people "from their property," but would always protect and sustain them.

COOKING AND KITCHENS

46:19 Now he brought me through the entrance, which *was* at the side of the gate, into the holy chambers of the priests which face toward the north; and there a place *was* situated at their extreme western end.
20 And he said to me, "This *is* the place where the priests shall boil the trespass offering and the sin offering, *and* where they shall bake the grain offering, so that they do not bring *them* out into the outer court to sanctify the people."
21 Then he brought me out into the outer court and caused me to pass by the four corners of the court; and in fact, in every corner of the court *there was another* court.
22 In the four corners of the court *were* enclosed courts, forty *cubits* long and thirty wide; all four corners *were* the same size.
23 *There was* a row *of building stones* all around in them, all around the four of them; and cooking hearths were made under the rows of stones all around.
24 And he said to me, "These *are* the kitchens where the ministers of the temple shall boil the sacrifices of the people."

Ezek. 46:19–24

Little need be said about this passage, which addresses a new but fairly simple topic, food preparation at the temple. We are reminded once again that worship and food went together in ancient Israel, as they do also in Christian worship in the observation of communion. Offering, butchering, and placing meat on the altar get the most attention in sections of the Scripture that deal with sacrifices, but cooking facilities, for baking, roasting, and boiling, were also very much needed to make it possible for many people to worship at only one altar. Breads, for example, were not baked on the sacrifice altar but in ovens (v. 20). Meat briefly and symbolically placed on the altar was probably taken off quickly to make room for other meat and actually cooked to eating tenderness in the pots of the kitchens (vv. 20, 23, 24). Alternatively, only the part for the priests was offered on the altar, the remainder being cooked from the start in one of the four outer court kitchens mentioned in verses 21–22.

The visionary tour of the future, symbolic temple complex is now almost complete. It is a temple laid out cleanly, with all in order for true worship. It will be served by priest and Levites who properly conduct all the rituals of worship. King and people will honor the Lord there by doing everything as they should so that their offerings are accepted and they incur no sin. It is thus a symbol of the true age to come, in which all is done as God wants it done, and His holiness brings holiness to all who belong to Him.

CHAPTER TWENTY-SIX

The New Promised Land

Ezekiel 47:1–48:35

This final section of the great vision of Chapters 40–48 takes the hearer/reader beyond the temple and its regulations to a description of the full promised land of the future and a concluding overview of the city of Jerusalem as a whole.

The descriptions found here result in a land and city very different from any Israel or Jerusalem, ancient or modern. This is entirely consistent with the rest of the great vision, the purpose of which is not to plan for a simple restoration of historical Israel, but to look symbolically to the wonderful future God has planned for those who love Him.

Naturally, the vision retains points of contact with the historical nation and describes the future in concrete terms familiar to the audience to whom Ezekiel was called to preach. For God to have inspired the prophet otherwise would have been to cut off His audience from the ability to appreciate what the vision was getting at. We all need to have things explained to us in terms we understand. Moving from the familiar to the unfamiliar is the way all education proceeds; no one can comprehend what is entirely new. So the vision of the new promised land is in some ways told in terms of the old promised land and in some ways is strikingly different from it.

There are four major subdivisions to these last two chapters of the book:

1. Life-giving waters (47:1–12)
2. Boundaries of the land (47:13–23)
3. Tribal and city allotments (48:1–29)
4. The city of God (48:30–35)

410

LIFE-GIVING WATERS

47:1 Then he brought me back to the door of the temple; and there was water, flowing from under the threshold of the temple toward the east, for the front of the temple faced east; the water was flowing from under the right side of the temple, south of the altar.

2 He brought me out by way of the north gate, and led me around on the outside to the outer gateway that faces east; and there was water, running out on the right side.

3 And when the man went out to the east with the line in his hand, he measured one thousand cubits, and he brought me through the waters; the water *came up to my* ankles.

4 Again he measured one thousand and brought me through the waters; the water *came up to my* knees. Again he measured one thousand and brought me through; the water *came up to my* waist.

5 Again he measured one thousand, *and it was* a river that I could not cross; for the water was too deep, water in which one must swim, a river that could not be crossed.

6 He said to me, "Son of man, have you seen *this?*" Then he brought me and returned me to the bank of the river.

7 When I returned, there, along the bank of the river, *were* very many trees on one side and the other.

8 Then he said to me: "This water flows toward the eastern region, goes down into the valley, and enters the sea. *When it* reaches the sea, *its* waters are healed.

9 "And it shall be *that* every living thing that moves, wherever the rivers go, will live. There will be a very great multitude of fish, because these waters go there; for they will be healed, and everything will live wherever the river goes.

10 "It shall be *that* fishermen will stand by it from En Gedi to En Eglaim; they will be *places* for spreading their nets. Their fish will be of the same kinds as the fish of the Great Sea, exceedingly many.

411

11 "But its swamps and marshes will not be healed; they will be given over to salt.

12 "Along the bank of the river, on this side and that, will grow all *kinds of* trees used for food; their leaves will not wither, and their fruit will not fail. They will bear fruit every month, because their water flows from the sanctuary. Their fruit will be for food, and their leaves for medicine.'

Ezek. 47:1–12

The theme of a river of life is found often in the Bible. Gen. 2:10–14 describes the flowing out into the whole earth of four rivers from one in the Garden of Eden. Ps. 46:4 alludes to the "river whose streams make glad the city of God." Ps. 65:9 speaks of the "streams of God" that provide water for the agriculture of the land. Isa. 33:20 foresees Zion as a place of "broad rivers and streams." Joel 3:18 envisions the "fountain that will flow out of the Lord's house," and Zech. 14:8 describes the "living water" that will flow out from Jerusalem heading east and the west. The river of life in Rev. 22:1–2 also parallels our present passage, to which it appears to have reference. These and similar passages make use of a fact of life in the ancient Near East: water was scarce yet necessary for life and scenes of abundance are therefore suggested by scenes of water. Moreover, a river —as opposed to a swamp, or a seasonally flowing stream, or an actual or potentially stagnant lake (like the Dead Sea), or the undrinkable ocean—was the most desirable water imaginable to most ancients. It flowed constantly, it was (usually) clean, drinkable, and usable for irrigation, and there was plenty of it. Rivers, by their very nature, give life.

Ezekiel was inspired to make use of this happy theme of a life-giving river not as a literal prediction, but again as a symbolic depiction of the coming age of abundance (cf. the similar hyperbole in many of the passages listed above, as well as Amos 9:13–14; Hos. 14:5–6; etc.). God is at the center of all the graces of the new age, and what better way to illustrate this than with a river that originates right in God's own house—the temple building—and flows through the barren land making it lush and productive?

After leaving the kitchens (46:19–24), Ezekiel was led by his angelic guide back to the front of the temple building where he saw the origin of the healing river in the form of a small stream coming from under the temple porch or vestibule (v. 1). It apparently went underground and reemerged from under the eastern gate (v. 2). As it continued through the city, into the countryside, toward the Jordan Valley, it became wider and deeper—supernaturally, of course—so that it was a great river eventually, sustaining much plant life (vv. 3–7). It flowed perpendicular to the Jordan, entering into the Dead Sea from the east rather than from the north as does the Jordan (v. 8), and providing agriculture, fishing, medicinal trees, fruit, etc. (vv. 9–12). The fresh water from the river did not entirely cleanse out the salt deposits of the Dead Sea, however (v. 11), since God's good provision allowed for the much-valued salt still to be available to His people.

Here, then, is a picture of what a good God does for His people. He gives what they need to live. He sustains them. By His supernatural grace He makes abundance appear where only desolation once prevailed. The work of Christ, who gives "living water," has begun the age seen in Ezekiel's vision. Heavenly life will fulfill it, as depicted in Revelation 22. We will enjoy the fruited abundance of Ezekiel's river. It will come from the Lord's house in the holy city, where we are already citizens if we truly know the Lord.

BOUNDARIES OF THE LAND

47:13 Thus says the Lord GOD: "These *are* the borders by which you shall divide the land as an inheritance among the twelve tribes of Israel. Joseph *shall have two* portions.

14 "You shall inherit it equally with one another; for I raised My hand in an oath to give it to your fathers, and this land shall fall to you as your inheritance.

15 "This *shall be* the border of the land on the north: from the Great Sea, *by* the road to Hethlon, as one goes to Zedad,

16 "Hamath, Berothah, Sibraim (which *is* between the border of Damascus and the border of Hamath), to Hazar Hatticon (which *is* on the border of Hauran).

17 "Thus the boundary shall be from the Sea to Hazar Enan, the border of Damascus; and as for the

north, northward, it is the border of Hamath. *This is* the north side.

18 "On the east side you shall mark out the border from between Hauran and Damascus, and between Gilead and the land of Israel, along the Jordan, and along the eastern side of the sea. *This is* the east side.

19 "The south side, toward the South, *shall be* from Tamar to the waters of Meribah by Kadesh, along the brook to the Great Sea. *This is* the south side, toward the South.

20 "The west side *shall be* the Great Sea, from the *southern* boundary until one comes to a point opposite Hamath. This *is* the west side.

21 "Thus you shall divide this land among your-selves according to the tribes of Israel.

22 "It shall be that you will divide it by lot as an inheritance for yourselves, and for the strangers who dwell among you and who bear children among you. They shall be to you as native-born among the chil-dren of Israel; they shall have an inheritance with you among the tribes of Israel.

23 "And it shall be *that* in whatever tribe the stranger dwells, there you shall give *him* his inherit-ance," says the Lord GOD.

Ezek. 47:13–23

In keeping with the interest that everything be done properly in the new age of restoration, Ezekiel's great vision includes prescrip-tions for the outer dimension of the promised land and for its fair distribution to native Israelites and non-Israelites alike. There are two special areas of attention in this passage: (1) the concern that God's people occupy their full boundaries, and (2) the concern that Gentiles will have an inheritance.

The land shown to Moses in Deuteronomy 34 and allotted among the tribes in Joshua 13–21 was never fully under Israelite control. Much of it was captured initially but abandoned to Canaanite reset-tlement during Joshua's incomplete conquest (cf. Judg. 1:21–36). Much of it was lost during the disastrous days of the Judges. David recaptured most of it, but by reason of the faithlessness of the people of God, much was again lost to neighbors, far or distant, during the days of the kings. All had been lost, of course, by Ezekiel's time in exile. And during his lifetime, Judah had been only a rump state, the ten northern tribal territories having been incorporated into the Assyrian provincial system. So the vision of a fully Israelite promised land, actually occupied by the people of God and under the Lord's control from border to border was a wonderful means of encouragement to a people for whom such a geopolitical situation was in human terms impossible.

The borders listed in the passage are similar to—although not exactly the same as—those specified in Num. 34:1–12 for the original land of promise, while the allocation to the tribes themselves in the following passage is very different. The western boundary, the Mediterranean, is an easy one to understand, as is the eastern boundary, the Jordan River and the Dead Sea. The northern boundary mentions some places that are no longer known to us (vv. 15–17), but it is clear that this boundary runs generally from Tyre on the Phoenician coast to the southern Syrian region north of the Sea of Galilee. The southern boundary runs from the Mediterranean to a point south of the Dead Sea, again along regions that are not entirely identifiable, since the modern place names are different from the ancient and because some of the ancient sites mentioned no longer exist (v. 19). What is perhaps most surprising about Ezekiel's visionary boundaries is that they include no land east of the Jordan, even though that area was originally settled by Reuben, Gad, and part of the tribe of Manasseh (Joshua 13). Once again, the vision departs from historical realities to convey symbolic symmetry and thus to remind us that a literalistic interpretation is not what Ezekiel or his audience would ever have assumed.

Verses 22–23 welcome the Gentiles into the people of promise. This is stated rather matter-of-factly but surely would have raised eyebrows among those who first heard these words, since we know from Jonah and other parts of the Old Testament that many Israelites had a rather narrow, self-interested view of the extent of the Lord's blessing. In fact, all the prophets who speak in detail of the age to come have something to say about the expansion of God's people beyond the numbers and influence of little ethnic Israel, and this part of the vision is merely one more instance of that expectation. The plan of God was always to have a people greater than one ethnic group in a particular location in the world, and Ezekiel's vision provides for inheritance of land by Gentiles right along with the various tribes, thus symbolizing what we call in technical language the doctrine of the "democratization of the chosen people." Gentiles, too, would have the right, by reason of their trust in the true God, to live in the land so full of the blessings already described in the vision. What the spread of the gospel has accomplished and will continue to accomplish is already foreshadowed in the regulations of Ezekiel's great vision.

TRIBAL AND CITY ALLOTMENTS

48:1 "Now these *are* the names of the tribes: From the northern border along the road to Hethlon at the entrance of Hamath, to Hazar Enan, the border of Damascus northward, in the direction of Hamath, *there shall be* one *section for* Dan from its east to its west side;

2 "by the border of Dan, from the east side to the west, one *section for* Asher;

3 "by the border of Asher, from the east side to the west, one *section for* Naphtali;

4 "by the border of Naphtali, from the east side to the west, one *section for* Manasseh;

5 "by the border of Manasseh, from the east side to the west, one *section for* Ephraim;

6 "by the border of Ephraim, from the east side to the west, one *section for* Reuben;

7 "by the border of Reuben, from the east side to the west, one *section for* Judah;

8 "by the border of Judah, from the east side to the west, shall be the district which you shall set apart, twenty-five thousand *cubits* in width, and *in* length the same as one of the *other* portions, from the east side to the west, with the sanctuary in the center.

9 "The district that you shall set apart for the LORD *shall be* twenty-five thousand *cubits* in length and ten thousand in width.

10 "To these—to the priests—the holy district shall belong: on the north twenty-five thousand *cubits in length*, on the west ten thousand in width, on the east ten thousand in width, and on the south twenty-five thousand in length. The sanctuary of the LORD shall be in the center.

11 *"It shall be* for the priests of the sons of Zadok, who are sanctified, who have kept My charge, who did not go astray when the children of Israel went astray, as the Levites went astray.

12 "And *this* district of land that is set apart shall be to them a thing most holy by the border of the Levites.

13 "Opposite the border of the priests, the Levites *shall have an area* twenty-five thousand *cubits* in length and ten thousand in width; its entire length *shall be* twenty-five thousand and its width ten thousand.

14 "And they shall not sell or exchange any of it; they may not alienate this best *part* of the land, for *it is* holy to the LORD.

15 "The five thousand *cubits* in width that remain, along the edge of the twenty-five thousand, shall be for general use by the city, for dwellings and common-land; and the city shall be in the center.

16 "These *shall be* its measurements: the north side four thousand five hundred *cubits*, the south side four thousand five hundred, the east side four thousand five hundred, and the west side four thousand five hundred.

17 "The common-land of the city shall be: to the north two hundred and fifty *cubits*, to the south two hundred and fifty, to the east two hundred and fifty, and to the west two hundred and fifty.

18 "The rest of the length, alongside the district of the holy *section, shall be* ten thousand *cubits* to the east and ten thousand to the west. It shall be adjacent to the district of the holy *section,* and its produce shall be food for the workers of the city.

19 "The workers of the city, from all the tribes of Israel, shall cultivate it.

20 "The entire district *shall be* twenty-five thousand *cubits* by twenty-five thousand *cubits*, foursquare. You shall set apart the holy district with the property of the city.

21 "The rest *shall belong* to the prince, on one side and on the other of the holy district and of the city's property, next to the twenty-five thousand *cubits* of

the *holy* district as far as the eastern border, and westward next to the twenty-five thousand as far as the western border, adjacent to the *tribal* portions; *it shall belong* to the prince. It shall be the holy district, and the sanctuary of the temple *shall be* in the center.

22 "Moreover, apart from the possession of the Levites and the possession of the city *which are* in the midst of what *belongs* to the prince, *the area* between the border of Judah and the border of Benjamin shall belong to the prince.

23 "As for the rest of the tribes, from the east side to the west, Benjamin *shall have* one *section;*

24 "by the border of Benjamin, from the east side to the west, Simeon *shall have* one *section;*

25 "by the border of Simeon, from the east side to the west, Issachar *shall have* one *section;*

26 "by the border of Issachar, from the east side to the west, Zebulun *shall have* one *section;*

27 "by the border of Zebulun, from the east side to the west, Gad *shall have* one *section;*

28 "by the border of Gad, on the south side, toward the South, the border shall be from Tamar *to* the waters of Meribah *by* Kadesh, along the brook to the Great Sea.

29 "This *is* the land which you shall divide by lot as an inheritance among the tribes of Israel, and these *are* their portions," says the Lord GOD.

Ezek. 48:1–29

The original tribal allotments accomplished during the days of Joshua were hardly symmetrical. Some tribes, such as Judah and Ephraim, had large territories. Others, such as Benjamin, Dan, and Issachar, had small districts to occupy. And Simeon was so soon absorbed into Judah that its theoretical boundaries were of little consequence. Moreover, there was no true equality among the tribes. A small territory for a tribe was not compensated for by the productivity of its land, or the like. Accordingly, pre-exilic Israel's territorial arrangement was somewhat analogous to that of the United States today, in which some states are rich in land, population, and wealth, and some states have relatively little of each.

In this part of the vision, Ezekiel sees a "fair and square" promised land, with everything laid out once again in a symmetry far different from historical reality but warmly symbolic of the orderliness and equity of the age to come. The original tribal boundaries twisted and turned along geographical features, with some tribes sandwiched in among others and all the tribal boundaries being oddly shaped. Not so in the new land. Seven equal tribal territories are situated north of the broad central east-west strip reserved for the city and the prince (vv. 2–8). In this configuration, Judah and Reuben, which were south of Jerusalem in actual fact, are placed north of the holy city. From north to south, each tribe has a horizontal (east-west) strip of territory going from the Mediterranean to the Jordan. Dan is at the top, then Asher, Naphtali, Manasseh, Ephraim, Reuben, and Judah as one travels south to the city.

Verses 9–22 repeat much of what was said in 45:1–8, although in somewhat greater detail. The broad central strip was a special territory for the temple, the city in general, the priests, the Levites, and the king. All of it was ultimately under the jurisdiction of the Lord and it was a kind of grand administrative district not allotted to any of the tribes, in the same sort of way that the District of Columbia in the United States is not allotted to any of the states. Verse 14 makes explicit what was implicit in 45:1–8, namely, that Levite territory can't be sold or transferred (in contrast to tribal or royal territories). Verses 15–20 give further details about the city district and who may cultivate it, not specifically touched on in Chapter 45.

Verses 23–29 continue the north-to-south order, with the five southern tribal allotments ranging in horizontal strips from Benjamin, just south of the central strip, to Simeon, Issachar, Zebulun, and finally Gad at the southernmost extreme of the land. Within these territories, the Israelites of the "new conquest" (accomplished by Christ, not by military means) will decide by casting lots which families get which shares. Again, this has no resemblance to historical fact, since only Judah and Simeon on the west of the Jordan and Reuben on the east of the Jordan were actually south of Jerusalem. It doesn't matter. This is not a real, earthly country; it is a symbolic country, designed to reflect a higher reality—the heavenly, eschatological reality that the New Testament so often witnesses to. This isn't the Israel of any human historical period. It is the true Israel of

God, where all is in His control and everyone enjoys equally the blessing of the Lord of Glory as heirs with Christ of the kingdom.

THE CITY OF GOD

48:30 "These *are* the exits of the city. One the north side, measuring four thousand five hundred *cubits*

31 "(the gates of the city *shall be* named after the tribes of Israel), the three gates northward: one gate for Reuben, one gate for Judah, and one gate for Levi;

32 "on the east side, four thousand five hundred *cubits*, three gates: one gate for Joseph, one gate for Benjamin, and one gate for Dan;

33 "on the south side, measuring four thousand five hundred *cubits*, three gates: one gate for Simeon, one gate for Issachar, and one gate for Zebulun;

34 "on the west side, four thousand five hundred *cubits* with their three gates: one gate for Gad, one gate for Asher, and one gate for Naphtali.

35 "All the way around *shall be* eighteen thousand cubits; and the name of the city from *that day shall be:* THE LORD *IS* THERE.'

Ezek. 48:30–35

The final passage returns to the city itself and its outer walls and gates, three on each side. This scheme is expanded upon in Revelation 21, which likewise uses the symbolism of the new city of Jerusalem as a means of speaking of the saints' eternal dwelling with God.

The gates are named after the twelve tribes, and we note some differences between the tribes mentioned here and in the preceding passage. The reason is simple: in verses 1–29 the priestly tribe of Levi has a special inheritance area and Joseph's two sons (Ephraim and Manasseh) are both given tribes (reflecting the historical situation to some degree). In the new holy city, however, the gates are named for people more than for regions, because everyone, whether of the priestly tribe or not, has access to the city, as symbolized by including all twelve of the original sons of Jacob in the naming of the gates. In other words, it is the *tribes* of Israel (v. 31), not the tribal *territories* of Israel, that have occasioned the names of the gates. Joseph's name therefore appears where Ephraim and Manasseh would have if this were a list of tribal territories. Levi's name appears where it would not be listed in a grouping of territories, since the Levites never had a strictly tribal allotment (cf. Num. 1:49; Deut. 10:9; 18:1; Josh. 13:14).

The name of the city, given in the very last verse of the book (v. 35), is not Jerusalem, or Zion, but *Yahweh Shammah*, Hebrew for "The Lord is there." To a considerable degree, this is the object of the entire vision. What God causes Ezekiel to see is a place where God is present. If He is there, all those accepted by Him into His presence will experience order, equity, continuing life, absence of the power of sin, and abundance of a sort not imaginable by usual standards. His presence is life itself, except, of course, to the wicked who oppose Him. To them, His presence is death. But this part of the vision is not addressing the question of how the presence of God can mean alternately life or death depending on who is in that presence. It envisions a time and a place where and when the division for or against the Lord has already occurred (chaps. 38, 39, etc.). The ultimate city and the eschatological promised land are for those who love the Lord and are His forever. He will be there, and they will finally be with Him, as they had faith they would be.

Bibliography

Ackroyd, Peter. *Exile and Restoration.* Philadelphia: Westminster Press, 1968.

Ahroni, R. "The Gog Prophecy and the Book of Ezekiel." *Hebrew Annual Review* 1 (1977): 1–27.

Albright, William Foxwell. "The Seal of Eliakim and the Latest Pre-exilic History of Judah, With Some Observations on Ezekiel." *Journal of Biblical Literature* 51 (1932): 77–106.

———. "What Were the Cherubim?" *Biblical Archaeologist* 1 (1938): 1–3.

Barnett, R. D. "Ezekiel and Tyre." *Eretz-Israel* 9 (1969): 6–13.

Berry, G. R. "The Composition of the Book of Ezekiel." *Journal of Biblical Literature* 58 (1939): 163–75.

———. "The Glory of Yahweh and the Temple." *Journal of Biblical Literature* 56 (1937): 115–17.

———. "Was Ezekiel in the Exile?" *Journal of Biblical Literature* 49 (1930): 83–93.

Bewer, Julius A. "Textual and Exegetical Notes on the Book of Ezekiel." *Journal of Biblical Literature* 72 (1953): 158–68.

Boadt, Larry. *Ezekiel's Oracles against Egypt.* Biblica et Orientalia 37. Rome: Biblicial Institute Press, 1980.

———. "Textual Problems in Ezekiel and Poetic Analysis of Paired Words." *Journal of Biblical Literature* 97 (1978): 489–99.

Browne, L. E. *Ezekiel and Alexander,* London: SPCK, 1952.

Brownlee, William H. "The Aftermath of the Fall of Judah according to the Prophet Ezekiel." *Journal of Biblical Literature* 89 (1970): 393–404.

———. "Ezekiel." *The Interpreter's One-Volume Commentary.* Ed. C. M. Laymon. Nashville: Abingdon Press, 1971.

———. *Ezekiel 1–19.* Word Biblical Commentary. Waco, Tex.: Word Books, 1986.

———. "Ezekiel's Parable of the Watchman and the Editing of Ezekiel." *Vetus Testamentum* 28 (1978): 392–408.

———. "'Son of Man, Set Your Face': Ezekiel the Refugee Prophet." *Hebrew Union College Annual* 54 (1983): 83–110.

———. "The Scroll of Ezekiel from the Eleventh Qumran Cave (with Facsimile)." *Revue de Qumran* 4 (1963): 11–28.

Burrows, Millar. *The Literary Relations of Ezekiel.* Philadelphia: Jewish Publication Society, 1925.

Buttenweiser, Moses. "The Character and Date of Ezekiel's Prophecies." *Hebrew Union College Annual* 7 (1930): 1–18.

Carley, K. W. *The Book of the Prophet Ezekiel.* The Cambridge Bible Commentary on the New English Bible. Cambridge: Cambridge University Press, 1974.

————. *Ezekiel among the Prophets.* London: SCM, 1975.

Cheyne, T. K. "The Image of Jealousy in Ezekiel." *Zeitschrift für die Alttestamentliche Wissenschaft* 21 (1901): 201–2.

Cooke, G. A. *A Critical and Exegetical Commentary on the Book of Ezekiel.* The International Critical Commentary. Edinburgh: T. and T. Clark, 1936.

Craghan, J. F. "Ezekiel: A Pastoral Theologian." *American Ecclesiastical Review* 166 (1972): 22–33.

Craigie, P. C. *Ezekiel.* Daily Study Bible. Philadelphia: Westminster, 1983.

Davidson, A. B. *The Book of the Prophet Ezekiel.* Rev. ed. The Cambridge Bible. Cambridge: Cambridge University Press, 1916.

DeVries, S. J. "Remembrance in Ezekiel. A Study of an Old Testament Theme." *Interpretation* 16 (1962): 58–64.

Dijk, H. J. van. *Ezekiel's Prophecy on Tyre (Ez. 26.1–28.19).* Biblica et Orientalia 20. Rome: Biblical Institute Press, 1960.

Driver, Godfrey Rolles. "Ezekiel: Linguistic and Textual Problems." *Biblica* 35 (1954): 145–59; 299–312.

————. "Linguistic and Textual Problems: Ezekiel." *Biblica* 19 (1938): 60–69; 175–87.

Eichrodt, W. *Ezekiel: A Commentary.* The Old Testament Library. Philadelphia: Westminster Press, 1970.

Ellison, H. L. *Ezekiel, the Man and His Message.* London: Paternoster Press, 1956.

Farmer, W. R. "The Geography of Ezekiel's River of Life." *Biblical Archaeologist* 19 (1956): 17–22.

Filson, Floyd V. "The Omission of Ezek. 12:26–28 and 36:23b–38 in Codex 967." *Journal of Biblical Literature* 62 (1943): 27–32.

Finegan, J. "The Chronology of Ezekiel." *Journal of Biblical Literature* 69 (1950): 61–66.

Fox, M. V. "The Rhetoric of Ezekiel's Vision of the Valley of the Bones." *Hebrew Union College Annual* 51 (1980): 1–15.

Freedman, David Noel. "The Book of Ezekiel." *Interpretation* 8 (1954): 446–71.

Gaster, Theodor. "Ezekiel and the Mysteries." *Journal of Biblical Literature* 60 (1941): 289–310.

Gehman, H. S. "The Relations between the Hebrew Text of Ezekiel and That of the John H. Scheide Papyri." *Journal of the American Oriental Society* 58 (1938): 92–102.

Greenberg, Moshe. *Ezekiel I–XX.* Anchor Bible. Garden City, N.Y.: Doubleday, 1983.

———. "Ezekiel 17 and the Policy of Psammetichus II." *Journal of Biblical Literature* 76 (1957): 304–9.

———. "On Ezekiel's Dumbness." *Journal of Biblical Literature* 77 (1958): 101–5.

Gruenthaner, M. J. "The Messianic Concepts of Ezekiel." *Theological Studies* 2 (1941): 1–18.

———. "Recent Theories about Ezekiel." *Catholic Biblical Quarterly* 7 (1945): 438–46.

Harford, John B. *Studies in the Book of Ezekiel.* Cambridge: Cambridge University Press, 1935.

Houk, C. B. "*Bn-ʿdm* Patterns as Literary Criteria in Ezekiel." *Journal of Biblical Literature* 88 (1969): 184–90.

Howie, C. G. *The Book of Ezekiel; The Book of Daniel.* The Layman's Bible Commentary. Richmond: John Knox Press, 1961.

———. *The Date and Composition of Ezekiel.* Journal of Biblical Literature Monograph Series 4. Philadelphia: Society of Biblical Literature, 1950.

Irwin, W. A. "Ezekiel Research Since 1943." *Vetus Testamentum* 3 (1953): 54–66.

———. *The Problem of Ezekiel.* Chicago: University of Chicago Press, 1943.

Johnson, A. C., H. S. Gehman, and E. H. Kase. *The John H. Scheide Biblical Papyri, Ezekiel.* Princeton, N.J.: Princeton University Press, 1938.

Johnson, Aubrey R. *The Vitality of the Individual in the Thought of Ancient Israel.* Cardiff: University of Wales Press, 1949.

Keil, K. F. *Biblical Commentary of the Prophecies of Ezekiel.* Tr. James Martin. Edinburgh: T. and T. Clark, 1876. Repr. Grand Rapids: Eerdmans, 1950.

Kelso, James L. "Ezekiel's Parable of the Corroded Copper Cauldron." *Journal of Biblical Literature* 64 (1954): 391–93.

Kenyon, Frederic G. *The Chester Beatty Biblical Papyri: Ezekiel, Daniel, Esther.* London: Walker, 1938.

Lang, B. "A Neglected Method in Ezekiel Research: Editorial Criticism." *Vetus Testamentum* 29 (1979): 39–44.

Levenson, Jon D. *Theology of the Program of Restoration of Ezekiel 40–48.* Harvard Semitic Monographs 10, Missoula, Mont.: Scholars Press, 1976.

Levey, S. H. "The Targum to Ezekiel." *Hebrew Union College Annual* 46 (1975): 139–58.

Lindars, Barnabas. "Ezekiel 18 and Individual Responsibility." *Vetus Testamentum* 15 (1965): 452–67.

Lust, J. "Ezekiel 36–40 in the Oldest Greek Manuscript." *Catholic Biblical Quarterly* 43 (1981): 517–33.

Matthews, I. G. *Ezekiel.* An American Commentary on the Old Testament. Philadelphia: Judson Press, 1939.

May, H. G. "The Departure of the Glory of Yahweh." *Journal of Biblical Literature* 56 (1937): 309–21.

———. *Ezekiel: Introduction and Exegesis.* Interpreter's Bible. Nashville: Abingdon Press, 1954.

Mays, James Luther. *Ezekiel, Second Isaiah.* Proclamation Commentaries. Philadelphia: Fortress Press, 1978.

Moran, William L. "Gen 49:10 and Its Use in Ez 21:32." *Biblica* 39 (1958): 405–25.

Muilenberg, J. "Ezekiel." *Peake's Commentary on the Bible.* Ed. M. Black and H. H. Rowley. Rev. ed. London: Thomas Nelson, 1962.

Mullo Weir, C. J. "Aspects of the Book of Ezekiel." *Vetus Testamentum* 2 (1952): 97–112.

Murray, J. J. "The Preacher's Use of Ezekiel." *Expository Times* 50 (1938–39): 314–16.

Myres, J. L. "Gog and the Danger from the North, in Ezekiel." *Palestine Exploration Quarterly* 64 (1932): 213–19.

Orlinsky, Harry. "Where Did Ezekiel Receive the Call to Prophecy?" *Bulletin of the American Schools of Oriental Research* 122 (1951): 34–36.

Parrot, André. *Babylon and the Old Testament.* Tr. B. E. Hooke. Studies in Biblical Archaeology 8. London: SCM, 1958.

Payne, J. Barton. "The Relationship of the Chester Beatty Papyri of Ezekiel to Codex Vaticanus." *Journal of Biblical Literature* 68 (1949): 251–65.

Robinson, H. Wheeler. "The Hebrew Conception of Corporate Personality." In *Werden und Wesen des Alten Testaments,* 49–62. Beihefte zur Zeitschrift für die Altestamentliche Wissenschaft 66. Berlin: Töpelmann, 1936.

———. *Two Hebrew Prophets.* London: Lutterworth Press, 1948.

Rowley, H. H. "The Book of Ezekiel in Modern Study." *Bulletin of the John Rylands Library* 36 (1953–54): 146–50.

Sherlock, C. "Ezekiel's Dumbness." *Expository Times* 94 (1983): 296–98.

Smith, James. *The Book of the Prophet Ezekiel.* New York: Macmillan, 1931.

Smith, Louise P. "The Eagle(s) of Ezekiel 17." *Journal of Biblical Literature* 58 (1939): 43–50.

Smith, M. "The Veracity of Ezekiel, the Sins of Manasseh, and Jeremiah 44, 18." *Zeitschrift für die Alttestamentliche Wissenschaft* 87 (1975): 1–16.

Smith, S. "The Ship Tyre." *Palestine Exploration Quarterly* 85 (1953): 97–110.

Snaith, Norman H. "The Dates in Ezekiel." *Expository Times* 59 (1947–48).

Spiegel, S. "Ezekiel or Pseudo-Ezekiel?" *Harvard Theological Revue* 24 (1931): 245–321.

————. "Toward Certainty in Ezekiel." *Journal of Biblical Literature* 54 (1935): 145–71.

Sullivan, K. "The Book of Ezekiel." *Worship* 29 (1954–55): 569–80.

Talmon, Shemaryahu, and Michael Fishbane. "The Structuring of Biblical Books: Studies in the Book of Ezekiel." *Annual of the Swedish Theological Institute* 10 (1976): 129–53.

Taylor, John. *Ezekiel: An Introduction and Commentary.* Tyndale Old Testament Commentaries. Downers Grove, Ill.: InterVarsity Press, 1969.

Te Stroete, G. A. "Ezekiel 24:15–27, The Meaning of a Symbolic Act." *Bijdragen* 38 (1977): 163–75.

Thackeray, Henry St. J. "The Greek Translators of Ezekiel." *Journal of Theological Studies* 4 (1903): 398–411.

Torrey, C. C. "Certainly Pseudo-Ezekiel." *Journal of Biblical Literature* 53 (1934): 291–320.

————. "Notes on Ezekiel." *Journal of Biblical Literature* 58 (1939): 69–86.

————. *Pseudo-Ezekiel and the Original Prophecy.* New Haven, Conn.: Yale University Press, 1930.

Toy, C. H. *The Book of the Prophet Ezekiel.* The Sacred Books of the Old Testament, 12. New York: Dodd, Mead, and Co., 1899.

Tsevat, Matitiahu. "The Neo-Assyrian and Neo-Babylonian Vassal Oaths and the Prophet Ezekiel." *Journal of Biblical Literature* 78 (1959): 199–204.

Turner, N. "The Greek Translators of Ezekiel." *Journal of Theological Studies* 7 (1956): 12–24.

Van Dyke Parunak, H. "The Literary Architecture of Ezekiel's *Mar'ot 'Elohîm.*" *Journal of Biblical Literature* 99 (1980): 61–74.

Van Zeller, H. *Ezekiel, Man of Signs.* London: Sands and Co., 1944.

Vogelstein, M. "Nebuchadnezzar's Reconquest of Phoenicia and Palestine and the Oracles of Ezekiel." *Hebrew Union College Annual* 23 (1950–51): 197–220.

Weitzman, M. "The Dates in Ezekiel." *Heythrop Journal* 17 (1976): 20–30.

Wevers, J. W. *Ezekiel.* New Century Bible. London: Oliphants, 1969.

Wilson, R. R. "An Interpretation of Ezekiel's Dumbness." *Vetus Testamentum* 22 (1972): 91–104.

Zimmerli, Walther. "The Message of the Prophet Ezekiel." *Interpretation* 23 (1969): 131–57.

————. "The Special Form- and Traditio-historical Character of Ezekiel's Prophecy." *Vetus Testamentum* 15 (1965): 515–27.

Zyl, A. H. van. "Solidarity and Individualism in Ezekiel." *Die Ou Testamentiese Werkgemeenskap in Suid-Afrika* (1961): 38–52.